Focus on Curriculum

Volume 5 in
Research on Sociocultural Influences on Motivation and Learning

Series Editors:
Dennis M. McInerney, *University of Western Sydney*
Shawn Van Etten, *State University of New York, Cortland*

Research on Sociocultural Influences on Motivation and Learning

Dennis M. McInerney and Shawn Van Etten, Series Editors

Volume 1: Research on Social Influences on Motivation and Learning (2001)
  edited by Dennis M. McInerney and Shawn Van Etten

Volume 2: Research on Social Influences on Motivation and Learning (2002)
  edited by Dennis M. McInerney and Shawn Van Etten

Volume 3: Sociocultural Influences and Teacher Education Programs (2003)
  edited by Dennis M. McInerney and Shawn Van Etten

Volume 4: Big Theories Revisited (2004)
  edited by Dennis M. McInerney and Shawn Van Etten

Focus on Curriculum

edited by
Dennis M. McInerney
University of Western Sydney

and

Shawn Van Etten
State University of New York, Cortland

INFORMATION AGE
PUBLISHING

Greenwich, Connecticut • www.infoagepub.com

Library of Congress Cataloging-in-Publication Data

Research on sociocultural influences on motivation and learning
  / edited by Dennis M. McInerney and Shawn Van Etten.
      p. cm.
   Includes bibliographical references and index.
   Contents: v. 1 [without special title] -- v. 2. [without
   special title] -- v. 3. Sociocultural influences and teacher
education programs -- v. 4. Big theories revisited -- v. 5.
Focus on curriculum.
ISBN 1-930608-63-2 (v. 1) -- ISBN 1-930608-62-4 (v. 1 : pbk.)
ISBN 1-931576-33-5 (v. 2) -- ISBN 1-931576-32-7 (v. 2 : pbk.)
ISBN 1-59311-051-0 (v. 3) -- ISBN 1-59311-050-2 (v. 3 : pbk.)
ISBN 1-59311-053-7 (v. 4) -- ISBN 1-59311-052-9 (v. 4 : pbk.)
ISBN 1-59311-208-4 (v. 5) -- ISBN 1-59311-207-6 (v. 5 : pbk.)
1. Motivation in education--Social aspects--Cross-cultural
studies. 2. Multicultural education--Cross-cultural studies.
I. McInerney, D. M. (Dennis M.), 1948- . II. Van Etten,
Shawn.
LB1065.R45 2001
370.15'4--dc21

                                    2002002157

Printed in the United States of America

CONTENTS

PART II
POSTSCHOOL CURRICULUM

INTRODUCTION: SOCIOCULTURAL FOCUS ON CURRICULUM

Dennis M. McInerney and Shawn Van Etten

The last two decades has seen the increasing development of teaching and curriculum programs that attempt to make education relevant to the wider sociocultural environment of learners. Volume 5 focuses on research on curriculum and teaching from a sociocultural perspective. In this volume we have chapters dealing with education from the earliest preschool levels through to adulthood. The chapters cover a wide range of important topics including reading and literacy, mathematics, science, social science, health education, language acquisition, religious education, and multicultural studies. The chapters represent research methodologies that are at the cutting edge of both quantitative and qualitative approaches. The authors discuss important examples of research on curriculum initiatives, teaching resources, and teaching approaches that reflect a concern for sociocultural issues broadly defined, while also mapping out implications, future issues, and future research agendas. It is interesting to note that there is a blend both across and within chapters of sociocultural issues derived from Vygotskian theorizing as well as cross-cultural and multicultural theorizing. The chapters are thought provoking, and to our minds as editors, represent not only the best examples of research and theory, but also thought-provoking philosophical considerations on the nature of enquiry within complex societies.

Part I deals with early childhood and school curricula and learning. Chapter 1 by Strom and Strom deals with play and creativity among young children and how this can be encouraged and supported through parental involvement. Nations have begun to assign higher priority to creative thinking in schools. Persons who possess creative abilities are more able to accommodate novelty, avoid boredom, cope with an abundance of consumer choices, accept complexity, tolerate ambiguity, make independent judgments, use leisure time constructively, and adapt to new knowledge. These assets are vital for societies characterized by rapid change. Creativity is most prominent when curiosity is encouraged, self-directed learning is practiced, and access to imagination is common. There is agreement that support for these conditions should begin at home during early childhood. However, many adults do not know how play affects development and, as a result, sometimes make unwise decisions on what child activities and behaviors to encourage.

Strom and Strom explain why children need to play with parents and how the benefits of this fantasy interaction differ from the advantages offered by peers. This presentation describes experiments with culturally diverse populations that reveal how mothers and fathers can rely on play as a medium to teach vocabulary, values, and social skills to preschool children. "Toy Talk" promotes reciprocal learning by merging the separate strengths of parent and child. The authors examine common apprehensions expressed by parents about the motives of young pretenders and the possible effects that certain kinds of toys might have on the formation of character. The progression of cognitive development is portrayed in a way that enables parents to accept motives of children at play and establish a mutually satisfying relationship.

In 1996 the New Zealand Ministry of Education published a national early childhood curriculum, Te Whäriki. This curriculum introduced a new, sociocultural lens to a sector that had looked mostly toward psychology for its perspectives and philosophies. Chapter 2 by Carr considers some of the implications of this shift for practice and for research. Carr describes the early childhood curriculum, highlighting those aspects that make it "sociocultural." She then traces her own journey as a teacher and researcher taking on a sociocultural lens, before Te Whäriki and after Te Whäriki. This journey is analyzed under three headings: learning outcomes, motivation, and assessment. Learning outcomes have foregrounded participation in a community of learners. Research by Carr has investigated the ways in which learning and performance goals (an aspect of motivation) appear to be situated in activity. And narrative modes of assessment are developing to establish within the new curriculum a coherent lens on learning. Stories about children in early childhood settings implementing Te Whāriki illustrate the chapter's themes and ideas.

In Chapter 3, Wigfield and Lutz discuss how sociocultural contexts of the classroom and characteristics of children influence their reading comprehension and engagement. They begin with definitions of reading comprehension and engagement, and then consider cultural influences on reading. They present some general points multicultural educators have made about culture's impact on learning, and also discuss sociocultural perspectives on literacy. Wigfield and Lutz describe instructional principles derived from these sociocultural perspectives, principles designed to help children from different cultural backgrounds succeed in school.

The authors then discuss two literacy instructional programs that are concerned with sociocultural contexts of classrooms and students' cultural backgrounds, albeit in different ways. One is Concept-Oriented Reading Instruction (CORI), a program that integrates science and reading at the elementary school level and works to increase students' reading engagement through a set of instructional principles designed to boost students' motivation, and strategy instruction designed to help children acquire the reading strategies needed to comprehend well. The second is the Kamehameha Elementary Education Program (KEEP), a whole literacy instructional program initially designed for native Hawaiian children. KEEP integrates reading and writing and has as a major goal fostering children's ownership of their own learning. Wigfield and Lutz describe each program, discuss how each considers sociocultural characteristics of classrooms and student cultural backgrounds, and present research evidence for each program. The chapter closes with a comparison of the two programs and suggestions for future research.

The fourth chapter, by Zacher, details the agentive identity work that urban fifth-grade children undertake in a 2-month-long literature study unit on Patricia and Frederick McKissack's (1992) *Sojourner Truth: Ain't I a Woman?* This ethnographic study highlights the race, gender, and social class negotiation in which children engage as they read, write, and talk about the slave narrative. In this case, the school itself has a focus on multiculturalism in general and the civil rights movement in particular, and students have studied key historical figures from that era each year in school. At the same time, the students in the classroom come from communities and homes that are socioeconomically and geographically diverse, and their lived experiences are often marked by extreme difference.

Zacher's analysis of student talk and writing around *Sojourner Truth* indicates that students have appropriated much of the multicultural discourse of the school community. At the same time, however, students construct their own definitions of race, social class, and other identity categories in their individual and small-group discussions, and in their written and performed texts about the book. They also bring to, develop, and take home interpretations that are embedded in the wider social environment in which they live. As Zacher points out, such interactions often take place under or outside of the teacher's radar, and the issues brought up in these interactions are seldom negotiated with the help of the teacher or other adults engaged in the teaching of the multicultural curriculum. In line with other scholars in the field of cultural studies, Zacher urges researchers and teachers to pay more attention to the places, everyday spaces, and spatial discourses, especially in relation to classrooms, in which children live. She argues that such attention can be critical in helping us understand how children make meaning out of school texts and how children's worlds are shaped by the spatial discourses of the school, classroom, and literature study unit.

Students' understanding of science and their difficulties in learning science are profoundly affected by a wide range of experiences and life circumstances that occur outside of the classroom. Their culture, economic status, language, race, gender, and any number of other factors all play a role in learning. In Chapter 5 Fong and Seigel look at how two teachers use their knowledge of students' sociocultural background to teach science. They explore how these teachers view the importance of student sociocultural background. Their chapter is based on case studies conducted in two life science classrooms in a large ethnically and racially diverse high school in Northern California. Fong and Seigel discuss teachers' awareness and valuing of students' sociocultural backgrounds, the types of strategies teachers use to investigate students' sociocultural background, how they use this information to inform their teaching, and any barriers that exist that might prevent investigation of student sociocultural backgrounds. Fong and Seigel situate their discussion within the framework of pedagogical content knowledge (PCK) and argue that a teacher's investigation and use of student sociocultural background information should be part of the implementation of PCK in science classrooms.

Mandinach and Honey, in Chapter 6, discuss research issues that impact the conduct of effective and informative research on educational technology. Educational technology has proliferated in school settings to the point of near ubiquity in some settings, whereas in other locations, it is far from common. Sociocultural factors such as the digital divide, gender equity, and organizational structure impact how technology is infused and implemented in school settings. There is no question that the digital divide continues to exist for many segments of the population, although for many groups, computer ownership and access to the Internet has increased. The authors' *leitmotif* is that context is critical to the understanding of how technology is implemented in schools and classrooms. Their chapter then examines the literature on three sociocultural variables--the digital divide, gender equity, and organizational structure--with respect to educational technology. Finally, three projects are highlighted and descriptions are provided about how sociocultural factors influence teaching and learning activities in technology-based environments.

In 1983, Howard Gardner proposed the theory of multiple intelligences (MI), in which he argued the need to adopt a pluralistic notion of intelligence. He posited seven discrete intelligences to which he later added an eighth. Although the theory had little impact in the field of psychology, it was warmly embraced by educators throughout the world. The ideas were used as the basis for designing individual teachers' classroom activities as well as for schoolwide reform; it was used to argue an alternative approach to the education of students with special needs and to suggest alternative approaches to the identification of gifted students. The 20-plus years since the theory was presented has seen a mushrooming of publications about the implementation of MI. Most of this work, however, has been descriptive and the literature needs to be supplemented by a more rigorous research base. In Chapter 7 Vialle reviews her research on MI conducted over the last 13 years in the United States and Australia; she also reviews the work of colleague June Maker, whose MI research covers a similar timeframe. Both researchers are drawn to the theory through their keen interest in finding solutions to the problem of the underrepresentation of cultural minority students in programs for the gifted. Vialle uses this research to argue that MI is an important tool to change the way teachers think about the students they teach. By recognizing the myriad ways in which people come to know, understand, and express their ideas, teachers come to appreciate the need to cater to all the diverse needs of their students. Vialle also reminds the reader that MI is not an educational panacea but its principles are complementary to other curricula approaches that may better serve the students of the 21st century.

In Chapter 8 McInerney, Dowson, and Yeung investigate Arabic students' perceptions of Personal Development Health and Physical Education (PDHPE) curricula. Arabic students' reactions to these curricula have been problematic, with many Arabic students withdrawing (tacitly or otherwise) from participation in PDHPE lessons and other school PDHPE activities (e.g., sporting carnivals) on the basis of their PDHPE perceptions. In this chapter, however, McInerney, Dowson, and Yeung suggest that, when investigating Arabic students' PDHPE perceptions, treating Arabic students as a homogeneous group may be misleading. Rather, by examining PDHPE perceptions with respect to religious and sex differences among Arabic students, a much more detailed and comprehensive picture emerges. Specifically, religion and sex differences appear to account for differences in Arabic students PDHPE perceptions that would not emerge if this level of analysis were not undertaken. The broader implication of the study is that within-culture differences may need to be more widely explored in sociocultural studies of education.

In a related chapter on religion, Chapter 9, Dowson explores the interaction between sociocultural context, type of religious education, and family religious orientation. He suggests that motivation and learning in religious education (RE) settings result from this interaction. The chapter provides a comprehensive framework for categorizing four types of sociocultural context (i.e., monoreligious, multireligious, secular-traditional, and secular-pluralistic) and three types of RE (education for religion, education about religion, and education from religion). The interaction of these types of context and RE can be used to predict how acceptable a particular type of RE will be in any given context. Moreover, the religious orientation of the family (typically reflected in the students' own religious orientation) may interact with both the wider sociocultural context and the type of RE encountered in school to substantially influence students' reactions to RE, including their motivational reactions and subsequent learning.

In Chapter 10 Suliman examines the issue of bilingualism among migrant children in Australia. Many children from migrant families are by necessity bilingual: they use a language at home that is not the main, social, academic, or political language used in the country in which they live. In Australia, a significant number of children come from such backgrounds and use another language at home alongside English. They often find themselves, from a very young age, in situations where they have to switch from one language to another or use both languages simultaneously to be able to communicate effectively. Suliman asks how proficient these children are in speaking, reading, and writing these two languages and what the implication is of this proficiency on their school achievement. The chapter addresses these language issues with particular reference to students from an Arabic-speaking background, highlighting the importance of developing the language proficiency of these children in both their first and second languages. Reference is made to language programs in schools, pointing out some models that can best develop the "bilingualism" of these children and enhance their school achievement.

In the final chapter of the first section of Volume 5 (Chapter 11), McGinley, Whitcomb, and Zerwin invite readers to take a view of literature reading that diverges from conventional approaches found in most secondary English language arts classrooms. It invites readers to envision instructional possibilities where whole-hearted reading is the norm, where the life-affirming qualities of literary conversation are the norm. Beginning with a reflection on a scene from *The Education of Little Tree*, in which one of the characters reads a passage from *Julius Caesar* and talks back to Shakespeare with an admixture of moral outrage and irreverence, the chapter raises questions about how we come to read literature in homes and communities and how that compares with those ways students are asked to read in school. In so doing, the chapter embraces and promotes a vision of literature reading that has roots in the hybrid, street-based engagement of literature experienced by working-class men and women in 19th-century England (as described by Willinsky) and in the heteroglossia of the carnival (as described by Bahktin). It stands in contrast with the academic traditions of English as a subject matter and with corporate book publishing. McGinley, Whitcomb, and Zerwin recount narratives of several teachers who reflect upon their development as teachers who challenged the traditional academic teaching of literature, and in so doing, created places where students engaged in more authentic conversation and dialogic with one another and with the texts. The authors challenge the status quo and provide images of the possible because they believe the text-based tradition of reading literature, which continues to dominate secondary English language arts classrooms, fails students and by extension the community. In sum, the chapter makes the case for an approach to literature reading in school that makes room for the transformative, saving power of literature to take hold.

Our second section on post-school education begins with a chapter by Burton, Dowling, Dorman, and Brodie dealing with student diversity at university and the factors that influence academic success. Chapter 12 describes a project that examines many of the different factors that shape how students perform at university. The aim of the project is to develop a model that can be used to achieve a better match between student learning styles and capabilities, and staff teaching styles and strategies, taking into account factors such as students' cultural norms and expectations, self-efficacy, individual learning preferences, language spoken, and ability level. The authors report on the results of a preliminary study of first-year engineering students, which examines the relationships between these sociocultural factors and their academic performance. The demographics of the University of Southern Queensland student cohort make this sample ideal, as it is diverse in terms of age, gender, language, ethnicity, educational and socioeconomic backgrounds, and life and work experiences. The authors believe that this type of research is significant because it helps teachers become more aware of the differences that students bring to the learning environment and helps them to identify adaptations to teaching methodologies and remedial programs that can help optimize student performance.

Richardson Bruna, in Chapter 13, challenges conventional narratives of the white teacher candidate's resistance to multicultural teacher education. The author draws on findings from her 3-year ethnographic study of a Cultural Diversity classroom to argue that the resistance of the white teacher candidate in learning about diversity is not adequately understood through an individualistic lens, but instead through the lens of social construction. The individualistic lens attributes resistance to the teacher candidate simply because of her white identity. The lens of social construction, however, attributes such resistance to the interactions between the teacher candidate and her multicultural teacher educator. The dynamic of these interactions is significantly influenced by what the author calls the force of cultural mismatch thinking. Cultural mismatch thinking, the idea that white teachers are innately ill-prepared because of their white identity to work with culturally and linguistically diverse students, results in pedagogical relations embroiled in disputes over the teacher candidate's self-perception as a "good white" and the teacher educator's inscription of her as a "bad white." The chapter showcases a snapshot of this socially constructed resistance and the role that the multicultural teacher educator's duplicitous use of reflection plays in actually achieving the opposition and demotivation of the white teacher candidate. Richardson Bruna asserts that these kinds of pedagogical relations result in the miseducation of the white teacher for cultural and linguistic diversity and in so doing work against the very goal of multicultural teacher education.

In Chapter 14 Horsley and Walker present a sociocultural analysis of curriculum and teaching in relation to South Pacific Islander students in the New South Wales school system (Pasifika Australia). Culture underpins both successful curriculum development and also the choice of pedagogies that reinforce and affirm the South Pacific student educational experience. Horsley and Walker consider curriculum activities and pedagogies that lead to successful learning for South Pacific Islanders. In particular, the authors discuss research projects concerning the curriculum and learning activities of South Pacific Island students. Their analyses demonstrate that there is a lack of alignment between Western perspectives of curriculum and teaching and perspectives from the culture of South Pacific Islanders. This lack of alignment is a major problem for South Pacific Island students, their teachers, and the school systems in which they study. It has lead to significant problems concerning the achievement of Pacific Island students. The chapter examines attempts to create alignments between the curriculum and teaching and the expectations of South Pacific Island students.

In Chapter 15, Kelly and Buxton describe a naturalistic inquiry that examines the importance of creating a community in an urban teacher education scholarship program for students of color. The authors believe that the creation of a community is important to provide a source of support for students as well as assisting them in forming identities as urban teachers. In exchange for scholarship support, students commit to teaching for 2 years in a high-need urban school. The program has been successful, with a graduation rate of 85%, while the college as a whole has a graduation rate of less than 40% for students of the same background. The creation of a supportive community is not an easy task, however, as it requires individuals from across the campus coming together in configurations not normally achieved in the institutional setting of a college campus. Involving students in field experiences is a second critical component in creating a community. The importance of campus-wide support and field experiences is presented through the words of students and graduates through course assignments, interviews, and correspondence with the program director.

Our final chapter (Chapter 16) by Ng examines curriculum and pedagogical development for building a community of learners among older Hong Kong Chinese adults in using ICT. This chapter focuses on researching how a selected group of anxious and unconfident novice learners have gradually developed into motivated experts capable of showcasing their computing achievement to others, and subsequently attracted other older adults to join the program, turning the elderly center into a hub for learning, sharing, and modeling the use of ICT knowledge and skills.

Data generated from a series of interviews, field visits, and classroom observation are utilized to show how specific curriculum and pedagogical features of the computer literacy program have successfully provided social scaffolds for learning computer knowledge and skills, opening up their ZPDs, and gradually fostering the development of a community of learners. The chapter indicates the importance of agency, reflection, collaboration, and culture as crucial factors for fostering the development of a community of learners. In addition, Ng argues that accommodating to the diverse needs of the learners (accommodation) and connecting with other communities (extension) are facilitative to the development of a community of learners among these older Chinese learners.

These 16 chapters present a wonderful kaleidoscope of cutting-edge research and theorizing on sociocultural influences on motivation and learning. Furthermore, each chapter illustrates the applied value of such theorizing and research for improving teaching and learning in very diverse sociocultural contexts. Shawn and I know that you will enjoy reading them, and enjoy learning from these authors' expertise. One acknowlegment: We would like to thank Martin Dowson for assistance with editorial work on this volume.

PART I

EARLY CHILDHOOD AND SCHOOL CURRICULUM

CHAPTER 1

TEACHING THROUGH PLAY AND RESPECTING THE MOTIVATION OF PRESCHOOLERS

Robert D. Strom and Paris S. Strom

Play is the dominant activity of preschoolers, their favorite way to spend time. Yet many parents are unsure about the importance of imaginative play and early childhood educators may not understand this initial expression of creativity well enough to ensure a prominent place for it in the curriculum. This presentation consists of two segments, each describing a separate aspect of the dynamics of play. First, we describe studies that make known the potential of play for teaching certain concepts more effectively than is possible when traditional forms of instruction are applied. Second, motives of preschool players are examined to identify misperceptions and replace these with awareness regarding normative mental development.

THE POTENTIAL OF PLAY FOR TEACHING

Our motivation to explore imaginative play was based on a desire to help parents join preschoolers in the forum they enjoy most. The literature sel-

Focus on Curriculum, 3–21

dom considered interpersonal variables, usually describing play as if the participants were interchangeable and represent the same potential for influence. In contrast, we assumed that play could yield differential benefits, depending on the players, whether the companions of young children were their parents, peers, or fantasy characters they invented during solitary play.

We needed a suitable environment in which to refine our assumptions and subject them to observation. A team of student architects was recruited along with a group of mothers with young children. Together they helped us plan and construct a colorful fantasy-oriented laboratory. Financial support to establish the work was provided by the Danforth Foundation, Rockefeller Foundation, General Mills, and the Toy Manufacturers of America. The initial sample consisted of 300 black, Hispanic, Native American, and white families from low- and middle-income neighborhoods. At the time we did not foresee that this local collaboration would one day evolve into a global venture that provides education for parents at every stage of their long-term role as teachers (P. Strom & Strom, 2002; R. Strom, 1995, 2002; R. Strom & Strom, 1998). An overview of current research and development can be examined at the Office of Parent Development International's Web site at http://www.public.asu.edu/~rdstrom

Defining the Challenge

Parents of preschoolers have a difficult teaching role because some goals must be accomplished through play. Reliance on play as a method for instruction may not appear demanding until it is recognized that parents (the teachers) have a shorter attention span than their children (the learners) for fantasy interaction. Then, too, young children more readily access imagination than is typical among adults. Given these conditions, the purposes of parents can best be achieved when they regard themselves as partners in play. Competition does not characterize a partnership. Instead, strengths of each partner are merged for mutual advantage. In fantasy play, a partnership can produce reciprocal learning and respect.

We wanted to honor the strengths that parents and preschoolers bring to their play and understand how these attributes can be combined. A related challenge was to figure out how the interactive process of pretending together could guide instruction. There was a corresponding need to discover how the lesser access of adults than children to imagination could be compensated for by reliance on other resources. Finally, it was necessary to decide on the kinds of lessons that should be emphasized during interactive play with 3- to 5-year-olds.

Play Preferences and Needs

One of our first observations indicated the preference of young children for repetition, their need to recreate certain play situations over and over again. By contrast, most adults who came to the play laboratory expressed feelings of boredom when placed in repetitive situations. To illustrate, when 4-year old John asked his father to play soldiers, his dad said, "But Johnny, we just played with these soldiers yesterday. Let's play something else, something different." Because adults are prone to boredom in repetitive settings, few of them are able to play with preschoolers for long periods. Indeed, laboratory observations suggested that, during parent–child fantasy play, adults have the shorter attention spans.

Some observers viewed the attention span differences between parents and their children as evidence of incompatibility. This conclusion was reinforced by colleagues who asked, "Why should children play with their parents anyway? When it comes to play, what children need most are friends their own age." At least this view seemed to be the prevailing opinion. Perhaps the play needs of children can be appreciated more by juxtaposing them with our own recreational needs. What kinds of games do we consider most exciting, the most fun to watch? Generally, adults agree that they prefer to watch a close game, one in which the outcome remains doubtful until near the end of the contest. When a football team outscores another 60 to 0, spectators may complain that what they witnessed was not a game at all. There was such an imbalance of power that the game eliminated uncertainty and consequent excitement over who would be the winner. When our team runs away with the score, we might encourage scoring by the opposition and find some pleasure in their success. Professional football and basketball teams initiated the annual draft recruitment policy for new players so that power would not become the exclusive realm of one team in the league. Promoters of sports realized that, if power were unilateral, fans would conclude, "Why watch?"

Some parents experience a similar motivation when they play games with their young children. The adults recognize their own competence is too great for the child to win, perhaps too powerful for the child to sense any satisfaction from the contest. Then, during a game of checkers, when the child begins to complain, threatens to quit, or seems ready to cry, the parent must decide what to do. Why do some parents decide to cheat in favor of their young opponent? Certainly it is not to teach dishonesty. The reason is to make the child feel powerful. The fact that young children are powerless in games that require rules means that these are not the best play activities for families to engage in together. There is a better way to respect children and become involved in their lives—through fantasy play (Taylor, 1999; Torrance, 1995).

We wanted to check our hunch that preschoolers need to play with parents so they can share dominance. Twenty-five parents agreed to participate with their 4-year-olds in fantasy interaction for 10 minutes each morning and evening. This schedule was followed for one week. During the following week, the parents were told to offer children excuses for being unable to play together. Throughout the experiment, each family kept a daily record of child misbehavior. As a group, the family records revealed an incidence of misconduct six times as great for non-play days as for the "child power" days of interactive play. The substantially less misbehavior on days when parents played with children suggested that certain power needs are met during family fantasy play (R. Strom, 1995).

Use of Play Themes

Generational differences in the preferred focus of play posed the task of discovering how children's wish for repetition could be reconciled with the adult desire for novelty. Toward this possibility, we exposed boys and girls to a wide array of toys that had been contributed to the laboratory by many of the 2,000 member companies in the Toy Manufacturers of America. The choice of toys and play themes preschoolers chose were identified by highest to lowest frequency of attention. The favorite themes implicated toys such as doctor's and nurse's kits, action figure dolls, trucks, airplanes, soldiers, boats, and prehistoric animals. Experiments revealed that during play, adults were able to accept the child's preference for repetition without enduring monotony. This was accomplished by focusing on one general theme related to the playthings selected by children but revising a theme each time in subtle ways. To illustrate, during play with doctor's and nurse's kits, we were able to extend our attention spans by reliance on these subthemes:

We must find the brown dog that bit the little boy.

The witch doctor wants to have a job at the hospital.

The martian has never been to see a doctor before.

Nurse, the hospital is full of noises and I can't sleep.

His family is needed to help him so he gets well again.

The patient must be hiding around here somewhere.

I want my dog to be with me while I am in the hospital.

Lots of things happen in the hospital emergency ward.

Animals are working as doctors in this animal hospital.

Let's try to help the elephant mother to have her baby.

We need to visit sick people who are in the hospital.

It soon became obvious that while children want to pursue familiar themes, they will readily accept an incremental variety of subthemes. In this way parent desire for novelty can be met without giving up the favorite play theme of a child. This approach implicated use of improvisation, being able to think quickly of subthematic variations on the spot. However, most adults that we observed, including preschool and primary teachers, performed poorly in generating alternative subthemes. Still, it was evident that the attention span of adults had to increase, to become long enough so parents would find enjoyment in fantasy play and make use of fantasy interaction to teach without suffering boredom.

How could subtheme variations be provided for adult players who yearn for greater novelty than they themselves are able to spontaneously produce? At the outset, we brainstormed lists of subthemes and placed them beside parents on the floor while they were observed during scheduled play periods with their child. Fifty subthemes were provided with toy airplanes and the general theme of "The airplanes are ready."

Airplanes can find the people who are lost in the desert.

All of the passengers have to be checked for weapons.

Passengers want Chicago but the hijacker says Mexico.

Our suitcases did not come with us on the same plane.

This airplane will be flying with animal stewardesses.

The children are working together in the control tower.

There are not enough soft drinks on board for everyone.

By providing this structure and easy access to versions of a theme, we hoped to diminish the parent polar responses of coercion and concession that typified their play with children. Coercion and concession are inappropriate ways to share dominance. Still, some parents suppose that, if they are using toys, their coercive interaction can be called play. In an opposite way, concession-oriented parents continually look to their children to provide them with direction about what to do next or say because they are unable to think of options on their own.

Subtheme lists were helpful but they presented limitations as well. The incidence of coercion declined but some parents felt overwhelmed with the wide range of subtheme options given to them. Other parents with a strong need to complete one task before going on to another reported feeling frustrated when they could not finish all of the subthemes they were provided prior to a play session. Classroom teachers sometimes

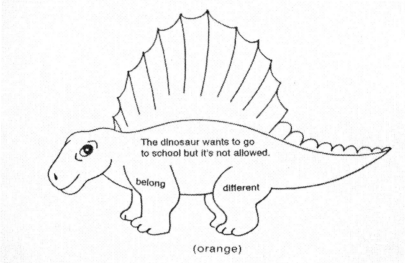

The dinosaur wants to go to school but it's not allowed.

belong

different

(orange)

Figure 1.1.   Examples of dinosaur cutout.

experience similar frustrations when they have more lessons to cover than there is time in the schedule.

At that point an insight led us to abandon subtheme lists. The replacement method was to write one subtheme on separate cutout figural forms. This change was intended to eliminate parent feelings of over choice but preserve access to novel ideas. In addition to many subthemes, there was diversity of figural shapes. Figure 1.1 shows one of the five dinosaur shapes made of colored construction paper. Children were less distracted as parents referred to a colorful paper figure on which a play subtheme was written than when adults had to turn to subtheme lists. To summarize, the purpose for placing one subtheme on each paper dinosaur is to provide parents a continuing source of ideas to sustain their involvement while preventing boredom. Five shapes of paper figures of airplanes, boats, doctors, and soldiers are provided when corresponding toys are found to be of greatest interest to the children. In every case, the couple plays with actual toys, not with the construction paper figures incorporated solely as a guide for parents. This approach is effective in structuring resource ideas that promote fantasy interaction. And, make no mistake about it—adults need structure.

Parent Goals for Teaching

Before parents can use subthemes effectively, they should feel comfortable with this process as a way to achieve some personal goals for child guidance. We start by acquainting them with the possibilities for teaching values, that realm of child learning for which most parents consider themselves accountable and want to be successful. For example, dinosaur play is introduced to parents in this manner:

This is dinosaur country. Most of us do not realize how hard it is to be a dinosaur these days. The fact is, except for the children, hardly anyone pays much attention to dinosaurs anymore. I got to thinking that maybe things would be different if the population of dinosaurs could increase so they would not be such a small group. After some persuasion, the 25 dinosaurs you see displayed on the wall agreed to come here with the expectation that you will help increase their numbers to start the population boom they need.

As you might suppose, dinosaurs are not all alike. The best way to tell them apart is not by appearance but by the values they support. These differing values are shown by separate colors. For example, regardless of their shape, pink dinosaurs all believe that the most important lesson for early learning is the "constructive use of power." Dinosaurs whose color is blue are united in believing that "sharing fears and anxieties" deserves the greatest attention. Green dinosaurs are convinced that "understanding the needs and feelings of others" deserve the highest priority. Yellow dinosaurs place their greatest emphasis on "cooperation with others," while orange ones think that "expressing differences verbally" should be the dominant aspect of teaching.

All of the dinosaurs will now be taken down from the wall and placed in groups according to their color. You are asked to join one group whose goal focus you wish to support. In addition to figures with subthemes, your team will have two dinosaurs with no theme written on them. Bear in mind that, to belong to any group as well as add to the dinosaur population, these unmarked dinosaurs must acquire a subtheme. So, in the next 15 minutes, the task of your team is to brainstorm possible subthemes and choose the two most preferable that will be assigned to give dinosaurs a sense of identity.

Consider the five goals and 25 subthemes that accompany them.

Play Theme: This is Dinosaur Country

Parent Goal: Teaching Constructive Use of Power (Pink Dinosaurs)

Subthemes

The boy is teaching the dinosaur how to swim.

We can cross the river on the dinosaur's back.

Let's ask him to help tear down old buildings.

Tell the dinosaur family the hunters are coming.

The biggest dinosaur is stuck in the mud.

Parent Goal: Sharing Fears and Worries (Blue Dinosaurs)

Subthemes

It's dark and he hears a noise outside the cave.
It's an earthquake and trees are falling down.
She woke up crying from a bad dream.
She is trying to find her way home.
People are running away to hide from him.

Parent Goal: Understanding the Needs and Feelings of Others
(Green Dinosaurs)

Subthemes

My best friend has to move to another place.
She's sad because she can't fit on the merry-go-round.
He's not been chosen for the animal parade.
She needs to make lots of noise but it bothers people.
He wants to play but no one will let him out of his cage.

Parent Goal: Cooperating with Others (Yellow Dinosaurs)

Subthemes

My friend cut his leg and we can't find a big-enough bandage.
This is the world's only dinosaur circus.
He can help us at the school playground.
Climb his tail so we can pick fruit from the trees.
Teach the dinosaur to cook so he won't be hungry.

Parent Goal: Expressing Differences with Others (Orange Dinosaurs)

Subthemes

The dinosaur wants to go to school but it's not allowed.
He is a friendly dinosaur but only the children know.
The cave people have become angry at the dinosaurs.
He just wants to sit and watch television all day long.
The little dinosaur tells his parents he will run away.

After the parents generate alternatives, they choose five of the sub-theme figures to take home for trial. The only recommendations that are given to them at this stage are:

1. Play with your preschooler a few minutes every day for the next week.

2. Schedule all of the play sessions at a time when you are fresh and have energy rather than being tired out.

3. Write your thoughts in a notebook after each play period.

Generally, parents report that using the subthemes enables them to interact for longer periods with their children. As the parents share their experiences, they commonly acknowledge their discovery that children are the best models for showing how to engage in fantasy play. Once this conclusion has been reached and the corresponding respect for children is evident, parents are ready to assume a more influential teaching role.

What are the benefits of using subthemes for instruction? First, it is well known that helping children perceive options is essential to divergent thinking. This way of looking at things can offer greater advantage than either/or thinking, the my-way or your-way kind of outlook. The impression that there are two sides to every issue is an underestimate in a society that promotes differences. Instead, if everyone can look at situations in a variety of ways, the chances of conciliation, getting along, sharing dominance, and living together even though we are different is much improved. Children need to develop an ability to see many possibilities in situations if they are to do well in problem solving as well as conflict resolution, areas of achievement in which too few people are able to excel. What we have in the subtheme approach is a way to increase duration of parent–child play, a way to practice sensing alternatives, and a way in which the child can learn to use assertion as well as compromise. Unlike a child's immature peers, parents offer a more mature model of how to express and accept differences.

Second, we should take advantage of the identification phase of early childhood. Using play subthemes that are colored according to personality (affective) goals allows parents to assume certain positive roles that daily affairs might prevent them from modeling. Some values that parents hold dear ordinarily are displayed in response to situations that seldom occur when children are around to observe. Children could follow their parents for weeks and never witness some of the values parents consider most important. However, play offers a unique opportunity to invent situations that permit parents to demonstrate their values in a consistent way.

The illustration of parental values has more effect on children than does an imposition of values. Consequently, it is recommended that, instead of settling for a random positive model of our values, parents choose a deliberate and consistent model. Goals for teaching values combined with the subtheme approach allow mothers and fathers to do so during play. The primary limitation of this method, which we refer to as "Toy Talk," relates to the age of the children. Until boys and girls are about 3½ years old, they do not have a sufficient language base and the concentration necessary to sustain thematic interaction. Parents continue to report mutual benefits from kindergarten through grade 3. The upper age limit for using Toy Talk seems to be 10, when soldiers and space toys serve as the last dominant themes.

Vocabulary and Language Development

When parents begin to enjoy fantasy play, as reflected by an increased attention span to a minimum of 12 minutes, and they can model values during play, we concentrate next on vocabulary development. In deciding about the words to convey, it is important to share language that is context relevant. This means respecting the vocabulary that is used by parents rather than prescribing "appropriate" words for them to teach children. The words should be ones used in the home, a factor that varies with education of parents and their socioeconomic status. Accordingly, parents choose from vocabulary lists the words they want to teach. The selected words are then applied to subtheme figures representing the play focus chosen by their child, such as airplanes, boats, soldiers, doctors and nurses, or dinosaurs. Figure 1.1 includes words that apply to a subtheme for one of the goals parents can choose to emphasize in play with dinosaurs.

For each word a parent selects, suggestions are given for ways to enact the definition in context. To illustrate:

1. Accident: something bad happens without being planned
    a.   The caveman fell off the mountain. It was an accident.
    b.   The caveman cut himself with a rock. It was an accident.
2. Afraid: feeling that something is going to hurt you
    a.   A big mean dinosaur is coming toward her and she feels afraid.
    b.   The cavemen are afraid and running away from the dinosaurs.
3. Alone: without anyone else nearby, to be by oneself
    a.   The baby dinosaur is sleeping alone under the tree.
    b.   The cavemen go to the lake together. They do not swim alone.

Similarly, during the course of a 10-minute "flight" with airplane subthemes, a parent might introduce and try to define words such as passenger, destination, delay, schedule, luggage, search, ticket, weapons, altitude, terrorist, afraid, rescue, negotiate, and reunion. Or, while on a submarine voyage to find treasures, the child might be exposed to the meaning of words like buried, search, sailing, submerge, map, compass, surface, depth, pirate, oxygen, ocean, unknown, and sink. Whatever the play theme, parents can enlarge their child's understand vocabulary (that is always larger than their spoken vocabulary) by defining relevant words in context. Usually we recommend emphasizing a small number of words per week. Using words in more than a single subtheme should reinforce the meanings.

By the time children arrive in kindergarten, there is a great disparity in word power among them. It is estimated that, in terms of sentence structure, a child's spoken language reaches 90% of its mature level by age 6; a first grader uses every part of speech and forms of a sentence. Speaking three-word sentences, telling stories, sharing ideas, and telling first name, last name, and age are skills that develop between 2 and 3 years of age. Three- to four-year-olds make sentences of four to five words and ask lots of questions. Most 4- to 5-year-olds can define common words, count to 20, and enjoy looking at books.

The methodology we have described is called "Toy Talk." This is one way parents can meet their responsibility for contributing to child language. Toy Talk is an activity where children at play are given the opportunity to learn at least one meaning for each of a number of words and use these words in a relevant setting. Toy Talk can also help build positive attitudes and values through play.

Although it is possible to communicate feelings and thoughts with a minimum of vocabulary, the more words at one's command, the richer and more exact the speech. Each person depends on language facility to express their ideas, to label thoughts, to urge the consideration of feelings, to describe emotions, and to compare experiences. Everyone has been in the situation of trying to convey an idea when the appropriate words seemed fugitive. The problem is more acute for persons whose speech has been developed in settings where restricted language tends to be prevalent. Students from such backgrounds often find themselves less able to understand and to make themselves understood than do their peers who come to school with facility in the language of the dominant culture. The greater the access to vocabulary, the less frequently all these frustrations occur.

Before parents start teaching language through play, we help them learn to assess their child's vocabulary. Otherwise, they lack the means to determine whether they've taught the child anything the child did not already know. Here it is important to underscore the self-concept of parents as the first teachers of their child. The possibility of confirming the effectiveness of their teaching helps them offset feelings of insecurity in the instructional role. Figure 1.2 illustrates the techniques that we devised to check comprehension. The questions parents ask children before and after they teach vocabulary words (called pre/post testing) are the same for each word. However, different pictures are used on the pre- and post-test. Children are asked to identify, explain, and elaborate the meaning of each word. This broad-based procedure provides a more accurate assessment of comprehension than is common in traditional vocabulary testing for this age group. Our studies show that over 90% of 3-year-olds comprehend the pictures.

PRETEST

A   B   C

DIFFERENT: not alike
1.   Which picture shows someone who is being different?
2.   Why did you choose that one?
3.   What do you do to be different?

POSTTEST

A   B   C

DIFFERENT: not alike
1.   Which picture shows someone who is being different?
2.   Why did you choose that one?
3.   What do you do to be different?

Figure 1.2.   Vocabulary assessment.

Summary of the Studies

Parents benefit from learning to pretend with their young children. Some critics regard imaginative play as an unimportant activity that is only appropriate for children. The view we maintain is quite different. Our studies indicate that interactive fantasy play can contribute to mental health at every age. Play is an especially powerful tool on which parents can rely for teaching values, social skills and vocabulary to their children. Play requires creativity, and adults should regularly exercise their imagination to remain viable. Perhaps Michel Montaigne, the French philosopher, said it best: "The play of children is their most serious business." We recommend that participation in this serious business should become a more common aspect of the parent experience.

ACCEPTING THE MOTIVES OF YOUNG CHILDREN

The second segment of this presentation concerns motives of preschoolers in fantasy play. We believe that the prevailing opinion about how boys and girls see things is inconsistent with what is known of normal cognitive development. One way to begin is by recalling the first "television war." This 1991 conflict was fought in the Persian Gulf when many nations opposed the Iraqi annexation of Kuwait. People wanted to watch everything they could of the continuous news coverage even though they feared what was happening. There were frequent briefings from officials at the Pentagon and military leaders in coalition forces. A photographic record of target damage from the pilot's view was included in the daily report of bombing raids. Service men and women were interviewed in the battle zone about their particular roles and impressions of the progress. Defense experts talked about the strategies of warfare, explained capability and performance of various armaments, and posed scenarios about events that might occur next.

Shortly thereafter, television networks provided children with an orientation to the war and joined parents in trying to respond to the broad range of questions that were expressed by youngsters. What can we do to support the troops? Should our family go to the shopping mall if that is the kind of place terrorists would strike? Why don't we treat the prisoners we capture the same way as they do? Who will take care of the single-parent children and those who have two parents in the war? What do the Muslim soldiers believe about dying in a battle? Can anything be done to save the birds and wildlife we see dripping with oil? How will the burning oil wells affect the rest of the world? Are the people of Iraq our enemy, or is just Saddam Hussein, the man who is their leader?

Differences between Real and Pretend War

Parents expressed many concerns too and they wondered how watching the war would influence their children. Some were uncertain about allowing sons and daughters to play with toy weapons or military games. Barbara is a 35-year-old mother of two preschoolers. Even before the war, Barbara and her husband felt that violent toys breed lawlessness: "We knew that the decision to deny them weapon toys would be difficult for our boys to understand. It would be easy to conform to the majority opinion, but to us that would mean a lowering of our personal standards of integrity."

Denise had misgivings about war toys when her fifth-grade son, Ben, got a laser tag set. This game requires a gun that shoots an infrared light beam. The gun is aimed at a red "star sensor" target worn by an opponent. When a sensor is hit, it lights up and plays an electronic series of sounds. After six hits, the sensor signals an end to the game. The light that is emitted is not an actual laser beam. It is a safe infrared light enabling children to play in the dark. Ben says that he likes it mostly because for the first time he can play tag and know for certain when someone has been hit. Denise feels there is more to the game than tag, causing the mock killing of another person to be viewed as a form of achievement. She has similar complaints about the video war games that Ben wants, particularly one that features a shootout with terrorists trying to blow up an airport.

During our parent education class discussions, we listened to many adults opposed to children playing war. They believe this activity can cause the rise of aggression, support impulsive behavior, and teach children to discount the value of human life. The worry is that children may come to view war as enjoyable and killing an enemy as justifiable so long as it is being done for patriotic reasons. A frequent comment is that there is already too much crime on television and in the community without being reminded of it by children at play.

Children's Understanding of Death

Those who oppose play warfare state that their goal is simply to discourage a reliance on weapons as the way to resolve disputes. They contend that gunplay in childhood could result in the desire for immediate revenge instead of the fair-trial, innocent-until-proven-guilty philosophy that we expect of grownups. Jane, the mother of a 4-year-old boy, expresses this perspective:

After overhearing my child tell his cowboy companions he was going to shoot and kill them, I felt compelled to say, "Donnie, you don't really mean that." I reconsidered and thought maybe I should sit him down and explain that when you kill someone they are dead, and they will never breathe again. Then I wondered, if I don't let Donnie play with guns, it might give him the feeling that we are convinced he is so violent he requires different toys from everyone else. Finally, not knowing what to do or say, I ignored him and went on feeling guilty.

Jane's dilemma is a common one. Perhaps we can reduce the problem by more closely examining just what young children mean when they talk about killing and dying. Preschoolers view death as a reversible process. Whether they play Hide-and-Go-Seek or Cowboys and Indians, all the dead people are expected to recover quickly and live again. The conventional television cartoon reinforces this notion when the rabbit runs and then falls off a high cliff, hits the ground with a thud, and, in keeping with the child's reversible concept of death, is brought back to life. The same thing happens whenever children watch a television actor die on one program and later miraculously appear as a guest on a talk show. Some time ago, when Paris was a preschooler, we had this conversation:

Paris: Dad, I'm going to dress up like an army man.

Dad: You look just like a soldier. I was a soldier once.

Paris: Why?

Dad: Because the country needed me. We were having a war in Asia.

Paris: Dad, did you die?

Dad: No, I was lucky.

The realization that death is permanent develops in stages. Between ages 3 to 5, there is a lot of curiosity and questioning about death. Unfortunately, many adults suppress this curiosity, and think it is impolite for a child to ask old Mrs. Thompson when she is going to die. In contrast, several generations ago, it was common for children to witness at least one deathbed event, usually the death of a grandparent. Yet, the preschooler believes death is not final; it is like being less alive; just as sleeping people can wake up and people on a trip can return, so too a dead person can come back to life. The coffin limits their movement, but dead people must continue to eat and breathe. People buried at the cemetery know what is happening on the earth, they are sad for themselves and feel it whenever someone thinks of them. Dying disturbs the preschooler, since life in the grave is seen as boring and unpleasant. But, most of all, it bothers the child because death separates people from one another. And, at this age, a child's greatest fear is separation from parents.

Preschoolers are self-centered and preoccupied by present events, so they are unable to recognize how a death in the family may impose future demands on them, including the permanent loss of someone's presence, their comfort, love, encouragement, and perhaps, financial support. Because these understandings do not come until a later age, young children may not express grief immediately, or even cry like their adult relatives and friends. In fact, it is common for adults to mistakenly conclude that a child is coping well with the loss of a loved one. But, bear in mind that young children are unable to fully comprehend the situation and they can only tolerate short periods of sadness. Because it is easy for them to be distracted, they may appear to be finished with the grief and mourning process earlier than is actually the case.

Even young children recognize that words are an insufficient way to help someone in grief and that what matters most is just being there to console them. To illustrate, 4-year-old Amanda did not come in from the backyard when she was first called by her mother. Later, when her mother asked Amanda to explain why she was late, the little girl replied, "I was helping Judy." Mother wanted more information. "What were you doing?" Amanda said, "Well, her doll's head got crushed." Mother wondered aloud, "How could you help fix that?" Amanda had a good answer and said, "I was helping her cry."

Children between 5 to 9 years of age tend to personify death, seeing it as an angelic character that makes rounds in the night to start life for some individuals and end it for others. The big shift in the child's thinking from the first stage to this one is that death is recognized as possibly being final. It is no longer seen as just a reduced form of life. This view of death emerges with increasing personal experiences, which suggest that certain separations are permanent. When the pet goldfish dies, the mother buys a new one because, she says, the other one is gone forever. Claude Cattaert's (1963) book *Where Do Goldfish Go?* shows how children can become upset by adults whose insensitive reaction to animal death is that pets can be replaced. When Valerie's goldfish unexpectedly dies, no one is bothered except Valerie; yet the family is overcome with sorrow when her grandfather dies, even though his death had been anticipated for years.

It is not just families that need to become more aware and sensitive to children's feelings about death. In conversations with prospective kindergarten and first-grade teachers, we asked, "What would you do if some morning at school the class goldfish were found dead?" The range of responses included these comments: I would deliver a eulogy; declare a day of mourning; conduct a burial; discuss the virtues of the deceased;

consider the after-life of fish; invite testimonials from friends; talk about human death and its meaning; or flush the fish and say, "Take out your books, it's time for oral reading."

Parents know that they cannot guarantee a long life for pets, but hope they can reduce the amount of exposure their children have to death on television. The outcome of this decision to protect youngsters usually is a refusal to let them watch detective and police programs, censorship of some aggressive cartoons, and ambivalence about viewing the local news, which frequently portrays violence or death in the community.

The typical 5- to 9-year-old child believes that the cause of death is external, and they personify death as being an outside agent. Since they conceive of death as a person, children feel it is possible to avoid death if protective measures are taken. Thus, one child may claim that his grandfather won't die because the family is taking good care of him. Children of single parents admit they worry most about "What will happen to me if my mother dies?" It is reassuring for them to know that plans have been made so they will be taken care of in the event of an unexpected death.

Finally, about ages 9 to 10, children realize that death is not only final but also inevitable. It will happen to them too, no matter how clever they are or how well they take care of themselves. Instead of imagining death as being controlled by an external agent, they now recognize that internal, biological forces are involved. As children begin to accept the universality and certainty of death, some changes can be observed. They begin to show concern about the meaning of life, their purposes for being on earth, and ways to achieve those purposes. This means that values become important in governing their behavior.

Many children throughout the world are growing up in the midst of death and threat of destruction. They see death on television with such regularity that war has become a common fear. Children look to adults for answers about death, but our attitude is the most important response. Certainly you will want to explain your beliefs about what happens after death. But, bear in mind that youngsters love mystery, and they will adopt our sense of wonder and uncertainty if we are willing to express it.

Child Perceptions of Toys

There are many playthings parents believe children could do without. Some dislike all military toys because they reflect violence. Others oppose stunt-oriented toys that might encourage taking risks on bicycles. Crash cars that fall apart on impact and then can quickly be reconstructed are thought to sanction a disregard for safety, and martial arts dolls create reliance on an irrational method for resolving conflicts. Parents expressing these complaints are often ambivalent because they want to purchase toys that reflect their own values, but they should also recognize that children require opportunities in decision making to develop their own value system. And where is it more appropriate for children to be given options than in their realm of play?

Grownups can justify making some decisions for children such as whether they will attend school, if they will go to the doctor, and when it is time for bed. Parents will also determine how much money can be spent on entertainment and toys for children. On the other hand, to claim that boys and girls need coherent values but deny them practice in making some personal choices is unreasonable. So, parents are bothered about the priority they should assign to feelings of their children in selecting toys for them.

Instead of declaring your values by choosing children's toys or by censoring the content of their fantasy, try to enact your values while you participate in pretend-type play with them. The imposition of values always has less influence than the illustration of values. If you feel that war tends to be glorified while the darker sides of battle are overlooked, give some attention to the aftermath of war and the importance of the peacemaker role in your play.

Most people share the aspiration that international disarmament will rid us of the threat of nuclear war. But, while peace means the end of war, it does not mean an end to differences of opinion. Since there is a critical distinction between the fantasy wars enacted by children and the bloody wars carried out by adults, it is a serious error to misread the motives of the preschool soldier. Grownups who suppose that preschoolers playing soldiers have the same purposes as the warring men and women they imitate misinterpret the motives of children and their level of understanding about violence and death. Parents should strive to see favorable possibilities in their children's choice of playthings.

Conflict toys and games can serve to meet certain needs of boys and girls. This kind of play offers relief from feelings of powerlessness and dependence that accounts for much of a child's experience. Surely there is nothing strange about the desire to control others, especially those who exercise power over you daily. Children delight when they can assert themselves in play and make Daddy run away or fall down because he has been shot. Then, too, conflict playthings offer a safe setting in which to express normally disapproved feelings like anger, fear, frustration and jealousy. In many homes these feelings are met by punishment, ridicule, or shame. Danger play also provides an opportunity to repeatedly confront fearful issues, such as war, death, and injury. Although these subjects are of universal concern to youngsters, many adults avoid talking about them and, in the process, increase the anxiety of children.

Taking risks requires practice in a low-cost setting. In danger play children can afford to take chances, to see what it is like to rebel, to be the bad guy or outcast. These are risks they dare not take in daily family life. In this connection, it is worth noting that war play is the only context in which some children can conduct conflict without guilt. Even though parents should teach how to settle disputes in constructive ways, some boys and girls learn instead to feel guilty whenever they oppose an authority figure. For many kids fighting off the mutual "enemy" fosters competition needs. War play also allows children to experience leadership, to take charge and command others as well as to become heroes like their favorite television characters. Finally, conflict toys and games are enjoyable, a fact that should be appreciated by a leisure-oriented society.

The Influence of Toys and Players

Safety should always be a parent consideration when they buy toys for their children. However, instead of overemphasizing the effect of toys, it is important to understand that the adults who play with children also can have a significant influence. Otherwise, the value of playthings is exaggerated and the impact of players is underestimated. Relatives cannot fulfill their guidance role merely by purchasing the right kind of toys or forbidding the wrong ones.

Adults complain that children are inclined to believe whatever they see advertised on television. Is the adult condition better if we believe everything we read on toy packaging? For example, exposure to so-called educational or creative toys will not necessarily support imaginative behavior. Creativity does not reside in certain toys because of their design, but mostly in the interaction between the persons who play with them. Research on creative behavior and modeling shows that parents should play with their children; they should get involved instead of limiting themselves to judging the merits of playthings. The assumption that certain toys can have a disabling effect on the personality of children is unwarranted. But the view that adults can have an impact through play has been demonstrated.

Parents and grandparents should discontinue the practice of censoring the content of children's fantasy play, except in instances of bodily danger. Once the direction of children's pretending becomes the choice of adults, boys and girls are no longer the decision-makers. And, in fantasy play, making choices is essential for participation (Taylor, 1999). Adults can share in determining the agenda if they are willing to accept the role of a play partner. It is unfair to interpret the content of children's play as representing adult motives. When an actor portrays the role of a killer in a film or a stage play, the audience may say the performance was convincing and therefore successful. However, when a pretending child chooses to play the same type of violent role, the reasons for deciding to act like or become that particular character may receive greater attention than the performance. This pessimistic interpretation of child's play leads to unfair inferences and the attribution of motives that children do not possess. The motives of children who kill each other temporarily using toy weapons are unrelated to motivation for violent activity in adult life.

CONCLUSION

Creative thinking is becoming a more prominent goal for education. Everyone possesses creative abilities to some degree. Most of what little children learn before schooling comes from guessing, questioning, searching, manipulating, and playing. These activities define the creative thinking process and characterize the method of instruction that we call Toy Talk. Given the natural creativity of children, the main concern of parents should be to preserve and enrich this priceless asset that supports adjustment and success throughout life. Robert Louis Stevenson (1915) urged adults to always keep in mind the child view of how play stimulates imagination:

When I was sick and lay a-bed,
I had two pillows at my head,
And all my toys beside me lay
To keep me happy all the day.

And sometimes for an hour or so
I watched my leaden soldiers go,
With different uniforms and drills,
Among the bed clothes, through the hills.

And sometimes sent my ships in fleets
All up and down among the sheets,
Or brought my trees and houses out,
And planted cities all about.

I was the giant great and still
That sits upon the pillow-hill,
And sees before him, dale and plain,
The pleasant land of counterpane.

REFERENCES

Cattaert, C. (1963). *Where do goldfish go?* New York: Crown.

Stevenson, R. (1915). *A child's garden of verses*. New York: Holt.

Strom, P., & Strom, R. (2002). *Interpersonal Intelligence Inventory*. Bensenville, IL: Scholastic Testing Service.

Strom, R. (1995). *Parent As A Teacher Inventory*. Bensenville, IL: Scholastic Testing Service.

Strom, R. (2002, March). Too busy to play. *Parenting for High Potential*, pp. 18–25.

Strom, R., & Strom, S. (1998). *Parent Success Indicator*. Bensenville, IL: Scholastic Testing Service.

Taylor, M. (1999). *Imaginary companions and the children who create them*. New York: Oxford University Press.

Torrance, E. P. (1995). *Why fly? A philosophy of creativity*. Norwood, NJ: Ablex.

CHAPTER 2

CHANGING THE LENS

Sociocultural Curriculum and Research in Early Childhood in New Zealand[1]

Margaret Carr

In 1996 the New Zealand Ministry of Education published a national early childhood curriculum, Te Whāriki (New Zealand Ministry of Education, 1996). This curriculum introduced a new, sociocultural lens to a sector that had looked mostly toward psychology for its perspectives and philosophies, and this chapter considers some of the implications of this shift for practice and for research. While early childhood education has constructed educational responses that belong in New Zealand, the view expressed in this chapter is that our early childhood experience has implications for learning outcomes, motivation, and assessment in other countries and in other sectors of education.

THE EARLY CHILDHOOD CURRICULUM: *TE WHĀRIKI*

The national curiculum for the early childhood sector in New Zealand was entitled *Te Whāriki*, a Māori (indigenous population) word meaning

Focus on Curriculum, 25–41

"woven mat." The title represents a weaving metaphor for a national curriculum in which the Ministry of Education provides the key strands of principles and direction, while early childhood settings weave their own local patterns into this, constructing their own "woven mats" for their service and for their community. Early childhood is a voluntary sector, characterized by a great diversity of services: sessional kindergartens for 3- and 4-year-olds, childcare centres and settings for children from birth to age 5, parent-run play centers, whānau-based Kōhanga reo (extended-family-based Māori immersion early childhood settings), Montessori centers, Steiner centers, and so on. The national curriculum was developed by a curriculum development team, including, significantly, representatives from the Māori and the Pacific nations educational community in New Zealand. Helen May and the author were the directors of the curriculum development project, but tribute must especially be paid to Tamati Reedy and Tilly Reedy who so generously and knowledgeably guided us as we navigated into bicultural waters and who assisted us to collaboratively develop such a radically different curriculum document. Key contributors were also the early childhood teachers who were part of the consultation process up and down the country, responding to position papers, arguing about curriculum—and whether play was work—and digging their toes in about the label *preschooler*. The sector wanted an early childhood document, not a "preschool" or preparation for school document, and their responses to the draft indicated that they also wanted a uniquely New Zealand document (Murrow, 1995). Tilly Reedy said at the time: "For me, Te Whāriki encapsulates my horizon and the dreams I have for my mokopuna's heritage.... It validates my belief systems and your belief systems. It is also 'home-grown'" (1995/2003, p. 74). As it turned out, the ideas in Te Whāriki are relevant to teaching and learning across all sectors, and the curriculum has been of international interest (Fleer, 2003).

There is always some debate about whether it is wise to have a national curriculum for early childhood, or whether it stifles local and creative initiatives. But Te Whāriki is, as its name suggests, an invitation to a weaving, with some basic strands set in place. The strands of learning outcome are about well-being and *mana atua*, belonging and *mana whenua*, communication and *mana te reo*, contribution and *mana tangata*, exploration and *mana te ao tūroa*. The Māori titles are not translations; they are parallel concepts that have their own cultural history and connections. These strands developed a vision of education as participation in a learning community, as caring, connecting, communicating, contributing, and critical enquiry. They are interwoven with four curriculum principles: (1) protecting and enhancing children's identities as competent learners and communicators, (2) taking a holistic approach to curriculum, (3) involving families and community, and (4) seeing teaching and learning as responsive and reciprocal relationships with people, places, and things.

Te Whāriki is now 10 years old, and local initiatives have been woven into programs in exciting and interesting ways. Here are some examples of involving family and community in curriculum:

- An early childhood center has developed a close relationship with the local hospital for the elderly. They arrange reciprocal visits, and the children's portfolios of "learning stories" (a narrative mode of documentation of learning that often includes photographs; Carr, 2001a) have provided opportunities for conversations with the elders.
- Rangiatea, a 146-year-old historic church in a small community, burned down in 1995. The rebuilding involved the entire community, including the local kindergarten. The children visited the rebuilding regularly, together with their families, documenting the progress and telling stories of the past.
- A "mozaic" project has continued off and on in a kindergarten for more than 2 years. It began from the interest of one family, and a parent coming to teach the children how to mosaic tiles and pots. Older children taught younger children the skills they needed. The ongoing project included the children making mozaic tiles for a newly developed outside area. They sketched their designs, attached shells, broken china, and tiles, mixed and applied the grout, smashed the china, and were often assisted by the visiting expert mozaic tile-maker (a parent). In response to demand, the teachers also provided a workshop for parents, and the local tile company displayed the children's work in their foyer.

The Te Whāriki lens is centrally about the principle of *ngā hononga*, connecting relationships—in this case, teaching and learning as responsive and reciprocal relationships with people, places, and things. This curriculum principle describes an essentially sociocultural perspective. Gordon Wells (2002) has called the unit of analysis for this sort of approach learning-and-teaching, joined by hyphens. James Wersch (1991) called it individual(s)-acting-with-mediational-means. Gavriel Salomon (1993) called it "distributed cognition." This sociocultural, or "situative," view acknowledges that learning is distributed across, stretched over, cultural tools and other people (people places and things). David Perkins (1992) describes this as the "person-plus" perspective. The surround—the immediate physical, social and symbolic resources outside the person—participates in the competence. Competence is situated within communities of learners or cultural communities; it includes intention and therefore "intentional action" rather than "behavior" has become the unit of interest. In this view, learners become more adept at participating in distributed cognitive systems. It focuses on

> engagement that maintains the person's interpersonal relations and identity in communities in which the individual has a significant personal investment. This view emphasises how people's very identities derive from their participatory relationships in communities. According to this view students can become engaged in learning by participating in communities where learning is valued. (Greeno, Collins, & Resnick, 1996, p. 26)

Barbara Rogoff (1997, 2003) has tackled the cultural context of development and learning by outlining a *transformation-of-participation* perspective. She analyzes participation in terms of personal, interpersonal, and cultural processes that can be foregrounded or backgrounded.

> Together, the interpersonal, personal and cultural-institutional aspects of (an) event constitute the activity.... Analysis of interpersonal arrangements could not occur without background understanding of community processes (such as the historical and cultural roles and changing practices of schools and families).... (T)he distinctions between what is in the foreground and what is in the background lie in our analysis and are not assumed to be separate entities in reality. (Rogoff, 2003, p. 58)

It is interesting that we were guided by Māori advisors, for whom the word *ako* means both teaching and learning, and Lev Vygotsky had in his lexicon the Russian word *obuchenie*, which also means both teaching and learning (Mercer, 2002). This is not a new lens. What is new is that it has now been translated into a national early childhood curriculum that has survived 10 years and significantly influenced the formats of assessment practice. It has also been endorsed by the early childhood sector for the next 10 years (New Zealand Ministry of Education, 2002).

Lenses are honed for a particular purpose, to select and sharpen a field of view. One of the activities I greatly enjoyed as a geography student at university was looking at photographs of landscapes through a double lens. Suddenly, the mountains and the gullies popped up and down, and you felt you could reach out and touch them. I think this is what happened in the 1990s in early childhood in this country. Te Whāriki has provided us with a lens through which responsive and reciprocal relationships come into sharper view, and we notice, recognize and respond to children's learning in a different way. The rest of this chapter gives a personal perspective on this shift to a new lens; it tells the story of my own journey, from kindergarten teacher before Te Whāriki, to working with teachers after Te Whāriki. I comment on the shift, from "before Te

Whäriki" to "after Te Whäriki," in terms of three aspects of my teaching and research: outcomes, motivation, and assessment.

BEFORE TE WHÄRIKI: LEARNING OUTCOMES, MOTIVATION, AND ASSESSMENT

Teachers of young children are inevitably educational researchers, and I was implicitly researching learning outcomes for 3- and 4-year-olds, working out how to motivate them and informally assessing them along the way. We had no formal curriculum. In hindsight I can now put some names and frames to some of those ideas about learning outcomes, motivation, and assessment.

Learning Outcomes: An Interest in an Individual's Skills and Attitudes

My first academic paper for early childhood was written while I was still a kindergarten teacher (Carr, 1987). It tells the story of how one of the children invented a carpentry drill, which was greatly superior to the traditional brace-and-bit and egg-beater designs where the children had to press down firmly, keep the drill upright, and turn the drill. Daniel was winding up a G clamp, upside down, and he shouted out to me: "Margaret, look, I'm drilling into the table!", very pleased with his discovery. The G clamp cap that grips the table had come off, and he was indeed drilling a hole into the top of our table. Retelling old stories allows us to put a positive light on our lives, and my memory now tells me that I said something like, "How clever, that's going to be a useful invention." And indeed, we did ask a parent to use Daniel's invention to make a drill where the only action is to turn the drill handle. Many early childhood centers adopted this new drill—and some still use it. (Nowadays, children in New Zealand centers also use electric drills and glue guns.)

In hindsight, this is an example of shifting the perspective, changing the lens: turning something upside down and noticing recognizing, and responding to it differently. But what is interesting here is how I analyzed the learning, what outcomes I focused on. The outcomes I highlighted were the independent skills that this tool afforded, and later I began a research project with exactly that topic in mind. When I wrote the drill story I also pointed out: "There are added bonuses: the 5mm drill sends up a fascinating spiral of wood shavings" (p. 4). I was interested in skills and attitudes, but I didn't combine them.

Motivation: An Interest in Learning and Performance Goals

The second feature of my educational understanding at this time, before Te Whāriki, was to do with motivation. When I was teaching, the following are the kinds of remarks that I began to hear and notice. I later tape-recorded some of the children's interactions. One of the 4-year-olds, Laura, said, "I do the things I know how to do"; and Trevor advised his friend that if you make a mistake you should just "leave it" (Carr, 2001a, pp. 31–32). Below is one of the tape-recorded conversations (later published in Carr, 2001a, p. 31). I asked Susie why she doesn't want to have a go at screenprinting. She explains:

Susie: It's too hard. I don't know how to cut out things. I don't know what to cut out.

Me: Right.

Susie: But I've done one when Alison [a previous teacher] was here. But I can't remember how I wanted to do it.

Me: Right.

Susie: I did a girl with two [pause] eyes. And Alison cut out the eyes. It looked really good but I don't know how to do it any more.

Me: Right. Right. So you don't want to have another go at it?

Susie: No.

Me: Mmhm.

Susie: 'Cause I might make a mistake.

Me: You might make a mistake. And then what would happen?

Susie: It, um, 'cause sometimes when somebody can put the paint on I actually even put too much on. So I don't want to ever do that again.

Looking back, and knowing what I know today, I think I was interested in learning and performance goals. Carol Dweck and her colleagues (e.g., Smiley & Dweck, 1994), in an impressive program of research over 20 years, have described children developing an orientation toward "learning goals" or "performance goals" at a very early age. Laura, Trevor, and Susie appeared to be developing an orientation toward "performance goals" in which learners interpret failure and error as revealing that they are unable or incompetent. Learning-goal children, on the other hand,

experience more positive affect during challenging tasks, make self-instructing and self-motivating statements, focus on effort and strategies, and maintain or enhance their on-task performance. Following such experiences, they accurately recall past performance, they maintain positive self-evaluations of ability, and their expectations for future performance are high. (Smiley & Dweck, 1994, p. 1723)

I didn't know about Carol Dweck's work when I was teaching. Kathy Sylva sought it out in 1992 in her search for the influence of early childhood and school experience on later learning. Paul Black and Dylan Wiliam (1998) also cited Carol Dweck's work on performance and learning goals to seek an explanation for why self-assessment appears to be so influential on learning achievement.

Assessment

The third aspect of education that I want to highlight here is assessment. We did no formal assessment in early childhood in the 1980s, except that just before the children went to school we had a list of about 10 items of knowledge and skill that we tested for, in order to check that the children were ready for school. This was last-minute summative assessment, although I remember some heavy-duty drilling of the skills if the children failed the test. Later, I have come to realize that we were actually preparing the children for a significantly influential mediating device: the new-entrant teacher's expectations (Timperley & Robinson, 1996), and that the consequences of this assessment had nothing to do with learning strategies or dispositions that might be described as contributing to learning at school.

AFTER TE WHĀRIKI: LEARNING OUTCOMES, MOTIVATION, AND ASSESSMENT

Te Whāriki was published in 1996, and ushered in a very different lens for outcomes, motivation and assessment. It changed the way we viewed learning and teaching. To summarize, the Te Whāriki lens:

- Took learners-acting-with-mediational means rather than individual mental functioning as a unit of analysis (Wertsch, 1991).
- Sited learning in local activity settings where participants are actively engaged. It was interested in participation (Rogoff, 2003).
- Took an interest in working theories and the children's developing identity as learners (Gipps, 2002; Wenger, 1998)

- Saw *whänau* (extended family) and community as part of the curriculum.

After Te Whäriki, I became involved in a number of research projects that investigated the implications of this new lens. The examples are from these projects.

Learning Outcomes

Learning outcomes are now about well-being, belonging, contribution, communication, exploration. They are also about identity and participation (Bronfenbrenner, 1979; Rogoff, 1997, 2003; Wenger, 1998). Te Whäriki set out a vision for early childhood education, for children

> to grow up as competent and confident learners and communicators, healthy in mind, body and spirit, secure in their sense of belonging and in the knowledge that they make a valued contribution to society. (New Zealand Ministry of Education, 1996, p. 9)

James Greeno (1997) sums up a similar view on learning outcomes in the form of a question: "Should we consider the major goals and outcomes of learning primarily as collections of sub skills or as successful participation in socially organised activity and the development of students' identities as learners?" (p. 9).

And Etienne Wenger and others have suggested that "Identity is the vehicle that carries our experiences from context to context" (1998 p. 268). An example comes from a project where we are collecting exemplars of assessment from early childhood centers: the Early Childhood Learning and Assessment Exemplar Project (Carr, Jones, & Lee, in press).

> Ezra (aged four years) announced to his teachers that he wanted to "make something real." Over several days he constructed a number of trucks from boxes, tyres, and a range of resources; on one occasion he added a kitchen. He was joined by co-drivers and co-constructors. The teachers decided to invite some experts in—the local road works team—and the children tried out their gear, the cab of the truck, and prepared questions beforehand that they would ask. The teachers took photographs and wrote up the stories, and this documentation was therefore able to be revisited by Ezra (who could read and tell the story from the photographs). The learning was recorded because it was valued. It described a learner as someone who: initiates projects, calls on resources to achieve a goal, adapts the goal to accommodate the people and resources available, collaborates and negotiates with others, consults with experts, and asks the experts questions of moment.

The learning outcomes are summarized in Te Whāriki as working theories and learning dispositions. I am currently involved in a research project where we are looking at the implications of applying a sociocultural lens to learning dispositions. As we collect data for the Dispositions in Social Context project, a joint project between the Children's Issues Center in Otago and researchers in the Waikato, funded by the Royal Society Marsden Fund, we are tracking 27 4-year-olds from their experience over time in early childhood education and into school, looking at three clusters of learning dispositions: reciprocity, resilience, and imagination (Carr et al., in preparation). We are beginning to notice and recognize the three parts to a learning disposition. David Perkins and his colleagues have called them inclination, sensitivity to occasion, and ability (Perkins, Jay, & Tishman, 1993). Guy Claxton and I have called them being ready, willing, and able (Carr, 2001a; Claxton & Carr, 2004). David Perkins later described "sensitivity to occasion" as alertness (Perkins, 2001). At the Breakthroughs' 9th international conference on thinking in Auckland in 2001 he said that attitude, alertness, and ability are "closely entangled" and his research had indicated that alertness is the bottleneck to "good" thinking. Barbara Rogoff commented (2003, p. 253) that generalizing experience from one situation to another involves knowing "which strategies are helpful in what circumstances."

The "sensitive to occasion" dimension grafts a sociocultural approach onto what has been essentially an individual and psychological unit of analysis—a learning disposition. It requires close attention to the relationship between the learner and their surroundings and to accept that the manifestation of learning dispositions will be very closely linked to the learning opportunities, affordances, and constraints available in each new setting (Carr & Claxton, 2002, p. 12). Another example from the Exemplar project illustrates this. Fuka, a 4-year-old, was the star player. Before this event, Fuka did not talk very much to the other children at the early childhood center; English was an additional language for her and her family.

> Fuka's father brought her to the early childhood center, and they decided to bring the family's hen with them. Numerous photographs recorded Fuka with the hen, Fuka's father, and the children holding, feeding, and running after the hen. After the visit, a decision was made to write a book from the photographs, using the children's words. The book was made and given to Fuka. It provided a talking point, a site for conversations, remembering, and laughter.

Together with her father and the teachers Fuka was developing participation repertoires to do with reciprocity in an early childhood center. These repertoires connected her family to the early childhood setting and were unique to both the family and to the center. These repertoires included strategies for communication and contribution and the development of a sense of belonging.

Motivation

During my time as a kindergarten teacher, I had become interested in children like Susie who were apparently avoiding difficulty and challenge in order to be seen as capable. Later, my research on children's interactions in construction and art activities in a kindergarten started out looking at skills, became interested in orientation, and finally led me into terrain that considered story, identity and working theories about the self (see Gee, 1992). A research study of children learning with everyday technology suggested that Carol Dweck's performance and learning goals appeared to have become attached, over time, to activity and often to place (Carr, 2001b). And I observed that every now and then a learner is pushed out of a preferred or privileged performance-oriented niche, to try a challenge or to take a risk. In other words, these orientations were situated, and could change. An example comes from that research study (Carr, 2002):

> Nell arrived at Jason's marble painting activity (which he had innovatively turned into a painting-tray-making activity), and asked him how to make a tray, admitting that she didn't know how to do it. Jason showed her how. He had taken the lead to socialize this activity toward "learning" goals, and Nell appeared to be experimenting with a new orientation or disposition toward technical difficulty and risk of error—this was the first time that she had been heard to say that she didn't know how to do something. She persevered with this challenging task, and later taught another child, Jinny, how to make a tray for marble painting, reminding her about some of the difficulties along the way. In this activity, Jason may have changed the descriptor of "being a technologist" to one in which challenge is interesting and sociable, and "being a friend" can be part of this.

I concluded from that study that performance and learning goals are themselves enmeshed within a complex and shifting pattern of socioculturally and historically derived social schemas, identities, or intents, that children favor certain social identities, and these identities form mediating devices that assist them to select from and edit the curriculum on offer. I described these social identities as being a friend, being nearly 5, being good, being a girl, being a boy, being a technologist.

Assessment

We became aware, after Te Whäriki was written and its framework mandated, that assessment would have to keep up. By 1998, it had become mandatory for early childhood services to have evidence of documented assessments that contribute to learning. A sociocultural curriculum would need a sociocultural assessment practice. What might that look like? Very different from my earlier preschool test, certainly.

Caroline Gipps (2002) has described a sociocultural approach to assessment. She said that it would be about best performance, distributed across cultural tools and teachers. She also suggested that it would be holistic, not separating out the social emotional and cognitive aspects of learning. And she emphasized the role of assessment in identity formation.

> The language of assessment and evaluation is one of the routes by which the identity of young persons is formed—for school purposes at least.... If identity is conceived as concerned with persuading others and oneself about who one is, and what one is able to do, the judgement of others is crucial. (p. 80)

Te Whäriki has added another feature: assessment will involve families, in the widest sense.

In a research project with teachers in a number of different settings (Carr, 1998, 2001a), we developed an assessment framework called Learning Stories. Learning Stories as a tool for assessment has the capacity to

- Keep the learning distributed across people places and things—the teachers, the activity and its purpose, the tools, and the discursive practices. Noting not only the competence, but the circumstances as well.
- Provide an account that the learner and family can revisit. One of the purposes of writing it down is that during the revisiting children can accurately recall past performance and maintain positive self-evaluations of ability and high expectations for future performance (characteristics of learning goals, according to Dweck). Learning stories also enable the construction of continuity of learning.
- Encourage children and families to be involved in assessments: writing or telling their own stories and becoming involved in self-assessment. They widen the community of learners.

As a result of research during the Exemplar Project, Bronwen Cowie and I described the consequences of sociocultural assessment as community, competence, and continuity. We suggest that (1) assessments act as a "conscription device" (a recruitment) for participants, establishing the membership of a social *community* of learners and teachers: children, families, and staff; (2) assessments are a means by which *competence* and competent learners are constructed; and (3) assessments illustrate and support *continuity* in learning. They provide a venue for the negotiation and navigation of individual and collective learning trajectories. They invite participants to discuss together what is being learned and to decide what might come next. This storying and restorying constructs multiple pathways of learning as "work in progress" (Cowie & Carr, 2004, p. 96). Children are beginning to dictate their own learning stories. An example of this, from the Exemplar Project, is Lachlan, who has spent some time perfecting the art of hula-hooping. He calls out to the teacher: "Write about my moves. I keep wriggling to keep it moving. When it goes lower I have to go faster, see?" The teacher comments, "Lachlan shows me how fast he has to go to keep the hula-hoop turning." The teacher takes photographs to accompany her commentary (initiated and partly dictated by Lachlan) and adds an analysis of the learning.

Narrative frameworks owe much to the work of Vivian Gussin Paley, of whom Jerome Bruner has said:

> She's one of those marvelous characters who has this intuitive gift for knowing how to get into the domain of children.... I keep thinking I wish she had taught my children; then I think, I wish she had taught me! (quoted in Mahany, 1995, p. 15)

Paley herself has said; "Any classroom—I know the kindergarten best—should develop into a close-knit community of people who care deeply about each other" (Mahany, 1995, p. 28). Her concern for justice and fairness, her focus on the children's sense of belonging, and her passion for story have been an inspiration to many of us in early childhood. In *The Boy Who Would be a Helicopter*, she writes about Jason, who has spent much of his time in the classroom being a helicopter, and not interacting with others. Paley writes about the occasion when Edward tells a story that includes Jason, and Jason responds:

> Jason smiles and says, "Y'wanna hear my story? The helicopter flies in the night. Edward is in the airplane."
> Jason has glimpsed the reciprocal connections between storytellers: I'll put you in my story if you put me in yours. How does this understanding come about? The weight of experience must be the main factor in developing this essential component in the learning process. You listen to my idea, and I'll listen to yours. (Paley, 1990, p. 104)

Paley alternates reflection with the telling of the children's stories as she attempts to make meaning from what she has observed and heard. Learning Stories tries to do the same.

IMPLICATIONS

I have found it a fascinating journey exploring the implications of the Te Whäriki lens, and many other researchers are on this journey too. We still have a way to go. I hope that, 10 years from now, Te Whäriki will not lose its promise of education for social justice, nor its capacity to encourage intuitive teachers and intuitive children who, in the words of Guy Claxton (1995), have developed a "nose" for learning.

Outcomes, motivation and assessment are, of course, closely connected. There is research evidence that assessment of the kind that takes away the control from the learner increases performance goals and leads to 'surface' learning (Harlen & Deakin Crick, 2003, p.171). Mihaly Csik-szentmihayi (1996) interviewed 91 "creative" people, including 14 Nobel Prize winners. He argued that creativity needs close attention and much effort. He commented (p. 158) that none of these individuals were prodigies or even gifted children as we now define them, "but they had a tremendous interest, a burning curiosity, concerning at least one aspect of their environment"...and "they seem to have become committed early to the exploration and discovery of some part of their world." Peter Fensham and Ference Marton (1992) analyzed interview data from 83 Nobel laureates in physics, chemistry, and medicine. Seventy two of them commented on the importance of intuition. One of them commented (p. 119) with concern that students

> get the impression that what really matters is being right or wrong—in science above all.... And I like to stress to my students that they're very much like research scientists: that we don't know how to get the right answer; we're working in areas where we don't know the right answer.

If our vision for education is about participation and identity, then it is clear that the focus of teaching will not be just on the acquisition of the right answer.

Research tells us that activities in many classrooms (and early childhood centers) focus on orderliness (Black & Wiliam, 1998), summative assessments (Harlen & Deakin Crick, 2003), convergent tasks (Torrance & Pryor, 1998), and, in the first year of school, may be centrally concerned with rules and routines (Cullen & St George, 1996) and writing. A current review of the New Zealand school curriculum will, I hope, reduce the press for content coverage, and allow teachers to give more time to help-ing students to develop participation repertoires and identities as learn-ers. Otherwise, children may have to seek out opportunities for meaning-making in the small spaces between set activities and evaluative work-sheets.

With this in mind, I want to conclude with an observation of Joseph when I was in his new-entrant classroom a few weeks ago. Joseph was being asked to set up a baseline for self-assessment. The teacher reads the sheet to him: "I will get better at.... What do you want to write here?" she asks, pointing to the ruled lines underneath. He has been at school for a few months now, and she anticipates that he will want her to write some-thing about reading letters, writing words, or counting to 200. Joseph has had experience that enables him to make sense of this worksheet. "The sick bay," he says confidently.

NOTE

1.   This chapter is adapted from the Jean Herbison lecture to the AARE and NZARE Conference, Auckland, December 2003.

ACKNOWLEDGMENTS

The stories in this chapter are included with permission from the families and teachers involved in the Early Childhood Learning and Assessment Exemplar Project, funded by the Ministry of Education, and the Disposi-tions in Social Context project, funded by the Royal Society of New Zealand Marsden Fund. The Ministry of Education also funded the Assessing Children's Experiences in Early Childhood Project, which began the assessment research. Many thanks to the children, families, and teachers in these projects, and to the Ministry of Education and the Royal Society of New Zealand.

REFERENCES

Black, P., & Wiliam, D. (1998). Assessment and classroom learning. *Assessment in Education*, 5(1), 7–74.
Bronfenbrenner, U. (1979). *The ecology of human development*. Cambridge, MA: Harvard University Press.
Carr, M. (1987). A pre-school "drill" for problem-solving? *Investigating*, 3(1), 3–5.
Carr, M. (1998). *Assessing Children's experiences in early childhood*. Final Report to the Ministry of Education. Wellington, New Zealand: Ministry of Education

Carr, M. (2001a). *Assessment in early childhood settings: Learning stories*. London: Paul Chapman.

Carr, M. (2001b). A sociocultural approach to learning orientation in an early childhood setting. *Qualitative Studies in Education, 14*(4), 525–542.

Carr, M. (2002). Emerging learning narratives: a perspective from early childhood education. In G. Wells & G. L. Claxton (Eds.), *Learning for life in the 21st century: Sociocultural perspectives on the future of education*. Oxford, UK: Blackwell.

Carr, M., & Claxton, G. L. (2002). Tracking the development of learning dispositions. *Assessment in Education, 9*(1), 9–37.

Carr, M., Jones, C., & Lee, W. (in press). *Kei tua o te pae. Assessment for learning: early childhood exemplars*. Wellington, New Zealand: Learning Media.

Carr, M., Smith, A.B., Duncan, J., Jones, C., Lee, W., & Marshall, K. (in preparation). *Dispositions in social context*. Final report to the Royal Society of New Zealand. Wellington: Royal Society of New Zealand.

Claxton, G. L. (1995). What kind of learning does self-assessment drive? Developing a 'nose' for quality: comments on Klenowski. *Assessment in Education, 2*(3), 339–343.

Claxton, G., & Carr, M. (2004). A framework for teaching learning: learning dispositions. *Early Years International Journal of Research and Development. 24*(1), 87–97.

Cowie, B., & Carr, M. (2004). Consequences of sociocultural assessment in early childhood settings: community, competence and continuity. In A. Anning, J. Cullen, & M. Fleer (Eds.), *Early childhood education: Society and culture* (pp. 95–106). London: Sage.

Csikszentmihalyi, M. (1996). *Creativity: flow and the psychology of discovery and invention*. New York: HarperCollins.

Cullen, J., & St George, A. (1996). Scripts for Learning: reflecting dynamics of classroom life. *Journal for Australian Research in Early Childhood Education. 1*, 10–19.

Fensham, P., & Marton, F. (1992). What has happened to intuition in science education? *Research in Science Education, 22*, 114–122.

Fleer, M. (2003). The many voices of Te Whāriki: kaupapa Māori, socio-cultural, developmental, constructivist, and...? Australians listen carefully. In J. Nuttall (Ed.), *Weaving Te Whāriki: Aotearoa New Zealand's early childhood curriculum document in theory and practice* (pp. 243–268). Wellington, New Zealand: NZCER.

Gee, J. P. (1992). *The social mind: Language, ideology, and social practice*. New York: Bergin & Harvey.

Gipps, C. (2002). Sociocultural perspectives on assessment. In G. Wells & G. Claxton (Eds.), *Learning for life in the 21st century: Sociocultural perspectives on the future of education* (pp. 73–83). Oxford: Blackwell.

Greeno, J. G. (1997). On claims that answer the wrong questions. *Educational Researcher. 26*(1), 5–17.

Greeno, J. G., Collins, A. M., & Resnick, L. B. (1996). Cognition and learning. In D. C. Berliner & R. C. Calfee (Eds.), *Handbook of educational psychology* (pp. 15–46). New York: Simon & Schuster Macmillan.

Harlen, W., & Deakin Crick, R. (2003). Testing and motivation for learning. *Assessment in Education, 10*(2), 169–207.

Mahany, B. (1995, June 25). Mrs. Paley's Lessons. *Chicago Tribune Magazine*, Section 10, pp. 12–20, 28–29.

Mercer, N. (2002). Developing dialogues. In G. Wells & G. Claxton (Eds.), *Learning for life in the 21st century: Sociocultural perspectives on the future of education.* (pp. 141–153). Oxford: Blackwell.

Murrow, K. (1985). *Early childhood workers' opinions on the draft document Te Whāriki* (Research Section Report Series No. 5). Wellington, New Zealand: Ministry of Education.

New Zealand Ministry of Education. (1996). *Te Whāriki. He Whāriki Mātauranga mö ngā Mokopuna o Aotearoa:* Early childhood curriculum. Wellington, New Zealnd: Learning Media.

New Zealand Ministry of Education. (2002). *Pathways to the future: Ngā Huarahi Arataki.* Wellington, New Zealand: Learning Media.

Paley, V. G. (1990). *The boy who would be a helicopter.* Cambridge, UK: Cambridge University Press.

Perkins, D. (1992). *Smart schools: Better thinking and learning for every child.* New York: The Free Press.

Perkins, D. (2001, January) *Intelligence in the wild.* Paper presented at "Breakthroughs" Ninth International Conference on Thinking, Auckland.

Perkins, D. N., Jay, E., & Tishman, S. (1993). Beyond Abilities: a dispositional theory of thinking. *Merrill-Palmer Quarterly, 39*(1), 1–21.

Reedy, T. (1995/2003). Toku Rangatiratanga na te Mana-Mātauranga "Knowledge and Power Set me Free…" In J. Nuttall (Ed.), *Weaving Te Whāriki: Aotearoa New Zealand's early childhood curriculum document in theory and practice* (pp. 51–77). Wellington, New Zealand: NZCER.

Rogoff, B. (1997). Evaluating development in the process of participation: theory, methods and practice building on eachother. In E. Amsel & K. A. Renninger (Eds.), *Change and development: issues of theory, method and application* (pp. 265–285). Mahwah, NJ: Erlbaum.

Rogoff, B. (2003). *The cultural nature of human development.* New York: Oxford University Press.

Salomon, G. (1993). No distribution without individual's cognition: a dynamic interactional view. In G. Salomon (Ed.), *Distributed cognitions: Psychological and educational considerations* (pp. 111-138). Cambridge, UK: Cambridge University Press.

Smiley, P. A., & Dweck, C. S. (1994). Individual differences in achievement goals among young children. *Child Development. 65*, 1723–1743.

Sylva, K. (1994). School influences on children's development. *Journal of Child Psychology and Psychiatry, 34*(1), 85–98.

Timperley, H. S., & Robinson, V. M. J. (1996). Achieving school improvement through challenging and changing teachers' schema. *Journal of Educational Change, 2*, 281–300.

Torrance, H., & Pryor, J. (1998) *Investigating formative assessment:Tteaching learning and assessment in the classroom.* Buckingham, UK: Open University Press.

Wells, G. (2002). Inquiry as an orientation for learning, teaching and teacher education. In G. Wells & G. Claxton (Eds.), *Learning for life in the 21st century: Sociocultural perspectives on the future of education* (pp. 197–210). Oxford, UK: Blackwell.

Wenger, E. (1998). *Communities of practice: Learning, meaning and identity.* Cambridge, UK: Cambridge University Press.

Wertsch, J. (1991). *Voices of the mind: A sociocultural approach to mediated action.* Cambridge, MA: Harvard University Press.

CHAPTER 3

READING INSTRUCTION IN SOCIOCULTURAL CONTEXT

Impact on Reading Comprehension and Engagement

Allan Wigfield and Susan Lutz

Cheryl is entering fourth grade this fall. Although she appears to be a bright student with a number of different interests, she struggled with reading in both the first and second grades, where phonics, decoding, and word recognition were emphasized. In third grade the reading program in Cheryl's school began to focus on reading comprehension. Because Cheryl still had some difficulties with the more basic aspects of reading, her comprehension did not develop quickly. Although she was placed in the "middle" reading group in her classroom, she often felt that she did not understand the material as well as many of the other children in her group. The third-grade reading program in Cheryl's school relies primarily on a basal reader for comprehension instruction, and Cheryl did not find too many of the stories in the basal interesting or exciting. Cheryl's third-grade teacher was traditional in the sense of following the basal reader and her curriculum closely, directing most of the teaching

Focus on Curriculum, 43–76
Copyright © 2005 by Information Age Publishing
All rights of reproduction in any form reserved.

activities in reading, and focusing on reading as something children do individually. Many of the activities that the class did in reading were not appealing to Cheryl, and so she was not highly engaged in them. Moreover, the student population in Cheryl's school was diverse, but the staff was primarily white and middle class. Cheryl's third-grade teacher did not seem especially comfortable with the cultural diversity in her classroom, nor did she have a strong understanding of the backgrounds of her students and how they impacted the students' approach to reading and comprehension of the materials presented in class.

By the end of third grade Cheryl read only during reading instruction time in class, her reading grades slipped, and her test scores showed little gain. Her teacher wondered whether she should recommend to the fourth-grade team that Cheryl be placed in the lowest reading group. Cheryl was relieved when the school year ended, and enjoyed her summer activities. She engaged in some literacy activities over the summer, but not many of the kind that she did in school. As Labor Day approached, Cheryl wondered what fourth grade would be like, and how much she would like her teacher and the kinds of activities that they would do in different subject areas. She hoped the reading materials she encountered would be more engaging than those from her third-grade year.

CHAPTER OVERVIEW

Researchers and policymakers have expressed concern about many children's lack of engagement in reading and other academic activities, and their low levels of reading comprehension (Fredricks, Blumenfeld, & Paris, 2004; National Reading Panel, 2000; National Research Council, 2004). Children's engagement in reading is important for a variety of reasons: children who are actively involved in reading comprehend better, achieve better in school, and have more opportunities later in life (Guthrie & Wigfield, 2000). Thus a number of authors discuss the importance of maintaining and enhancing children's engagement in reading and other academic activities as a way to ensure that their cognitive skills in different areas grow as well (Fredricks et al., 2004; Guthrie & Wigfield, 2000).

As children go through the elementary school years, reading comprehension becomes an increasingly important part of the reading instruction they receive, with this emphasis typically beginning in the third grade. The emphasis on reading comprehension instruction in the later elementary grades means a greater focus on deriving meaning from longer sections of text rather than focusing on decoding individual words.

In general, we have a better understanding of children's letter and word recognition processes than we do of their broader reading comprehension skills. Developing effective reading comprehension programs is currently a high national priority (National Reading Panel, 2000).

There are a variety of influences on both reading engagement and reading comprehension. These include psychological processes within the child, children's social and cultural backgrounds, and the kinds of instructional practices and programs children experience. The latter two kinds of influences can be considered broadly as sociocultural influences, and it is these kinds of influence that we focus on in this chapter. We begin with definitions of reading comprehension and reading engagement, and then turn to a brief consideration of multicultural education and its implications for literacy instruction. We then discuss sociocultural perspectives on reading, with a specific focus on the implications of these perspectives for literacy instruction. Next we present in greater detail two approaches to literacy instruction that focus in particular (albeit different) ways on sociocultural influences and their impact on reading comprehension and engagement. The programs, Concept-Oriented Reading Instruction (CORI) and the Kamehameha Elementary Education Program (KEEP), were chosen because of their focus on culture, a programmatic approach to reading instruction, and also because each has strong research support.

Defining Reading Comprehension and Reading Engagement

A complete review of the theoretical and empirical work on reading comprehension is well beyond the scope of this chapter. However, we thought it important to provide a working definition of reading comprehension, as we focus in this chapter on instructional programs designed to increase it. Broadly, reading comprehension can be defined as the processes involved in deriving or constructing meaning from text (Goldman & Rakestraw, 2000; Kintsch, 1988, 1998; National Reading Panel, 2000; Pressley, 2000). Most reading researchers now assume that comprehension implies active construction of meaning rather than passive reception of information from text. For instance, Pressley and Afflerbach (1995) reviewed evidence showing clearly that expert readers who comprehend well are exceptionally active cognitively as they read. They interpret and reflect on the text, have goals for their reading, read selectively, and integrate what they are learning with their prior knowledge, to name just a few of the processes in which they engage.

Reading comprehension builds from children's ability to decode symbols and words and read fluently, but clearly goes beyond these basic reading skills and involves much more elaborate cognitive representations and inferences about the text. The individual's prior knowledge has a strong influence on their comprehension of new information from text, as does (as we discuss in more detail below) their cultural background. Various properties and structures of particular texts can influence comprehension, including, for example, surface structures. Surface structures of text are the ways in which texts are organized and presented on the page, including organizing phrases such as "in summary" or "we next discuss" and other features of the printed page. When these structures match well with the potential meaning intended by the author, comprehension is facilitated; if the match is not good, then comprehension suffers (Goldman & Rakestraw, 2000). For instance, clear use of headers and organizing phrases can help readers discover the meaning of a passage; if these features are absent or used poorly, then readers may miss the author's intended message.

There are a variety of cognitive strategies in which readers engage that can facilitate their comprehension. These include posing questions about the text, monitoring one's comprehension, summarizing the (potential) main ideas, developing graphic or other kinds of organizers of the material, and activating one's background knowledge, to name just a few (National Reading Panel, 2000). Some of these strategies are described in more detail below when we discuss the CORI program.

Reading comprehension primarily involves cognitive processes. By contrast, reading engagement is defined as the "simultaneous functioning of motivation, conceptual knowledge, strategies, and social interactions during literacy activities" (Baker, Dreher, & Guthrie, 2000, p. ix). Engaged readers are motivated, which means they enjoy reading, believe they are capable of reading well, have purposes for reading, and spend significant amounts of time reading. Engaged readers also have various cognitive competencies that allow them to read well, including relevant background knowledge, cognitive strategies for reading and learning, and the ability to organize and synthesize the new knowledge they generate. These competencies help engaged readers utilize well the reading strategies they learn to use. Finally, engaged readers interact frequently with others during reading, sharing information as well as discussing what they like and don't like about different books, and they view reading as a social activity (for further discussion, see Guthrie, 2004a; Wigfield & Tonks, 2004).

This definition emphasizes behavioral and cognitive aspects of engagement. Fredricks and colleagues (2004), in their discussion of engagement, also included emotional engagement, which they defined as students' affective reactions in the classroom. Engaged students experience a variety of positive affects while they read and in other learning situations, including interest, happiness, and identification with learning and one's school. Such positive emotions can impact students' achievement in meaningful ways, in part by motivating them to read more frequently.

How does reading engagement relate to reading comprehension? There is a growing body of evidence showing that engaged students' reading comprehension and achievement increase more strongly than does the comprehension and achievement of less engaged students (Guthrie & Cox, 2001; Guthrie et al., 1998). Students who read frequently and who are engaged deeply in their reading benefit in many ways from their reading. Because comprehension is such an effortful set of processes, engagement (and particularly the motivational aspects of engagement) may be a necessary condition for comprehension to occur in its richest forms. An important implication of this point is that reading programs, which aim to foster comprehension, also need to foster children's motivation and engagement in reading. We return to this point later.

CULTURE AND READING COMPREHENSION

Multicultural Education and its Implications for Literacy Instruction

Much has been written about the growing ethnic and cultural diversity of the student population in American schools, diversity that will continue to increase each year. This growing diversity is one of the most exciting changes taking place in American schools, but also one of the most challenging. As the diversity of the student population has increased, so too has the "achievement gap" in reading and other areas between different groups of students, particularly between poor and affluent students, and students from some minority groups in comparison to students from other minority groups (Au, 2000; Lee, 2004; Strickland & Alvermann, 2004). Although the student population's diversity continues to increase, the same cannot be said of teachers in many elementary schools, who remain primarily female, white, and middle class in many areas (Alvermann & Phelps, 1998; Au & Raphael, 2000).

There has been much discussion among educators, researchers, and policymakers about the various issues associated with the increasing ethnic and cultural diversity in our schools, and also the stubborn achievement gap between some of these different groups, as we try to both understand the gap and eliminate it. Multicultural educators have made significant contributions to our understanding of these issues, and we next present briefly some of their ideas. A complete recent review of many aspects of multicultural education can be found in the edited volume by Banks and Banks (2004).

Multicultural educators are interested in the education of different groups of children (females and males, exceptional children, children from different racial and ethnic groups), with a particular concern that students from these and other groups all have an equal chance of succeeding in school (Banks, 2001; Gay, 2003, 2004). Banks, Gay, and many others have discussed how the cultural backgrounds and knowledge of different groups of children often do not match well with the culture and knowledge of many schools, which means that they may not have an equal chance of school success. Gay (2004) discussed several different kinds of knowledge characteristic of children and schools: personal and cultural knowledge that comes from the home, family, and community; mainstream academic knowledge coming primarily from research done in Western cultures; and school knowledge, which is based primarily on mainstream academic knowledge. For some children and groups of children there is a good match between the knowledge required to do well in school and their personal and cultural knowledge, and when this occurs success in school may be more likely. This match is especially likely to occur for children whose cultural backgrounds match the cultural backgrounds of those producing the school-based knowledge. For other children and groups, there is a potential mismatch in these kinds of knowledge; if this mismatch occurs, school success can be more difficult for these children to achieve. These difficulties are compounded when schools devalue or negate the personal and cultural knowledge that children bring; a primary example of this is language and ways of speaking, and what are appropriate ways of speaking in school. For example, Hawaiian American children like to talk simultaneously when discussing stories; many European American teachers find this practice to be inappropriate, and so attempt to control it. We return to this example later when discussing KEEP.

For the purposes of this chapter, we take two fundamental points from multicultural educators about culture and learning. First, they argue strongly and convincingly that instruction in our schools needs to be culturally sensitive so that the knowledge and behaviors that different groups of children bring to school is understood and accepted, rather than negated (Banks, 2001; Gay, 2003, 2004; Gray, 2003; Hacket, 2003). Culturally sensitive instruction is more likely to reach more students in diverse classrooms, providing them with better opportunities to do well in school. Also, when students' cultural backgrounds and knowledge are understood and accepted, their engagement and identification with school very likely will increase, with potential for influencing their reading comprehension and achievement. Second, multicultural educators discuss how knowledge is socially and culturally constructed through different lenses, rather than passively received in similar ways by all individuals, or based solely in psychological processes. Extrapolating this point to literacy instruction means that such instruction must consider how children's social and cultural backgrounds influence their reading comprehension. Those taking a sociocultural approach to reading also argue that knowledge is socially and culturally constructed, and we turn to this work next.

Sociocultural Approaches to Reading

A variety of researchers take a sociocultural approach to reading, building on some of the points raised by multicultural educators and extending them in interesting ways to the areas of reading and literacy. As with multicultural education, a complete review of sociocultural approaches to reading and literacy is beyond the scope of this chapter (see Au, in press, for further review). Instead, we present some major points from this work to provide a context for the reading instruction programs that we describe later in this chapter. One fundamental point from this work is that learning to read, and learning to become literate more broadly defined, must be understood within the sociocultural contexts of different classrooms. These sociocultural contexts involve teaching practices in reading and other subject areas, linguistic practices of students and teachers, interaction patterns between teachers and students and among students, and so on. Reading is not something that can be separated out from these practices, but is an integral part of them and can only be understood in these larger contexts (Alvermann & Phelps, 1998; Gee, 1996, 2004; Santa Barbara Discourse Group, 1994).

A second major point that derives from the first is that reading (and literacy) is much more than a set of psychological processes. The definition of reading comprehension that we provided earlier stresses active psychological processes as fundamental to reading comprehension. For those taking a sociocultural perspective on reading, such psychological processes are one important part of reading, but only one part. Rather than being individually and psychologically constructed, reading instead is socially and culturally constructed, through interactions with others in different environments (O'Brien, Moje, & Stewart, 2001). This approach to conceptualizing reading is based in part on a Vygotskian (1978) perspective on the nature of development in different areas, and reflects the belief that reading is far more than a set of cognitive strategies and processes. It also is based in cultural anthropological approaches (e.g., Heath, 1994). A similarity in the sociocultural and psychological views is the focus on activity on the part of the reader as crucial to reading comprehension; however, those taking a sociocultural approach see this activity as including much more than active cognitive processing.

A third point is that reading and literacy should be broadly defined, and that literacy occurs in many different ways. The term "multiple literacies" perhaps best captures this point (Au & Raphael, 2000). Reading is much more than interacting with a printed page in a book in a classroom, but occurs with many kinds of media in many situations in and out of school (e.g., Alvermann & Phelps, 1998; Kelly, 2001). A narrow focus on reading as a school-based activity with limited reading materials may negate the literacy experiences of many children in and out of our schools. Moreover, definitions of reading and literacy and reading practices vary widely across different groups. This point has been documented in many ways, but perhaps most clearly by Heath (1994) and Moll (1994). Heath observed literacy practices among African American families in one community that she called Trackton, describing the ways in which language was used to communicate in a variety of settings, and the kinds of reading and literacy practices different families used. Moll provided a rich description of literacy practices in some Latino households. One major point each researcher made is that the kinds of rich literacy practices that occurred in the households in each study often did not match well with the school literacy practices the children of these families encountered, meaning that the kinds of competencies that children had developed at home did not help them much with in-school literacy practices. This mismatch can have a strong impact on both school engagement and school achievement.

What are some of the instructional implications of these points, particularly for literacy instruction? Au and Raphael (2000) provide a cogent set of suggestions. First, they suggest that we need both an expanded definition of literacy to include the multiple literacies that many children experience. Literacy has often been defined too narrowly, particularly in school, and to reach different groups of children, different kinds of literacy experiences must be explored. Second, Au and Raphael emphasize that literacy instruction that makes connections to students' own lives and is rich with meaning leads to greater student involvement with literacy activities. This is true for all children, but may be especially true for children who traditionally have been marginalized in our society, and students like Cheryl who do not feel strong connections to school literacy activities. Third, literacy instruction for all children should be at a high cognitive level; too often children struggling with reading in traditional classrooms receive very low-level instruction that does not promote either comprehension or engagement. Fourth, literacy instruction needs to engage students actively in their own learning, rather than being a "transmission" model of instruction. Viewing learners as active participants in their own learning is a hallmark of both modern psychological and sociocultural views of reading and literacy. Fifth, classrooms should be communities of learners in which children have many opportunities to interact with one another and with the teacher.

Au and Raphael (2000) and others taking a sociocultural perspective on reading provide many ideas for how literacy instruction can be expanded beyond a focus on individual psychological processing of text. We turn next to a detailed presentation of two reading comprehension instruction programs that emphasize sociocultural contexts of classrooms and how they impact literacy, albeit in different ways. One program is Concept Oriented Reading Instruction, a reading instructional program that focuses on integrating reading with other content areas like science and social studies, and promoting children's reading engagement (Guthrie, Wigfield, & Perencevich, 2004a). The other program is the Kamehameha Elementary Education Program (KEEP) based in Hawaii (see Au, 1997a; Au & Carroll, 1997). This program was developed to foster the reading and writing engagement and achievement of native Hawaiian children, a group of children who have done poorly in many traditional schools in Hawaii. Thus this program focuses on literacy, not just reading. We also briefly discuss how KEEP became adapted for Navajo students attending Rough Rock Elementary School on the Navajo reservation in Arizona. As noted earlier, we chose these programs because of their focus on sociocultural issues, and also because they have research support for their effectiveness. We do not mean to imply that these are the only two programs attending to classroom sociocultural contexts, but instead use them as exemplars for different ways in which classroom sociocultural contexts can be considered.

Concept-Oriented Reading Instruction (CORI)

The CORI program, an evolving collaboration among university researchers and elementary school teachers since 1993, integrates reading comprehension instruction with a focus on a conceptual theme or themes related to science or social studies (Guthrie et al., 2004a; Swan, 2003). CORI is designed to foster the reading comprehension as well as the reading engagement of all children through the kinds of instructional practices implemented by CORI teachers. These practices, as we will discuss, fit well with the recommendations made by Au and Raphael (2000) with respect to sociocultural perspectives on teaching reading. First, however, we will describe these practices and other elements of the CORI framework.

To date, CORI has been implemented in the third through fifth grades for a length of 12 weeks to an entire school year. The conceptual themes that are a hallmark of CORI provide a basis for organizing instruction (see Guthrie, 2004a). These themes might include, but are certainly not limited to, the life of animals and plants in different places, the solar system, weather, discrimination, or countries around the world (Guthrie, 2004a; Swan, 2003). Teachers guide students through exploration of the conceptual theme in four sequential phases: *Observe and Personalize*, in which students experience real-world interactions and identify their individual interests within the theme; *Search and Retrieve*, in which students learn how to gather information related to their questions and interests; *Comprehend and Integrate*, in which students learn how to synthesize information gleaned from multiple sources; and *Communicate to Others*, in which students share their new understanding with their classmates, students in another class, or another audience in their community. Within each of these phases, teachers simultaneously support student development of reading comprehension and engagement by teaching reading strategies, facilitating motivational processes, implementing inquiry science or social studies activities, and helping students make connections between what they have read and what they have learned through observation or other non-text-based activities (Guthrie, 2004a).

The reading strategies that teachers teach and the ways in which they facilitate motivation are formally conceptualized in the CORI framework as sets of instructional practices for creating a classroom context that promotes reading comprehension and engagement for many different kinds of texts. These sets of practices are summarized in Table 3.1. One set includes instruction in six reading comprehension strategies: (1) activating background knowledge, (2) summarizing, (3) searching for information, (4) graphic organizing, (5) questioning, and (6) comprehension monitoring; these strategies are all highlighted in the National Reading Panel (2000) report as effectively improving children's reading comprehension. During the first several weeks of CORI, the strategies are introduced individually. In later weeks, once students have become adept at applying single strategies, they learn how to use them in combination. Different strategies are emphasized at different grade levels; for instance, comprehension monitoring becomes particularly important at fifth grade (see Guthrie & Taboada, 2004, for a detailed discussion of these strategies and how they are implemented in CORI).

The other set of instructional practices focuses on building students' engagement and motivation in reading. First, teachers emphasize the conceptual themes and provide clear learning and knowledge goals based on them in order to give students clear purposes for their learning. Second, teachers utilize real-world or hands-on interactions related to the

Table 3.1.   Instructional Practices in CORI

Reading Strategies Taught	Engagement Supportive Practices
Activating background knowledge	Content goals for instruction
Questioning	Hand-on activities
Searching for information	Support for student autonomy
Summarizing	Provision of interesting texts
Graphic organizing	Collaboration support
Comprehension monitoring	

theme to engage students' interest and connect the theme to their own lives. These interactions include nature walks, observations of plants and animals in the classroom, and other activities. From these activities students generate their own questions for which they want to search for answers. Third, there are many interesting texts from different genres (both informational and literary) tied directly to the theme available to students in the classroom, so that they can find answers to their questions. The wide variety of texts available means that students from many different backgrounds can find books to which they can connect. Fourth, teachers support student autonomy by allowing them many choices about which books they read and what kinds of activities they do, as well as by encouraging them to generate and answer their own questions. Fifth, teachers support student collaboration by having them work together on a variety of reading and other activities (for more detailed discussion of these practices, see Guthrie, Wigfield, & Perencevich, 2004b; Wigfield & Tonks, 2004).

Exemplification of Recommendations for Quality Reading Instruction From Au and Raphael's Sociocultural Perspective on Literacy Instruction

As delineated earlier, Au and Raphael (2000) emphasized five instructional implications of their sociocultural approach to literacy. These include: (1) broader definitions of literacy and the realization that literacy comes in multiple forms; (2) the importance of connecting learning to students' lives; (3) the need for instruction to be at a high cognitive level for all students; (4) the importance of engaging students actively in their learning; and (5) the need to create communities of learners with opportunities to interact with each other frequently. We next connect CORI to each of these implications.

Multiple Literacies

In CORI, literacy means much more than being able to decode text fluently or supply facts after reading a single story to answer what, when, and why something happened. Rather, being literate means being cognitively, motivationally, and socially engaged in reading for the purposes of understanding conceptual knowledge and being able to share that understanding with others. It also means being able to apply use of strategies that enable one to derive understanding in one area to countless other areas (Guthrie, 2004a).

In CORI classrooms, approximately equal amounts of time are devoted to comprehending informational texts and to literary texts related to the central conceptual theme (Davis & Tonks, 2004; Guthrie, 2004a; Perencevich, 2004). As noted above, the use of different text genres can help diverse students connect to reading. Due to evidence that the availability of interesting texts especially prompts intrinsic motivation for reading (Hidi & Harackiewicz, 2000), an abundance of informational texts are accessible to students in CORI classrooms, including science and social studies trade books on specific topics, reference books such as encyclopedias, almanacs and field guides, magazine articles, websites, and other multimedia sources; they hardly include traditional textbooks. Literary texts are likewise made available in abundance, including all genres of novels, storybooks, poems, legends from a variety of cultures, and personal narratives; they hardly include basal readers unless the stories within them relate to the conceptual theme (Perencevich, 2004). Furthermore, diverse levels of texts in these categories are available in all classrooms, particularly books for struggling readers containing colorful, detailed pictures, which these students can use to help them build their literacy (Guthrie, 2004b; Swan, 2003). For listings of appropriate informational and literary texts of diverse levels for the themes Birds Around the World and Survival in Freshwater Habitats, as well as a list of Internet directories for children, see Davis and Tonks (2004).

Another way CORI utilizes multiple literacies is through the different kinds of reading activities done in and out of CORI classrooms. Students often read expressively to other students, which supports oral traditions in literacy and gives students a chance to express their voices while reading. There are reading pair shares in which two students read together and talk about what they read, larger groups of students reading together, and times for students to read alone.

Connecting to Students' Lives

CORI's emphasis on real-world interactions clearly meshes with Au and Raphael's (2000) second recommendation that a connection to students' lives leads to greater student involvement. For example, during the

Observe and Personalize phase of CORI, the theme Survival of Life on Land and Water, which has been implemented in third-grade classrooms in Maryland, has lent itself to a walk in nearby woods to generate interest in the local array of plants and animals, thus addressing children's motivational needs (Guthrie, 2004a). In this first phase, students are taught the reading strategy of activating background knowledge; that is, students learn to recognize and share what they know about the text topic before reading, so that they might discover how new content links to this prior knowledge (Guthrie & Taboada, 2004). In our example, students might contribute observations based simply on their experiences playing in their own backyards or neighborhoods, and related to these observations, they might form high-level questions, another strategy emphasized in CORI. Thus, real-world interactions permit cognitive skill development as well as enhance motivation, and they also allow students to connect what they are learning to their own diverse backgrounds and experiences. Students can bring the CORI books home, which allows them to share the books with their families and thus connect their school reading experiences to their home reading experiences.

Even students themselves recognize the value of having personal experiences related to the topics about which they will be reading. A major hands-on activity in the third-grade version of CORI is an owl pellet dissection, an activity that students find fascinating. After guiding her students through the dissection of owl pellets and sharing books with them that helped them identify the bones they found within the pellet, one teacher commented:

> When they see it in a book, they make the connection, "Oh wow, we've seen this." I asked them, "Why didn't I just show you the book? Why did we actually tear the owl pellet apart?"..."You know what they said? 'Because we wouldn't have learned as much or been as interested in the book. It wouldn't have been as exciting.'" (Perencevich, 2004, p. 35)

Furthermore, science activities related to the conceptual themes, such as exploring wetlands close to the school, help all students understand the environments in which they live and what kinds of things affect them, helping to create a common classroom culture to which all children can relate. Yet the students can still differentiate their particular interests within this shared culture.

In addition, conceptual themes may provide an avenue for children to explore topics related to their own backgrounds and in that way uniquely contribute to the class's learning on a particular theme. For example, one CORI teacher with a racially diverse class in a school where both student and parent disengagement was a rampant problem chose the theme of civil rights. She gave her students the choice of exploring the civil rights experiences of African Americans, Mexican Americans, Native Americans or women, with the overarching goal for her students being for them to discover links between the meaning of civil rights for these groups and the meaning of civil rights to individuals. The students responded enthusiastically, as did their parents, wanting to know why their children were suddenly so eager to go to school, even on the day they had off for parent–teacher conferences (Swan, 2003).

Cognitively Engaging All Children

Reading instructional programs often provide cognitively challenging activities and materials for readers who read well, and this is true for CORI. Many programs do this less well for struggling readers, who often have to read simple texts that do not present complex or interesting ideas. Within CORI, however, a modified format has been developed especially for struggling readers, specifically children in the third and fourth grades who are not yet fluent decoders, that does not limit the opportunity these students have to gain meaningful conceptual knowledge, the primary cognitive goal of CORI for students of all achievement levels (see Guthrie, 2004b). Struggling readers receive a half hour of small-group instruction each day as part of the 90-minute to 2-hour block of CORI the whole class receives each day. During the first 15 minutes, struggling readers participate in expressive reading of the text on which they will be practicing comprehension strategies that day, followed by somewhat simplified strategy instruction on the same strategies that the other children are learning. For example, for summarizing, struggling readers may be asked to summarize a shorter section of text than students who are average- or above-average readers. In addition, the teacher may model a strategy for struggling readers 8–10 times, whereas for other students she may model it only 2 or 3 times before asking them to apply the strategy independently.

Furthermore, as mentioned previously, there are interesting texts included in each classroom for students of diverse reading capabilities. Materials that avoid the common problem of texts for struggling readers of oversimplifying concepts to the point of being inaccurate or uninteresting are sought. Also, special care is taken to find books that have fewer words per sentence and sentences per page and illustrations that can help students confirm the meaning they derive from the text, but that still possess text features, such as a table of contents, subtitles, and an index, that make them appropriate for application of the comprehension strategies that are taught. For instance, for students at a beginning third-grade level, appropriate texts typically have 7 to 11 words per sentence, 1 to 4 sentences per page, and illustrations covering about half of each section (Guthrie, 2004b; Russell & Guthrie, 2003). In this way struggling readers connect to the same rich conceptual themes, and learn the same comprehension strategies, as the other children in the class, in order to maximize their cognitive growth and engagement in reading.

Encouraging Students to Construct their Own Learning

In CORI, learning becomes ever more student-directed rather than teacher-directed as classes proceed through the four phases of the instructional framework (Guthrie, McGough, Bennett, & Rice, 1996; Guthrie et al., 2004b). In a sense, the purpose of teaching students strategies for comprehension is to support their development into autonomous learners who understand concepts thoroughly and communicate this understanding articulately, rather than automatons who recite isolated facts transmitted to them by their teachers. Teachers gradually decrease their level of scaffolding for the comprehension strategies, from full modeling to guided practice to simply prompting their application until students initiate use of the strategy, as needed, to help them fulfill their learning and knowledge goals (Guthrie & Taboada, 2004).

Students also become active in their own learning because they have received scaffolding for motivation (Guthrie et al., 2004b). For example, one way teachers foster children's autonomy is by gradually increasing the scope of the choices they give them related to CORI activities, as research has strongly demonstrated that meaningful choices increase students' intrinsic motivation for academic activities (Reeve, 2002; Reeve, Bolt, & Cai, 1999). More specifically, the teacher might initially direct the student to read a particular section of text within a book, then later might let them choose which section of the text they would like to read, and eventually might let them choose which text is most appropriate for answering their self-devised questions, questions perhaps based on the unique observations they made during real-world interactions. Students also gradually may be given more and more voice in selecting topics within the conceptual theme, a sequence for activities, or a method of expression (Guthrie & McCann, 1997).

Furthermore, students also may be active in monitoring their own progress and effort. For example, one CORI teacher made a chart for her students to use in monitoring how well they were satisfying the criteria for written reports and group projects on the weather. If they satisfied the criteria, which included meeting their goals, using at least three references, complete thoughts and complete sentences, original writing (i.e., not copied from books), illustrations, and oral presentations, they received an A, which all students did (Swan, 2003).

Fostering Communities of Learners

Although CORI provides support for autonomy, becoming autonomous does not preclude becoming part of a community of learners. Indeed, one of the principles on which CORI is based is the idea that engaged readers engage not only with text but also with their peers, teachers, and members of their broader school and home communities in deriving meaning from text; hence, collaboration support is a key contextual feature of CORI classrooms.

Students have the opportunity to interact cooperatively with each other in all four phases of CORI. When classes have studied Survival in Freshwater Habitats, students have collaborated during the Observe and Personalize phase to build aquariums (yet were autonomous in devising the questions they sought answers to based on their observations of the snails, insects, fish, and plants in those aquariums; Guthrie, 2004a). In another classroom in which the conceptual theme was the solar system, students formed interest groups during the Search and Retrieve phase based on the particular planets they were researching (Guthrie al., 1996). Exemplifying collaboration in the Comprehend and Integrate phase, students in one CORI classroom regularly met in editing groups of four, in which students' jobs depended on the color pencil they received from their teacher, with roles rotating each time the group meets: red for spelling, blue for capitalization and punctuation, green for overall story sense, and purple for paragraph finding (Sikorski, 2004). Lastly, in the Communicate to Others phase, students might, for instance, collaborate on oral presentations; in the class that studied weather, each group of students selected one type of weather, such as hurricanes or tornadoes, and decided among themselves which member of their group would report on which aspect of their group's weather type (Swan, 2003). Often students choose weather types most likely to affect their own areas, which again helps create a common culture of learning.

Social interaction related to learning, however, is not merely initiated by the CORI teacher. In the CORI class studying the weather, the students' shared engagement in this topic seemed to naturally stimulate positive social relations. Since the teacher posted students names alongside their personal questions relating to weather, all students became familiar with the specific topics that their peers were studying. Thus, when they came across information on another student's topic in the midst of their own searching, they excitedly shared the information with that other student and sometimes the whole class. Students especially became excited when they found information that helped a classmate who had chosen the relatively "obscure" topic of tsunamis, and he welcomed their input (Swan, 2003).

Collaborations in CORI include pairs of students, groups of students, and whole-class collaborations. Teachers create different groups of students for various collaborative activities, and students also choose different students to work with for different projects. Thus students from different backgrounds and experiences get to know each other as they are doing their CORI work. CORI classrooms become communities of learners, with all students included in the ongoing activities.

Research Evidence

Research has documented CORI's effectiveness in enhancing students' reading comprehension and reading motivation. Several of these studies have been done in diverse classrooms containing a high percentage of students from ethnic minority backgrounds, particularly African American and Latina students. Both Guthrie and colleagues (1998) and Guthrie, Anderson, Alao, and Rinehart (1999) showed that third and fifth grade CORI students had higher reading comprehension scores than students in traditional reading instruction classrooms, and transferred these strategies to new tasks more effectively than did students in traditional classrooms. CORI students also have more positive motivation for reading than do students in traditional classrooms (Guthrie, Wigfield, & Von Secker, 2000).

Most recently Guthrie, Wigfield, Barbosa, and colleagues (2004) studied the impact of CORI, a strategy instruction (SI) program that taught the same reading strategies as CORI but did not provide the motivation/engagement supporting practices and traditional reading instruction (TI) on third-grade students' reading comprehension and reading motivation. Students participating in this research were diverse racially and economically. In two studies, third-grade students who had received CORI for 12 weeks scored higher than SI students on a measure of passage comprehension that compared students' knowledge structures with that of experts on the topic, multiple text comprehension based on a packet of articles related to two ecological biomes, and the standardized Gates–McGinitie Reading Comprehension Test. They also scored higher than TI students on passage comprehension and the Gates–McGinitie test. In regard to engagement, CORI students reported more motivation than SI students, and were also rated as being more motivated to read by their teachers. A composite measure of CORI students' strategy use (including activating background knowledge, searching for information, and organizing information) showed that they improved in this regard more than SI students.

Taken together, these findings provide substantial evidence that CORI enhances students' reading comprehension and motivation. Guthrie, Wigfield, Barbosa, and colleagues (2004) argue that it is the combined and interactive effects of the motivational and reading strategy instruction practices that lead to the greater gains in comprehension and motivation. From the perspective of this chapter, many of these practices reflect a concern for how children's backgrounds and the sociocultural contexts of classroom influence children's literacy engagement, and relate in particular to Au and Raphael's (2000) sociocultural perspective on literacy instruction. That is, instructional practices in CORI emphasizing multiple literacies, connections to students' lives, high levels of cognitive demands, active engagement in learning, and creating opportunities for student interactions and collaborations facilitated students' motivation for reading and reading comprehension.

Kamehameha Elementary Education Program (KEEP)

The structure and practices used in the KEEP program also cohere well with the recommendations made by Au and Raphael (2000) for using sociocultural perspectives to guide reading instruction. As we did with CORI, first we present an overview of the program, then discuss how specific features of KEEP link with each of Au and Raphael's recommendations, and describe the research evidence for KEEP. Finally, we discuss how KEEP educators collaborated with Navajo teachers to adapt KEEP for Navajo students.

Supported by a private educational trust established in 1887 in the will of the last heir of the royal Hawaiian Kamehameha family, KEEP operated from 1970 to 1995 as a research and development effort to address Hawaiian American children's low academic achievement (Jordan, 1995). Initially, many thought the students' lack of motivation and misbehavior in the classroom explained why they were routinely scoring in the bottom quartile on national standardized measures of achievement. Thus, when the first KEEP laboratory school opened in 1972, teachers were instructed to positively reinforce individual students, while teaching reading through a widely used basal-based phonics curriculum (Vogt, Jordan, & Tharp, 1987). Gradually, however, applied ethnographic research revealed that incompatibility of the school curriculum and classroom organization with the children's home cultural experiences was largely breeding the students' disinterest and poor performance (Jordan, 1985; Vogt et al., 1987). As a result, in 1982 KEEP classrooms were reorganized to reflect the especially prominent role that peers and siblings take in caring for and teaching one another outside of school, in contrast to how adults typically fulfill these roles for children in European American culture (D'Amato, 1988; Weisner, Gallimore, & Jordan, 1988).

Over the years KEEP's approach to literacy instruction shifted from a phonics emphasis to a stronger emphasis on reading comprehension and equal stress on reading and writing in the curriculum, due to findings that gains obtained on test scores for younger students were not enduring in the higher grades (Au & Asam, 1996). As will be discussed below, the overarching goal of the latest curriculum, termed "whole literacy," is ownership of reading and writing (Vogt & Au, 1995). This curriculum, which is grounded in the perspective that literacy has important affective as well as cognitive dimensions, was disseminated to 160 K–6 teachers in nine public schools in Hawaii between 1989 and 1995. The majority, if not all, of the students in each of the KEEP classrooms were from low-income Hawaiian American families (Au, 1997a, 1997b; Valencia & Au, 1997).

In KEEP, which is implemented for the full school year, whole-literacy instruction occurs in two daily blocks, the readers' and writers' workshops. The readers' workshop typically begins with the teacher reading aloud or conducting a minilesson related to comprehension with the whole class. Then the teacher guides small-group discussions of literature, while students who are not meeting with the teacher work on other tasks such as writing in their literature response logs, reading independently or with a partner, or working on individual or small-group projects (Au & Asam, 1996). Teachers stress reading for information and reading for enjoyment equally (Au, 1997b; Au & Carroll, 1997). The writers' workshop likewise might begin with a minilesson for the whole class on a topic such as writing an interesting lead, after which students work on writing using the process approach as described by Calkins (1991) and Graves (1983). During the writing period, students frequently engage in editing conferences with their teacher or peers. Teachers provide instruction in grammar and spelling skills within this context where the emphasis is on application to students' own compositions, rather than through isolated workbook exercises (Au, 1997b). Toward the end of the writers' workshop, the whole class typically gathers around the author's chair (Graves & Hansen, 1983) to hear and comment on other children's drafts or "published" books (Au & Carroll, 1997).

Exemplification of Recommendations for Quality Reading Instruction From Au and Raphael's Sociocultural Perspective on Literacy Instruction

Multiple Literacies

As in CORI, literacy in KEEP encompasses much more than simply being able to read aloud fluently or answer factual questions about a basal story. A variety of kinds of literacy activities and materials are used in KEEP, which means that the concept of multiple literacies is embraced in the program. These materials and activities connect to children's cultural backgrounds in important ways, and the kinds of literacy activities they experience in settings outside of school also connect to the school-based materials and activities.

There are six aspects of whole literacy emphasized in the KEEP curriculum, including the central goal of ownership of reading and writing, which is defined as positive attitudes toward literacy and participation in literacy activities in daily life outside of school. Such emphasis is placed on ownership of important skills because it helps children realize the immediate benefits of schooling, which may be especially important for minority children like native Hawaiians whose family and cultural histories may not readily evidence links between education and future positive outcomes (Au, 1997a, 1997b; Au & Kawakami, 1991).

The other dimensions of literacy emphasized in KEEP include reading comprehension, which itself includes text interpretation, response to text, and ability to recognize links between the text and one's own life, and the writing process, which consists of planning, drafting, revising, editing, and publishing. Language and vocabulary knowledge (stressing the importance of grammatical structure and proper word usage in both spoken and written English), word-reading and spelling strategies, and voluntary reading of self-selected materials are the other major aspects of literacy in KEEP. Proficiency or participation in these latter five aspects of literacy support the development of ownership, at the same time as the developing sense of ownership fosters greater student investment in the processes of learning to read and write (Au, 1997a, 1997b).

Connecting to Students' Lives

In order to develop ownership of reading and writing, children need to feel that their teachers at school value the literacy activities they engage in at home, and they need to see the relevancy of what they read in class to their lives outside of school. KEEP teachers partially satisfy the former need by encouraging students to talk about their favorite books from home and they partially accomplish the latter by allowing students to choose their own topics for writing based on their personal experiences and interests (Au & Kawakami, 1991).

Teachers also help students make connections between what they are reading and their own lives by using the Experience–Text–Relationship (E-T-R) approach for reading comprehension. In the E phase, teachers briefly introduce a storybook or novel and ask students how their own past experiences might relate to the book. For example, students immediately related to a story in which the child characters had both Japanese and English names, since most of them possessed both Hawaiian and English names. In the T phase, students read the text silently or aloud, pausing after short sections to participate in discussions initiated by the teacher. They speculate on questions such as the significance of the story's title and compare predictions they made about what would happen in each section with what actually occurred. Lastly, in the R phase, the students and teacher decide on the theme of the story and identify relationships between the text and students' own experiences (Au & Kawakami, 1991; Kawakami & Au, 1986).

The interaction style among students and teachers during reading comprehension lessons also helps children make connections between literacy experiences inside and outside of school. They discuss what they are reading in a manner resembling the Hawaiian community event known as "talk story," in which individuals jointly relate a tale, building upon each other's contributions in a fast-paced manner with frequent overlapping speech. In class, while the teacher chooses the initial topic for discussion and may occasionally slow the pace of conversation, the students respond freely, extending each other's comments as they see fit (Au & Kawakami, 1991; Au & Mason, 1983). This interaction style contrasts with the traditional Initiate–Response–Evaluate (I-R-E) method, in which teachers spotlight one child at a time, a particularly uncomfortable position for Hawaiian children (D'Amato, 1988) and a method that has been found to be less engaging for Hawaiian students than the talk story method (Au & Mason, 1981, 1983).

Cognitively Engaging All Students

Regardless of children's ability level, the KEEP curriculum gives central prominence to authentic reading and writing activities. For all students, word reading, vocabulary, and spelling are not taught as isolated skills, but are taught in relation to the stories children are reading for comprehension and the pieces they are composing in the writers' workshop. For example, during the readers' workshop, teachers instruct students to find new, interesting words and to use these vocabulary words in their oral discussions and written summaries (Au, 1997b).

Recognizing the negative effects of fixed ability grouping for reading (see Graham & Harris, 2000), KEEP teachers avoid this practice as much as possible. In the primary grades about half the teachers do group their students by reading ability, since students in these grades may need different levels of word-reading strategy instruction. However, many primary-grade teachers and the vast majority of upper-grade teachers group their students by their interests in different novels and topics of study (Au, 1997b; Au & Carroll, 1997).

Encouraging Students to Construct their Own Learning

KEEP's central goal of literacy ownership depends largely on students taking an active role in their own learning. Although teachers lead the text discussion in reading groups, student input on the direction of the discussion is welcome and valued, and teachers often open small-group sessions by asking their students to share their literature responses. For example, for a story about how a grandmother helps her grandchildren witness a caterpillar's transformation into a moth, the teacher had initially identified the theme as "learning from grandparents." However, once she realized that the children had distinguished a theme more interesting and meaningful to them, "need for freedom," from the events in the story leading to the moth flying away, she changed her questions to facilitate discussion of this alternative theme (Au, 1997b; Au & Kawakami, 1991).

KEEP also fosters ownership and engagement in reading by encouraging students to make meaningful choices related to their activities. One KEEP teacher gradually introduced her students to six different methods of literature response, including writing a letter from one story character to another or writing about one's favorite part of the story, so that eventually these students could select which one of the six options they preferred (Au, 1997b). Students also select their own books for a period of silent reading during each school day, and their daily homework almost always includes reading from a book of one's choice for 10 to 30 minutes, which may be picked from the classroom library or another source.

Fostering Communities of Learners

As discussed above, teachers interact with their students during reading comprehension lessons in a style termed "talk story." Not only does this method provide a link to students' cultural background, it is also instrumental in promoting the formation of a community of learners. This method, based on the Hawaiian community speech event in which "the skilled speaker is one who knows how to involve others in conversation, not one who holds the floor alone" (Au, 1997b, p. 197), encourages students to work together to form full, thoughtful responses to their teacher's questions. It deemphasizes the values of individualism and competition promoted by the traditional I-R-E method, instead enforcing the value of cooperation for the 'ohana, or extended family, fostered at home (Au, 1997b).

KEEP teachers also support development of harmonious learning communities by adjusting their classroom management practices to reflect the prominent role of sibling caretaking and peer interaction, including teaching activities, with little direct adult supervision in native Hawaiian children's lives in comparison to that in European American children's (Weisner et al., 1988). KEEP teachers thus allow their students to seek and give assistance to their classmates as they desire. They also typically permit students to assign their own roles when working in small groups, finding that children work very effectively together when they do so, perhaps due to the children's complex organization of leaders and followers in their peer groups, yet their desire to maintain equality and fair treatment among their peers (Au, 1997b; D'Amato, 1988).

Teachers in KEEP classrooms are also encouraged to show their students that they too are learners. To promote voluntary reading, they give book talks to the whole class about stories they have enjoyed (Au, 1997b) and during the writers' workshop they may share their own compositions. One teacher not only read her finished stories about childhood memories and tales of recent events, but also used her drafts in minilessons on the writing process, requesting editing input from her students (Au, 1997a).

Research Evidence

Assessment of the effectiveness of KEEP's whole literacy curriculum primarily was based on student progress as documented in portfolios. The initial evaluation of KEEP's whole literacy format, based on data from the 1990–91 and 1991–92 school years, showed that two-thirds of the 2,000 students in grades K–3 who received this curriculum met or exceeded the benchmarks for literacy ownership. However, only one-third met or exceeded the benchmarks for reading comprehension, language and vocabulary knowledge, and the writing process, whereas one-half satisfied or surpassed the criteria for voluntary reading and word-reading strategies (Au & Asam, 1996; Au & Carroll, 1997).

After finding these somewhat disappointing results, KEEP consultant staff decided to work closely with 13 teachers during the following school year to implement either the readers' or writers' workshop in their classrooms as fully as possible. Teachers were given the choice of which workshop to concentrate on, and the majority (11) selected the writers' workshop. In the second year of this "demonstration" project, of the 20 additional teachers who participated, 18 chose the writers' workshop. Thus, only achievement and ownership data related to writing were analyzed for these 2 years. The results were much more striking; for example, after the first year of this focused implementation, writing process assessments showed that 68% of 234 students in grades K–6 (over 60% of whom were of native Hawaiian ancestry) were at or above grade level, whereas at pre-implementation (for which data for 7 of the 11 teachers' students were available), nearly the reverse was true: 60% were below grade level. For ownership of writing, 88% percent of these students were at or above grade level after implementation, whereas before implementation 42% were below grade level (Au & Asam; Au & Carroll, 1997).

These results, combined with observations showing, for example, that students were much more attentive, discussed more text ideas, and made more logical inferences during talk story style lessons than those employing the I-R-E method (Au & Mason, 1981, 1983), suggest that KEEP effectively facilitated improvements in literacy achievement and engagement through practices that exemplify Au and Raphael's (2000) recommendations for instruction based in sociocultural theory. However, although these results are promising, more research on how KEEP influences children's reading comprehension is needed.

The KEEP-Rough Rock Demonstration School Collaboration

In the late 1970s and early 1980s, when the KEEP curriculum focused on reading comprehension but had not yet developed the whole literacy curriculum with its equal emphasis on reading and writing, KEEP students were typically scoring in the 50th percentile on national standardized tests, a great improvement from the years prior to and during the early implementation of KEEP when scores in the bottom quartile were typical (Jordan, 1985). As KEEP appeared to be positively influencing Hawaiian students' academic progress as well as their motivation for learning (Au & Mason, 1981, 1983), a debate arose regarding whether the improvements were due to the way in which KEEP practices coordinated specifically with Hawaiian culture, or due to the fact that the practices embodied general features of quality education. Thus, in 1983, KEEP staff members initiated collaboration with Rough Rock Demonstration School, a K–12 school in northeastern Arizona where the students as well as nearly all faculty and staff are native Navajos. While the school had included Navajo culture and language in its curriculum since its inception in 1966, teachers used the same instructional practices focusing on basic skills, which their own majority-culture teachers had employed, and as in Hawaii, students were faring quite poorly academically (McCarty & Dick, 2003; Vogt et al., 1987).

In the third-grade classroom in which KEEP was first implemented at Rough Rock, it quickly became apparent that modifications were needed to realize the goals of the curriculum for Navajo students. For example, the Navajo students only worked well together when given the opportunity to collaborate with one or two other students of the same gender and ability, unlike the Hawaiian students who delighted in working in larger groups of boys and girls where they could easily provide help and receive it from students of different skill levels. Eventually, the staff realized that the Hawaiian grouping pattern violated the Navajo cultural norm of gender separation in work activities (even though the children were only 8 years old) as well as conflicted with Navajo children's familiarity with working alone or with just one other person from a young age, in jobs such as sheep herding (Jordan, 1995; Vogt et al., 1987).

Additionally, in contrast to Hawaiian students, Navajo students preferred to discuss a book only after having read the entire story, not responding well to the KEEP method of alternating reading of short sections with discussion of those units and prediction of future events. While one KEEP teacher then struggled to outline the plot of a story in such holistic, nonlinear fashion, a Navajo teacher developed a flower-like diagram for describing the story, with the central problem encircled by petals containing each of the events related to it. As in KEEP, student input on reading activities was welcomed; for example, one third grader provided an alternative idea for diagramming the story, suggesting that it could be shown as a spiral with the main problem at the center with the related events winding out from it (Vogt et al., 1987).

Furthermore, Rough Rock educators were particularly interested in providing children a strong background in Navajo language and culture, in contrast to Hawaii, where instruction occurred in Standard English, although Hawaiian themes were highlighted. Therefore, Rough Rock faculty began writing and publishing their own children's storybooks in Navajo based on their own experiences and local stories (McCarty & Dick, 2003). They likewise focused on selecting culturally relevant themes, especially ones that provided connecting points among disciplines. For example, the theme of Navajo creation stories, which feature insects and insect people, provided a natural link to science lessons on entomology (Begay et al., 1995). Thus, while KEEP inspired the initial changes in the curriculum at Rough Rock, over the years Rough Rock teachers took more and more initiative in designing their own program (and achievement assessments), now known as the Rough Rock English-Navajo Language Arts Program (RRENLAP), the development of which is detailed in Begay and colleagues (1995; see also McCarty, 2002).

To date, Rough Rock educators and researchers have studied the effects of this continually evolving literacy curriculum on students' biliteracy, self-efficacy, and academic achievement, finding significant improvements in all areas (McCarty & Dick, 2003). For example, at the end of the 1992–1993 school year, 71% of K–3 students scored at the mastery level for English reading, with students averaging a gain of 13 percentage points on the locally developed assessment from fall to spring (Begay et al., 1995). In addition, K–6 students in RRENLAP consistently performed higher on standardized reading tests than local students who had not received RRENLAP (McCarty, 2002).

Similarities and Differences between CORI and KEEP

CORI and KEEP are instructional programs that take into careful consideration how the sociocultural contexts of classrooms and students' backgrounds and experiences influence the development of their reading comprehension and engagement, and development of broader literacy skills. Research has documented the effectiveness of each program on a variety of indicators of reading and writing skills, motivation, and engagement.

There are interesting similarities and differences in the programs. The similarities are most apparent in some of the practices designed to boost children's engagement. KEEP's focus on ownership and working to help children take charge of their own literacy learning and literacy activities in and out of school is similar to the CORI practice of supporting student autonomy to the greatest extent possible. In KEEP this is done by fostering active learning, providing meaningful learning activities, and encouraging student choice of the kinds of books read and activities done in class. Similar practices are used in CORI to develop students' control over their own learning. Both programs also focus on connecting school literacy experiences to children's lives, and making literacy activities as personally meaningful as possible for children. KEEP does this through the Experience–Text–Relationship approach, and CORI does so through activities that connect to students' experiences. Each program also emphasizes collaboration and interactions among students, although the ways in which this is done differs across the program, in large part because KEEP was designed for Hawaiian American children and so emphasizes practices such as the talk story.

There are some important differences across the programs as well. At the broadest level, the approach to culture varies between the programs. With respect to cultural background, KEEP was designed with a specific cultural group of children in mind, Hawaiian American children, and a number of the practices in KEEP (such as the talk story) are included in order to connect specifically to this group of children. When KEEP was implemented with Navajo children, some of the culturally specific practices were changed to correspond to the cultural background of these children. Although CORI focuses on sociocultural contexts of classrooms (at least as discussed by Au & Raphael, 2000), to date the same strategy and engagement practices in CORI are utilized with all children in the classroom. Struggling readers receive a modified set of practices, but they are designed to teach the same reading strategies and to engage these children fully in reading. The experiences and cultural backgrounds of individual children are taken into account through the kinds of book choices available to children, and choices about which kinds of assignments to do, which books to read, and (sometimes) with whom to work. To date, however, different kinds of CORI practices for different cultural groups of children have not been developed.

This issue could be addressed in CORI programs integrating social studies and reading. In such applications, activities relevant to the social and cultural backgrounds of different groups of children could be structured into CORI, with connections to books and then the other CORI instructional practices. As discussed earlier, this currently is being done by having different genres of books and legends from many different cultures included in the readings, but the materials could be tailored more specifically to certain cultural groups depending on the cultural composition of the classrooms. It would be interesting in future work with CORI to assess whether different kinds of instructional practices or activities may work better or worse for different groups of children.

There are other, more specific differences between the programs. CORI focuses on the integration of different content areas in the curriculum and the use of conceptual themes in particular subject areas to a greater extent than KEEP does. KEEP has daily components devoted to reading and to writing, whereas CORI focuses more on reading. However, writing becomes an increasingly important part of literacy instruction in CORI as children move through the elementary grades. KEEP is implemented at all grades in elementary school; to date, CORI has been implemented in grades 3–5. CORI uses direct instruction to a greater extent, particularly for the teaching of reading strategies. KEEP teachers use some direct instruction to teach skills, but to a lesser extent than do CORI teachers (see Au, in press, for discussion of direct strategy instruction in culturally diverse classrooms). Finally, CORI presents a particular set of motivational practices to foster children's engagement in reading. KEEP emphasizes motivation, but does not directly present a set of motivational instructional practices.

The similarities and differences between CORI and KEEP are fascinating, and we believe they are much in the spirit of sociocultural approaches to reading, in the sense that the programs carefully consider how children's backgrounds influence their learning, and work to make learning meaningful for all children. The specific ways each program does this vary, but each attends to these issues.

CONCLUSIONS AND DIRECTIONS FOR FUTURE RESEARCH

We discussed in this chapter important premises from cultural approaches to learning, beginning with some general points from the literature on multicultural education and then turning to specific ideas and recommendations from researchers who take a sociocultural approach to literacy and literacy instruction. Sociocultural approaches to literacy have made important contributions to our understanding of how children's reading and literacy skills and engagement develop. They provide a more inclusive perspective on the nature of literacy in and out of school, and emphasize how reading and literacy are not an isolated set of psychological processes but instead depend heavily on sociocultural contexts of classrooms. Theorists and researchers adopting these perspectives also provide a variety of recommendations for how literacy instruction in school can be more responsive to the developmental needs of diverse learners, as well as suggestions for how practitioners can be sensitive to the impact of sociocultural aspects of instructional practices and how these influence different children. These suggestions can help students like Cheryl become more engaged in literacy activities, and maintain that engagement.

We presented two instructional programs, CORI and KEEP, that focus in different ways on sociocultural aspects of classrooms and the cultural backgrounds of learners. We chose these because of their programmatic nature, and support by research. There is evidence showing that each program fosters the development of children's reading and writing skills, and engagement in reading and writing activities. There are similarities across these programs with respect to the ways in which they work to foster student control over their own learning, build collaboration among children as fostering engagement and learning, and emphasize how important it is for literacy activities to be meaningful and connect to students' backgrounds. There also are important differences in these programs with respect to certain instructional strategies and focus on the cultural backgrounds of students.

Although there is a growing research base for each program, more work is needed. We close with several suggestions for each program. With respect to KEEP, there is more information available on its impact on students' ownership of their reading and writing activities, rather than on students' cognitive skills in these areas. Ownership is an important outcome of literacy programs, but it also would be helpful to know more about how children's reading and writing skills are affected. Initially, KEEP was designed to help narrow the achievement gap in Hawaii between Hawaiian American children on the islands and other children there, and it would be informative to know if this goal was met. KEEP was designed for Hawaiian American children and has been extended to Navajo children. It now would be interesting to know how effective it is for other groups of children, and what kinds of modifications need to be made in KEEP for it to be effective with different groups. In Hawaii KEEP was implemented across grades K through 6; it would be interesting to examine its relative effectiveness at different grade levels.

CORI has been implemented in third- through fifth-grade classrooms, and has been shown to be effective at each of these grade levels. It would be interesting to determine if CORI could be extended to the primary grades, and also to middle school, and there is interest on the part of researchers and practitioners to do so. Important modifications would have to be made in the reading strategies taught, but the engagement practices may function well with younger and older children. To give one example, comprehension monitoring probably would not be emphasized in the primary grades as part of strategy instruction, but would receive increasing emphasis in the later elementary and middle school years. By contrast, provision of interesting texts and meaningful learning activities should occur at all grades.

To date, assessments of CORI have focused on all children, with some analyses of its effectiveness with struggling readers. It would be informative to begin to determine CORI's effectiveness for different groups of children, including children from different cultural groups, and also boys and girls. Studies focusing on such differences would provide information about the generality of CORI's effects, and (like the work on KEEP) might provide suggestions for how CORI could be modified to be more effective with different groups, if that needs to be done.

NOTES

1. Students in TI classes were not assessed for multiple text comprehension, motivation, or strategy use.
2. As mentioned briefly in the overview of KEEP, the whole literacy curriculum was implemented in 1989 because these earlier gains in achievement did not endure.

ACKNOWLEDGMENTS

The writing of this chapter was supported in part by Grant No. 008295 from the Interagency Educational Research Initiative to John Guthrie, Allan Wigfield, and Pedro Barbosa. Thanks to the Reading Engagement Team (John Guthrie, Kathy Perencevich, Ana Taboada, Angela McRae, Cassie Shular, Stephen Tonks, and Laurel Wagner) for comments on an earlier draft of this chapter.

REFERENCES

Alvermann, D. E., & Phelps, S. F. (1998). *Content reading and literacy: Succeeding in today's diverse classrooms*. Boston: Allyn & Bacon.

Au, K. H. (1997a). Ownership, literacy achievement, and students of diverse cultural backgrounds. In J. T. Guthrie & A. Wigfield (Eds.), *Reading engagement: Motivating readers through integrated instruction* (pp. 168–182). Newark, DE: International Reading Association.

Au, K. H. (1997b). A sociocultural model of reading instruction: The Kamehameha Elementary Education Program. In S. A. Stahl & D. A. Hayes (Eds.), *Instructional models in reading* (pp. 181–202). Mahwah, NJ: Erlbaum.

Au, K. H. (2000). A multicultural perspective on policies for improving literacy achievement: Equity and excellence. In M. L. Kamil, P. B. Mosenthal, P. D. Pearson, & R. Barr (Eds.), *Handbook of reading research* (Vol. 3, pp. 835–851). Mahwah, NJ: Erlbaum.

Au, K. H. (in press). *Multicultural issues and literacy achievement.* Mahwah, NJ: Erlbaum.

Au, K. H., & Asam. C. L. (1996). Improving the literacy achievement of low-income students of diverse backgrounds. In M. F. Graves, P. van den Broek, & B. M Taylor (Eds.), *The first R: Every child's right to read* (pp. 199–223). New York: Teachers College Press.

Au, K. H., & Carroll, J. H. (1997). Improving literacy achievement through a constructivist approach: The KEEP demonstration classroom project. *Elementary School Journal, 97*, 203–221.

Au, K. H., & Kawakami, A. J. (1991). Culture and ownership: Schooling of minority students. *Childhood Education, 67*, 280–284.

Au, K. H., & Mason, J. M. (1981). Social organizational factors in learning to read: The balance of rights hypothesis. *Reading Research Quarterly, 17*, 115–152.

Au, K. H., & Mason, J. M. (1983). Cultural congruence in classroom participation structures: Achieving a balance of rights. *Discourse Processes, 6*, 145–167.

Au, K. H., & Raphael, T. E. (2000). Equity and literacy in the next millennium. *Reading Research Quarterly, 35*, 170–188.

Baker, L., Dreher, M. J., & Guthrie, J. T. (2000). Preface. In L. Baker, M. J. Dreher, & J. T. Guthrie (Eds.), *Engaging young readers: Promoting achievement and motivation* (pp. ix–x). New York: Guilford Press.

Banks, J. A. (2001). Multicultural education: Characteristics and goals. In J. A. Banks & C. A. M. Banks (Eds.), *Multicultural education: Issues and perspectives* (4th ed.). Boston: Allyn & Bacon.

Banks, J. A., & Banks, C. A. M. (2004). *Handbook of research on multicultural education* (2nd ed.). San Francisco: Jossey-Bass.

Begay, S., Dick, G. S., Estell, D. W., Estell, J., McCarty, T. L., & Sells, A. (1995). Change from the inside out: A story of transformation in a Navajo community school. *Bilingual Research Journal, 19*(1), 121–139.

Calkins, L. M. (1991). *Living between the lines.* Portsmouth, NH: Heinemann.

D'Amato, J. (1988). "Acting": Hawaiian children's resistance to teachers. *Elementary School Journal, 88*, 529–544.

Davis, M. H., & Tonks, S. (2004). Diverse texts and technology for reading. In J. T. Guthrie, A. Wigfield, & K. C. Perencevich (Eds.), *Motivating reading comprehension: Concept-Oriented Reading Instruction* (pp. 143–172). Mahwah, NJ: Erlbaum.

Fredricks, J., A., Blumenfeld, P. B., & Paris, A. H. (2004). School engagement: Potential of the concept, state of the evidence. *Review of Educational Research, 74*, 59–109.

Gay, G. (2003). *Becoming multicultural educators*. San Francisco: Jossey-Bass.

Gay, G. (2004). Curriculum theory and multicultural education. In J. A. Banks & C. A. M. Banks, *Handbook of research on multicultural education* (2nd ed., pp. 30–49). San Francisco: Jossey-Bass.

Gee, J. E. (1996). *Social linguistics and literacy: Ideology in discourses* (2nd ed.). London: Taylor & Francis.

Gee, J. E. (2004). Reading as situated language: A sociocognitive perspective. In R. B. Ruddell & N. J. Unrau (Eds.), *Theoretical models and processes of reading* (5th ed., pp. 116–132). Newark, DE: International Reading Association.

Goldman, S. E., & Rakestraw, J. A. (2000). Structural aspects of constructing meaning from text. In M. Kamil, P. B. Mosenthal, P. D. Pearson, & R. Barr (Eds.), *Handbook of reading research* (Volume III, pp. 311–336). Mahwah, NJ: Erlbaum.

Graham, S., & Harris, K. R. (2000). Helping children who experience reading difficulties: Prevention and intervention. In L. Baker, M. J. Dreher, & J. T. Guthrie (Eds.), *Engaging young readers: Promoting achievement and motivation* (pp. 43–67). New York: Guilford Press.

Graves, D. (1983). *Writing: Teachers and children at work*. Exeter, NH: Heinemann.

Graves, D., & Hansen, J. (1983). The author's chair. *Language Arts, 60*, 176–183.

Gray, A. L. (2003). Conversations with transformative encounters. In G. Gay (Ed.), *Becoming multicultural educators* (pp. 67–90). San Francisco: Jossey-Bass.

Guthrie, J. T. (2004a). Classroom contexts for engaged reading: An overview. In J. T. Guthrie, A. Wigfield, & K. C. Perencevich (Eds.), *Motivating reading comprehension: Concept-Oriented Reading Instruction* (pp. 1–24). Mahwah, NJ: Erlbaum.

Guthrie, J. T. (2004b). Differentiating instruction for struggling readers within the CORI classroom. In J. T. Guthrie, A. Wigfield, & K. Perencevich (Eds.), *Motivating reading comprehension: Concept-Oriented Reading Instruction* (pp. 173–193). Mahwah, NJ: Erlbaum.

Guthrie, J. T., Anderson, E., Alao, S., & Rinehart, J. (1999). Influences of Concept-Oriented Reading Instruction on strategy use and conceptual learning from text. *Elementary School Journal, 99*, 343–366.

Guthrie, J. T., & Cox, K. E. (2001). Classroom conditions for motivation and engagement in reading. *Educational Psychology Review, 13*, 283–302.

Guthrie, J. T., & McCann, A. D. (1997). Characteristics of classrooms that promote motivations and strategies for learning. In J. T. Guthrie & A. Wigfield (Eds.), *Reading engagement: Motivating readers through integrated instruction* (pp. 128–148). Newark, DE: International Reading Association.

Guthrie, J. T., McGough, K., Bennett, L., & Rice, M. E. (1996). Concept-Oriented Reading Instruction: An integrated curriculum to develop motivations and strategies for reading. In L. Baker, P. Afflerbach, & D. Reinking (Eds.), *Developing engaged readers in school and home communities* (pp. 165–190). Mahwah, NJ: Erlbaum.

Guthrie, J. T., Van Meter, P., Hancock, G. R., McCann, A., Anderson, E., & Alao, S. (1998). Does Concept-Oriented Reading Instruction increase strategy use and conceptual learning from text? *Journal of Educational Psychology, 90*, 261–278.

Guthrie, J. T., & Taboada, A. (2004). Fostering the cognitive strategies of reading comprehension. In J. T. Guthrie, A. Wigfield, & K. C. Perencevich (Eds.), *Motivating reading comprehension: Concept-Oriented Reading Instruction* (pp. 87–112). Mahwah, NJ: Erlbaum.

Guthrie, J. T., & Wigfield, A. (2000). Engagement and motivation in reading. In M. Kamil & P. Mosenthal (Eds.), *Handbook of reading research* (Vol. 3, pp. 403–422). Mahwah, NJ: Erlbaum.

Guthrie, J. T., Wigfield, A., Barbosa, P., Perencevich, K. C., Taboada, A., Davis, M. H., Scafiddi, N. T., & Tonks, S. (2004). Increasing reading comprehension and engagement through Concept-Oriented Reading Instruction. *Journal of Educational Psychology.*

Guthrie, J. T., Wigfield, A., & Perencevich, K. C. (Eds.). (2004a). *Motivating reading comprehension: Concept-Oriented Reading Instruction.* Mahwah, NJ: Erlbaum.

Guthrie, J. T., Wigfield, A., & Perencevich, K. C. (2004b). Scaffolding for motivation and engagement in reading. In J. T. Guthrie, A. Wigfield, & K. C. Perencevich (Eds.), *Motivating reading comprehension: Concept-Oriented Reading Instruction* (pp. 55–86). Mahwah, NJ: Erlbaum.

Guthrie, J. T., Wigfield, A., & Von Secker, C. (2000). Effects of integrated instruction on motivation and strategy use in reading. *Journal of Educational Psychology, 92*, 331–341.

Hackett, T. L. (2003). Teaching them through who they are. In G. Gay (Ed.), *Becoming multicultural educators* (pp. 315–340). San Francisco: Jossey-Bass.

Heath, S. B. (1994). The children of Trackton's children: Spoken and written language in social change. In R. B. Ruddell, M. R. Ruddell, & H. Singer (Eds.), *Theoretical models and processes of reading* (4th ed., pp. 208–230). Newark, DE: International Reading Association.

Hidi, S., & Harackiewicz, J. M. (2000). Motivating the academically unmotivated: A critical issue for the 21st century. *Review of Educational Research, 70*, 151–179.

Jordan, C. (1985). Translating culture: From ethnographic information to educational program. *Anthropology and Education Quarterly, 16*, 105–123.

Jordan, C. (1995). Creating cultures of schooling: Historical and conceptual background of the KEEP/Rough Rock collaboration. *Bilingual Research Journal, 19*(1), 83–100.

Kawakami, A. J., & Au, K. H. (1986). Encouraging reading and language development in cultural minority children. *Topics in Language Disorders, 6*, 71–80.

Kelly, M. M. (2001). The education of African American youth: Literacy practices and identity representation in church and school. In E. B. Moje & D. G. O'Brien (Eds.), *Constructions of literacy: Studies of teaching and learning in and out of secondary schools* (pp. 239–259). Mahwah, NJ: Erlbaum.

Kintsch, W. (1988). The role of knowledge in discourse comprehension: A construction-integration model. *Psychological Review, 95*, 163–182.

Kintsch, W. (1998). *Comprehension: A paradigm for cognition*. New York: Cambridge University Press.

Lee, C. D. (2004). African American students and literacy. In D. S. Strickland & D. E. Alvermann (Eds.), *Bridging the literacy gap, grades 4–12* (pp. 70–85). Mahwah, NJ: Erlbaum.

McCarty, T. L. (2002). *A place to be Navajo: Rough Rock and the struggle for self-determination in indigenous schooling*. Mahwah, NJ: Erlbaum.

McCarty, T. L., & Dick, G. S. (2003). Telling the people's stories: Literacy practices and processes in a Navajo community school. In A. I. Willis, G. E. Garcia, R. Barrera, & V. J. Harris (Eds.), *Multicultural issues in literacy research and practice* (pp. 101–122). Mahwah, NJ: Erlbaum.

Moll, L. C. (1994). Literacy research in community and classrooms: A sociocultural approach. In R. B. Ruddell, M. R. Ruddell, & H. Singer (Eds.), *Theoretical models and processes of reading* (4th ed., pp. 179–207). Newark, DE: International Reading Association.

National Reading Panel. (2000). *Report of the National Reading Panel: Teaching children to read--an evidence-based assessment of the scientific research literature on reading and its implications for reading instruction* (NIH Publication No. 00-4769). Jessup, MD: National Institute for Literacy.

National Research Council. (2004). *Engaging schools: Fostering high school students' motivation to learn*. Washington, DC: National Academies Press.

O'Brien, D. G., Moje, E. B., & Stewart, R. A. (2001). Exploring the context of secondary literacy: Literacy in people's everyday school lives. In E. B. Moje & D. G. O'Brien (Eds.), *Constructions of literacy: Studies of teaching and learning in and out of secondary schools* (pp. 27–48). Mahwah, NJ: Erlbaum.

Perencevich, K. C. (2004). How the CORI framework looks in the classroom. In J. T. Guthrie, A. Wigfield, & K. C. Perencevich (Eds.), *Motivating reading comprehension: Concept-Oriented Reading Instruction* (pp. 24–53). Mahwah, NJ: Erlbaum.

Pressley, G. M. (2000). What should comprehension instruction be the instruction OF? In M. Kamil, P. B. Mosenthal, P. D. Pearson, & R. Barr (Eds.), *Handbook of reading research* (Volume III, pp. 3545–562). Mahwah, NJ: Erlbaum.

Pressley, G. M., & Afflerbach, P. (1995). *Verbal protocols of reading: The nature of constructively responsive reading*. Hillsdale, NJ: Erlbaum.

Reeve, J. (2002). Self-determination theory applied to educational settings. In E. L. Deci & R. M. Ryan (Eds.), *Handbook of self-determination theory research* (pp. 183–203). Rochester, NY: University of Rochester Press.

Reeve, J., Bolt, E., & Cai, Y. (1999). Autonomy supportive teachers: How they teach and motivate students. *Journal of Educational Psychology, 91*, 537–548.

Russell, S. L., & Guthrie, J. T. (2003). *Engaging struggling readers: Supporting fluency, comprehension strategies, and knowledge acquisition*. Manuscript submitted for publication, University of Maryland, College Park.

Santa Barbara Discourse Group. (1994). Constructing literacy in classrooms: Literate activities as social accomplishment. In R. B. Ruddell, M. R. Ruddell, & H. Singer (Eds.), *Theoretical models and processes of reading* (4th ed., pp. 124–154). Newark, DE: International Reading Association.

Sikorski, M. P. (2004). Inside Mrs. O'Hara's CORI classroom. In J. T. Guthrie, A. Wigfield, & K. C. Perencevich (Eds.), *Motivating reading comprehension: Concept-Oriented Reading Instruction* (pp. 195–223). Mahwah, NJ: Erlbaum.

Strickland, D. S., & Alvermann, D. E. Learning and teaching literacy in grades 4-12: Issues and challenges. In D. S. Strickland & D. E. Alvermann (Eds.), *Bridging the literacy gap, grades 4–12* (pp. 1–13). Mahwah, NJ: Erlbaum.

Swan, E. A. (2003). *Concept-Oriented Reading Instruction: Engaging classrooms, lifelong learners.* New York: Guilford Press.

Valencia, S. W., & Au, K. H. (1997). Portfolios across educational contexts: Issues of evaluation, teacher development, and system validity. *Educational Assessment 4*, 1–35.

Vogt, L. A., & Au, K. H. (1995). The role of teachers' guided reflection in effecting positive program change. *Bilingual Research Journal, 19*, 101–120.

Vogt, L. A., Jordan, C., & Tharp, R. G. (1987). Explaining school failure, producing school success: Two cases. *Anthropology and Education Quarterly, 18*, 276–286.

Vygotsky, L. S. (1978). *Mind in society.* Cambridge, MA: Harvard University Press.

Weisner, T. S., Gallimore, R., & Jordan, C. (1988). Unpackaging cultural effects on classroom learning: Native Hawaiian peer assistance and child-generated activity. *Anthropology & Education Quarterly, 19*, 327–352.

Wigfield, A., & Tonks, S. (2004). The development of motivation for reading and how it is influenced by CORI. In J. T. Guthrie, A. Wigfield, & K. C. Perencevich (Eds.), *Motivating reading comprehension: Concept-Oriented Reading Instruction* (pp. 249–272). Mahwah, NJ: Erlbaum.

CHAPTER 4

EFFECTS OF A MULTICULTURAL LITERACY CURRICULUM IN A RACIALLY AND SOCIOECONOMICALLY DIVERSE FIFTH-GRADE CLASSROOM

Jessica C. Zacher

A MULTICULTURAL CURRICULUM AND A DIVERSE STUDENT BODY

The teachers at Gonzales Elementary,[1] a racially diverse urban public school in northern California, employed a multicultural literacy curriculum (Harris, 1997) that celebrated diversity and taught about the Civil Rights Movement at every grade level, while meeting state standards for social studies and language arts curricula. As this chapter unfolds, I examine that curriculum—and its effects on students' identity work—through a close examination of student talk and writing about the slave biography *Sojourner Truth: Ain't I a Woman?* (McKissack & McKissack, 1992). Such attention is critical because choices about what to include in literacy curricula are ideologically laden; "texts build up 'possible worlds,' versions of the social and natural world," and "children construct their identities and

Focus on Curriculum, 77–99
Copyright © 2005 by Information Age Publishing

life trajectories in relation to the cultural texts that they encounter" (Luke, 1994, p. 33).

The teachers and principal at Gonzales strove to include a variety of life stories in their curricula, from novels like *Esperanza Rising* (Ryan, 2002) about migrant farm workers to histories of Native American persecution like *Navajo Long Walk* (Armstrong, 2001). As a result of those efforts, the school stood as a place where multiracial and multilingual diversity was, at least on the surface, an asset to the children. This ethnographic study highlights the race, gender, and social class negotiation in which children engaged as they read these stories. The students studied key historical figures from the Civil Rights era each year in school, and they came from communities and homes that were socioeconomically and geographically diverse.

This analysis of student talk and writing around *Sojourner Truth* indicates that students appropriated much of the multicultural discourse of the school community. At the same time, however, they constructed their own definitions of race, social class, and other identity categories in their individual and small-group discussions and in their written and performed texts about class books. Such interactions often took place under or outside of the teacher's radar, and the issues brought up in them were seldom negotiated with the help of the teacher or other adults engaged in the teaching of the multicultural curriculum. To illustrate these complexities, I open this chapter with a short vignette, a mere snippet of classroom conversation between two friends that reveals some layers of the students' ongoing identity construction in relation to multicultural texts (cf. Banks, 1995; Cai & Bishop, 1994).

In this scene, some tensions between how students see themselves and how they interpret what they learn from their curriculum are palpable— we can practically feel the discomfort that the conversation engenders, and breathe a sigh of relief when it is safely over. After this introduction, to contextualize my findings, I highlight some recent studies about the various ways that multicultural curricula are being deployed in multicultural settings. The meat of this chapter, my description of the very practices through which children constructed differences in their talk and writing, is followed by an illustrative vignette of students talking in more depth about Sojourner Truth's biography. I close with some ideas for how we might begin to reconceive the many implications of using multicultural curricula in diverse settings.

"If there was still slavery...": A Conversation

It was mid-February in Room 126, a fifth-grade classroom. Ms. Jean (the classroom teacher) and her students had just read the first chapter of

Sojourner Truth's biography as a class. They had broken into small groups in which students were responsible for summarizing and illustrating the chapter, as well as responding personally to events in it. Christina (a girl labeled by the school as White, but who identified as Latina) and her best friend Vanessa (who was both classified and identified as Latina) sat near the windows, working on their assigned vocabulary words (drawn from the book's first chapter). Vanessa and Christina were talking about "if there was still slavery."

Christina: If there was still slavery, um, we would be washing the floors.
Vanessa: You?
Christina: (*nodding vigorously*) Yeah.
Vanessa: <u>You?</u>
Christina: <u>Yeah.</u>
Vanessa: (*shaking her head*) No. No, but you're <u>White</u>, okay?

There was a momentary pause.

Christina: I could be washing the floors.

The girls look at each other for a moment.

Christina: How do you shape your eyebrows?
Vanessa: I want to shave them.

Vanessa pointed at Christina's eyebrows and started to talk about where she would pluck them.

In this classroom, children like Vanessa and Christina constructed their identities, and the meanings of texts, in various spaces, with various peers and adults, in complicated nets of social interaction. In this particular conversation, Vanessa and Christina jointly *historicized* slavery and its injustices; that is, the comment "if there was still slavery" indicates their understanding that slavery was an injustice of the past, left in the past. As an ethnographer visiting Gonzales, I set out to describe and understand the salience of Christina, Vanessa, and other children's chosen identity categories, categories that I interpreted based on these students' expressible relationships with others. I recorded conversations in the language arts and social studies periods and analyzed my data based on the understanding that their identities were dialogic at listening, speaking, and writing moments (Bakhtin, 1981; Holquist, 1990). That is, in a fundamental way, they narrated their very selves as they spoke to each other about slavery, about racism, about critical social issues of historical and present importance.

In addition, I viewed these students as subjects who, like all of us, were hailed by or drawn to particular discourses, ways of talking, being, and doing (Gee, 1996). In turn, they invested in those discourses and acted out certain subject positions. Stuart Hall (1996) refers to this process of hailing (being drawn to certain ways of being/doing) and at the same time investing in them (acting out those ways of being) as a "suturing...an *articulation*, rather than a one-sided process" (p. 6). Like their identities themselves, this articulation was visible in students' dialogues with peers about texts. Below, I argue that difference from one's peers was interpreted and expressed dialogically, in conversations and written texts, and that the constructions of otherness played out in students' interpretations of the books from the multicultural curricular materials.

For example, Christina's comment about washing the floors may initially seem to function only to *historicize* the injustice of slavery, to remove it from the girls' present social world. However, through her use of the pronoun "we," she signified her affinity with slaves—victims of "all of the terrible things that went on"—despite the vast differences of race and social class that Vanessa immediately chose to *highlight*. I use the term *highlight* to specify instances when students drew their peers' attention to differences in a subtle fashion, usually in lieu of labeling them outright. In other situations, gender was the most physically obvious difference for these students, but it was rarely *highlighted*, and was often less salient than variations in race, perceived social class (these students, like most, were aware of and sometimes vocal about their peers' relative poverty and wealth), neighborhood associations, popular culture tastes, and numerous other differences.

When Vanessa *highlighted* Christina's otherness, asking "you?" twice, she was engaging in an identity-building dialog with Christina. Vanessa followed her highlighting by *naming*, or labeling, Christina racially: "no, but you're White, okay?" Christina did not reply directly to Vanessa's label; instead, she repeated her slightly less emphatic claim that she herself "*could* be washing the floors" (the first time, she said that she *and* Vanessa "*would* be washing the floors"). After this comment, when the girls seemed to be at an impasse about Christina's assertion, Christina changed the subject by bringing up a shared cultural activity, the practice of eyebrow shaping.

Throughout their conversation, Christina and Vanessa constructed and interpreted meanings in both a school text and their lives by *naming* and *historicizing* injustices, and *highlighting* difference and sameness. I define the special valance that I give these terms below as I detail the "construction of otherness" that took place at Gonzales amidst children's ongoing identity work. Conversations like these, where students mixed personal claims like "I could be washing the floors," signifying some allegiance with slaves, and historical notations including the remark, "if there was still slavery" took place frequently. These students were, I argue, pushing the boundaries of established identity categories by trying to affiliate with those who were, on the surface, different. They did this work, this negotiation, through the multicultural curriculum, which I discuss in more detail in the following section.

Learning about Difference through a Multicultural Literacy Curriculum

At Gonzales, otherness was interpreted and expressed discursively, as well as textually, in students' and adults' literacy practices. Students negotiated more than textual meanings as they constructed notions of otherness and difference; as in the exchange above, they also negotiated their identities. Through this analytic lens, everyone was an "other," and racial, class, and gender identities were open to and for interpretation and reinterpretation by members of the school community at different times. Below, I describe the discursive practices through which otherness was constructed and maintained by students and teachers at Gonzales. Within this analytical frame, we can see how students and teachers created meanings across multiple conversational strands and literacy events (Street, 1995, 2000). As the vignettes in this chapter illustrate, these practices enabled participants to hang meaning together in temporary constellations (Massey, 1998) that bridged local and global contexts and settings.

Although elements of these practices were visible across the school day in the talk, writing, and actions of all of those actors, the combined language arts/social studies period in the fifth-grade classroom was an especially fertile site for the construction and maintenance of this particular way of talking about otherness. This construction was not an official or "center stage" discourse (Finders, 1997; Goffman, 1959)[2] somehow set up in opposition to, or alongside of, a "backstage" or "offstage" discourse (Scott, 1990) that students created and maintained on their own. Instead, otherness was negotiated and interpreted by the use of discursive tools and textual practices that students used most often—but not only—when they were engaged in conversations with adults about texts. Students who engaged in such negotiations drew on a variety of meanings across space and time.

This constant (re)interpretation of texts and identities could not have happened without the underlying structure of Ms. Jean's antiracist pedagogy, through which she attempted to demonstrate, in one scholar's words, "that the views we hold about race have different historical and ideological weight, forged in asymmetrical relations of power, and that they always embody interests that shape social practices in particular ways" (Giroux, 1993). The pedagogy was undergirded by a rich multicultural social studies and language arts curriculum, for which Ms. Jean brought in such books as *Sojourner Truth* and *Number the Stars* (Lowry, 1989). The former biography illuminates Sojourner Truth's life as a slave owned by a New York Dutch family, her eventual release from slavery, and her work as an "activist for the rights of Blacks and women," as one student described her. The latter book, *Number the Stars*, tells the story of a Danish Christian family that helped a 10-year-old Danish Jewish girl escape to Sweden in the midst of the Nazi invasion in 1943. She used these and several other books as springboards for discussions about otherness, as we will see below.

Ms. Jean's curriculum, broad though it was, was only one "fund of knowledge" (Moll, Amanti, Neff, & Gonzalez, 1992) from which the students in Room 126 drew. In the next section, I organize and connect some recent studies that address the use of multicultural texts in the elementary classroom as well as some research findings that dovetail with my own about how children understand difference through the lenses of various texts. In the subsequent section I draw out the analytic terms that comprise the "construction of otherness" through which students and adults negotiated relationships, read texts, and built identities. I then relate these practices to one particular curricular segment of the classroom language arts/social studies curriculum, the biography *Sojourner Truth: Ain't I a Woman?* (McKissack & McKissack, 1992). Throughout, I argue that the practices entailed in the construction of otherness centered around the official texts that students read throughout the year and the antiracist pedagogy through which they read them (Giroux, 1993).

Literature on Social Justice Issues: The Future of Multiculturalism

As Bishop (1997) explains, "multicultural literature is one of the most powerful components of a multicultural education curriculum, the underlying purpose of which is to help make society a more equitable one" (p. 40). The larger, book-length study through which these data were collected began from a sociocultural perspective on literacy development (Bakhtin, 1981; Heath, 1982b; Vygotsky, 1986), one that goes hand-in-hand with the notion of a multicultural curriculum that can work toward social justice. From a Bakhtinian (1981) perspective, the addressivity of written and oral texts—the ways they are always contextualized in human relationships—makes them sites of active identity negotiation in relation to other readers, authors, and peers. Building on past sociocultural work,

I also drew on identity theory (Hall & du Gay, 1996) and research in the field of cultural studies (Holloway & Valentine, 2000; Massey, 1998; McRobbie, 1991) to make sense of what the racially and socioeconomically diverse children of Gonzales were doing as they read multicultural literature together. In sum, I viewed these 10-year-old children as agents who negotiated their identities as they worked together in everyday literacy events, occasions where a piece of text was central to social interactions (Heath, 1982a).

These basic premises led me to an investigation of the ways in which the multicultural literature that students read contributed to their conceptions of difference—and of the salience of their identity categories—in school contexts. In these times, when "even the baseline discourses and tenets of multiculturalism...have been destabilized by cultural and economic globalization" (Luke, 2003), researchers and educators must continue to try new ways to teach and reach multicultural and multilingual populations. Some researchers, like Daiute (2000), claim that the acts of reading literature about social justice (in this case, the texts *Mayfield Crossing* [Nelson, 1993]) and *Felita* [Mohr, 1979]) and writing narratives that extend and complicate those texts can impact the social consciousness of middle-year children. Others have turned to popular culture texts (e.g., mainstream movies and rap music lyrics) to link children's in-school and out-of-school worlds and develop "critical literacies" (Morrell, 2002). They argue that this attention is "culturally and socially relevant" (ibid., p. 75) because it can and does "engage student writers" as they work through issues of legitimization and representation in popular culture texts (Mahiri, 1996).

Researchers like Dyson (1997, 2003) describe children as meaning negotiators who work through ideological assumptions as they create texts that draw on both in-school and out-of-school worlds. There is a growing body of work on the ways that children's identities shape their "textual and literate practices," and in turn, their literate practices "play a role in their positioning" (McCarthey & Moje, 2002). This kind of work, in combination with ongoing discussions about cultural authenticity and cultural relevance (cf. Bartolomé, 1994), offers us new ways for thinking about how children interact with school curricula, how they "identify" with what they are asked to read, and how their identifications—as in Christina and Vanessa's above conversation—shape the ways that they interpret texts that have been chosen for their authentically multicultural characters and social justice–oriented plots.

This research is warranted, especially since multicultural education's boundaries were "set over 30 years ago by U.S. Civil rights and school desegregation legislation, framed by the Bernstein/Labov debate and Cazden, Johns, and Hymes' (1972) prototypical work on the ethnography of speaking" (Luke, 2003, p. 134). In these newer times, as we design curriculum for groups whose demographics shift rapidly, we must concentrate on the interaction between diverse students and the diverse texts and characters in texts that we offer in the service of multicultural education. My findings indicate that children at Gonzales had varied understandings of what it meant to be an "other," to be "multicultural," to be discriminated against, to be entitled. In addition, they constructed those understandings based partially on what their teacher, and their school, asked them to read as part of a social justice–oriented multicultural curriculum. These students' varied conclusions about difference offer an example of how children in classrooms today interpret such work, and indicates the sense they make of otherness in their very diverse worlds.

CONTEXT OF STUDY

Methodological Orientation

The goal of my larger project was to investigate the salience of particular identity categories in literacy events "from the various points of view of the actors themselves" (Erickson, 1986). In order to accomplish this, the major research method used in the larger dissertation study was ethnography: specifically, participant-observation sessions two to three times a week, for 2 hours each day, over the course of the 2-month-long literature study unit. Throughout the project, I relied on a combination of anthropological notions of "thick description" a là Geertz (1973) and interpretive methods (Erickson, 1986). The larger study incorporated textual and thematic analyses, discourse analysis of key events, and visual analysis of photographs (of students across contexts, throughout the school day) and student-generated diagrams. Here, I rely primarily on textual and thematic analyses of field notes and collected student work (Bogdan & Biklen, 1998) to make my argument about the nature of students' identity work in the context of a multiculturally-oriented language arts classroom.

Research Questions

The main question guiding this research was, What are the salient identity categories for these students, and when do they matter to participants in literacy events in this classroom? Subsequent questions were crafted to address issues of children's identity work—how children articulated their senses of self in relation to others—in a variety of textual and spatial arenas. These included: (1) How do the texts that students read and compose reflect and/or influence their multiple identities, and, by extension, their positioning in relation to issues of gender, race, and class? (2) How do children conduct their identity work, and develop their identities, in relation to both the curriculum and their social hierarchies? and (3) How do ideas from multicultural social studies and language arts curricula get used by students in diverse settings, and what do these findings suggest for the way we organize classroom instruction?

Introducing Room 126 and Gonzales Elementary School

I use the following moment to introduce the students, teacher, and, literally, the halls of Gonzales Elementary because it is fairly typical of both the tenor and content of discussions about language arts and social studies texts in this school. Located in a commercial and residential neighborhood in a major city in the San Francisco Bay Area, Gonzales served approximately 250 students from all over the city. About 75 percent of the student body was bussed from several different neighborhoods in the city (three fifth-graders took public transportation to school); the rest lived in the neighborhood and were either walked or driven to school. The school had 11 classrooms: two each of kindergarten through third grade, one fourth, one split fourth/fifth grade, and one fifth grade (my research site). Out of 12 full-time teachers, 11 were certified, and one was completing her credential. The story related here is an introduction to Room 126; like the opening scene, it is indented to set it off from the text.

In early February, before the conversation reported above between Christina and Vanessa took place, Ms. Jean stopped the whole class in the hallway on their way in from the playground. She asked them what they had talked about the day before, and someone said "Sojourner Truth." The class stood in front of a set of two 5-foot square timelines color coded by topics that included women's rights, slavery and abolition, Native American history, and more. Ms. Jean pointed to the earlier timeline (covering the years 1400 to 1900) and asked the class what period Sojourner Truth had lived in. Jaime answered, "the 1800s." Ms. Jean had DeAndre read part of the chart, which was divided up after the large sections into small boxes. He chose a box in the "Women's" section with a blurb about Sojourner.

DeAndre read that Sojourner Truth was "a former slave, a spokeswoman for racial and sexual equality." Someone in the back of the group giggled—probably about the word "sexual"—and Ms. Jean asked for another word for "sexual." Cody called out "gender." Keisha asked why the information was placed there instead of in the slavery and abolition section. Ms. Jean said that "slavery and women's rights," were "connected," and that the kids would have to see "what that's about." She went on to talk a bit more about the chart, and had Adam read the first box about slavery. She pointed out the spot in 1619 when, as she said, the United States "got our first boatload" of slaves. She pointed out that in 1829 there were both slaves and free African Americans, like Daniel Walker, who was on the chart for his writing about freedom.

Moments like this occurred all year long. Ms. Jean never hesitated to stop students in their tracks, to talk about a current issue, to look at a poster on the wall, to examine other students' work, in short, to discuss anything that she noticed might feed into the ongoing conversation about social justice. She was a native Californian, a White woman who spoke fluent Spanish. She and I earned our teaching credentials from a local school several years prior to the larger study, and she welcomed me into her classroom when I proposed this project. Although elements of the construction of otherness were visible across the school day in the talk, writing, and actions of all of those actors, the combined language arts/social studies period in the fifth-grade classroom was an especially fruitful site for the construction and maintenance of this particular way of talking about otherness. Ms. Jean graciously shared her daily schedule with me, as far ahead as she was able, so that I could plan to be on site during those periods.

Of the 25 fifth-grade students, approximately nine were African American, nine Latino/a, four White, and three Asian American. Like most schools in the district, Gonzales was "full inclusion," with minimal pull-out instruction for students with special needs; one student in Room 126 had severe special needs and several others had learning disability–related individualized education plans (IEPs). Out of these 25, I had taught at least seven in my own kindergarten class 5 years ago, and knew at least 10 more from my 3 years as a teacher at Gonzales and 3 further years as a relatively regular visitor and ethnographer. About half the students were girls and about half of the students in the class came from families whose incomes qualified their children for free lunches; another third qualified for reduced-price lunches.

Data Collection

Data used in this manuscript were gathered two to three times a week, each time students gathered as a group to read the books aloud and discuss the lessons with the teacher, and when small groups of students were assigned certain activities related to the books or the unit of study (i.e., writing summaries, responses, drawing illustrations, finding vocabulary definitions). My data sources were numerous, and include my field notes (Bogdan & Biklen, 1998; Emerson, Fretz, & Shaw, 1995) taken at each whole and small-group session; tape recordings and transcriptions of each session; copies of all student work done about the books during the language arts period; copies of students' take-home reading journals with comments about the books; digital photographs taken during each whole- and small-group session as well as later on each day; interviews with eight focal students (Weiss, 1994); and field notes taken throughout the day after the end of the language arts period (during recess, math, lunch, etc.).

Data Analysis

Data analysis began in the second month of data collection, when I started to write biweekly analytic memos (brief memos based on reviews of field notes to date) that identified possible themes and coding categories. After data collection ended, I systematically reviewed the entire corpus of data, conceived of coding categories, and tested those categories. In this process, I employed two main methods of analysis. First, I conducted *multilevel analyses of literacy events*: based on the sociocultural framework described above, I used interpretive methods to analyze dialogic interactions where a piece of text was central to social interaction. I started by noting what children said about themselves to me, as well as what others said about them and did to them. I began to note that students talked as much about other students and people being different—from each other and from themselves—as they did about their own identities. After more refining work, as I reread my field notes from one of the lessons in the Cycle of Oppression, I realized that the key student talk was not just about "race" or other identity categories at all, but differences across the board.

Second, I conducted *broad thematic analyses* of content and genre of written artifacts. I read all student work about Sojourner Truth's life story and traced larger themes I found across the papers; examples from their work support my findings about how otherness was constructed at Gonzales. As I did this, and coded for instances of teachers and students talking and writing about difference, using the terms *naming, historicizing, empathizing,* and *flipping,* I began to simultaneously code for instances when students showed, through actions or words, that differences did indeed matter to them. The categories that comprise the "construction of otherness" emerged out of this process, as did another set of analysis categories through which I described how children "signified their affiliation along axes of difference" in and out of the classroom. Many of these axes were those lines along which students constructed difference, including race, gender, social class, popular culture tastes, after-school activity choices, and so on. The vignettes reported below are examples of this large-scale analysis, and it was as I wrote up such events that I began coding the data for instances of what I finally termed the "construction of otherness."

RESULTS: CONSTRUCTING THE "OTHER"

In the opening exchange, as Christina and Vanessa negotiated the possibility that Christina "could" have been a slave, they were constructing each other as others. As we saw, Christina also signified her affiliation with Vanessa and with slaves. This kind of exchange, where otherness was negotiated *and* students signified their allegiances, was typical of small group literacy events in Room 126. The practices of what I term *naming, historicizing,* and *highlighting* difference, combined with an emphasis on *empathizing* with victims of injustice, the occasional *flipping* of officially recognized categories of difference, and the provision of some *counteractions* for dealing with injustice on a day-to-day basis, comprised the "construction of otherness" prevalent in most language arts and social studies conversations in this classroom, and in school-wide events as well.[3]

In a partial answer to my last research question, I view these practices as one consequence of the deployment of a multicultural curriculum in a multicultural classroom. Sometimes the effects of them on the children's learning and identity-building had positive outcomes (when, for instance, children could claim they had advocated for a friend in the face of a problem); sometimes, when racism seemed confined mostly to the past, these practices might have limited students' available options for thinking about social justice. These categories are meant mostly to describe what went on, to show in specific ways how students built identities through talk and writing around the school's texts and curriculum. Below, I describe each of the analytic terms I use to describe this construction of otherness, with some examples; the chapter closes with a vignette that exemplifies these practices in action.

Naming injustices and people. The most common talk about difference in this classroom and the school was the outright *naming* of discriminatory acts and past and present injustices. Names are powerful, and in the act of naming an insidious –ism, students seemed to take away some of its power to hurt their peers, themselves, and people they read about. They had a keen grasp of historical and present injustices, and they almost always named the issue at hand before dealing with it by what I call *historicizing,* or by enacting *counteractions.* In addition to naming such injustices as homophobia—"it's against gay people," said one boy—they named racism, sexism, and other –isms, as well as heroic attempts to counter them.

Students and teachers were equally adept at naming *people* by a variety of identity markers. This kind of naming was their way of defining "otherness"; students were accustomed to naming people by race, gender, age, country of origin, and other differences. Describing and ultimately naming such differences accounted, I believe, for the way that all students became "other," became used to being seen as different in some way—however small or large—from their peers. For example, Ms. Jean frequently named students by gender and race, often for organizing children's bodies (i.e., "girls line up first"). DeAndre, writing about Sojourner Truth's interactions with Whites on her quest for her own freedom, named Quakers as "very good abolitionists" who "don't believe in slavery." When students and adults named others, they usually did so with explicit language, as when Vanessa asked her friend Christina: "But you're White, aren't you?"

Historicizing injustices and otherness. Emphasizing that such injustices took place mostly in the past was the lynchpin of the construction of otherness. Through it, students and adults set up almost every kind of perfidious "ism" as a thing of the past. Ms. Jean constantly struggled with this practice because it was her job to teach about the vicissitudes and triumphs of American history while *simultaneously* bringing students together in a new, supposedly more tolerant community of learners. *Historicizing* was almost inevitable because of the subject matter: students studied tumultuous historical eras, and one way that they were able to deal with their present multicultural context was to place the negative actions of their forebears—all of those who committed wrongs against others and all of those who were victims—in the past.

The most pointed example of this practice occurred when Vanessa described slavery to Christina, after reading the first chapter of the Sojourner Truth biography, as "All of the terrible things that went on..." Christina went on to write this phrase into her chapter summary, augmenting it so that it read: "All of the terrible things that went on back then with slavery." In this kind of writing and talk, students and teachers treated injustices like slavery as historical facts, and sometimes linked them to present realities. For instance, Saria once wrote that Sojourner Truth's son Peter—who had joined a gang, gotten in fights with rival gang members, stolen a saddle, and ultimately been imprisoned—was less imperiled as a gang member in his own time than he would have been now, "because if he got into a fight with other gang members [now] they might have got a gun out and shot him."

Students and teachers engaged in this practice at a fairly equal rate, in relation to texts like *Sojourner Truth* and *Number the Stars* as well as to issues brought up by the study of what Ms. Jean called the "Cycle of Oppression." In discussions of how women fought for the right to vote, assumptions about gender differences were historicized as ideologies of the past, not problems of the present. When the students discussed sexism, Ms. Jean asked, "Were women allowed to vote *at that time*?" and several kids answered "no;" one or two shook their heads. Particular individuals were subject to *historicization* more so than groups. When the class was talking about Harvey Milk, a famous gay rights activist, the teacher said, "Harvey Milk was a pi-uh-" and paused, looking intently at the students. After a moment, several students said "neer!" ("pioneer"). When the teacher entertained a discussion about Sojourner Truth's name change (from Isabella Van Wagener, also called Belle), DeAndre announced "Malcolm X did that, too." Christina later wrote that Sojourner Truth was "an advocate and abolitionist for Black and women's rights."

The practice of *historicization* occurred both in students' spoken conversations and written texts, and was visible in both teacher-driven assignments and students' personal writing projects (done in the classroom writing center). Ms. Jean and other school personnel historicized difference in class discussions, assemblies, and school events; as we saw above, posters and other material on the walls of the classroom and school fortified this practice. For example, a "Civil Rights" timeline that decorated the upper-grade hallway was separated into clusters: women's rights, abolitionism, immigration, and so on, across 400 years of U.S. history. These approaches ensured that students and adults had ample time to *historicize* injustices in their community, in the school, and in the country, and, in fact, almost every student in the classroom made at least one verbal or written comment that *historicized* some aspect of otherness.

Highlighting injustices and otherness. There were times when the students and teacher did not directly *name* an injustice, or someone's distinct identity marker, but instead *highlighted* difference. When students sat as a group on the meeting carpet, the teacher asked, "How are you segregated this morning?" A few students answered her—gender was the overriding factor that day—and then resorted themselves in a more integrated fashion (see *integration*, below). Highlighting was different than *naming* because it was more oblique, less direct, and was often used to draw someone else's attention to a situation that might or might not be changeable. In this sense it was a tool with which students could either highlight—or downplay—injustices and otherness. For example, in Vanessa and Christina's opening dialog, Vanessa highlighted Christina's otherness gently as Christina negotiated her claim to washing the floors, and, more subtly, her identity.

In a lesson about teasing and its role in the Cycle of Oppression, students were asked to write down two things about themselves that they could not change that they got teased about. Keisha wrote "I can't change my color, and I can't change my height." Although the point of the larger exercise was to empathize with others, these responses allowed Keisha to *highlight* some differences. Other students highlighted things including their "color" and their size. This complex pointing-out-without-changing way of addressing difference was a subtle but integral part of the construction of otherness. Highlighting was also a way for the teacher to help students imagine *counteractions* that would ameliorate injustices in front of her students (see below).

Empathizing with victims of injustice. The students and the teacher empathized with victims of injustice in both broad and specific ways. The written and spoken results of this practice were one of the most positive results of the curriculum and the construction of otherness that took place through it. In a lesson on the Cycle of Oppression, students had to tap into their own feelings about being teased, and empathize with the victims of teasing. They were asked to write "responses" to each chapter of each book that they read for literature circles. Prompts for the responses included "If I was __, I would feel ___" and "I can imagine ___." These were intended, the teacher explained to me, to make students draw personal connections between themselves and the story characters. Ms. Jean modeled empathetic language around "hard" terms, saying that it was "hard to refer to people as "owned,"" and honoring one student for reading a sentence aloud in which some slaves called Truth "the White man's nigger." The teacher said that they "all" knew "how hard it [was] to use that term."

Sojourner Truth's life story provoked empathizing across the book; students wanted to know such personal details as "whether she have a boyfriend or a husband." When Truth maimed her hand, someone said, "She didn't even care 'cause she just wanted her freedom!" When they learned of the age of Truth's twice-enslaved son, Peter—6 years old—one student said "Oh my God!" The teacher read aloud that Sojourner "vowed not to let another child of hers live in slavery again," and two girls cheered "Wooh!" Students had the chance to write about their empathy with her each week, when it was their turn to write the "response" segment of their group's literature circle work. Examples of their responses included: "I would be very very sad if I was sold away from my parents" and "I would run away too if I was Sojourner."

Flipping. The students in Room 126 often read about racial and other slurs in their books, and (perhaps because of the near-constant attention to difference, or perhaps because of the diversity of the student body) there were occasions when racial slurs might have been made between students. To protect each other from such possibilities, and to defuse such situations, students sometimes *flipped* the meaning of an officially recognized category of difference, or *flipped* a racial insult. When an African American girl named Mabel called Shirley, the young Chinese immigrant protagonist of *In the Year of the Boar and Jackie Robinson* (Lord, 1986), "a

Puerto Rican coconut," and heaped other "racist" names on Shirley, the teacher *highlighted* the fact that Mabel used "racist names." In response to the highlighting and to that particular insult, John, an African American student, said "Puerto Rican coconut!" with a large and apparently nonmalicious smile to his friend, Arturo, who was of Puerto Rican descent. Arturo laughed along with his friend, and the talk went on, but for a moment, a student had *flipped* the negative connotation and negative outcomes of racist teasing on its head, and made his friend smile. As we will see below, they also occasionally *flipped* the teacher's ideas to offer new perspectives.

Counteractions: General. The practices of the construction of otherness afforded some explicit counteractions with which students (and adults) could combat "isms" and work for justice in their daily lives. Some of these were teacher-generated, while others were thought of, and enacted, by students themselves. For example, Ms. Jean offered hypothetical situations: "Say there's a bully. What would the bully say when…" She set up situations in which the children could take turns advocating for each other when someone teased them, and offered specific lines they could say to the bully, including "How would you like it if someone called you that?" Students incorporated these examples into skits that they made as part of the study unit to exemplify different –isms, and they also created their own extensions of the examples.

For example, in a skit about lookism, Christina told her peers that they should say "Ooh, please don't play that!" when she and her friend insulted their looks. In addition, the classroom and school walls held posters of the lyrics of positive songs and raps, including "There's no room for hate in our world," and "I'm young, and I'm positive." The lyrics celebrated diversity and decried hatred. These counteractions, some of which were arrived at by teacher and students as difference was *highlighted* or *named*, were picked up and used more in class sessions when the teacher was present than in her absence, where students submitted to and created more hierarchical and (perhaps) less socially just structures for interaction through their own affiliation practices.

Counteractions: Integration. Over the year, Ms. Jean actively encouraged students to *integrate*, sometimes by *highlighting* their segregated seating patterns, but more often by telling them that they could not sit with their prior partners (who were usually same-sex friends). Texts like *In the Year of the Boar and Jackie Robinson* provided positive examples of integration, or at least of racial harmony, and the teacher *highlighted* those incidents when they appeared. In the Lord book, after a liberal dose of racial insults, including "Puerto Rican coconut," Mabel gave Shirley two black eyes, yet Shirley refused to tell on Mabel. A few days later, it was raining at school, and Shirley offered Mabel her umbrella. They were friends—

across racial and linguistic lines—from that day forward. Integration was ubiquitous; it was offered to the students as a *counteraction* and adults helped them practice this in countless events to combat various forms of segregation across the year.

Constructing Notions of Difference in Relation to Sojourner Truth's Story

In the following vignette, I look at how the students and teacher in Room 126 constructed notions of otherness, emphasizing the practices detailed above. Prior to opening *Sojourner Truth*, the class had made "K-W-L" charts that remained on the walls around the carpet area for the entire length of the unit. At this point in the unit, as the class prepared to move into Chapter 3, the "K" charts were about half-full of things students "knew" about Sojourner's life, or had learned in the first chapters. The "W" charts were as full as they had been when the students first made the list of things they "wanted" to learn about her, and the "L" chart, for things they had "Learned," had seven or eight lines of text on it in different students' handwriting.

As part of their language arts small-group rotations, different groups of children wrote about the events of each chapter on a revolving schedule. The groups were responsible for a summary, a response, an illustration of a key moment, and for definitions of vocabulary words they had picked out for each chapter. Ms. Jean kept this work in a binder that she held on her lap, open to the previous week's illustration. What follows is my rendition of events, with my analytic categories and comments interspersed between segments.

> Ms. Jean showed the class Ella's picture of Robert, Sojourner's first boy-friend, being beaten by his owner. She asked who Robert was, if everyone remembered, and Vanessa said, "I know, I know, the lover of Belle." Ms. Jean asked, "Yeah, but what was the problem?" Cody said something about how Robert was Sojourner's boyfriend, that he had been beaten because of his affair with Belle, and that he had another arranged marriage. Ms. Jean, pointing to the illustration of Robert being beaten with a knife-tipped metal wire, said it was a "kind of brutal" scene. She pointed at the caption: "Isabella, sad, watching her boyfriend get beat," and added that it was "very detailed."

As the class began to work through the events of this chapter, Ms. Jean helped them *empathize* with Robert, whose beating (and the illustration thereof) was "brutal." She then prompted students to talk more about what had happened in Sojourner's life up to that point.

Arturo said "Sojourner, in this chapter somewhere, her brother got sold—" Ms. Jean repeated him, nodding, "her brother got sold—" and then Arturo said, "She got sold to a Mr. Dumont, and then the mom, the wife [of Mr. Dumont], she was pretty bad to her."

Ms. Jean asked Arturo, "The wife was pretty bad to what?" Arturo answered, "To Sojourner," and a few other kids—DeAndre among them—said "Oh!" Ms. Jean asked, "Okay, you guys remembering now?" Arturo continued, "and then she got…" but then he drifted off.

John raised his hand, and Ms. Jean nodded at him. He said, "Belle met this guy [Robert, being beaten above], and she wanted to marry him, but the master said she couldn't marry him, that he would find somebody to marry her." Ms. Jean asked, "Why was it that they didn't want people—slaves—to get married? What was the problem with having these two individuals get married?" Max said "Oh!" And Ms. Jean called on him. Max said, "When their kids get there, the kids would be Dumont's slaves." Ms. Jean said, "Who would have ownership?" and Max answered "Dumont." Ms. Jean said to the class that it was "hard to refer to people" as owners.

Here, John *empathized* a bit with Belle's marital problems as he rehashed the plot. At the same time, Ms. Jean *historicized* the denial of marital rights to slaves, and Max continued to *historicize* this injustice by explaining his perception of the thinking behind the marriage prohibition. In fact, he *flipped* Ms. Jean's assumption—that marriage was bad for slaves because of the ties slaves might form despite their owners' wishes—by viewing the problem of marriage and children from the slaves' perspective. Ms. Jean appeared not to notice his *flip*, and *empathized* again, this time with the students, about how "hard" it was to talk about owning other people. This *empathy* with her current students' discomfort in turn made the past injustices seem even more removed and located in the past.

Adam was called on next, and said something about how one of the maids had put something in the soup. Ms. Jean said, "Oh! That was when—" as a few other kids started talking at the same time. Adam went on, explaining that the maid had put ashes in the family soup (to frame Sojourner, who had previously had a bit of the family's goodwill), and Ms. Jean repeated "ashes."

Ms. Jean asked who had "helped her out" in that situation, and DeAndre said "the daughter." Ms. Jean asked, "That was the first time that what had happened to Sojourner?" She called on Marta, whose hand was raised, and Marta replied, "That a White person helped her." Ms. Jean agreed, and said "no one White had ever helped her."

As the story rehashing continued, Adam brought up a scene in which a White maid, an indentured servant, had put ashes into the family soup, to frame Sojourner. DeAndre chimed in with more details, collaborating with Adam. Ms. Jean then *highlighted* a startling event in the text, and

Marta, in reply, *named* the otherness inherent in a White person helping a slave at that particular historical time.

IMPLICATIONS FOR RESEARCH:
MULTICULTURAL CURRICULA AT GONZALES AND AT LARGE

Within certain constraints (Appiah, 1994), children at Gonzales, like children across the nation, continue to be faced with a growing diversity of plausible identity categories, possible ways of affiliating with different ethnic, linguistic, and even racial groups. One possible result of the conjunction of increasing multiplicity and a multicultural curriculum is the case of Room 126, where students and adults jointly constructed notions of otherness in literacy events through textual analyses. At Gonzales, the construction of otherness was so pervasive—and yet so unanalyzed—that difference itself was defining. As a result, students internalized a sense of "other," and were able to *name, historicize,* and *highlight* different categories of their own identities, at the same time as they did so to injustices and facts about which they read in books.

The students of Room 126 drew on a variety of resources to make sense of what they read and wrote in school. From this perspective, the exploration of the relationship between Vanessa's gloss on slavery to the whole group—"all of the terrible things that went on"—and her private comments to her friends about the intimate details of Sojourner Truth's life, including how Truth might rescue her son and how Truth's illicit lover was punished, is a vital part of classroom research. Although my subject has been the ways that students constructed otherness in their conversations and writing about school texts, such research can lead us, eventually, to the ways in which students created "points of temporary attachment to subject positions" (Hall, 1996, p. 6) as they read such texts. That is, through such projects, we can look at how children may form their identities in conjunction with or in opposition to classroom texts in *and* out of the formal spaces created for discussion of the book.

Such a multidisciplinary approach to a study of children's literacy and identity practices in a teacher-driven literature unit—viewing student comments and writing in multiple spaces, and thinking about how their discussions contribute to their identity work—affords us one main advantage. We avoid stark dichotomies, and may instead focus on "social space as the hybrid product of relations and interconnections from the very local to the intercontinental" (Massey, 1998, p. 125). This emphasis on children's literature reading, literacy practices, and identity work as hybrid and interconnected opens up space for us to conceive of these as "constellations" (Massey, 1998) instead of compartmentalized practices.

For example, students discussed race, gender, morality, and sexuality in relation to *Sojourner Truth* in both teacher-sanctioned whole- and small-group discussions and in non-teacher-sanctioned events. It is easy to then trace children's writing and talk about Truth's life story to their local and global understandings of slavery and race, and thereby gain a larger picture of how children construct meaning through the text across contexts.

This research adds to a growing body of work on these interconnected issues (Daiute, 2000; Moje & Sutherland, 2003), but the field can only benefit from more investigation into students' identity formation, especially in multicultural schools, in relation to assigned texts. In short, these findings help us understand how such multiplicity affects students' literacy development, and in turn how multicultural curricula in the integrated classroom impact students' identity construction. We must continue along this path if we want to know more about how children make meaning out of school texts, how their worlds are shaped by multicultural curricula, and what the relationship might be between such curricula and the lived experiences of diverse groups of students.

NOTES

1. All names in this paper have been changed to protect the anonymity of the research site and subjects.
2. Margaret Finders's 1997 book about the "hidden literacies" of two groups of junior high school girls is premised on Goffman's (1959) division of performances into public and private, or center stage and backstage. Finders also relies on Scott's (1990) use of the term "offstage" to construct a dichotomous relationship between the texts and textual practices of her preteen subjects in arenas that she labeled "offstage" and "public" (pp. 9–10).
3. These events included, but were not limited to, whole-school assemblies for Thanksgiving, Black History Month, a Mexican folk dancing exhibition, a hip-hop dance show, a production about recycling, and a principal-led march to protest the war that culminated in the students singing a 1960s peace song at a busy commercial intersection while holding a banner that read "Peace."

ACKNOWLEDGMENTS

This research was supported in part by a grant from the Graduate Division of the University of California, Berkeley, and in part by a Spencer Foundation Research Training Fellowship. The research itself is part of a larger dissertation study. The author thanks Christian Zacher, Glynda Hull, and Mollie Blackburn for their insightful comments, and is grateful to Maren Aukerman and Paige Daniel Ware for their editorial help and general support.

REFERENCES

Appiah, K. A. (1994). Identity, authenticity, and survival: Multicultural societies and social reproduction. In A. Gutman (Ed.), *Multiculturalism: Examining the politics of recognition* (pp. 149-164). Princeton, NJ: Princeton University Press.

Armstrong, N. M. (2001). *Navajo long walk (the Council for Indian Education)*. New York: Robert Reinhardts.

Bakhtin, M. M. (1981). *The dialogic imagination* (C. Emerson & M. Holquist, Trans.). Austin: University of Texas Press.

Banks, J. A. (1995). Multicultural education: Historical development, dimensions, and practice. In J. A. Banks (Ed.), *Handbook of research on multicultural education* (pp. 3–24). New York: Macmillan.

Bartolomé, L. (1994). Beyond the methods fetish: Toward a humanizing pedagogy. *Harvard Educational Review, 64*, 173–194.

Bishop, R. S. (1997). Multicultural literature for children: Making informed choices. In V. J. Harris (Ed.), *Teaching multicultural literature in grades K–8* (pp. 37–53). Norwood, MA: Christopher-Gordon.

Bogdan, R., & Biklen, S. (1998). *Qualitative research in education: an introduction to theory and methods* (3rd ed.). Needham Heights, MA: Allyn & Bacon.

Cai, M., & Bishop, R. S. (1994). Multicultural literature for children: Towards a clarification of the concept. In A. H. Dyson & C. Genishi (Eds.), *The need for story: Cultural diversity in classroom and community* (pp. 57-71). Urbana, IL: NCTE.

Daiute, C. (2000). Narrative sites for youths' construction of social consciousness. In L. Weis & M. Fine (Eds.), *Construction sites: Excavating race, class, and gender among urban youth* (pp. 211–234). New York: Teachers College Press.

Dyson, A. H. (1997). *Writing superheroes: Contemporary childhood, popular culture, and classroom literacy.* New York: Teachers College Press.

Dyson, A. H. (2003). *The brothers and the sisters learn to write: Popular literacies in childhood and school cultures.* New York: Teacher's College Press.

Emerson, R., Fretz, R., & Shaw, L. (1995). *Writing ethnographic field notes.* Chicago: University of Chicago Press.

Erickson, F. (1986). Qualitative methods in research on teaching. In M. C. Wittrock (Ed.), *Handbook of research on teaching* (pp. 119-161). New York: McMillan.

Finders, M. J. (1997). *Just girls: Hidden literacies and life in junior high.* New York: Teachers College Press.

Gee, J. P. (1996). Discourses and literacies, *Social linguistics and literacies: Ideology in discourses* (2nd ed.). London: Taylor & Francis.

Geertz, C. (1973). Thick description: Toward an interpretive theory of culture. In *The interpretation of cultures* (pp. 3–32). New York: Basic Books.

Giroux, H. (1993). Postmodernism as border pedagogy: Redefining the boundaries of race and ethnicity. In J. Natoli & L. Hutcheon (Eds.), *A postmodern reader* (pp. 452-496). Albany: State University of New York Press.

Goffman, E. (1959). *The presentation of self in everyday life.* New York: Doubleday.

Hall, S. (1996). Introduction: Who needs identity? In S. Hall & P. du Gay (Eds.), *Questions of cultural identity* (pp. 1–17). London: Sage.

Hall, S., & du Gay, P. (Eds.). (1996). *Questions of cultural identity.* London: Sage.

Harris, V. (Ed.). (1997). *Using multiethnic literature in the K-8 classroom.* Norwood, MA: Christopher-Gordon.

Heath, S. B. (1982a). Protean shapes in literacy events. In D. Tannen (Ed.), *Spoken and written language: Exploring orality and literacy* (pp. 348-370). Norwood, NJ: Ablex.

Heath, S. B. (1982b). What no bedtime story means: Narrative skills at home and school. *Language in Society, 11*, 49–76.

Holloway, S., & Valentine, G. (2000). Children's geographies and the new social studies of childhood. In S. Holloway & G. Valentine (Eds.), *Children's geographies: Playing, living, learning* (pp. 1–28). London: Routledge.

Holquist, M. (1990). *Dialogism: Bakhtin and his world.* London: Routledge.

Lord, B. B. (1986). *In the year of the boar and Jackie Robinson.* New York: Harper Trophy.

Lowry, L. (1989). *Number the stars.* New York: Dell.

Luke, A. (1994). *The social construction of literacy in primary school.* South Melbourne, Australia: Macmillan.

Luke, A. (2003). Literacy and the other: A sociological approach to literacy research and policy in multilingual societies. *Reading Research Quarterly, 38,* 132–143.

Mahiri, J. (1996). Writing, rap, and representation. In P. Mortensen & G. E. Kirsch (Eds.), *Ethics and representation in qualitative studies of literacy* (pp. 228-240). Urbana, IL: National Council of Teachers of English.

Massey, D. (1998). The spatial construction of youth places. In T. Skelton & G. Valentine (Eds.), *Cool places: Geographies of youth cultures* (pp. 121–129). London: Routledge.

McCarthey, S., & Moje, E. B. (2002). Identity matters. *Reading Research Quarterly, 37*(2), 228–238.

McKissack, P., & McKissack, F. (1992). *Sojourner Truth: Ain't I a woman?* New York: Scholastic.

McRobbie, A. (1991). *Feminism and youth culture: From "Jackie" to "just seventeen."* Boston: Unwin Hyman.

Mohr, N. (1979). *Felita.* New York: Bantam.

Moje, E. B., & Sutherland, L. M. (2003). The future of middle school literacy education. *English Education, January,* 149–164.

Moll, L., Amanti, C., Neff, D., & Gonzalez, N. (1992). Funds of knowledge for teaching: Using a qualitative approach to connect homes and classrooms. *Theory Into Practice, 31*(2), 132–141.

Morrell, E. (2002). Toward a critical pedagogy of popular culture: Literacy development among urban youth. *Journal of Adolescent and Adult Literacy, 46*(1), 72–77.

Nelson, V. M. (1993). *Mayfield Crossing*. New York: Avon.

Ryan, P. M. (2002). *Esperanza Rising*. New York: Scholastic.

Scott, J. (1990). *Domination and the arts of resistance: Hidden transcripts*. New Haven, CT: Yale University Press.

Street, B. (1995). *Social literacies: Critical approaches to literacy in development, ethnography, and education*. New York: Longman.

Street, B. (2000). Literacy "events" and literacy "practices": Theory and practice in the "New Literacy Studies." In M. Martin-Jones & K. Jones (Eds.), *Multilingual literacies: Reading and writing different worlds*. Amsterdam/Philadelphia: John Benjamins.

Vygotsky, L. (1986). *Thought and Language* (A. Kozulin, Trans.). Cambridge, MA: MIT Press.

Weiss, R. S. (1994). *Learning from strangers: The art and method of qualitative interview studies*. New York: The Free Press.

CHAPTER 5

TEACHING WELL

Science Teachers' Investigation and Use of Student Sociocultural Background

Steven Ramirez Fong and Marcelle A. Siegel

What does it mean to be a "good" teacher? This question has great relevance for teacher preparation, professional development, and the perception of teachers that exists in our society today. Efforts to characterize "good teaching" by educational researchers have resulted in a category of teacher knowledge known as pedagogical content knowledge (PCK). PCK defines those skills and strategies used by teachers in their instruction within a particular content area. This study seeks to further elaborate on the general PCK model within the content area of science. Specifically, this chapter begins to describe an additional component of PCK specifically focusing on teachers' knowledge of student sociocultural background and the use of such knowledge to inform more inclusive teaching.

The importance of culture to learning has become an increasingly studied area of educational research. When entering the classroom and engaging in the learning process, students bring much more than just their prior academic experience. They bring their language, race, gender, socioeconomic status, and a host of other sociocultural aspects of their

Focus on Curriculum, 101–128
Copyright © 2005 by Information Age Publishing
All rights of reproduction in any form reserved.

lives. Never has this fact been more apparent or obvious than the present. Within a single classroom population there might be 10 different home languages, students reading at a wide range of grade levels, and students who have parents of vastly different educational experience and economic means. For many teachers, this diversity is markedly different from what they have encountered in their personal schooling and other life experiences. This situation creates an environment in which students who differ from the majority have difficulty understanding and relating to the content and instruction. Essentially, we as educators are failing students by neglecting to embrace and utilize the cultural resources that they bring with them to the classroom (hooks, 1994).

A first step in utilizing the cultural resources students bring with them to the classroom is the assessment and investigation of those resources. Only after we are knowledgeable about what students have to offer can we begin to work toward bridging the disjuncture between home and school. Thus, it is useful to have some method or strategy of investigating students' sociocultural background. Furthermore, by explicitly characterizing such methods and strategies, we can expand our understanding of what constitutes good teaching.

"It may be worth inquiring how it is that most of us are able to remember great teachers, but do not have routine ways to talk about what great teaching is. And if we cannot talk about it, it is surely difficult to build into research/practice on learning" (Lave, 1996). Lave's comment elaborates the idea that we need to be more explicit about what constitutes "great" teaching. Practices, such as the investigation of students' sociocultural background, are key steps in the process of creating an effective learning environment and developing successful lessons and activities. Specifically characterizing these types of practices and their associated knowledge further refines our definition of "good teaching," and thus our ability to inform teacher preparation and educational research. One body of research that has attempted to do this is that dealing with PCK. In the next section, we document teacher behaviors and knowledge that might further our understanding of what "good teaching" is and possibly provide support for further characterization of PCK.

THEORETICAL BACKGROUND

The first major area of research this study draws from is research surrounding the importance of students' prior knowledge to teaching and learning. It is often the case that a student's past experiences outside the classroom are more important in determining how they respond to instruction than their formal schooling. As was found by Solano-Flores and Nelson-Barber:

> The way students interpret science items and respond to them may be more influenced by personal experience than formal school learning experience. Frequently, everyday life experiences seem to be what first comes to students' minds when they respond to science items. (2000, p. 559)

This indicates that in addition to students' prior *school* knowledge being important, their prior life experience is also very relevant. It is not only students' preconceptions about specific topics that affect their understanding in the classroom, but also the wide range of experiences, beliefs, and values they bring with them as part of their personal backgrounds. As Magnusson, Borko, and Krajcik (1999, p. 10) described, "For some science topics, learning is difficult because the concepts are very abstract and/or they lack any connection to the students' common experiences." When concepts and instructional activities lack any connection to the common experiences of our students (sociocultural background), it is likely that they will have trouble understanding (cognitive understanding).

This connection of cognitive understanding to sociocultural background relates directly to a concept referred to by Lareau (1987) as cultural capital. Students' sociocultural experiences are seen as assets that are accumulated and developed over time. Students use these assets in the classroom as they engage in the learning process. Lareau is basically asserting that students have a base of capital that they can "spend" in the classroom. If the instruction they are given connects to their background, their capital has value and they have a higher potential for success. If the instruction does not acknowledge their background, the capital they have accumulated over time is useless and they stand at a disadvantage. This issue cannot be overstated, as the increasingly diverse demographics of schools present a situation in which teachers are confronted with a wide range of cultures and backgrounds on a daily basis. Educators could in effect negate the cultural capital such that students' assets are useless, and in some circumstances detrimental to success.

The second area of research forming the basis of this study is that surrounding PCK. PCK is an area of research that has increased in visibility during recent years and is still the subject of much debate. For the purpose of clarity, we will rely primarily on the definition of PCK set forth by Magnusson and colleagues in their 1999 paper: "A teacher's understanding of how to help students understand specific subject matter." The authors further examined PCK and described it in terms of five specific components. These components include: (1) orientations toward science teaching, (2) knowledge and beliefs about science curricula, (3) knowledge and beliefs about students' understanding of specific science topics, (4) knowledge and beliefs about assessment in science, and (5) knowledge and beliefs about instructional strategies for teaching science.

Teachers also need to have knowledge of students' languages, cultures, and other aspects of their sociocultural background. Furthermore, it is useful for them to have methods of investigating students' backgrounds so that they might obtain such knowledge. It is this aspect of PCK on which we focus.

The current body of PCK research is very broad and may be considered by some to be ill-defined. Relatively few studies offer concrete examples of PCK or specifically define PCK and its components. Loughran, Mulhall, and Berry (2004) offer three reasons for this lacking in their attempt to further articulate PCK. The first reason they give for PCK being so hard to define is its complex nature. As they describe, "The development of a teacher's PCK is multifaceted and not linear; therefore, it is a complex task to capture and portray PCK despite the fact that PCK itself is an almost unquestioned academic construct." A second reason given that PCK is difficult to define is that it is largely internal and tacit in nature, making it extremely difficult to capture via observation. Related to this issue is the third reason: even if an aspect of PCK is explicit enough for teachers to be able to discuss, they often lack the vocabulary to do so. Loughran explains, "Teachers commonly share activities, teaching procedures, and clever insights into teaching and learning that have implicit purposes in practice, but rarely articulate the reasons behind them." For all these reasons, PCK has been difficult to define—a fact reflected by the lack of concrete examples in the literature.

While it has been difficult to capture, PCK is important to study because it has great potential to impact teacher education and professional development. PCK describes those qualities that make a teacher successful in their specific subject matter. It follows that if we can clearly define these qualities, we might be able to incorporate them into teacher education. Often seen as a job that "anyone can do," successful teachers possess a specific set of skills that have only just begun to be defined.

The third and final body of research that this study draws from is that concerning cultural validity. Cultural validity refers to the idea that instruction needs to take into account the effects a student's sociocultural background has on their learning. Scientific learning is NOT an activity that can be isolated from the rest of the world and it is important to recognize the role culture can play in the learning process. As Lemke (2001) stated, "We need to see scientific learning as the acquisition of cultural tools and practices. As learning to participate in very specific and often specialized forms of human activity" (p. 1). We rely on the definition presented by Solano-Flores and Nelson-Barber in their 2001 study: "By cultural validity we refer to the effectiveness with which science [instruction] addresses the sociocultural influences that shape student thinking and the ways in which students make sense of some items and respond to them" (p. 555). To be culturally valid, a teacher must consider how a student's background might affect their learning. This seems obvious, but has time and again proven to be something that not all teachers are aware of.

A classic example is that presented by Bransford (2000) in a discussion of a student being asked to complete a specific math problem. The problem posed to the student is one involving fractions and asks the student to consider a pumpkin pie. The student could not solve the problem due to the fact that they were thrown off by the context of the pumpkin pie. They had never heard of, seen, nor tasted a pumpkin pie (for them it had always been sweet potato pie) and could not progress past that point. Operating from a cultural validity perspective allows teachers to both prepare to prevent such situations as well as diagnose and address them should they occur.[1]

When considered with the bodies of research in prior knowledge and PCK, sociocultural validity can be seen as the lens through which the first two are interpreted and implemented. In the case of prior knowledge, we can begin to look specifically and critically at the sociocultural aspects of a student's background and how those might function as a type of prior knowledge. In creating a constructivist classroom, a student's sociocultural background thus becomes equally important to their academic background. Using the lens of sociocultural validity, PCK might be modified to include the importance of teachers understanding specific aspects of a student's sociocultural background and considering how it might impact their understanding of science topics. Aspects of student sociocultural background, such as language, economics, race, gender, and others, all become explicit sources of prior knowledge that affect how a student will respond to instruction. Through this lens, a student becomes much more than their "misconceptions" and academic experience, but rather a complex being that needs to be investigated and understood in all facets of their life.

RESEARCH QUESTIONS AND METHODS

In the interest of building upon current understandings of PCK, we conducted case studies of two teachers in two life science classrooms in a large California high school. We investigated the following questions:

1. How do teachers view the importance of student sociocultural background?

   • Are teachers aware of student sociocultural background as a source of PCK?

   • What value do teachers place on student sociocultural background as a source of knowledge?

2. What strategies do teachers use to investigate student sociocultural background?

3. In what ways do teachers use their knowledge of student sociocultural background to inform inclusive teaching?

4. Do teachers identify barriers that prevent their investigation of student sociocultural background?

   • What specific barriers exist and what are their causes?

   • What suggestions/recommendations do teachers have for overcoming these barriers?

Both classes in the study were Advanced Biology courses and a different teacher taught each. The first teacher, who will be referred to as Teacher A, was in his eighth year of teaching and had taught only at the current high school. He had taught Advanced Biology for several years, a basic biology course, a biotechnology class that was part of a campus vocational program, and Integrated Science to English learners. The specific Advanced Biology class in this study was composed of 32 students, 15 males and 17 females. In discussing his own sociocultural background, Teacher A described being raised in a homogeneous environment in which most of his community was racially white and Catholic. He experienced heavy parental involvement in most aspects of his academic progress. His parents were a constant presence in making sure he was "on track" and "doing the right thing." They did this by checking in with him regularly to make sure his homework was completed and that he was meeting all expectations set forth by the teachers. He described this scenario as "the typical Midwestern experience," through which he developed a very disciplined work ethic and the need for personal academic success.

The second teacher, who will be referred to as Teacher B, had 4 years of previous experience, with 3 of those years at the high school level and 1 year at a middle school. He was in his second year of teaching Advanced Biology and was also teaching Advanced Placement (AP) Biology. Previously, he had taught courses in Anatomy and Integrated Science. The specific Advanced Biology class used for this study was composed of 28 students, 18 males and 10 females. Teacher B described his sociocultural background primarily in terms of his family. His mother, who was constantly working and busy, was his primary caretaker. She was a first-generation American whose family had come to America from Europe following World War II. Teacher B describes himself as Jewish, both ethnically and religiously. In terms of socioeconomics, Teacher B noted that he paid his own way through college by working throughout his studies. This was a formative part of his experience and significantly affected his values and perspectives.

In terms of racial and ethnic breakdown, the student body of the school at large is relatively diverse. With 37% white students, 32% African American students, 11% Latino students, 9% Asian students, and 11% "multiethnic" students, there is no standout majority group present. As a rough measure of socioeconomic composition, based on the 2001 Academic Performance Index Base Report, 12% of the school's students participate in a free or reduced-price lunch program. In addition, the school has a large amount of linguistic diversity. Seventeen percent of students report a primary language other than English and 10% of students are designated as English learners. These statistics are relevant not only for the information they give about the teachers' larger working environment, but their accurate reflection in the two specific classes observed for this study. The classes were selected to reflect the diversity of the high school, rather than one of the more homogenous classes, and the teachers were selected specifically for their previous successes in dealing with issues of sociocultural diversity.

Data Sources and Collection

Throughout the study, daily classroom observations were conducted and course materials and teacher work were collected. At specific points in the study teacher interviews were conducted. The overall length of the study was 5 weeks.

Classroom observations were conducted in both Advanced Biology classes on a daily basis throughout the duration of a 4-week period. Observations were conducted in a nonparticipant fashion (i.e., the researcher positioned himself in the rear of the room to observe and did not interact with the teacher or the students). Though no formal observation instrument was used, observations were made with specific goals in mind. Observations were made of specific ways in which the teachers assessed student background, displayed awareness of sociocultural issues, and addressed sociocultural issues in their instruction. The recording of data was done in a particular format, which in turn helped to later shape the discussion of results. Teacher–student interaction was monitored closely for four sequential events. These included:

- Teacher assessment of student sociocultural background;
- Teacher identification (or lack thereof) of a student learning need;
- Teacher use of knowledge of student sociocultural background to address student learning needs; and
- Outcome of teacher's efforts to address student learning needs.

Early in the study following the first few days of classroom observations, initial teacher interviews were conducted. These interviews were designed to determine general teacher awareness of sociocultural issues, including the ways in which they addressed such issues in their daily instruction. While they were informal in nature, the interviews did follow a specific structure. The teachers were first asked a series of questions to obtain a general sense of their personal and professional experiences. These questions ranged from those dealing with number of years taught and site of their degree/credential to inquiries about their family and religious beliefs. The teachers were next shown a list of "top classroom issues," including gender, race, discipline, grading, socioeconomics, and so on, and asked to quantify their relative importance to daily lesson planning. To do this they were asked to rank each issue on a scale of 1 to 3, with one signifying an issue of great importance that they carefully considered and factored into their lesson planning on a daily basis. A rank of three signified an issue that, while still important, might be "lower on their radar" and not a significant factor in their day-to-day teaching. They were also asked to explain *why* they had ranked each the way they did. This portion of the interview was also intended to prompt discussion of each "classroom issue." Following their ranking and explanation for that ranking, the teachers were asked follow-up questions based on their response. For instance, if they mentioned that gender was something they thought about from time to time yet did not consider a large part of their daily lesson planning, they were asked a series of questions to further explore that issue. The interviews lasted approximately 45–50 minutes each and took place during the teachers' preparatory periods. All interviews were recorded on audiotape and transcribed for later review.

Directly after conducting teacher interviews, student surveys were distributed to both classes. The confidential questions focused on students' personal and academic background and how those factors influenced their experience in science classes. In all, 40 surveys were collected from the two classes. Next, over the course of the second and third weeks of the study, student interviews were conducted. In total, eight interviews were conducted, with four students from each class being interviewed. These interviews lasted approximately 20–25 minutes each and were held both during class periods as well as after school. The goal of these interviews was to expand upon the answers given by the students in their surveys.

Following all student interviews and completion of the fourth week of classroom observations, final teacher interviews were conducted. The results of previous teacher interviews, student interviews, student surveys, and classroom observations all aided in shaping the questions asked during the final teacher interview. The goal of this interview was to specifically discuss the issue of student background and the way in which teachers assessed it and used their assessment in shaping their instruction. The primary method of accomplishing this was to introduce examples from the classroom observations, student interviews, and student surveys and have the teachers respond to them. This format allowed the teachers to reflect on specific examples of their own practice and discuss the rationale, thought, and decisions for each example. As in the student interviews, each teacher was asked questions based on their own classes, yet both were prompted to discuss the same broad topics. These included the following:

- How knowledge of student sociocultural background helps to form instruction;
- Specific strategies used to gain knowledge of student sociocultural background;
- Barriers to gaining knowledge of student sociocultural background;
- Strategies/techniques for gaining knowledge of student sociocultural background that would be ideal but have not as yet been implemented;
- How the results presented affect their perception of teaching and how they might change their teaching; and
- Identification of the "most valuable" aspects of student sociocultural background for a teacher to assess.

These final interviews lasted approximately 45 minutes and, similar to all other interviews, were recorded on audiotape and transcribed for later analysis.

RESULTS AND DISCUSSION

Awareness and Valuing of Student Sociocultural Background as a Source of PCK

The two teachers in this study were highly aware of student sociocultural background and its importance to pedagogy. They cited specific examples where sociocultural background played an important role, elaborated upon specific aspects of sociocultural background they would like to assess, and discussed the limitations and inherent dangers with regard to taking a sociocultural approach. For instance, in discussing the relevance of student background to him as a teacher, Teacher A commented,

> What kind of examples are they really going to get that would be meaningful to them—that I could really tailor to their knowledge so they get it and don't have to struggle with my Midwestern white guy example? Like snow— they've never seen snow so you have to know your audience.

In making this statement, teacher A is revealing his thought process for choosing specific examples to use when presenting science content. Prior to using a particular example, he reflects on how that example might be interpreted and/or understood by students based on their own contextual experience. For students in the Bay Area who have not had the occasion to visit a location where snow is common, a classroom example involving snow may be ineffective. This scenario is very similar to one about mountains presented by Solano-Flores and Nelson-Barber (2001) in his study of cultural validity as part of science assessment construction.

In discussing socioeconomics, Teacher B stated, "I'm definitely aware of the kids who can afford tutors and come to me and ask if I have any tutors I can recommend and those kids that can't afford tutors." He went on to describe how this disparity is definitely something that affects the decisions he makes about his availability to students. Teacher A discussed parental educational level as a significant aspect of sociocultural background in his comment, "The amount of science schooling that parents had is one of the bigger factors all the way through high school. Some parents can't help their kids." These and others including gender, race, and religion all demonstrate further that the teachers were aware of student sociocultural background as an important factor affecting their pedagogy and that they did attribute some value to gaining knowledge of such background.

Both teachers elaborated by discussing specific aspects of student background that they would like to investigate and how they might like to use that knowledge to improve their practice. In response to the interview question "What do you see as being the most important aspects of student background for a teacher to know about?", both teachers identified parental involvement as the single most important aspect. Teacher A discussed the relevance of knowing about parental circumstances:

> I would think first is parental involvement—how often are your parents asking you to do your homework, how often are they helping you to do your homework, what was their educational level, how often are they home at

night, how often are they asking where you are going, just stuff like that. I don't want to make it sound like I'm blaming them. A lot of them don't have a choice because they're working late at night just to keep the kids housed and fed. But if we could find that out you could target and give a little extra attention to those who need it.

Teacher B shared similar feelings indicating that for him, it needs to start with "having their actual phone numbers." The school attracts students from all over the region, including many who are not in the actual school district. Many of these students use alternate addresses and contact information to gain entry into the district, which ordinarily would not accept them. With parent contact already an extremely difficult endeavor, this subterfuge makes it nearly impossible at times. Teacher B went on to mention more specific things he would like to know, including "which kids were in a group home or homeless or stuff like that" and "which kids were not getting enough food." Though one might think that aspects of student background such as these would be quite obvious, both teachers reported that in fact, the opposite it true. Especially in more extreme cases, such as homelessness, poverty, and malnutrition, students can be very reluctant to share information because they are embarrassed and ashamed.

Another part of the teachers' perception of student sociocultural background was their ability to discuss the limitations and inherent dangers in taking a sociocultural approach. Beyond simply recognizing the importance of student background, they critically evaluated the ways in which knowledge of student background might constrain a teacher or impact pedagogy in a negative manner. Teacher B expressed these concerns in his description of the "danger of going in with a prejudice based on knowledge." In his view, one of the dangers of investigating student sociocultural background was that the knowledge gained might be used not to create more specific and relevant pedagogy, but to form more general and homogenized instruction based on stereotypes. Teacher B commented, "One of the biggest problems in high school is I know certain teachers attach a label and make their curriculum easier and make exceptions— stuff that ends up hurting the kids." This issue cannot be understated, as it demonstrates the easy way in which knowledge of students' sociocultural background can be misused and reinforces the need for very careful and explicit pedagogy in this area. The goal is *not* to create profiles of particular groups and thus implement standardized ways of instructing all members of such groups. Rather, the goal is to gain a greater understanding of every one of our individual students and find ways of tailoring our instruction to address each of them.

A second concern raised by Teacher B was the ever-changing nature of our students. As he described, "I certainly don't think they're static—they're going to change day to day. Even if they say one thing it might not be true of them a week later." Student background is not something we can assess at a single point and assume that we know all there is to know. As teachers, checking in with students and continuing in our pursuit to investigate their sociocultural background should be a habit and a practice. As soon as we cease to do so, we put ourselves in danger of relying on assumed qualities and stereotypes.

Use of Specific Strategies to Investigate Student Sociocultural Background

A second aspect of PCK that both teachers demonstrated was the use and knowledge of strategies for investigating student sociocultural background. These strategies ranged from techniques that could be considered relatively common in most classrooms to involvement outside the classroom in extracurricular activities and the community, all with the common intent to find out about student background.

The first strategy for investigating student sociocultural background mentioned by both teachers was the use of introductory "get-to-know-you" activities and student surveys. These activities are often a staple of any classroom, yet they are not always implemented with the same intent. As teacher A described,

> In the beginning of the semester I hand out a "you" sheet and it's says "YOU" on top and it asks a few basic questions like: Do you have a job after school or are you planning on getting one? What is it? Do you play sports? What do you like to do when you're not studying? What do you want to do and are you planning on going to college? Do you like to travel or do you want to just get a job? Just a super-easy way to get stuff coming at you right away because they'll write stuff down that they won't talk about because they're too nervous or they're too shy about being in a new group of kids and being in a new class.

Additional examples of such activities used by Teacher A were also described. He mentioned an activity he uses that is a variation on the common "Two Truths and a Lie" game in which students are required to share various pieces of information about themselves with their classmates and the teacher. He also described an activity that he uses involving the passing out of squares of toilet paper upon which students have to write down different "fun facts" about themselves.

The teachers in this study reflected upon the purpose of the activities and discussed them not merely as a means of obtaining student contact information or learning names, but a genuine opportunity to gain insight into students' lives and begin to lay a foundation of knowledge of student sociocultural background upon which they could build the rest of the year. As seen in the example of the "You" sheet, Teacher A was able to discuss the fact that he is able to learn things about students that they are not willing to share verbally or won't yet share because it's so early in the semester. In this comment, teacher A demonstrates an explicit and investigatory purpose behind the use of the sheet in his classroom. It is not only serving to provide standard information needed by the teacher, but is offering a safe and protected forum in which students can share aspects of their lives and themselves that they might not be comfortable sharing otherwise.

A second strategy used by teachers was explicit conversation, meaning socializing, which is intended specifically to gather information about students. While it is true that due to the nature of their jobs, teachers will come into contact with a large number of students on a daily basis, the nature of this contact is at the discretion of the teacher. The teachers in this study reported the explicit use of conversation as a method of gathering information on student background. This conversation took the form of built-in time during class as well as outside-of-class interactions. For instance, Teacher B incorporated conversation into his daily homework stamping routine. He described, "Every day at the beginning of class I take 5 minutes or so to go around and stamp homework. But it's also to see how they're doing." In classroom observations of Teacher B, this was observed on a regular basis and often more than 5 minutes was allotted to this process. Teacher B would circulate around the room, often on his skateboard, which the students enjoyed immensely, and engage in intentional conversations while stamping their completed assignments. During one such conversation, Teacher B was heard talking to a pair of students about their recent trip to Italy. The two students, who were brothers, had recently traveled to Italy to visit their grandmother and extended family. This brief exchange developed into an extended discussion of their family history, their learning of their family language, and culture. The two students excitedly showed photos of their trip including many of their grandmother. This conversation continued at various points during that day's class and was brought up a number of other times throughout the week.

Teacher A also described his efforts to incorporate explicit conversation while stamping homework. As in the case of the beginning of year activities, the stamping of homework is not something specific to the teachers in this study alone. This is a very common process that most teachers engage in at one time or another. However, relatively few teachers likely consider this activity as a way to gather information on student background. Outside-of-class conversation occurred during lunch hours, after school, and before school. Both teachers made themselves available to students outside of class on a regular basis and explicitly used this time to socialize with students and learn more about their background. Teacher A stated, "Just by spending time with people is how I get to know them. Just by sharing things about your life and hearing things about their life is how I come to know them."

An important point made by both teachers was that the process of explicit conversation can be long and arduous. Building the trust of students and developing rapport is something that takes time and cannot be rushed. However, once a student's trust is earned, they are often more willing to share things about themselves that they would not before. As Teacher B states, "It takes time, and once they start to trust you, stuff starts to come up naturally in class. Just that they know I'm interested." This was a key finding from the study. Without gaining a student's trust, it is useless to think about investigating their sociocultural background. They will not share the intimate details of their life history with someone who they do not perceive as supportive and trustworthy. As teachers, gaining the trust of our students should be a primary concern and prerequisite to gathering information on their sociocultural background.

A third strategy used by the teachers to investigate students' sociocultural background was targeted questioning. This term refers to the act of asking questions directed toward a specific student or students that the teacher seeks to know more about. It can be done both in and out of class and can take many different forms. For example, Teacher A, in his quest for developing new analogies that are effective and relevant for his students, would constantly ask groups of them about particular songs, music videos, or movies. He would then use this knowledge to enhance his rapport with them and create relevant, contextual examples. Teacher B often directed his questions at students in a very informal and specific way. For example, he was observed talking with a student about Spanish as her primary language and how it affected her learning of the vocabulary words in the current lesson. In fact, Teacher B initiated the entire conversation in his questioning of the student regarding how to say particular vocabulary words in Spanish. This action by Teacher B suggests that he does in fact attribute value to student sociocultural background, this being demonstrated by his specific attention and attempt to speak the student's home language. Students reported that this experience was very powerful for them, as not many teachers take the time to specifically ask them about aspects of their life other than academics.

To investigate student sociocultural background, the teachers also discussed the assignment of specific projects intended to gather information.

For example, Teacher A described, "As the year goes by, you assign projects that help you get to know the kids. Kids will do videos, drawings, or pictures, or whatever. So you can start to see how they do their project is a reflection of what they like to do or their skills and their talents." This comment was made specifically concerning a cell model project Teacher A had assigned. He went on to describe it as, "A cell translation activity where they have to take the parts of the cell and translate them into some part of their life. You can actually learn quite a lot about some kids." Examples of cell analogies included sports teams, industrial plants, and supermarkets. Again, this analogy activity is probably relatively common in most biology classrooms. However, it is the intentionality with which the teachers in this study assigned these typical activities that make them useful for investigating student background.

The teachers also cited extracurricular activity as a means of interacting with students in a specific context allowing for the investigation of student sociocultural background. They reported that serving as athletic coaches, club advisors, and general resources for specific groups of students allowed them access to populations they might not have contact with inside the classroom environment. Teacher A said, "Outside of class I used to coach, that's a great way to get to know kids you might not have in your class and expand the base. Sports attract different types of students—socioeconomically, racially, and academic abilities." Teacher A at different times coached football and golf, two sports that typically draw from very separate socioeconomic pools. He recognized this and discussed the benefit of exposing himself to these different sociocultural groups. In addition to his coaching, Teacher A involved himself in a number of other activities that gave him the opportunity to interact with students and learn more about their background. During the period of this study, he was currently an advisor for a new student group that was focused on aiding the local children's hospital. In his classroom were prominently displayed pictures of him at student dances, and he attended numerous community events in which his students participate.

In his discussion of using extracurricular activities as a way of investigating student background, Teacher B described how a teacher might accomplish this without serving as an official coach and/or advisor. As someone of Jewish descent himself, Teacher B had established a relationship with students involved in the Jewish Student Organization and offered himself as a source of support. Additionally, there are many other types of extracurricular activities teachers might involve themselves in as a means of investigating student sociocultural background. Activities such as community service, class advising, student group support, academic teams, spirit competitions, and many others all provide teachers with rich opportunities to learn more about their own and other students.

A final strategy cited by the teachers as a major means of assessing their students' sociocultural background was interaction and involvement within their students' home community. Teacher A confirmed this value in his statement, "I think that it's definitely helped that I've lived in this community and know this community so we have a lot of the same experiences like what stores we go to and I may see kids around on the street." In his comment, Teacher A hits upon an important point—that not only can teachers come to understand some of the experiences students go through by living and/or visiting their community, but they can *have* some of the same experiences. It is difficult to imagine a more authentic way of coming to understand the background of students than actually going through some of the experiences oneself. This manner of investigating student sociocultural background has the potential to be infinitely more meaningful to the teacher, and will likely give the teacher much greater validity and credibility when discussing sociocultural experiences with students.

In summary, strategies to learn about student sociocultural background include:

- Introductory "get to know you" activities;
- Initial student surveys/informational sheets;
- Explicitly conversing with students;
- Projects specifically intended to provide insight into students' sociocultural background;
- Involvement in extracurricular activities;
- Involvement in the communities where students live;
- Specifically questioning particular students to gain insight into their background; and
- General socialization time in which teacher–student informal interaction is possible.

Use of Knowledge of Student Sociocultural Background to Inform Inclusive Teaching

Having outlined some of the various strategies that teachers use to assess their students' sociocultural background, the following section discusses several of the ways in which participating teachers used the knowledge gained through those strategies to inform more inclusive teaching. These included the adjustment of expectations, use of specific analogies and contextual examples, validating student interest and building trust, focusing on the language demands of biology, and giving extra attention to address student-specific problems.

The first method of utilizing knowledge of student sociocultural background that the teachers discussed was the adjustment of behavioral and academic performance expectations. Teacher A described how he found knowledge of student background useful. "It makes classroom management so much better when I know that because I know exactly what's going on with them. They may be having to work a night job and drop their little brother or sister off to school in the morning." It might be something as small as not calling on a student during a particularly rough week and allowing him or her some extra time to turn in assignments. And yet it could also be something as involved as developing an individual study plan for a student who has to miss a significant number of days due to a personal problem. Teacher A described a situation in which he sensed that a particular student was having a very difficult week. He based this on his observations of him/her during and outside of class. After talking with him/her, he found that s/he was having personal problems. Teacher A gave her/him some extra time to turn in homework and did not demand as much during class time. Teacher A went on to state, "That's where I use their actual life circumstances to actually deal with them, like how far should I actually push them and what should I be pushing them on. How strict should I be and how understanding can I be?" Teacher A's comment emphasizes the important idea that instruction need not be standardized. As is often said, "Equal does not mean fair." Treating all students the same assumes that all students are coming from the exact same background and dealing with the same set of life circumstances.

A second major way that the participating teachers used knowledge of student background to inform their pedagogy was through the use of specific analogies and contextual examples. The use of analogies based on knowledge of student background was seen on a daily and frequent basis during observations of Teacher A's classroom. For example, during a single lesson covering the basics of RNA translation, Teacher A used a wide variety of analogies and examples to explain the quite complicated molecular process. He likened mRNA and tRNA to opposite sides of Velcro, sites on the ribosome to "nestled little pockets inside a beanbag chair," and the action of a ribosome to a cassette player. He then used an extended example of movie editing to explain the process of RNA splicing. In this example, he discussed the *Lord of the Rings*, a film that had recently premiered in theaters. This example was powerful not only in that it used an analogy, but it also tapped into a context that the students found highly engaging. Observing Teacher A's class over an extended time period revealed that this day was no exception. His use of analogies was constant and seemed to play a central role in his instruction. He commented on this during his interview. "Their actual background knowledge I like to use in teaching the class in any examples I give or any analogies I use because I teach a lot by analogy." He later went on to discuss the value of analogies and their instructional power. "There's just so many different comparisons out there that it seems easiest for everybody, not just people in the different ethnic classes or different socioeconomic classes."

Teacher B also explicitly stated that he likes to "explain things in a number of different ways," and he often used similar student-friendly examples as Teacher A. For example, he compared the cell cycle to a football team. He described mitosis as "the quarterback of the cell cycle—it gets all the action." To explain the concept of crossing over or recombination during meiosis, he brought up a story about a hand transplant in which the doctors had placed the incorrect hand on a patient. He likened this to the tips of chromosomes exchanging and thus ending up on the "other" arm. These and other examples were received well by students not only because they provided analogies that placed the concept in another context, but the contexts themselves were those that students could relate to. Use of contexts that students themselves are interested in increases the likelihood that the examples will be understood.

The comment by teacher A that analogies "seem easiest for everybody" demonstrates that he recognizes the value of analogies for all students and not just specific groups. Yet, a comment he made later and observations of his instruction demonstrated that he also recognized the value of using analogies that were student-specific when necessary. He stated, "At times I'll come up with analogies that are student-specific—that no one else in the class gets but that doesn't matter at the time." This was observed in classroom observations on a number of occasions. Teacher A would mention a student by name and make a specific point pertaining to something he knew about his or her life. Whether specific to the student or generalized for the entire class, by tapping into personal background a teacher can be much more specific in their activation of prior knowledge and is much more likely to increase student engagement.

Also employed by both teachers was the frequent referencing of pop culture in their instruction. In embracing pop culture, the teachers acknowledged that they felt students' interests were valuable and relevant. Teacher B described his technique of bringing pop culture into the classroom:

> I'm always bringing up things that are in pop culture, even though I'm not totally into them. I'm always just making stuff up that I read in the newspaper. But then I make it sound REALLY nerdy so they think I'm a total fool and that bridges the gap a little.

Many examples of this were observed in both teachers' classrooms. For instance, teacher B constantly would refer to a song that was currently very popular among the students. Dubbed by him as the "Salt Shaker Song," he would frequently work a reference of the song into his lectures and conversations with students. To talk about the "goals of cell division," he mentioned the well-known Univision announcer Andres Cantor who shouts "GOOOOOOOOOAL," every time a soccer player scores a goal. He referred to chromosomes being wound tight as "hella tight," this being a slang term often used by students. Teacher B even incorporated aspects of the local community such as the "unicycle man." Unicycle man is an individual who is known to all the students due to his antics on the major street where most of the students get lunch and travel to and from school. Teacher A utilized pop culture frequently as well. Examples of his incorporation of pop culture included his references to the *Lord of the Rings* movies, X-Men movies, and comics, current fashion, local restaurants that students frequented, and Starbucks.

In teacher A's mention of how he makes himself sound "nerdy," he is highlighting something that is seemingly simple yet reveals some important aspects of bringing pop culture into the classroom. First, and most important, is that one need not be "into" something to bring it into the classroom. More important is that the students be interested and excited. In fact, the chance that we as teachers will be "into" everything we find out about our students in our investigations of their sociocultural background is extremely low. It can be to our advantage, like Teacher B, to seek out aspects of pop culture that we may not personally enjoy but recognize as being relevant and engaging for our students. A second point emerging from Teacher B's statement is that it can sometimes be useful to play the role of the ignorant observer when it comes to students" interests. As a teacher, simply demonstrating that one is aware of certain singers, actors, or programs can make you wholly credible and "cool." Attempting to know everything about such topics and trying to interact with students in that capacity may give the impression of "trying too hard" and actually result in a loss of credibility. Playing the role of the "nerd" allows the teacher to demonstrate that she is aware of something and at the same time provides students with the opportunity to serve as experts and explain what is really going on. Examples included his mention of Nelly, a popular rapper, and skateboarding, a popular activity. He would then make a few comments that were intended to indicate that he had no idea what the topic was really about. The students would instantly want to provide a complete and accurate explanation of the topic. This relates directly to the second major benefit to referencing pop culture— increasing student engagement. By utilizing references and examples that we <u>know</u> students will be interested in based on our investigation of their background, we greatly increase our chances of generating and maintaining engagement.

Teacher B was observed using his knowledge of student background to aid in his instruction of scientific vocabulary. During lectures/discussions, he would point out particular words that were difficult or raised questions among students. When possible, he would break these words down and discuss their roots, origins, and meanings. For instance, in talking about words such as *chromosome* and *telophase* as part of a unit on cell division, he broke apart the words into *chromo*, *some*, *telo*, and *phase*. He then discussed the fact that *chromo* signified color and *soma* was the root for *body*. He went on to talk about the languages where these terms originated and other interesting facts. Finally, he gave additional examples where the same prefixes/roots were used. At times these were words the students were familiar with from everyday experience and at other times they were other, relevant vocabulary words from the same unit, such as *chromatid* and *chromatin*. A second aspect of Teacher B's focus on language issues was his referencing of specific languages during instruction. When possible, he would demonstrate how the root of a word could be seen as a cognate for a similar word in Spanish. He did this to aid the students in his class who spoke Spanish as a second language and, in some cases, as their first language. Furthermore, Teacher B was observed approaching students that he knew spoke Spanish as a second or first language and asking them about their language. He asked them how they might say certain words in Spanish, what certain words meant in Spanish, and talked about the Spanish language in general.

As discussed in his interview, Teacher B used these language techniques because of his awareness of the high language demands presented by biology. Almost all students, regardless of their English language ability, struggle with the large vocabulary and academic language demands that science classes such as biology entail. Teacher B's awareness of this fact and attempt to alleviate the demands was recognized multiple times in student survey results and interview data. Students noted teacher B's efforts to constantly define words, break words down, and link similarly structured words to others that they had already learned. Teacher B's attention to students' home language, in this case Spanish, opened a dialogue with students who typically said little during class. It should be noted that this focus by Teacher B was possibly due to the fact that he already possessed a familiarity with the Spanish language and that he was not able to provide the same focus for other home languages. However, for those students who did speak Spanish, his efforts to link the instruction and vocabulary to their home language was observed to be well received and a positive factor in aiding their understanding.

A final example of teachers using their knowledge of student background to inform their practice was the giving of special and extra attention to students in need. While seemingly vague, this example relates to cases in which teachers have potential for the greatest impact. Both teachers in the study were able to share examples of how knowledge of student background caused them to take a proactive approach to dealing with real-life issues. Teacher A described his approach by stating, "I might give a little extra backup or hints and suggestions about how kids should get to class. Not because of the way they look or what their culture is, but if they start falling into the culture of failure." Instead of simply writing off a student as "late" and disciplining them accordingly, Teacher A acknowledges that something larger may be going on and attempts to discuss alternatives and solutions with the student appropriate to their specific need. Teacher B shared an example that while seemingly different, illustrates the same point. He said, "Last year I helped a kid get on the free lunch thing. He was too embarrassed to do it, but he wasn't eating any food." This statement is deceptive in that it seems like the process of placing the student in the free lunch program was quite simple. In fact, the process involved Teacher A investigating the student's background sufficiently to discover that he was not eating enough, approaching the student in a nonthreatening manner, broaching the subject of free lunches, and convincing the student to participate in the program. However, whether simple or complex, the point of the process was the teacher's investigation of the student's background and use of the knowledge gained to address their need.

In the above cases it may be questioned whether the examples have strayed too far from the initial definition of "inclusive teaching." Yet if one allows for a perception of teaching that includes all aspects of affecting students" lives and not just transmission of content, then it seems less out of place. Going above and beyond the call of duty, such as Teacher B did in helping his student apply to the lunch program, represents the essence of being inclusive. He discovered a specific need that student had and went out of his way to address that need. And if we consider "teaching" to be the process of working toward the personal, academic, and social development of students, then what Teacher B did can certainly be considered as a successful teaching act.

In reflecting on the various ways that teachers used their knowledge of student sociocultural background to inform their practice, some common themes can be identified. First and most important, all the techniques used by teachers stemmed directly from specific things they had learned about their students through their investigatory strategies. In the use of specific analogies, focus on particular words and languages, and referencing of pop culture, the teachers took what they knew about their students and used it in a very intentional manner. A second commonality was the way the teachers used these techniques to tap into students' prior knowledge.

Identification of Barriers that Prevent Investigation of Student Sociocultural Background

Both teachers commented on the barriers that often prevented them from appropriately investigating student background. Their descriptions revealed these barriers to be both logistical as well as personal on the part of teachers and students. The ability to engage in critical analysis of one's situation is a valuable skill in any setting, and the development of PCK is no exception. Being able to identify and understand these barriers is the first step in determining how to overcome them.

Perhaps most common of all barriers to investigating student sociocultural background is the restrictions that come with increased class size and reduced class time. As Teacher B stated of investigating student background, "It would definitely be better if I had a smaller class size. Thirty to 40 kids per class makes it difficult." Teacher A also identified lack of time as a significant factor impeding his ability to implement strategies for investigating student background. He stated, "One of the big things I miss about double periods is that chance to get to know the kids better and really find out about their background." Teachers also discussed the effects of the statewide financial crisis, which had resulted in much larger class sizes. Also, they mentioned the large number of administrative tasks expected of teachers such as meetings, documentation, and committees.

A second identified barrier related to the curricular demands placed on teachers and students by certain courses, in this case Advanced Placement (AP) Biology. In discussing some of his other courses, Teacher B commented on the greater difficulty he had investigating the background of his AP students. This scenario is quite relevant as it is becoming an increasing source of concern for all teachers, even those who do not teach AP or accelerated classes. With the rising implementation of standardized tests in the United States, the need to race through content quickly has numerous frightening consequences.

Another type of barrier to investigating student background is that presented by the students themselves. Teacher A and B both commented extensively that, "Those kids who need it the most are often the hardest to find out about." "Those kids" are the shy students, the stressed-out students, the students who rarely come to class, and the students who are too embarrassed about their situation to discuss it. The issue of student-derived barriers is important in that this discussion might have led one to believe that once initiated, a teacher's efforts to investigate student background are always met with immediate success. On the contrary, it is more likely that a teacher's attempts to delve into the sociocultural experiences and circumstances of a student will be met with resistance, avoidance, and even hostility. Students can be extremely protective of their personal situation and react strongly to those who are attempting to question them about it.

To overcome barriers such as this, Teachers A and B used specific strategies. One such strategy was simple persistence. With a high probability of resistance after a first, second, and even third attempt, they emphasized the need to persist as long as they feel they can still gain something from knowing more about the student. A second strategy was alternating the methods of investigation. The teachers explained that if directly approaching the student was met with limited success, using another technique such as a specifically designed project or getting involved with a particular extracurricular activity might provide the "in" needed to access that student fully. Once the student's trust had been gained through alternate means, a teacher might then be able to return to a direct approach.

Teacher A provided a very apt description of another barrier to investigating student sociocultural background in his statement,

> I think the big barrier that teachers have is that rigid "professional distance" that they have to keep. People get so concerned with keeping their personal life so completely separate from their professional life. And I think it keeps you exactly that—it keeps you distant from the kids so they don't really get a feel for what you're going through in your life.

This point relates directly to the previous discussion. For these teachers, a large part of investigating student background and using that knowledge to inform their instruction are the processes of building trust and developing rapport. Through the building of trust, teachers gain increased entry into their students' lives and a greater understanding of how a student's experiences affect them within the classroom. Additionally, gaining a student's trust increases the likelihood that a specifically designed instructional approach will be well received and result in success. For a teacher who is reluctant to engage in trust-building activities such as socialization and out-of-class experiences, the probability that they will acquire the same knowledge and understanding of students is very low. According to both teachers, a key part of getting to know students and understanding them is allowing them to know you as an individual. Only by taking the first step and putting your trust in them will you make them feel comfortable enough to put their trust in you.

Another barrier that both teachers recognized as existing within the teaching community at large was that of prejudice and stereotypes. By relying on generalized information found in an investigation of a particular group of students, a teacher may completely negate a student's individuality while at the same time feel that they are effectively addressing the needs of specific populations. This was an issue noticed by students as well as teachers. In their interview one student stated, "In some classes you know there's stereotypes of blacks and Latinos. Like [the teacher] might be surprised that somebody is smart. It's not so much race but how they dress or the kind of music they listen to and stuff like that." Another effect that stereotypes and prejudices might have is to preclude a teacher from conducting an investigation of student background in the first place.

The final barrier to investigating student background that the teachers in this study mentioned was the limitation of their own sociocultural experience. The teachers recognized that the majority of their students were from a very different set of life circumstances than the ones they had experienced growing up. As Teacher A stated, "Being from Wisconsin I have big gaps in my inner-city knowledge and different ethnic and cultural knowledge. But there are certain things that are common of teenagers anywhere you go." This comment reveals two thought processes on the part of Teacher A, both of which are key aspects of identifying and beginning to overcome barriers to investigating student' sociocultural background. The first is the recognition that one's own experience is vastly different than that of the students being taught in the classroom. Especially in a situation where a teacher from a middle-class, suburban, white background is teaching a student population that is urban, socioeconomically disadvantaged, and in the minority for both race and ethnicity, such recognition is key. It is the first step in acknowledging that a great deal of investigation needs to be done if one is to understand even a fraction of the students' situations and life experiences that they bring to the classroom. The second point revealed in Teacher A's comment is that no matter how different a teacher may be from their students, there will always be some commonalities that provide a place to start interacting and investigating student background. No teacher should feel that they are so out of place that they cannot relate to their students. There is always some point of reference or something to latch onto for each and every student that can be used to take the first step in increasing our understanding of their sociocultural background.

In summary, barriers that prevent investigation of student sociocultural background that were identified by the teachers include:

- Increased class size;
- Reduced class time;
- External curricular demands (e.g., standardized testing);

- Student resistance;
- Need for "professional distance" between teacher and student;
- Prejudices and/or stereotyping by teachers; and
- Limitations of teachers' own sociocultural experience and/or knowledge.

CONCLUSIONS:
A PRELIMINARY ADDITION TO THE PCK MODEL

We have outlined the specific ways in which the two teachers in this study displayed and discussed practices related to investigating their students' sociocultural background. We propose to add a sixth component to the current PCK definition proposed by Magnusson and colleagues in their 1999 paper. This sixth form pertains specifically to teachers' investigation of student background. Drawing from the data collected in teacher interviews, classroom observations, student surveys, and student interviews, we suggest that teachers need to demonstrate proficiency in the following four areas:

1. Awareness and valuing of student sociocultural background as a source of PCK;
2. Use of specific strategies to investigate student sociocultural background;
3. Use of knowledge of student sociocultural background to inform inclusive teaching; and
4. Identification of barriers that prevent investigation of student sociocultural background.

By actively engaging in these ways of thinking and acting, teachers demonstrate their possession of the proposed sixth component of PCK and, in short, are practicing "good teaching."

However, it is also acknowledged that some of the results presented are most likely not specific to science alone. For instance, the teachers' use of pop culture, their involvement in extracurricular activities, and many of the barriers to investigating student background they identified might be found just as easily in an English classroom or a mathematics classroom. In this sense, some of the behaviors documented would be better classified as PK rather than PCK. Perhaps more examples of PCK would be found if more time were allowed for observation and more interviews were conducted. In fact, if one considers that it is necessary for PK to exist before PCK can be present for a specific subject, then the presence of PK might be taken as an indicator for potential PCK. In this case, this study's finding of a number of examples of PK might serve as a map for future examination of PCK.

In summary, we make four claims. First, the two teachers in this study did demonstrate behaviors that indicated that they are aware of and engage in the practices of investigating students' sociocultural background and using the knowledge gained to inform inclusive teaching. Second, there are examples within the results that are science specific and thus *do* suggest the presence of teacher PCK in the area of investigating student sociocultural background. This in turn offers support for the possible addition of an additional dimension of PCK. Third, a large portion of the results are not science specific and cannot be said to represent evidence of teacher PCK. They would be more appropriately termed PK and are largely generalizable across content areas. However, as discussed, this PK might in turn be an indicator of yet-to-be-uncovered PCK. Fourth and last, the results of this study can offer further insight into what constitutes "good teaching." The ability to investigate students' sociocultural background and use the knowledge gained to inform one's teaching is an important component of a teacher's practice, no matter what label is applied.

Educational Implications

By identifying and characterizing behaviors for teachers to investigate their students' sociocultural backgrounds, this study aids in the "discovery" of more ways to make teaching responsive to a classroom community that is diverse and heterogeneous. In order to build an educational environment that does not prescribe the same curriculum and methods for all students, it is necessary to give teachers ways of responding to their different students' needs. Part of this involves investigating and assessing students' backgrounds. Such knowledge should be made available through teacher preparation and professional development (Bristol, Blake, & Siegel, 2004). Three specific results of the study that could be used are: (1) the intentionality with which the participating teachers implemented strategies and techniques, (2) the ongoing nature of their investigation, and (3) their awareness of some potential pitfalls of using students' background to inform instruction. Communicating to teachers the importance of investigating their individual students' background and adjusting instruction to meet their needs could potentially result in much more inclusive classrooms.

When we, as educators, allow our pedagogy to be radically changed by our recognition of a multicultural world, we can give students the education they desire and deserve. (hooks, 1994)

This work could be more useful to educators by following several directions of research and development. One area of future research is the identification of specific aspects of student sociocultural background that are most relevant for science teachers to investigate. A second direction is the formalization and categorization of the strategies teachers use to investigate students' background. It would be useful to have an organized compendium of the different investigatory strategies available to teachers within a science classroom. For instance, if the teacher were just beginning the year, they might consult a listing of various introductory "get to know you" activities and survey questions to use during the first several days of class. Also important in future research would be the characterization of the process teachers use to translate their knowledge of student sociocultural background into effective and inclusive instruction. Ultimately, a model could be developed that delineates the process from investigation to instruction. A fourth direction of research this study points to is the continued identification, categorization, and characterization of barriers preventing science teachers from effectively investigating students' sociocultural background, and an elaboration of appropriate ways to overcome the barriers identified.

All of the above suggestions for future research fall under the umbrella of further characterizing PCK. As it is so difficult to capture and define, any future studies that either provide evidence of PCK, or add to its definition, have the potential to be of great significance in understanding "good teaching."

NOTE

1. We will use the terminology of "sociocultural validity," because for many "sociocultural" encompasses a wider range of factors than those denoted by the more specific term "cultural." For instance, "cultural" for many people implies one's ethnicity and the various customs, languages, and traditions that go along with it. In contrast, the term "sociocultural" is often perceived as implying not only ethnicity, but economic status, gender, sexuality, race, and a host of other factors.

REFERENCES

Bransford, J. (2000). *How people learn: Brain, mind, experience, and school: Expanded edition*. Washington, DC: National Academy Press.

Bristol, J., Blake, S., & Siegel, M.A. (2004). *Equity for all in science education: Elementary Science Teacher Leadership (ESTL) 4*. Berkeley, CA: SEPUP, Lawrence Hall of Science, University of California, Berkeley. Available online at http://sepuplhs.org

Fong, S.R. (2004). *Investigating pedagogical content knowledge: Teachers' knowledge of student sociocultural background.* Unpublished master's thesis, University of California, Berkeley.

hooks, B. (1994). *Teaching to transgress: Education as the practice of freedom*. New York: Routledge.

Lareau, A. (1987). Social class differences in family-school relationships: The importance of cultural capital. *Sociology of Education, 60*, 73-85.

Lave, J. (1996). Teaching, as learning, in practice. *Mind, Culture, and Activity, 3*(3), 149–164.

Lemke, J. (2001). Articulating communities: Sociocultural perspectives on science education. *Journal of Research in Science Teaching, 38*(3), 296–316.

Loughran, J., Mulhall, P., & Berry, A. (2004). In search of pedagogical content knowledge in science: Developing ways of articulating and documenting professional practice. *Journal of Research in Science Teaching, 41*(4), 370–391.

Magnusson, S. J., Borko, H., & Krajcik, J. S. (1999). Nature, sources, and development of pedagogical content knowledge for science teaching. In J. Gess-Newsome & N. Lederman (Eds.), *Examining pedgagogical content knowledge* (pp. 95–132). Boston: Kluwer.

Solano-Flores, G., & Nelson-Barber, S. (2001). On the cultural validity of science assessments. *Journal of Research in Science Teaching, 38*, 553–573.

CHAPTER 6

EDUCATIONAL TECHNOLOGY AND SOCIOCULTURAL INFLUENCES

Context Does Matter

Ellen B. Mandinach and Margaret Honey

This chapter examines how sociocultural variables in technology-based learning environments influence teaching and learning activities and organizational structure. It acknowledges an all-important principle that context matters. In order to understand and appreciate the interrelationships among variables in complex and dynamic educational settings, it is essential to take into consideration the context in which teaching and learning occur. In this chapter, we discuss the methodological perspectives that recognize the influence of contextual factors in education and we situate this discussion in current educational research and practice policies. Specifically, we discuss some of the key sociocultural issues in the study of educational technology and highlight a number of educational technology projects that illustrate contextual factors and their impact on teaching, learning, and organizational structure.

Focus on Curriculum, 129–169
Copyright © 2005 by Information Age Publishing

METHODOLOGICAL BACKGROUND:
THE NEED TO CONTEXTUALIZE

In tracing the transitions in thinking that have occurred in educational psychology, Berliner (2004) highlights the growing importance of socio-cultural influences and of adapting sociological and anthropological methods into the educational research. Accompanying this merger of fields was a paradigm shift from behavioral to cognitive psychology. As Berliner notes, the paradigm shift "was from the study of the individual to the study of the individual situated *in*, and bringing a socio-cultural history *to* a context that exerts powerful influences on the thoughts and actions of all those in the context" (p. 3). Psychometrician Lee Cronbach, perhaps the most eminent quantitative mind in psychological and educational research, made one of the first appeals to attend to context. In his seminal papers, *The Two Disciplines of Scientific Psychology* (1957) and *Beyond the Two Disciplines of Scientific Psychology* (1975), Cronbach discussed the merger of correlational and experimental psychology. Among the many important ideas in these papers, he described the need to examine the individual in context. Cronbach recognized the need to attend to local conditions, and more specifically to take into consideration that educational environments are comprised of numerous and complex interactions between sociocultural influences and individual differences. This complexity is precisely why Cronbach (1975) and later Berliner (2002, 2003) recognized education as the most difficult science.

The complexity and systemic nature of implementing technology-based applications requires sophisticated and sensitive evaluation methodologies. There is a delicate balance to be struck among several competing issues of design that reflects a trade-off between scientific rigor and practical validity. Educational evaluations must be:

- Rigorous, adhering to the standards set forth by the National Research Council (Shavelson & Towne, 2002).
- Relevant to multiple stakeholders, including practitioners, policy-makers, researchers, and funders.
- Constructive, providing feedback that can enable designers and implementers to make modifications.
- Responsive, making use of multiple methods while focusing on the dynamic interactions among multiple levels in school systems.

Furthermore, it is essential for research as well as evaluation to recognize the importance of context. In an article titled "Challenges of Educational Theory and Practice," Schoenfeld (1999) makes two essential points:

1. It is possible to conceptualize educational (and other) research in such a way that "pure" and "applied" work are not in conflict, but so that contributions to basic knowledge and contributions to practice can be seen as compatible and potentially synergistic dimensions of our work.

2. Educational research has evolved to the point where it is possible, much of the time, to conduct research in contexts that are of practical import, working on problems whose solutions help make things better *and* contribute to theoretical understanding. Finding and working on such problems is a high-leverage strategy for making a difference in the years to come. (p. 5)

Design Experiments

Brown, Collins, and Duguid (1989a, 1989b) argue that knowledge is a situated activity that is best understood within specific contexts and cultures. The same argument can be made for the examination of educational technology. Researchers working in the field of the learning sciences and educational technology have turned to a methodology known as design experiments as a means by which to recognize, examine, and include the complex sociocultural influences of the real world in their research designs (Brown, 1992; Collins, 1992). Design experiments, according to Barab (2004), use "iterative, systematic variation of context over time."

Collins, Joseph, and Bielaczyc (2004) provide two lengthy examples of design experiments. One is Brown and Campione's (1994, 1996) work on "Fostering a Community of Learners," a model that moves learning both horizontally across a classroom and vertically across grades. The second example is the concept of passion school, based on the principle of comprehensive progressive education that capitalizes on learner interests. Other examples can be found in the *Proceedings of the Sixth International Conference of the Learning Sciences* (Kafai, Sandoval, Enyedy, Scott Nelson, & Nerrera, 2004). For instance, Penuel, Yarnall, Koch, & Roschelle (2004) have designed software for handheld computers that enables teachers to capture students' questions and steer their curiosity toward student-led inquiry. The researchers have worked collaboratively with participating teachers to develop materials and the technology to support this process. Responses to the prototypes are fed back into the design process in an iterative manner, allowing for future prototypes to reflect teacher needs, not just the creative ideas of the researchers or developers.

The design experiment methodology enables the researcher to understand how the systematic changes affect practice. Design experiments overlap with other methodologies such as ethnography and formative evaluation by providing rich descriptions of the phenomena of interest, tracing its development over time, often as they are implemented and become infused into school settings. They do, however, differ from other methodologies in some fundamental ways. In the learning sciences, design researchers focus on the development of models of cognition and learning, not just program improvement (Barab & Squire, 2004). The approach is what distinguishes design research and evaluation, as is posited by the Design-Based Research Collective (2003):

> We do not claim that there is a single design-based research method, but the overarching, explicit concern in design-based research for using methods that link processes of enactment to outcomes has power to generate knowledge that directly applies to educational practice. The value of attending to context is not simply that it produces a better understanding of an intervention, but also that it can lead to improved theoretical accounts of teaching and learning. In this case, design-based research differs from evaluation research in the ways context and interventions are problematized. (p. 7)

These authors further distinguish that design research defines educational innovation as resulting from the interaction between the intervention and the context. Context does matter in evaluations.

As Collins (1999) notes, design experiments are conducted in messy, nonlaboratory settings, where there are many dependent measures and social interactions. These variables are viewed as contributing to the situation rather than factors that need to be controlled, as in an experiment. Design is characterized as flexible. Hypotheses are not tested. Instead, profiles are generated. Design experiments create collaborative roles for participants, rather than serving solely as research subjects.

A foundational principle that underlies the design experiment methodology is that context matters. It is important to understand the local dynamics of the phenomenon of interest. It also is essential to take into consideration refinement as well as viewing the phenomenon from multiple perspectives and at different levels. Refinement here means that the researchers will feed collected data back into the development and implementation process to make the application better or make the implementation more effective. Collins and colleagues (2004) specify three types of variables that are key to understanding in design research: climate, learning, and systemic. Examples of climate variables are engagement or cooperation. Learning variables include declarative knowledge or learning strategies. Systemic variables might include sustainability or scalability. Thus, the focus of investigation is a constantly changing phenomenon, placed within the context of local dynamics, thereby creating a moving target. Consequently while laboratory-based research sacrifices much essential understanding about a phenomenon when examining isolated variables, design research sacrifices its ability to provide reliable replications due to the constructivization or variability in context (Barab & Squire, 2004). As Collins and colleagues note, an effective design in one setting will not necessarily also be effective in other settings. Design experiments seek to understand complexity. This potential lack of generalizability raises the issue of the relative importance of internal versus external validity. Shavelson, Phillips, Towne, and Feuer (2003) further question the validity and replicability of claims based on primarily anecdotal evidence as well as the plethora of confounding variables that are likely to occur when using methodologies such as design experiments.

Formative Experiments

Similar to design experiments, Newman (1990) uses a methodology called the formative experiment to explore the impact of the environment, not just the technology. Formative experiments examine the process by which a goal is attained, rather than controlling treatments and observing outcomes. An essential component of the formative experiment is that the environment is the unit of analysis, not the technology. It examines process. The approach takes into consideration the context of the classroom, the school, or however the organizational structure is defined. It also promotes the use of a longitudinal perspective to enable the observation of process evolving over time. As Newman notes:

> The logic of a formative experiment in which the experimenter analyzes the support required to reach an initial goal must allow for the goals to change as the environment appropriates the technology. The technology is treated not as the cause of change but as something that can be used, by the school as well as the researcher, to support changes. (p. 12)

In more recent work, Newman and Cole (2004) consider the ecological validity of laboratory studies and their translations into real-world settings. Such studies are not limited solely to technology, but education more generally. They conclude that experimental controls have the potential to "lead researchers and decision-makers to the wrong conclusion." They suggest that there is a gap between laboratory research and actual practice, even in the wake of the push to use scientifically sound research to inform practice. "When complex educational programs are implemented on a scale large enough to show an effect, the effort of maintaining tight control over the implementation has the danger of introducing ecological invalidity" (Newman & Cole, 2004).

Much of the research on educational technology, particularly those that attend to sociocultural variables, are design or formative experiments. Such research considers contextual and sociocultural factors important to understanding the educational interventions or applications. These sociocultural and contextual factors may be ignored in the current climate of pressure toward rigorous scientific studies because they often cannot be controlled (see National Educational Technology Plan, 2004; What Works Clearinghouse, 2004; Whitehurst, 2003a, 2003b).

A FOCUS ON SOCIOCULTURAL ISSUES

Key Questions

In one of the most recent and comprehensive treatments of the sociology of educational technology, Kerr (2004) reviews the literature for the *Handbook of Educational Communications and Technology*. He identifies three types of sociological concerns with respect to educational technology: interactions and relationships, social problems, and changes to educational systems.

Interactions and Relationships

A first set of issues involves the effects of the technology on interactions and relationships. For example, one question that has been raised is the extent to which educational technology results in isolated learning. Is such isolation a valid concern? Does it lead to social problems? Much public attention has lamented the social isolation of the virtual learner, the Internet addict, or the computer geek. Technology need not be a solitary medium. Using technology can be a social event, whether the activity is accessing the Internet, communicating via email, participating in chat rooms, using instant messaging, or working in collaborative groups of students and teachers. In fact, one of the issues facing e-learning is that the very nature of the learning environment becomes a 24/7 activity for students and teachers (Mandinach, in press). Professors can communicate with their students with greater frequency at all hours of the day, stimulating far greater interaction than if they held traditional office hours. Professors report that they often have much more interaction with their students and virtually get to know them better virtually than in face-to-face interactions.

Social Problems

The second set of issues focuses on social problems such as gender inequities. Early research efforts in educational technology in classrooms attempted to focus on and isolate the effects of targeted sociocultural variables related to potential social problems. For example, a special issue of the journal *Sex Roles* examined emerging trends in gender differences in the use of computers shortly after they were first introduced in schools (Lockheed, 1985a). A strand of work from our organization has examined gender differences in the use of educational technology (Brunner, Bennett, & Honey, 1998; McMillan & Honey, 2002). Most recently, our colleagues have been creating applications that may help to stimulate interest in technology on the part of girls. In addition to gender inequities, the digital divide highlights social inequities and their educational consequences (International ICT Literacy Panel, 2002; National Telecommunications and Information Association, 1998, 1999, 2000; Organisation for Economic Co-operation and Development, 2000, 2001).

Efforts to ameliorate the digital divide, other than increasing the technological infrastructure, have largely focused on fostering the acquisition of information and communications technology (ICT) literacy skills through education and training. In particular, the International ICT Literacy Panel (2002) outlines the cognitive and technical proficiencies necessary to be effective in a knowledge society and charges schools, businesses, and governments with the responsibility to ensure that their students, workforce, and citizens have the skills to function as lifelong learners.

Changes to Educational Systems

Kerr's (2004) third set of issues focuses on the changes in educational systems stimulated by educational technology, such as promoting social improvement and suggesting new ways by which to carry out work. The introduction of technology into school systems affects the structure and functioning of the social organization. Two longitudinal projects traced such organizational impacts (Cline, 1989; Mandinach & Cline, 1994a; Sandholtz, Ringstaff, & Dwyer, 1997). Another fundamental recognition is that schools are complex learning organizations or systems comprised of dynamic and interrelated components (Mandinach & Cline, 1994a; Senge et al., 2000).

Schools as Learning Organizations

The implementation of technology applications within the context of the organizational system of a school is a complex and dynamic phenomenon with many interacting components. Mandinach and Cline (1994a) and Senge and colleagues (2000) recognize the importance of taking into consideration the multilevel or hierarchical structure of systems as organizational entities. Mandinach and Cline identify three levels of structure that may be analyzed: (1) the school as an organization, including administrators, policymakers, and the community; (2) the classroom, including the teacher, the curriculum, and the dynamic interactions between students and teacher and among students; and (3) the student, focusing on both learning outcomes as well as cognitive and affective processes. It is also necessary to examine across levels certain demographic/sociocultural characteristics such as socioeconomic status, ethnicity, gender, and locale. Such variables not only influence students' engagement with technology, but also influence how the classrooms and schools function organizationally.

Others have focused on the levels of school organization. Kozma (2003) describes a conceptual framework that includes micro, meso, and macro levels that all interact. Senge and colleagues (2000) refer to schools as nested systems of activity in which a critical issue is identifying the appropriate leverage point for systemic change for any intervention or innovation. Their first nested system is the learning classroom that includes teachers, students, and parents. Second is the learning school, comprised of superintendents, principals, school leaders, and school board members. Finally, there is the learning community made up of community members and life-long learners. As part of any comprehensive evaluation of technology, systems analysis can be used to parse out how those components (e.g., students, faculty, administration, infrastructure, etc.) interact.

A Review of Selected Sociocultural Findings

Before describing some highlighted projects in depth, we will examine the literature for three selected sociocultural issues that have become, in our opinion, some of the most salient and consistent with respect to educational technology. It is impossible to trace the entire history of such issues over the past 20 years, as the literature is too vast. Instead, we will provide a selective review of topics such as gender differences, the digital divide, and organizational change, the variables we have mentioned previously as being the focus in the professional literature and key issues in the effective implementation of educational technology.

Gender Differences

The educational technology literature is steeped in work on gender differences in part because of early recognition that the environment may be less conducive to fostering and supporting interest in females than males (Lockheed, 1985a). Our intent here is to provide snapshots in time that will provide the reader with a picture of the path of evolution in this constantly morphing field. We explore some of the early statistical trends, describe initial studies, and then provide relatively current enrollment and participation statistics. Among the highlighted projects described later in this chapter, we survey the gender differences work that our organization, the Center for Children and Technology (CCT), has done over its 25-year history.

Early Studies and Statistics

Even the earliest educational technology studies focused on gender differences in response to computer learning environments. Research examined differences in programming, game playing, cognitive effects, interests, and other related issues. Whether an early assumption or recognition that males were more likely to use computers than females, data began to emerge that confirmed this premise. Lockheed (1985b) summarized results that indicated that males use computers more for programming and game playing than do females, but that this finding does not hold for other applications. Despite this finding, the cognitive effects for males and females apparently are similar. That is, performance in courses or on specific tasks indicated little if any gender differences. Although there were early disparities in bachelor degrees awarded to women in computer science (Strober & Arnold, 1984), there was a recognition by high school girls that computers would be an important part of the educational and employment future (Fetler, 1985). While there was the recognition of technology's importance, this perception did not translate into equity in the voluntary use of computers in courses (Revelle, Honey, Amsel, Schauble, & Levine, 1984; Rock, Ekstrom, Goertz, Pollack, & Hilton, 1985), computer course enrollment (Linn, 1985), attendance at computer camps (Hess & Miura, 1985), or at computer centers (Collis, 1984; Lockheed, Nielsen, & Stone, 1983). Males were more likely to have positive attitudes toward computers than were females (Collis, 1984; Wilder, Mackie, & Cooper, 1985), spend more time playing computer games

(Kiesler, Sproull, & Eccles, 1983; Lockheed et al., 1983), and use different strategies and interact differently with educational games (Mandinach, 1984; Mandinach & Corno, 1985).

In terms of cognitive outcomes, Lockheed, Nielsen, and Stone (1985) found that boys outperformed girls on measures of high school computer literacy. Fetler (1985) also found that boys outperformed girls on indices of computer literacy and computer science achievement on a statewide assessment of computer literacy in California. Given the newness of computers when this study was conducted, Fetler also noted that achievement overall was fairly low for both males and females. In studies of middle schools also in California during the same period of time, findings indicated that once females enrolled in computer classes, their performance was found to be equal to that of the males (Linn & Dalbey, 1985; Mandinach & Fisher, 1985). Mandinach and Linn (1987) conducted a study of middle school programming performance and reviewed the existing literature. They concluded that although more boys enrolled in programming courses, there were no differences in programming performance. Thus, when given the opportunity and access, girls can succeed in computer classes.

In terms of problem-solving strategies, early studies indicated that boys' and girls' approaches differ. In a computer problem-solving game environment, boys tend to go beyond the scope of the game, breaking its code, to find tactical shortcuts to solutions (Mandinach, 1984; Mandinach & Corno, 1985). They were more likely to use active and strong forms of cognitive engagement, whereas girls used weaker or passive engagement strategies. Boys also tended to shift strategies based on computer feedback, while girls stuck with a strategy regardless of the degree of success or the task demands. Boys were more successful than girls across instructional sessions with the game. Student ability interacted with this finding. High-ability students were more successful than low-ability students. Thus both student ability and gender were related to differences in task approach, cognitive engagement, and performance outcomes. Furthermore, males who were unsuccessful reverted to arcade-like strategies, executing moves impulsively and without reflection, whereas females continued with a more methodical style of interaction.

Recent Statistical Trends

More recent statistics provide insights into the continuing gender inequities. According to data released by the American Association of University Women Educational Foundation (2000), females take fewer technology courses at both the high school and college levels. They are less likely to obtain degrees in technology fields, less likely to pursue postgraduate training in technology, and are underrepresented in higher end technology jobs. Females do, however, use technology applications such as the Internet and email at a rate equal to males, indicating that although they are users, they are not working at the most sophisticated levels. The College Board (2001) reports that only 17% of test-takers who took the Advanced Placement Computer Science A test were females. The figures were even lower for the more advanced Computer Science AB test, with only 11% female test-takers. At the college level, only 31% of computer science majors were female (U.S. Department of Education, 2000), as were only 16% of computer science doctorates in 1994 (U.S. Department of Education, 1996). The outcome of these trends is that only a quarter of the professionals in the information technology (IT) fields are women (American Association of University Women Educational Foundation, 2000). Panteli, Stack, and Ramsay (2001) confirm the continuation of these findings.

Recent statistics published by the U.S. Department of Education (2002) indicate that only 27.7% of the bachelor's degrees conferred in computer and information sciences in 2000–2001 were granted to females; 33.9% of master's degrees; and 17.7% of doctorates. These data were broken down further into specific categories that included computer and information science, general; computer programming; data processing technology/technician; information science and systems; computer systems analysis; and computer and information sciences, other. Females were most highly represented in the information science and systems category, with 36.4, 40.4, and 42.8% of the degrees conferred, respectively. The 2001–2002 statistics were the most recently available data published in the *Chronicle of Higher Education* (2004) and indicate that the trends are fairly stable. Although women receive 60% of associate degrees across disciplines, they received only 36% of those conferred in computer and information sciences. At the bachelor level, women receive 57.4% of all degrees but only 27.6% in computing. They receive a third of the computing master's degrees and 22.8% of the doctorates, compared to 58.7 and 46.3% of the total master's and doctorates

The Digital Divide

Statistical Trends

From local to national to international, and from the public to the private sectors, few would disagree that technology affects and will continue to play a fundamental role in the economic, social, and educational development of countries and their workforce, citizens, and students (Commission on Technology and Adult Learning, 2001; Committee for Economic Development, 2003; Committee on Information Technology Literacy,

1999; Education Development Center, 2000; Information Technology Association of America, 2000; International ICT Literacy Panel, 2002; National Telecommunications and Information Administration, 1998, 1999, 2000; Organisation for Economic Co-operation and Development, 2000, 2001; Plomp, Anderson, Law, & Quale, 2003). ICT is a key driver in the economic development of countries, making the acquisition of ICT skills and knowledge critical for its citizens, workforce, and students. The digital divide focuses on the gap between individuals and societies who have access to technology compared to those who do not.

The digital divide is about inequities across different groups based on socioeconomic status, gender, ethnicity, and poverty. The divide generally focuses on limitations in access to information (Light, 2001; Norris, 2001), with some members of society having access to information while others do not. Access to technology is only part of the digital divide problem. Technology is useless if individuals do not have the appropriate ICT skills to benefit from the hardware and software (International ICT Literacy Panel, 2002; McNair, 2000). It also is about the world of information and communication (Venezky, 2000). As Light (2002) notes, the digital divide goes beyond the presence or absence of technology to a consideration of sociotechnical relations, namely, "who controls the technology and information, which technologies, with what capabilities and, ultimately, the relation between people and information" (p. 48).

Light (2002) further delineates three dimensions of the digital divide: the economic divide; democracy and virtual civil society; and the information consumer. The economic divide, which has received the most attention in articles about the digital divide, focuses on the necessity for societies to have technologically literate citizens to form a workforce with skills to meet the constantly evolving technology. The digital divide in a virtual society focuses on individuals who have instantaneous access to information and are therefore advantaged, in comparison to others who cannot participate in the information society as fully or equally. The final dimension focuses on individuals who will only be able to consume information, rather than produce information, thereby not affording them opportunities for full participation in the emerging society.

Ba, McMillan Culp, Green, Henríquez, and Honey (2001) identify four component of equitable access. The first is universal access to hardware. The second dimension is community organization around access. A third dimension for equitable access is perceived control of the technology and communication. The final dimension involves giving and making meaning of access.

It is apparent that the digital divide is defined according to income, race/ethnicity, education, location of living, and age. Papadakis (2000), in an American study, noted that nearly half the white families owned computers, whereas under a quarter of African American families had home computers. From 1994 to 1997 the gap widened by 7%, although the percent of home computers grew for both groups. The National Telecommunications and Information Administration (NTIA; 1999, 2000) published data in 1999 and 2000 chronicling issues of inclusion around the digital divide. Not surprisingly in the earlier report (NTIA, 1999), race, income, education, and location were identified as affecting the likelihood of owning a personal computer or having Internet access. Computer ownership and Internet access increased with income and level of education. Asian Americans and whites far surpassed blacks and Hispanics in computer ownership and Internet access. The gap between whites and Hispanics and whites and blacks was 5% larger than the gap in 1997. The gap also widened for education (25 percent) and income (29%). Controlling for income level, poor whites were three times more likely than poor Hispanics and four times more likely than poor blacks to have computers and Internet access. The data also indicated that rural areas lagged behind other areas for Internet access. Light (2002) notes an often-overlooked demographic variable in terms of the digital divide is age. Nearly all children under 16 years of age have had experience using the Internet, while a much smaller portion of the adult population have had Internet experience or are likely to have a home computer. The NTIA (1999) report concurred, noting that senior citizens are the least likely age group to have a personal computer or have Internet access.

Trends remained the same but progress was noted when the second NTIA (2000) report was published in October 2000. By August 2000, 41.5% of the households had Internet access and 51% had home computers. Internet users rose. NTIA (2000) summarized its findings by noting: "The rapid uptake of new technologies is occurring among most groups of Americans, regardless of income, education, race or ethnicity, location, age, or gender, suggesting that digital inclusion is a realizable goal. *Groups that have traditionally been digital "have nots" are now making dramatic gains*" (p. xv). Increased access and ownership were noted across all groups—income levels, education levels, and rural households. Blacks and Hispanics have made gains but still lag behind whites and Asian Americans. By 2000, 46.1% of the white families and 56.8% of Asian American families had home computers, while only 23.5% of black families and 23.6% of Hispanic families had home computers. For computer ownership, the divide still exists but has stabilized. Senior citizens remain the least likely group to use the Internet. The gender disparity in computer ownership and access has disappeared.

The OECD Secretariat (2000) recognizes other sectors of the population as at risk in terms of the digital divide. In addition to those who are socially and economically deprived, linguistic and ethnic minorities, the geographically remote, and older citizens, the Secretariat notes the need to attend to individuals with special needs or physical disabilities, groups suffering from social exclusion, and technologically alienated persons.

Steps toward Amelioration

Attention has been given to the digital divide in schools locally, nationally, and internationally. Fulton (1999) outlined the Clinton Administration's foundations to technology literacy in the United States, called the four pillars. For all schools to bridge the divide, they must be connected to one another and the outside world, have computers accessible to every student, have teachers competent with ICT, and have appropriate and engaging content. *Education Week* (1997, 1998, 1999, 2001, 2002, 2003, 2004) annually publishes *Technology Counts*, which traces trends and provides state-by-state comparisons of technology infrastructure, access, professional development, and equity issues. The 2001 issue, entitled *The New Divides: Looking Beneath the Numbers to Reveal Digital Inequities*, examined seven "dividing lines": money, race, gender, academic record, location, special needs, and language barriers. The most recent issue examined global trends (*Education Week*, 2004). Just as the digital divide exists within local education agencies, even more dire divides exist internationally in terms of curricula and teacher professional development (Law & Plomp, 2003), technological infrastructure (Quale, 2003), and educational policies (Anderson, 2003; Plomp et al., 2003).

Organizational Change

An Overview

Schools are social organizations made up of multiple levels that interact in dynamic and complex ways. Because of this complexity, it is difficult and time-intensive to capture the nuances of how the introduction and infusion of technology into schools affect the structure and functioning of the organization. Studies have examined organizational change (Cline, 1989; Collins, 1991), the social organization of classrooms and schools as technology is introduced (Hawkins, Sheingold, Gearhart, & Berger, 1982; Light, 2002; Light, McDermott, & Honey, 2002a, 2002b; Schofield, 1995), and the role changes that technology stimulates (Gearhart, Herman, Baker, Novak, & Whittaker, 1994; Mandinach & Cline, 1994a; Sandholtz et al., 1997). What distinguishes these studies from others is that they tend to be longitudinal and more in-depth than the typical investigation. Such methodological emphases were necessary to capture the complexity and dynamic nature of the organizational change. As Mandinach and Cline (1994a) note, change rarely happens quickly or dramatically.

The STACI^N Project

An organizational substudy (Cline, 1989) was conducted as part of a larger longitudinal effort in the Systems Thinking and Curriculum Innovation Network Project (STACI^N), an examination of the impact of a technology-based curriculum innovation on teaching, learning, and organizational change. The substudy focused on changes in the structure and functioning of the school as an organization that might be attributable to the introduction of technology and systems thinking. Variables of interest were changes in work assignments, patterns of authority and influence among administrators and faculty, changes in communication networks, work satisfaction, morale, and productivity. Over the extended duration of the project, substantial changes were observed for all of these variables (Mandinach & Cline, 1994a). Perhaps the most striking change occurred in the communications patterns where teachers within schools began talking to and collaborating with other members of the faculty beyond departmental boundaries. Because of the structure of the project, in which eight schools across the country were participating, these teachers also established collaborations outside the boundaries of their schools, districts, and states, oftentimes beyond the participating schools. The introduction of email made this possible. Teachers would exchange curriculum materials and discuss effective and less effective pedagogical techniques.

Participation in the project and working with the technology became so important that, when one district's teachers went on strike, the participating teachers continued to work on project activities despite prohibitions from their union. The teachers were convinced of the professional worth of the technology-based effort and how it was transforming the way they conceived of, approached, and carried out their instructional activities. Teacher values had evolved. Similar transformations occurred, crossing levels of the school to administrators, stakeholders, and students. A more in-depth description of two of the project sites will be provided in the section on highlighted projects.

ACOT

Sandholtz and colleagues (1997) conducted a longitudinal project in schools across the country for Apple Classrooms of Tomorrow (ACOT). The perspective ACOT took was that technology should serve as a tool to support the curricula. It was ACOT's belief that the key to technology infusion was the teachers. They make it happen. Just as Mandinach and Cline (1994a) differentiate between traditional instruction and systems thinking, ACOT distinguishes between instruction and construction. The following are the dimensions along which didactic/traditional instruction versus constructivist technology-based learning environments differ: classroom activity, teacher role, student role, instructional emphasis, concept of knowledge, demonstration of success, assessment, and technology use. These dimensions translate into an environment that is interactive, learner centered, and collaborative. Constructivist learning environments emphasize inquiry and the transformation of facts, demonstrated by the quality of understanding in portfolios and performances rather than the quantity measured by traditional forms of assessment.

The ACOT work also contributed to the literature on a five-stage model of instructional evolution that was noted in their technology-based classrooms, but certainly can be applied more generally. The stages are entry, adoption, adaptation, appropriation, and invention. This model traces the direction of classroom activities from traditional, teacher-centered delivery to more innovative and constructivist applications. The evolution delineates not only general classroom activity but also the transformations that occur in classroom management, reflecting in teachers' knowledge of the technology.

General Trends

As Doyle (1980) notes, issues of classroom management evolve as context changes. Multidimensionality, simultaneity, immediacy, and unpredictability are four issues that arise in technology-based environments. Teachers have to juggle many activities that are often unpredictable simultaneously and immediately.

Both the ACOT and STACI^N Projects found similar results in terms of student and teacher role changes. Because students became more active and engaged learners in the computer-based environments, they took more responsibility for their own learning. Students formed collaborative groups, often fostered by the small groups working at each computer. Students would help other students, creating peer tutoring situations. Students also would provide technical assistance to teachers. Classrooms became less teacher-centered. Teachers no longer served as the sole provider of information, but rather the coach, mentor, or guide. Teachers would look to students for assistance. They were less likely to hesitate if a student asked a question for which they did not have an answer. This became the impetus for inquiry learning. Teachers also engaged in team teaching and consultation with colleagues about technical matters, pedagogical strategies, and other evolving issues. Their collaborations often crossed disciplinary and departmental boundaries. It is important to note that not all teachers, however, were amenable to or capable of making these transformations. For some teachers, it was impossible to relinquish control of the classroom, often due to fear that students might ask questions to which they did not have answers. For other teachers, the constructivist environment provided a new and exciting pedagogical approach, thereby renewing their enthusiasm for the educational process.

Schofield (1995) spent 2 years examining the impact of computers on the classroom culture of a large urban high school. This work recognized the interactive relationship between computer and classroom. That is, the organization of the school and classrooms affects how computers are used, while the computers influence the structure and functioning on the classroom. Schofield found three sociocultural shifts that confirm findings from similar projects (Mandinach & Cline, 1994a; Sandholtz et al., 1997). A first finding is the role changes that occur for students and teachers. Classrooms become student-centered rather than teacher-directed. A second and corresponding finding is the change in peer interaction patterns where students tend to become more collaborative. The third finding is the increase in student motivation. Schofield also noted an unintended consequence of technology infusion. It further divided the haves from the have-nots. The more gifted students tended to have more interaction with the technology than did other students.

Mutations and Transformations

Schofield's work also concurs with findings that Brown and Campione (1996) noted in terms of the curriculum. Namely, that implementation does not always go as planned. Thus there is the need to distinguish among intended, potentially implemented, and implemented curricula. The same principle applies with respect to implementing computer applications. This is related to what Brown and Campione refer to as "lethal mutation." Often in technology implementation projects, things do not go as planned. The technology infrastructure may not be adequate. Professional development activities may be delayed. Administrative support may be lacking. Such implementation problems may cause lethal mutation; that is, the infusion of technology and the accompanying curriculum may become compromised by the problems. In the context of this chapter, it is clear that parallels can be made between curriculum and ICT implementation, especially as it is embedded within curricula. All too often, the expectations for technology's impact are too high and the implementation fails to take advantage of the affordances and potentials of the technology. All too often problems prevent implementation from occurring as designed or on schedule.

In an article fairly early in the history of educational technology, Cohen (1988) raises the issue of the extent to which technology is a transformative medium. He notes that even incremental change presents a challenge in educational settings. It is interesting to note that the International ICT Literacy Panel (2002) purposefully selected the term "transformative" to convey their belief that the merger of cognitive and ICT proficiencies is a transformative skill for lifelong learning. As Schofield (1995) and Mandinach and Cline (1994a) note, simply placing technology in schools is an inadequate approach. Much more is needed in terms of supportive structures and resources for innovation or transformation to occur. Schofield focuses on the need for professional development and for teachers to recognize how technology can be used to meet their objectives. Mandinach and Cline concur but take the requisites further in developing a draft systems model of the complex relationships in school systems that affect the introduction, implementation, and sustained infusion of technology in classroom-based settings.

HIGHLIGHTED PROJECTS

We now turn to descriptions of a small number of highlighted projects that provide depictions of how the introduction and infusion of technology can affect teaching and learning activities, how the curricula are carried out, the organizational structure of a school, and how sociocultural issues embedded in classrooms, schools, and districts can affect these processes. We begin with an example from a recent project at CCT that examines inequities in digital literacy as a form of digital divide. We then turn to CCT's programmatic examination of gender and technology and the implications for design. Finally, we present two case studies from a longitudinal project conducted by one of us (Mandinach) while at Educational Testing Service. This project introduced a technology-based curriculum innovation into eight schools around the country and observed as the implementation occurred over an 8-year timeframe. The focus was on the impact of technology on students, teachers, and the school as a learning organization.

DIGITAL LITERACY AND THE DIGITAL DIVIDE

The first highlighted project is a comparative study of how low- and middle-income children use computers. It explores digital divide issues, but moves away from the traditional notions and definitions of digital divide. Ba, Tally, and Tsikalas (2002) reconceptualize the digital divide as a digital literacy issue; that is, they see the divide as more than simply an issue of access. According to this work, "information technologies are viewed as cognitive and cultural tools used to manipulate symbols and share meaning" (p. 4). The authors sought to explore potential differences of how children of different socioeconomic backgrounds use technology at home for learning, social activities, fun, and work. The researchers defined five kinds of dimensions of digital literacy and questions that they sought to investigate: (a) what kinds of troubleshooting strategies do children use?;

(b) what are their purposes for using technology?; (c) what comprises the children's skill sets?; (d) what is communication literacy?; and (e) what is Web literacy?

The study compared the patterns of technology use of nine low-income families and 10 middle-income families over the course of a year. Researchers made frequent home visits and observed the home environments and computing practices of the families. They observed as children engaged in computing activities and interviewed family members. Data were analyzed to discern patterns of the five dimensions of literacy mentioned previously.

Results from the study indicate distinct patterns of technology use between the two groups that reflect home environmental influences. There were, however, some commonalities. Both low- and middle-income children used computers for homework. They also spent 2–3 hours using technology for hobby-related activities, communication, and playing games. All of the children attained basic literacy with email, the use of the Web, and word processing.

Differences, however, can be seen across the five dimensions of literacy. Results indicated that the low-income children had fewer resources available to them for troubleshooting technical problems. These children sought assistance from project staff or teachers, whereas the middle-income children were able to seek help from peers, parents, extended family members, or solved problems themselves. The groups also used technology for different purposes. The low-income children primarily used their computers for schoolwork, and then email communication and recreation. In comparison, the middle-income children used their computers constantly for communication with friends through instant messaging. They also played games, browsed websites, and downloaded files. A final use was for schoolwork.

All the children demonstrated a functional level of literacy with the tools—the word processor, email, the Internet browser, and games. The low-income students, however, demonstrated only a surface-level of fluency with tool use, whereas the middle-income children had fluency with more advanced features of the tools. They also were able to individualize some of the tool functions to enhance their personal use. Additionally, differences were noted in the children's communications literacy. Whereas the low-income children used email, the middle-income children used instant messaging and also were familiar with chatrooms, bulletin boards, and email. Similar patterns were discerned for Web literacy. The low-income children were able to conduct basic Web searches and file management activities, whereas the middle-income children were also able to move beyond these basic functions to evaluation and authoring skills.

In addition to the findings about differential performance, the study also identified several local circumstances that influence how the children used technology. These factors included: (a) length of time a family had a home computer; (b) the ability to have stable connectivity; (c) the number and location of home computers; (d) parents' attitudes toward computers; (e) children's leisure time; (f) computing habits of peers; (g) technical expertise of individuals surrounding the family; (h) homework; and (i) instruction in school. The first three factors directly affected children's technology use, whereas the other factors influenced it to lesser degrees.

The study illustrates how environmental, social, and familial factors influence children's use of technology and their subsequent ability to attain digital literacy skills. Even from this small sample of low- and middle-income families, distinct patterns of usage and skills emerge, and it is clear that early environmental influences can have substantial impact on children's differential ability to use technology in effective ways for school, recreation, and communication.

The findings of this study have direct links to classroom applications. The study delineates the kinds of contexts in which students acquire digital literacy skills. For low-income children, schools can play a critical role in supporting the deep acquisition of digital literacy skills. Such school-based support can help to provide some of the necessary environmental influences that facilitate the acquisition of digital literacy skills.

This research helped to delineate the intricate relationship among family income, social capital, and technology use that raises questions about the factors that support or complicate children's and family's uses of technology in different social settings. Researchers and policymakers are barely aware of the new ecologies of childhood learning that are emerging in homes, schools, peer groups, and community centers. We can learn much more about closing the digital divide through research that attends to all of these settings. This work has generated a holistic and complex picture of both access to and use of technology for young people, what it means for youth to engage with technology across their schools, families, peer groups, community spaces, and organizations, and how these institutions can enhance educational and social experiences for these children.

GENDER AND TECHNOLOGY: A THEME FOR RESEARCH AND DESIGN AT CCT

Work in the area of gender differences in technology has a long history and has been a central theme at CCT. This research examines the ways adults and children "construct meanings in relation to different technological environments" (Bennett, Brunner, & Honey, 1996). The work has attempted to determine social and cultural barriers that influence how technology is used and perceived, recognizing that gender shapes how individuals engage the technology (Brunner, Bennett, & Honey, 1998).

CCT researchers have explored the multiple, interlocking factors that influence the interpretation and use of technology. The factors are seen as interconnected and their interactions must be considered, rather than examined individually. The factors include sociological issues, economic factors, and psychological factors. The sociological issues "have to do with the fact that girls and students of color still opt out of advanced level science and math courses at a greater rate than do Caucasian males. As a result, scientific, engineering, and technological fields that are responsible for technological design are still largely dominated by men" (Bennett et al., 1996). The economic factors include issues like the products that have already shown commercial success and the further development of products that perpetuate similar visions of technology. Psychological factors reflect the stereotypes of gender that technology creates and perpetuates. They "suggest there are ways in which we, as consumers, have been strongly encouraged to collude in the kinds of narratives and story lines that the vast majority of interactive products offer—particularly in relationship to the gaming industry" (Bennett et al., 1996). The ultimate objective is to design technological environments that can engage diverse learners.

Bennett and colleagues (1996) note that much of the work conducted in the field has assumed a deficit model; that is, women lack the necessary experience and knowledge base to interact effectively with technology. CCT's work takes a different perspective. It suggests that males and females make meaning differently, and those differences manifest themselves in distinct ways when interacting with technology. Such differences have direct impact on children's responses to technology in school and other settings.

Metaphor

Some of the earliest work established an enduring theme—that males and females approach technology in fundamentally different ways (Brunner et al., 1990; Hawkins, Brunner, Clements, Honey, & Moeller, 1990; Honey et al., 1991). These studies explored the metaphors males and females use as they interact with technology. Females tend to see technology as communicative and collaborative devices that can broaden social and personal networks. For them, technology can facilitate human interactions and help solve everyday problems (Brunner et al., 1998; McMillan

Culp & Honey, 2002). In contrast, males see technology as an extension of their power. Technology is about greater control, speed, and efficiency.

Bennett and colleagues (1996) asked men and women to fantasize about technology and noted 10 major differences. Women fantasize about technology as a medium; men fantasize about a product. Women see technology as a tool; men see it as a weapon. Women want to use it for communication, while men want to use it for control. Women are impressed with its potential for creation, while men are impressed with its potential for power. Women are attracted by its flexibility, men by its speed. Women are concerned about effectiveness; men are concerned about its efficiency. Women are attracted by technology's ability to facilitate sharing; men are attracted by the autonomy. Women focus on integrating it into their personal lives, while men are intent on consuming the technology. Women find empowerment through technology, while men seek transcendence.

Brunner and Bennett (1997) noted additional differences. They found that girls are more ambivalent about technology, whereas boys are more positive and excited. Bennett and colleagues (1996) found that even women who are experts with technology have different expectations and feelings about technology than do men who are experts. The women are concerned about the aspects of technology that are useful and accessible to others. The men are more focused on the machines themselves. These fundamental differences stimulated a sequence of projects to design interfaces that capitalize on the metaphors, particularly for females, to stimulate their interest in technology. Designing for Equity: The Imagine Project (Bennett et al., 1996) developed a computer-based graphics program that enabled girls to create devices of their own imagination. The software provided an environment in which girls could envision themselves as designers and inventors of technology. Imagination Place! (Bennett & Brunner, n.d.; Brunner & Bennett, 2002) engaged girls in collaborative activities to explore engineering and invention in everyday life. The environment provided a virtual design center in which students use problem-solving skills and principles of technology design to create technological invention.

The Gender Paradox

Questions continue to exist among technology designers about how to deal with gender in the design of learning and recreational environments (McMillan Culp & Honey, 2002). They ask: "Should game design ignore gender? Should it focus on the preferences that we think boys and girls have? What would it mean to build environments that do not privilege gendered fantasies?" (p. 35). McMillan Culp and Honey refer to this as the gender paradox.

Both McMillan (1999) and Honey (1988) explored questions of gender in different gaming environments. These studies examined how boys and girls fantasize, interpret, and establish relationships with and strategize and perform in a gaming environment. Honey used a game environment that privileges male fantasies. McMillan used a less gendered or gender-indeterminate environment. The Honey study found that boys outperformed girls strategically. They embraced the environment and were more sophisticated players than were the girls. In the less gendered environment, McMillan found no performance differences between the girls and boys. What did differentiate performance was an individual's ability to generate personal meaning though play. Because the environment was not overdetermined in terms of gender, boys and girls were equally likely to explore and make meaning from the gaming environment. The lesson to be learned from these studies is that fewer gender differences are likely to result from the design of environments that evoke varied and flexible metaphors.

Other CCT Projects

The goal of the Telementoring Project (Bennett, Hupert, Tsikalas, Meade, & Honey, 1998; Hupert, Bennett, Tsikalas, & Meade, 1997) was to encourage girls in secondary schools to enroll in technical courses and pursue careers in technology. This work provided girls with guidance and support through Internet-based telementoring communities that linked high school students with professional women in technical fields. This work created online environments where girls could share ideas and collaborate.

One recent project has focused on how metaphors affect the understanding of technical concepts (Bennett, Brunner, McDermott, & Green, 2003). This project created metaphors that prior research indicated could be more attractive to males and females. This research studied features of games that support girls' positive notions of the IT professions. The underlying premise of this work was that electronic games afford opportunities to develop new relationships to technology. In this experimental study, no differences in performance were found for middle school students. A follow-up study is developing an object-oriented programming environment, using ice skating as the visual metaphor for the programming task. This project is expected to enable girls in particular to develop a more comprehensive understanding of programming concepts. Once the development is completed, the environment will be tested in high school programming classes.

The objectives of all these research and development efforts is to explore differences in how males and females relate to technology environments and then translate those differences into ways to stimulate girls' interest in technology. Findings are then introduced into new curriculum materials and technology-based applications for use in schools, museums, clubhouses, and other interested institutions.

Educational Implications

This body of work, and the Brunner and Bennett study (1997) in particular, began to draw implications on gender differences and how they might impact classroom applications, noting that more formal research would be necessary. While females tend to look at technology's social functions, males focus on the machine itself. Thus, if technology is presented as an end in itself, such as a programming class, females are less likely to find such classes attractive. They should be more attracted to classes that use technology as a means to an end. Another way to attract females might be to emphasize technology as a means by which to solve social problems. Technology-based assignments also need to reflect the interests of all children, not just boys. Finally, the Internet has the potential to stimulate interest in girls by tapping into its communicative and collaborative features. The Internet enables students to share ideas and communicate with others.

Technology is now able to assist student exploration, interpretation, and communication. Through the process of discovery, students can build meaning and communicate their ideas. The challenge is to design and integrate new methods of teaching and learning into classrooms whereby the technology will stimulate such sharing of ideas and collaboration for all students.

THE STACI[N] PROJECT

The final highlighted project also illustrates the importance of organizational influences in the implementation of technology. It describes the impact of administrative support and digital divide issues, as well as other sociocultural influences.

The STACI[N] Project was an 8-year technology-based curriculum innovation effort in eight schools, and comprising nearly 100 teachers across the country. It used modeling and simulation-building software and the

Macintosh computer. STACI[N]'s teachers integrated a philosophical and instructional approach known as systems thinking into middle school and high school classrooms across the curriculum. According to Hulse (1995), systems thinking "is the study of how the behavior of systems arises from the mutual interactions of their component parts and processes. The need to understand such behavior is ubiquitous—a common intellectual thread unifying the study of the sciences, technology, economics, business, social systems, etc." The combination of the hardware, software, and systems thinking created a constructivist environment in which teachers and students could explore the systematic and dynamic nature of phenomena in various disciplines.

Systems thinking as an instructional perspective allows teachers and students to explore dynamic phenomena by examining how interrelated components of a system interact and change over time. Systems thinking helps to concretize abstract concepts that may be difficult for students to understand. An example is global warming. A systems approach would explore the causes of global warming and the consequences of not attending to the problem. Another example is the general concept of revolution. Students would study various wars and conflicts throughout history, determining why they occurred, the antecedents, consequences, and the similarities among such events as the U. S., Russian, and French revolutions.

Technology and Systems Thinking Proficiency Matrix

We describe how systems thinking and the technology impacted the teachers, presenting a description of a matrix that characterized the modes of adaptation used by teachers as they interacted with the technology (Mandinach & Cline, 1994a, 1994b). We then present brief case studies of two of the project schools to illustrate the impact the technology had on the sociocultural aspect of the selected schools.

The STACI[N] Project teachers were categorized according to their levels of proficiency with technology and with the systems thinking applications used in their classes. The systems dimension is described elsewhere (Mandinach & Cline, 1994a, 1994b). The technology proficiency dimension is based on ACOT's (Sandholtz, Ringstaff, & Dwyer, 1990) three stages of classroom management (survival, mastery, and impact). STACI[N] extended the dimension by adding a fourth category, termed *innovation*.

Table 6.1 delineates across the four categories of technological proficiency the activities that occur in technology-based and systems-based classrooms. The first column lists activities that are found in technology-based learning environments, as well as in systems-based classrooms. The

Table 6.1.   Teaching Activities in the STACI[N] Project across Stages of Proficiency with Technology and Systems Thinking

	Technology	*Systems Thinking*
Survival Stage	• Struggle with technology • Assailed by problems • Status quo in classrooms • Cannot anticipate problems • Teacher-directed • Unrealistic expectations • Management problems • Chaos	• Struggle to use systems thinking • Need for constant hand-holding • Trial-and-error model construction • Stop and wait for expert assistance • Textbook search for systems thinking topics
Mastery Stage	• Developing coping strategies • Increased tolerance • New forms of interactions • Increased technical competence • More engagement	• Less reliance on systems experts • Sounder curriculum modules • Increased ability to troubleshoot problems • Increased use of modeling
Impact Stage	• Infused technology • New working relationships and structures • Learner-centered • Teachers as facilitators of learning • Less threatened by technology • Technology-enhanced curriculum coverage	• No more funnels (i.e., cramming facts down students' throats) • Systems-infused curriculum • More varied use of systems applications
Innovation Stage	• Restructuring of curriculum and teaching and learning activities	• Curriculum revision based on systems thinking

Source: Adapted from Mandinach and Cline (1994a).

second column outlines activities specific to the systems thinking approach.

Teachers at the survival stage are marked with many types of problems, ranging from classroom management to technical issues. They are in constant need of support, advice, and hand-holding. Oftentimes, they are barely keeping their heads above water, looking to others, either colleagues or even students, for assistance. Although teachers may hold high expectations for what technology can bring to the classroom, the affordances and potentials of the technology are unattained. The classroom is teacher-directed.

Teachers at the mastery stage begin to develop coping strategies for the technology and the new style of classroom management. They have increased tolerance for the productive chaos of a constructivist learning environment. With their increasing experience and technical and pedagogical competence comes increased confidence.

At the impact stage, the classroom has evolved into a learner-centered environment where the teacher serves as the facilitator of learning, coach, mentor, or guide. This change creates opportunities for new working relationships with and among students. A new structure of the classroom emerges as the technology and constructivism are infused. Technology is used to address an increasing amount of the curriculum.

By the time a teacher reaches the innovation stage, technology is fully infused into the classroom culture. This innovation stimulates a restructuring of how teaching and learning activities occur, and even changes to the curricula.

The STACI^N Project observed and interviewed 41 of the project teachers, then classified them along the proficiency dimension part-way through the 8 years of the project. Even after a few years of work in the project, seven teachers were still struggling at the survival stage and three others bordered on the mastery stage. Another eight teachers were classified as at the mastery stage, with two bordering on the impact stage. Sixteen teachers had reached the impact stage, and five had totally innovated their classrooms using technology and systems thinking. There was not a perfect correlation between proficiency with technology and systems thinking. In at least one instance, a teacher was a systems thinker but was barely at the survival stage in terms of technical proficiency. This was a case where peer tutors in the class compensated for the teacher's lack of technical skill. Most teachers made steady progress over the course of the project, feeling more confident with the use of the technology and finding creative ways to integrate it into their classroom activities.

Case Study 1

This high school was one of three participating schools from a district that serves a multiethnic, working-class population in California. A high percentage of its students come from lower-SES, immigrant families, most from the Pacific Rim. As Mandinach and Cline (1994a) noted, this school was the "veritable ugly duckling story" (p. 171). Early in the project, this school and its teachers experienced all sorts of problems, but in the end, turned into a complete success, transformed by the work in the STACI^N Project. Part of the challenge was the principal, his leadership style, and his lack of vision in terms of technology. He was a long-time administrator who kept tight control over what was taught and by what methods. This principal was not interested in innovation and eschewed technology. His belief was that technology had no place in schools and that computers were of no value in teaching and learning. He had two reasons, however, for allowing the project access into his school. First, he was forced to participate by the superintendent who envisioned losses of substantial professional recognition as a progressive leader and of three computer laboratories. Second, he was politically savvy enough to know that he would be viewed as a forward-thinking educator if he allowed the project to go forward, even though the acceptance came grudgingly and with hostility.

The principal did not make things easy for project staff or the participating teachers. The room he assigned as the computer laboratory was poorly lighted with little ventilation and inadequate facilities. It was on the first floor of the main building where theft could easily occur and it did twice, losing computers, projection equipment, and other items from the room. The district had to replace the missing computers, and only after the second theft was the laboratory moved to a more secure location. The room was also not dedicated solely for computer use, with other classes being assigned to the rooms. Thus the computers took substantial abuse.

Luckily the principal retired soon after the second theft and was replaced by a strong proponent of technology and the project. The new principal purchased additional equipment and provided substantial resources and support for the project teachers and others who sought to use the technology. This principal soon left but his replacement became an even stronger supporter of the project work. She recognized the value of the technology in its potential to transform teaching and learning activities. Project teachers became the models for other teachers in the school.

Transformations among the participating teachers paralleled the value system and level of support provided by the three principals. The first principal hand-selected several pet teachers who were generally averse to technology and innovation but who would receive the project computers for their own use. These teachers had neither the pedagogical insights nor styles to work effectively with the technology or embrace constructivism. They soon became frustrated and resigned. Two of the initial teachers were young, enthusiastic, and saw immediate applications for systems and the technology in their science classes. Through a series of interviews and observations, we determined that they were constrained, however, by having to teach according to the principal's mandates if they wanted to receive tenure. Project staff worked intensively with these two teachers so that they could appease the principal, but also take advantage of the technology's affordances. Luckily these teachers outlasted the principal and subsequently thrived under the new administrators. They both developed into gifted educators, now both science department chairpersons in other districts. They mentored new teachers, showed unbounded enthusiasm, and produced outstanding curriculum materials and applications. They enhanced the school's technology by applying for and receiving a sequence of awards from local foundations. So convinced were they of the worth of their work in the STACI^N Project, these teachers crossed union picket lines to continue their participation when the district teachers went on strike.

Work on the project transformed the teachers, the school, and teaching and learning activities. Two of the participating teachers became intellectual leaders in the project and in the school. Although both have left the school to teach in other locations, technology and systems thinking continue to play a prominent role in their teaching and departmental chair activities.

These teachers and subsequently the students they reached using the technology-based science curriculum materials infused with systems thinking represent a success story. In the case of the STACI^N Project, we broadly defined technology both as the hardware and software, but also using the sociological definition, included the theoretical perspective of systems thinking as part of the technology. They are inextricably intertwined. The teachers did, however, move past just the systems thinking applications to infuse other technology into their instructional repertoires.

There are a number of implications that can be drawn from this case study. First, it illustrates the importance of strong and visionary leadership when attempting to implement educational innovation. Command commitment is important, without which it is more difficult for teachers to function. Without administrative support, teachers must deal with competing priorities and mandates. Teachers in the project acknowledged that having the support of the principal made a great deal of difference.

A second lesson is that teachers must be treated as professionals and provided with quality professional development. This was an underlying principle of the project. The teachers noted that their participation in STACI^N was one of the most important professional activities they have ever been privileged to engage in. The project provided the teachers intellectual challenges, renewed motivation, and new career paths, opportunities that they would not have had otherwise. The combination of the technology training and the pedagogical perspective transformed how the teachers functioned in the classroom as well as the structure of the science department and the school, more generally. The activities of these teachers and their successes illustrate what is possible when dedicated professionals are given the opportunity to flourish.

This case study illustrates how the structure of the school and the role changes among teachers and between teachers and administrators can be transformed through the infusion of technology. Visionary leadership played an important role here. But more important was the shared vision that a small number of teachers had about the potential impact of the technology and systems thinking. This shared vision and commitment to finding effective pedagogical strategies to reach their students influenced how the project teachers convinced the administration of the worth of their activities. The constructivist learning environment provided by the technology and the systems thinking perspective enabled the teachers to transform their classrooms into inquiry-based, learner-centered environments. Prior to that point, the administration had mandated a teacher-directed, didactic, and fact-focused model of pedagogy. The project teachers received attention from the administration for their work and were held up as role models. Instead of potentially leaving the teaching profession out of frustration, the project teachers regained their enthusiasm for the educational process and became even better practitioners.

Case Study 2

This Arizona high school was the last site to join the STACI^N Project. The school serves an extremely poor Hispanic population in a large, southwestern city. When the project began working in the school, only a small percent of the students graduated, and even fewer pursued any higher education. Students in this school often had to serve as the source of support for their families, working several jobs after school. The school was one of the first to have a full-time nursery onsite, to encourage teenage parents to continue their education and graduate.

STACI^N was situated in the mathematics department of the high school. Members of the department, led by the department chairman, decided to infuse systems thinking and technology throughout the mathematics curriculum as a way of reaching these at-risk students who heretofore had been turned off by traditional curricula. The project was fortunate to have a supportive principal, a department chair who was both a technological wiz and a visionary educator, and another teacher who captivated students through his creative and enthusiastic classroom practices.

One of the implicit goals of the project teachers was to use technology and systems thinking to engage and motivate their students to enhance their love of learning, not just in mathematics but more generally. Another implicit goal was to increase students' self-esteem so that they would become effective and productive citizens. The teachers were admired and respected by their students. They became role models and mentors.

They created a systems thinking and technology club to encourage students to go beyond the scope of the typical coursework. Students worked hard to gain membership in the club, as it became a privilege gained through hard work and interest. A visit to the campus would find students in the computer lab before school, between classes, and after school until the teachers had to close the department building to go home at night. Students made presentations to the school board, the superintendent, local businesses, and at national computing conferences. They dressed in business attire, had business cards drafted, and conducted themselves as young professionals, overcoming the stereotype that they were only kids from the barrio.

One particular anecdote illustrates the power of committed students, as the teachers and project staff approached the district administration about potential participation in STACI^N. The district was experiencing severe financial problems and feared that participation in the project would result in the expenditure of funds they could not devote to ancillary activities. The teachers were aware of the administration's concerns and reticence and so were the students, who by this time were fully committed to the technology and the pedagogical perspective. But they needed the support STACI^N could provide in terms of the technological infrastructure, money, resources, professional development, and other forms of support. The teachers and students decided that they needed to plead the case for technology and systems thinking to the district administration and the school board. The assistant superintendent requested that the students do a trial presentation with her before the school board meeting; the students had a true believer 10 minutes into the rehearsal. She became a staunch supporter of the project after observing the intellectual and motivational transformations that had occurred in the students. The subsequent presentation to the school board and the superintendent further confirmed the worth of the perspective and the work in which the teachers and students had been engaged.

A trend emerged slowly at first, and then with more consistency over time. Students, with their increased self-respect and motivation to succeed, became more interested in higher education. More students enrolled in college preparatory classes. They began to apply to colleges. The school's graduation rate increased. Over time there was a pipeline of students from this high school applying to and gaining admission to the mathematics, engineering, and science departments of the major state university only miles from the high school campus. These students often were the first members of their families to graduate from high school, and certainly the first to attend college. It is probably a safe bet that now, a decade later, these same students are productive professionals and responsible members of their community.

The students in the classes and the club understood and appreciated what the teachers were trying to accomplish. Technology may have been the medium and systems thinking the pedagogical approach, but what the work in this school was really about was respect, self-esteem, responsibility, and the importance of lifelong learning.

WHAT HAVE WE LEARNED ABOUT TECHNOLOGY'S IMPACT AND WHAT DOES THE FUTURE HOLD?

One lesson to be extracted from the highlighted projects is that context does matter, not just in technology-based projects, but education more generally. The complexities and dynamic nature of each of the settings only became apparent through in-depth, long-term, sustained research that uncovered the context in which the technology innovation efforts were situated. Researchers would have missed critical nuances, impacts, and the systemic nature of the schools as learning organizations if they had only conducted short-term experimental studies.

The implementation of any curriculum reform, whether technology-based or not, becomes situated within a complex and dynamic organizational structure. Students are nested within teachers and classrooms, which are in turn nested within schools, and again nested within districts. To understand such complex phenomena requires a systemic perspective. Conducting small, experimental studies will often cause the researcher to miss important information. Yet the practicalities of conducting longitudinal, more ethnographic research are daunting. A reasonable balance is necessary.

Another lesson that emerged from these studies is that researchers need to be flexible. Given the probability of unintended consequences, variations from design and implementation, lethal mutation, and other extraneous confounding factors, researchers need to adapt flexibly to the constraints imposed by the specific context. For example, the STACI[N] project originally was designed as a quasi-experiment (Cline & Mandinach, 2000). It took only 2 months to recognize the impossibility and the impracticality of the design. The evolving world of a school makes such tight design constraints difficult at best. The notions underlying both formative design experiments address this issue.

A major lesson to be drawn from these studies is that research questions and methods must be appropriately aligned and responsive to contextual factors. Much has been written recently on methodological fit and rigor or research in education (Coalition for Evidence-Based Policy, 2002; Cook, 2002; Jacob & White, 2002; Kelly, 2003; Mosteller & Boruch, 2002; U.S. Department of Education, 2003; Whitehurst, 2003a, 2003b). As Berliner (2002) convincingly notes, scientifically based educational research is difficult and challenging due to the dynamic myriad of social interactions in school contexts. These complex interactions cause context to be all important. All too often "scientific" findings miss the complexities of context because the studies are too narrowly defined. They answer different, but limited questions.

The studies examined here use various methodologies, but fundamentally used the practices of design experiments. They evolve as the target phenomena evolve. Data are fed back into the project to provide information for improvement. Experimental controls are neither possible nor practical as the questions being asked are much more contextual and require deeper investigation.

It is probably safe to say that design experiment studies like the ones described above as well as many others that have shaped the field would certainly fail to meet the criteria Cook (2002) outlined as necessary for acceptable scientific rigor in educational research. This finding has significant implications for how researchers will conduct future studies to gain in-depth insights into the complexities of implementing technology-based applications in real educational settings without manipulating and sacrificing the local validity of the context. Obtaining reliable and valid indicators of not just student learning and affect, but also pedagogical practices, classroom dynamics, sociocultural variables, and organizational variables is a challenging task. It is imperative that we align the research questions and methods, while paying close attention to the interrelations among variables across all levels of the school, the dynamic nature of schools as learning organizations, and context. Ignoring these factors will indeed cause not just lethal mutation but will be a fatal flaw.

REFERENCES

American Association of University Women Educational Foundation. (2000). *Tech-savvy: Educating girls in the new computer age.* Washington, DC: Author.

Anderson, R. E. (2003). Introduction. In T. Plomp, R. E. Anderson, N. Law, & A. Quale (Eds.), *Cross-national information and communication technology policy and practice in education* (pp. 3–13). Greenwich, CT: Information Age.

Ba, H., McMillan Culp, K., Green, L., Henríquez, A., & Honey, M. (2001). *Effective technology use in low-income communities: Research review for the America Connects Consortium.* New York: EDC Center for Children and Technology.

Ba, H., Tally, W., & Tsikalas, K. (2002). Investigating children's emerging digital literacies. *The Journal of Technology, Learning, and Assessment, 1*(4). Available online at http://www.jtla.org

Barab, S. (2004, June). *Ensuring rigor in the learning sciences: A call to arms.* Paper presented at the Sixth International Conference of the Learning Sciences, Santa Monica, CA.

Barab, S., & Squire, K. (2004). Design-based research: Putting a stake in the ground. *Journal of the Learning Sciences, 13*(1), 1–14.

Bennett, D. T., & Brunner, C. (n. d.). *The role of gender in the design of electronic learning environments for children.* Available online at http://www2.edc.org/CCT/publications_feature_summary_asp?numPubId_21

Bennett, D. T., Brunner, C., & Honey, M. (1996, June). *Gender and technology: Designing for diversity.* Paper written for the Regional Equity Forum on Math, Science, and Technology Education. Cosponsored by the EDC's WEEA Equity Resource Center, Northeastern University Comprehensive Resource Center for Minorities, TERC, and MassPep.

Bennett, D. T., Brunner, C., McDermott, M., & Green, L. (2003, October). Designing for diversity: Investigating electronic games as pathways for girls into information technology professions. In *Proceedings: The National Science Foundation's ITWF & ITR/EWF principle investigator conference* (pp. 34–38). Albuquerque, NM.

Bennett, D. T., Hupert, N., Tsikalas, K., Meade, T., & Honey, M. (1998). *The benefits of online mentoring for high school girls: Year three evaluation of the telementoring young women in science, engineering, and computing project.* New York: EDC Center for Children and Technology.

Berliner, D. C. (2002). Education research: The hardest science of them all. *Educational Researcher, 31*(8), 18–20.

Berliner, D. C. (2003). Educational psychology as a policy science, including some thoughts on the distinction between a discipline and a profession. Canadian *Journal of Education Administration and Policy, 26*(15). Available online at http://www.umanitoba.ca/publications/cjeap/articles/miscellaneousArticles/berlner.html

Berliner, D. C. (2004). *Toward a future as rich as our past.* Carnegie essays on the doctorate: Education/Educational psychology. Available online at http://www.carnegiefoundation.org/cid.

Brown, A. L. (1992). Design experiments: Theoretical and methodological challenges in creating complex interventions in classroom settings. *Journal of the Learning Sciences, 2*(2), 141–178.

Brown, A. L., & Campione, J. C. (1994). Guided discovery in a community of learners. In K. McGilly (Ed.), *Classroom lessons: Integrating cognitive theory and classroom practice* (pp. 229–270). Mahwah, NJ: Erlbaum.

Brown, A. L., & Campione, J. C. (1996). Psychological theory and the design of innovative learning environments: On procedures, principles, and systems. In L. Schauble & R. Glaser (Eds.), *Innovations in learning: New environments for education* (pp. 289–325). Mahwah, NJ: Erlbaum.

Brown, J. S., Collins, A., & Duguid, P. (1989a). Debating the situation: A rejoinder to Palinscar and Wineburg. *Educational Researcher, 18*(4), 10–12, 62.

Brown, J. S., Collins, A., & Duguid, P. (1989b). Situated cognition and the culture of learning. *Educational Researcher, 18*(1), 32–42.

Brunner, C., & Bennett, D. (1997). *Gender and technology.* New York: EDC Center for Children and Technology.

Brunner, C., & Bennett, D. (2002). The feminization of technology. In N. Yelland & A. Rubin (Eds.), *Ghosts in the machine* (pp. 71–96). New York: Peter Lang.

Brunner, C., Bennett, D., Clements, M., Hawkins, J., Honey, M., & Moeller, B. (1990). *Gender and technological imagination*. Paper presented at the annual meeting of the American Educational Research Association, Boston.

Brunner, C., Bennett, D., & Honey, M. (1998). Girl games and technological desire. In J. Cassell & H. Jenkins (Eds.), *From Barbie to Mortal Kombat* (pp. 72–88). Cambridge, MA: MIT Press.

Chronicle of Higher Education. (2004, August 27). *Chronicle of Higher Education Almanac Issue 2004–5*, p. 22.

Cline, H. F. (1989). *What happens when a school starts using a microcomputer laboratory: The impact of a science micro-computer program on the structure and functioning of a high school* (TR89-4). Cambridge, MA: Harvard Graduate School of Education, Educational Technology Center.

Cline, H. F., & Mandinach, E. B. (2000). The corruption of a research design: A case study of a curriculum innovation project. In A. E. Kelly & R. A. Lesh (Eds.), *Handbook of research design in mathematics and science education* (pp. 169–189). Mahwah, NJ: Erlbaum.

Coalition for Evidence-Based Policy. (2002). *Bringing evidence-driven progress to education: A recommended strategy for the U.S. Department of Education*. Available online at http://www.excelgov.org

Cohen, D. K. (1988). Educational technology and school organization. In R. S. Nickerson & P. P. Zodhiates (Eds.), *Technology in education: Looking toward 2020* (pp. 231–264). Hillsdale, NJ: Erlbaum.

College Board. (2001). *College Board, 2001*. New York: Author.

Collins, A. (1991). The role of computer technology in restructuring schools. *Phi Delta Kappan, 73*(1), 28–36.

Collins, A. (1992). Toward a design science of education. In E. Scanlon & T. O'Shea (Eds.), *New directions in educational technology* (pp. 15–22). Berlin: Springer-Verlag.

Collins, A. (1999). The changing infrastructure of education research. In E. Lagemann & L. S. Shulman (Eds.), *Issues in education research: Problems and possibilities* (pp. 289–298). San Francisco: Jossey-Bass.

Collins, A., Joseph, D., & Bielaczyc, K. (2004). Design research: Theoretical and methodological issues. *Journal of the Learning Sciences, 13*(1), 15–42.

Collis, B. A. (1984). *The development of an instrument to measure attitudes of secondary school males and females toward computers*. Unpublished doctoral dissertation, University of Victoria, British Columbia.

Commission on Technology and Adult Learning. (2001). *A vision of e-learning for America's workforce*. Alexandria, VA, and Washington, DC: American Society for Training and Development and the National Governors Association.

Committee for Economic Development. (2003). *Learning for the future: Changing the culture of math and science education to ensure a competitive workforce*. New York: Author.

Committee on Information Technology Literacy. (1999). *Being fluent with information technology*. Washington, DC: National Academy Press.

Cook, T. D. (2002). Randomized experiments in educational policy research: A critical examination of the reasons the educational evaluation community has offered for not doing them. *Educational Evaluation and Policy Analysis, 24*(3), 175–199.

Cronbach, L. J. (1957). The two disciplines of scientific psychology. *American Psychologist, 12,* 671–684.

Cronbach, L. J. (1975). Beyond the two disciplines of scientific psychology. *American Psychologist, 30*(2), 116–127.

Design-Based Research Collective. (2003). Design-based research: An emerging paradigm for educational inquiry. *Educational Researcher, 32*(1), 5–8.

Doyle, W. (1980). *Classroom management.* West Lafayette, IN: Kappa Delta Phi.

Education Development Center. (2000). *IT pathway pipeline model: Rethinking information technology learning in schools.* Newton, MA: Author.

Education Week. (1997, November 10). Schools and reform in the information age: Technology counts. *Education Week, 17*(11).

Education Week. (1998, October 1). Putting school technology to the test: Technology counts '98. *Education Week, 18*(5).

Education Week. (1999, September 23). Building the digital curriculum: Technology counts '99. *Education Week, 19*(4).

Education Week. (2001, May 10). The new divides: Looking beneath the numbers to reveal digital inequities: Technology counts 2001. *Education Week, 20*(35).

Education Week. (2002, May 9). E-defining education: Technology counts 2002. *Education Week, 21*(35).

Education Week. (2003, May 8). Pencils down: Technology's answer to testing: Technology counts 2003. *Education Week, 22*(35).

Education Week. (2004, May 6). Global links: Lessons from the world: Technology counts 2004. *Education Week, 23*(35).

Fetler, M. (1985). Sex differences on the California statewide assessment of computer literacy. Women, girls, and computers [Special issue]. *Sex Roles, 13*(3/4), 181–191.

Fulton, K. (1999, July). *Closing the gap: Delivering quality educational content in the digital age.* Report from the 1999 NCTET Tahoe Institute. Lake Tahoe, NV: National Coalition for Technology in Education and Training.

Gearhart, M., Herman, J. L., Baker, E. L., Novak, J. R., & Whittaker, A. K. (1994). A new mirror for the classroom: A technology-based tool for documenting the impact of technology on instruction. In E. L. Baker & H. F. O'Neil, Jr. (Eds.), *Technology assessment in education and training* (pp. 153–197). Hillsdale, NJ: Erlbaum.

Hawkins, J., Brunner, C., Clements, P., Honey, M., & Moeller, B. (1990). *Women and technology: A new basis for understanding.* New York: Bank Street College of Education, Center for Children and Technology.

Hawkins, J., Sheingold, K., Gearhart, M., & Berger, C. (1982). Microcomputers in schools: Impact on the social life of elementary classrooms. *Journal of Applied Developmental Psychology, 3,* 361–373.

Hess, R. D., & Miura, I. T. (1985). Gender differences in enrollment in computer camps and classes. Women, girls, and computers [Special issue]. *Sex Roles, 13*(3/4), 193–203.

Honey, M. (1988). *At play in the phallic universe.* Unpublished doctoral dissertation, Teachers College, Columbia University, New York.

Honey, M., Moeller, B., Brunner, C., Bennett, D., Clements, P., & Hawkins, J. (1991). *Girls and design: Exploring the question of technological imagination* (Technical Report No. 17). New York: Bank Street College of Education, Center for Technology in Education.

Hulse, R. A. (1995, September). *System dynamics and computer modeling for education: A physicist/computer modeler's perspective on what this is all about and why it is important for education.* Paper presented at the System Dynamics and Computer Modeling Conference, Princeton Plasma Physics Laboratory, Princeton, NJ.

Hupert, N., Bennett, D. T., Tsikalas, K., & Meade, T. (1997). The telementoring project: Taking a look at diversity on-line. *The Well Connected Educator* [Online]. Available: http://www.techlearning.com

Information Technology Association of America. (2000). *Bridging the gap: Information technology skills for a new millennium*. Arlington, VA: Author.

International ICT Literacy Panel. (2002). *Digital transformation: A framework for ICT literacy*. Princeton, NJ: Educational Testing Service.

Jacob, E., & White, C. S. (Eds.). (2002). Theme issue on scientific research in education. *Educational Researcher, 31*(8).

Kafai, Y. B., Sandoval, W A., Enyedy, N., Scott Nelson, A., & Herrera, F. (Eds.). (2004). *Proceedings of the sixth International Conference on the Learning Sciences: Embracing diversity in the learning sciences*. Mahwah, NJ: Erlbaum.

Kelly, A. E. (Ed.). (2003). Theme issue: The role of design in educational research. *Educational Researcher, 32*(1).

Kerr, S. T. (2004). Toward a sociology of educational technology. In D. H. Jonassen (Ed.), *Handbook for research for educational communications and technology* (2nd ed., pp. 113-142). Mahwah, NJ: Erlbaum.

Kiesler, S., Sproull, L., & Eccles, J. S. (1983, March). Second-class citizens? *Psychology Today*, pp. 41–48.

Kozma, R. B. (2003). ICT and educational change: A global phenomenon. In R. B. Kozma (Ed.), *Technology, innovation, and educational change: A global perspective* (pp. 1–18). Eugene, OR: International Society for Technology and Education.

Law, N., & Plomp, T. (2003). Curriculum and staff development for ICT in education. In T. Plomp, R. E. Anderson, N. Law, & A. Quale (Eds.), *Cross-national information and communication technology policy and practice in education* (pp. 15–30). Greenwich, CT: Information Age.

Light, D. (2002). *Information, knowledge, and technology in a real school*. Unpublished doctoral dissertation, New York University of the New School, New York.

Light, D., McDermott, M., & Honey, M. (2002a). *The impact of ubiquitous portable technology on an urban school: Project Hiller*. New York: EDC Center for Children and Technology.

Light, D., McDermott, M., & Honey, M. (2002b). *Project Hiller: The impact of ubiquitous portable technology on an urban school*. New York: EDC Center for Children and Technology.

Light, J. (2001). Rethinking the digital divide. *Harvard Educational Review, 71*(4), 709–733.

Linn, M. C. (1985). Fostering equitable consequences from computer learning environments. Women, girls, and computers [Special issue]. *Sex Roles, 13*(3/4), 229–240.

Linn, M. C., & Dalbey, J. (1985). Cognitive consequences of programming instruction: Instruction, access, and ability. *Educational Psychologist, 20,* 191–206.

Lockheed, M. E. (Ed.). (1985a). Women, girls, and computers [Special issue]. *Sex Roles, 13*(3/4).

Lockheed, M. E. (1985b). Women, girls, and computers: A first look at the evidence. Women, girls, and computers [Special issue]. *Sex Roles, 13*(3/4), 115–122.

Lockheed, M. E., Nielsen, A., & Stone, M. K. (1983). *Sex differences in microcomputer literacy.* Paper presented at the meeting of the National Educational Computer Conference, Baltimore.

Lockheed, M. E., Nielsen, A., & Stone, M. K. (1985). Determinants of microcomputer literacy in high school students. *Journal of Educational Computing Research, 1,* 81–96.

Mandinach, E. B. (1984). *The role of strategic planning and self-regulation in learning an intellectual computer game.* Unpublished doctoral dissertation, Stanford University, Stanford, CA.

Mandinach, E. B. (in press). The development of effective evaluation methods for e-learning: A concept paper and action plan. *Teachers College Record.*

Mandinach, E. B., & Cline, H. F. (1994a). *Classroom dynamics: Implementing a technology-based learning environment.* Hillsdale, NJ: Erlbaum.

Mandinach, E. B., & Cline, H, F. (1994b). Modeling and simulation in the secondary school curriculum: The impact on teachers. *Interactive Learning Environments, 4*(3), 271–289.

Mandinach, E. B., & Corno, L. (1985). Cognitive engagement variations among students of different ability level and sex in a computer problem solving game. Women, girls, and computers [Special issue]. *Sex Roles, 13*(3/4), 241–251.

Mandinach, E. B., & Fisher, C. W. (1985). *Individual differences and acquisition of computer programming skill* (ACCCEL Report). Berkeley, CA: University of California, Lawrence Hall of Science.

Mandinach, E. B., & Linn, M. C. (1987). Cognitive consequences of programming: Achievements of experienced and talented students. *Journal of Educational Computing Research, 3*(1), 53–72.

McMillan, K. (1999). *Gender and subjective experience in a virtual environment.* Unpublished doctoral dissertation, Teachers College, Columbia University, New York.

McMillan Culp, K., & Honey, M. (2002). Imagining less-gendered game worlds. In N. Yelland & A. Rubin (Eds.), *Ghosts in the machine* (pp. 33–53). New York: Peter Lang.

McNair, S. (2000). The emerging policy agenda. In OECD, *Schooling for tomorrow: Learning to bridge the digital divide* (pp. 9–19). Paris: Organisation for Economic Co-operation and Development.

Mosteller, F., & Boruch, R. (Eds.). (2002). *Evidence matters: Randomized trials in education research.* Washington, DC: Brookings Press.

National Educational Technology Plan. (2004). Available online at http://www.nationaledtechplan.org

National Telecommunications and Information Administration. (1998). *Falling through the net: A survey of the "have nots" in rural and urban America*. Washington, DC: U.S. Department of Commerce.

National Telecommunications and Information Administration. (1999). *Falling through the net: Defining the digital divide*. Washington, DC: U.S. Department of Commerce, Author.

National Telecommunications and Information Administration. (2000). *Falling through the net: Toward digital inclusion*. Washington, DC: U.S. Department of Commerce, Author.

Newman, D. (1990). Opportunities for research on the organizational impact of school computers. *Educational Researcher, 19*(3), 8–13.

Newman, D., & Cole, M. (2004). Can scientific research from the laboratory be of any help to teachers? *Theory Into Practice, 43*(4), 260-267.

Norris, P. (2001). Digital divide: *Civic engagement, information, poverty, and the Internet worldwide*. Cambridge, UK: Cambridge University Press.

Organisation for Economic Co-operation and Development. (2000). *Schooling for tomorrow: Learning to bridge the digital divide*. Paris: Author.

Organisation for Economic Co-operation and Development. (2001). *Understanding the digital divide*. Paris: Author.

OECD Secretariat. (2000). Emerging trends and issues: The nature of the digital divide in learning. In OECD, *Schooling for tomorrow: Learning to bridge the digital divide* (pp. 51–62). Paris: Organisation for Economic Co-operation and Development.

Panteli, N., Stack, J., & Ramsay, H. (2001). Gendered patterns in computing work in the late 1990s. *New Technology, Work and Employment, 16*, 3–17.

Papadakis, E. (2000). Environmental values and political action. *Journal of Sociology, 36*, 81–97.

Penuel, W. R., Yarnall, L., Koch, M., & Roschelle, J. (2004). Meeting teachers in the middle: Designing handheld computer-supported activities to improve student questioning. In Y. B. Kafai, W. A. Sandoval, N. Enyedy, A. Scott Nelson, & F. Herrera (Eds.), *Proceedings of the sixth International Conference on the Learning Sciences: Embracing diversity in the learning sciences* (pp. 404–411). Mahwah, NJ: Erlbaum.

Plomp, T., Anderson, R. E., Law, N., & Quale, A. (Eds.). (2003). *Cross-national information and communication technology policy and practice in education*. Greenwich, CT: Information Age.

Quale, A. (2003). Trends in instructional ICT infrastructure. In T. Plomp, R. E. Anderson, N. Law, & A. Quale (Eds.), *Cross-national information and communication technology policy and practice in education* (pp. 31–42). Greenwich, CT: Information Age.

Revelle, G., Honey, M., Amsel, E., Schauble, L., & Levine, G. (1984, April). *Sex differences in the use of computers*. Paper presented at the annual meeting of the American Educational Research Association, New Orleans, LA.

Rock, D., Ekstrom, R., Goertz, M., Pollack, J., & Hilton, T. (1985). *A study of excellence in high school education: Longitudinal study, 1980–82.* Washington, DC: National Center for Education Research.

Sandholtz, J. H., Ringstaff, C., & Dwyer, D. C. (1990). *Classroom management: Teaching in high-tech environments: Classroom management revisited first-fourth year findings* (ACOT Report #10). Cupertino, CA: Apple Computer, Inc., Advanced Technology Group, Apple Classrooms of Tomorrow.

Sandholtz, J. H., Ringstaff, C., & Dwyer, D. C. (1997). *Teaching with technology.* New York: Teachers College Press.

Schoenfeld, A. H. (1999). Looking toward the 21st century: Challenges of educational theory and practice. *Educational Researcher, 28*(7), 4–14.

Schofield, J. W. (1995). *Computers and classroom culture.* Cambridge, UK: Cambridge University Press.

Senge, P., Cambron-McCabe, N., Lucas, T., Smith, B., Dutton, J., & Kleiner, A. (2000). *Schools that learn: A fifth discipline fieldbook for educations, parents, and everyone who cares about education.* New York: Doubleday.

Shavelson, R. J., & Towne, L. (Eds.). (2002). *Scientific research in education.* Washington, DC: National Academy Press.

Shavelson, R,. J., Phillips, D. C., Towne, L., & Feuer, M. J. (2003). On the science of education: Design studies. *Educational Researcher, 32*(1), 25–28.

Strober, M. H., & Arnold, C. I. (1984). *Integrated circuits/segregated labor: Women in three computer-related occupations.* Stanford, CA: Stanford University, Institute for Research on Educational Finance and Governance.

U.S. Department of Education. (1996). *Digest of educational statistics, 1996.* Washington, DC: Author.

U.S. Department of Education. (2000). *1999–2000 National postsecondary student aid study.* Washington, DC: Author.

U.S. Department of Education. (2002). *Digest of education statistics, 2002.* Washington, DC: National Center for Education Statistics. Available online at http://www.nces.gov/programs/digest/d02/tables/dt255.asp

U.S. Department of Education. (2003). *Identifying and implementing educational practices supported by rigorous evidence: A user friendly guide.* Washington, DC: U.S. Department of Education Institute for Education Sciences National Center for Education Evaluation and Regional Assistance.

Venezky, R. L. (2000). The digital divide within formal school education: Causes and consequences. In OECD, *Schooling for tomorrow: Learning to bridge the digital divide* (pp. 63–76). Paris: Organisation for Economic Co-operation and Development.

What Works Clearinghouse. (2004). Available online at http://www.w-w-c.org

Whitehurst, G. J. (2003a, April). *The Institute for Education Sciences: New wine and new bottles.* Paper presented at the annual meeting of the American Educational Research Association, Chicago.

Whitehurst, G. J. (2003b, August). *Psychology and evidence-based education.* Paper presented at the annual meeting of the American Psychological Association, Toronto, Canada.

Wilder, G., Mackie, D., & Cooper, J. (1985). Gender and computers: Two surveys of computer-related attitudes. Women, girls, and computers [Special issue]. *Sex Roles, 13*(3/4), 215–228.

CHAPTER 7

MINDFUL CLASSROOMS

A Synthesis of Research on Multiple Intelligences Theory in Cross-Cultural Contexts

Wilma Vialle

The scene is a primary school in regional Australia that has a large proportion of students from non-English-speaking backgrounds (NESB). In one of these culturally diverse classrooms, I observed the following exchange at the beginning of a blustery Thursday with the students gathered together on the front mat. The teacher was quizzing her Grade 1 class on the days of the week. She held up flashcards and the children were asked to read the day. When she held up "Thursday," she drew attention to the "ur" sound and asked which other day also included the "ur" sound. After a few incorrect attempts from various class members, the answer of "Saturday" was given. As the teacher resumed "testing" the days of the week, James, a boy from Papua/New Guinea, said, "Turtle has the 'ur' sound, too." The teacher nodded at the child and continued with the days of the week when James again interrupted with, "And dinosaur. That ends with 'ur'." The teacher looked at him and with ill-humor, said, "Yes, but dinosaur doesn't make the 'ur' sound, does it?" before continuing with

Focus on Curriculum, 171–198
Copyright © 2005 by Information Age Publishing
All rights of reproduction in any form reserved.

the lesson. What interpretations can be made of this exchange? We could assume that this is a teacher who does not welcome interruptions that take the class "off-task" and this is certainly the explanation given after the lesson. In response, I commented to the teacher that James seemed to be a bright boy, to which she replied, "James is *too* smart. He gets us off task all the time." However, on a number of other occasions, I observed the teacher capitalizing on those "off-task" teaching moments when another child was responsible for the interruption, particularly when the "culprit" was a white girl.

CULTURAL DIVERSITY AND SCHOOL ACHIEVEMENT

The dinosaur example is illustrative of many similar examples from my data, collected over a decade of research in Australian schools, which indicate the relative unresponsiveness of the teacher to children from different cultural backgrounds. It is a powerful illustration that indicates, at best, a failure to be mindful of the diverse needs of students from diverse cultural groups, and, at worst, discrimination against such students. Furthermore, the dinosaur example illustrates the importance of teachers interacting with students in ways that not only permit, but also encourage, student initiative. In the dinosaur example, James's initiative was actively discouraged because it did not coincide with the teacher's agenda. Furthermore, while James possessed high linguistic intelligence, evident in his verbal exchanges, this ability was not always evident in written tasks and was therefore not fully appreciated. There is little chance for a teacher to establish intersubjectivity (Vygotsky, 1978)—that is, shared understanding—with children from culturally diverse groups unless the teacher values the ways of thinking and learning of all children and allows their diverse voices to be heard.

The dinosaur incident highlights why I believe Gardner's (1983) multiple intelligences (MI) theory is highly relevant for an education system that purports to develop the potential of all its culturally diverse students, and often fails to do so. The ideas reported in this chapter are motivated by the well-documented achievement gap between children from diverse cultural backgrounds and those from the mainstream culture (Au, 1998; Au & Mason, 1981, 1983; Ford, 2003; Howitt & Owusu-Bempah, 1994; Kozol, 1991, 1995; Mirza, 1992; Pallas, Natriello, & McDill, 1989; Wellman, 1993; Wetherell & Potter, 1992). This gap has often been attributed to the cultural differences between white middle-class school structures and children of cultural minority groups or low socioeconomic status (Boutte & DeFlorimonte, 1998; Heath, 1983; Tharp & Gallimore, 1988). Part of this cultural mismatch may be the differing cultural background of the teacher compared to the children (Ladson-Billings, 2001; Pigott & Cowen, 2000). Scrimsher and Tudge (2003) argue that responding to children's diversity involves not only awareness of the children's backgrounds but also "the specific approaches to learning and communicating with others that children bring with them to school" (p. 303). This chapter argues that MI theory provides a tool for teachers that assists them in recognizing, valuing, and accommodating the diversity among their students.

CULTURAL DIVERSITY AND GIFTEDNESS

My interest in MI theory was initially stimulated by the underrepresentation of culturally diverse students in programs for the gifted, a situation that largely arises from the over-dependence on IQ-type testing in selection processes. The broader conceptualization of intelligence inherent in MI theory offered promise for identifying giftedness in children who did not perform well on a standard IQ test. MI theory, then, is consistent with a shift to more inclusive and broadened notions of giftedness (Gallagher, 2003; Shore, Cornell, Robinson, & Ward, 1991). My research has demonstrated that it is an effective framework for identifying giftedness in students from cultural minorities (Vialle, 1991, 1994b, 1995).

When I started circulating these ideas over a decade ago, I encountered a hostile reception from many people in gifted education. For some people in the field, MI theory was perceived as a threat to gifted education because it broadened the base of intelligence and relegated the IQ test to a less lofty status. Despite these critics, several practitioners in gifted education welcomed the theory and utilized it predominantly in the design of learning activities for gifted students.

My research and practical experience have convinced me that MI theory can speak to some of the debates that face gifted educators. Rather than undermine gifted education, MI theory offers the potential to reconceptualize the field in issues such as defining giftedness, identification procedures, and equity versus elitism, particularly as they relate to the underrepresentation of culturally diverse students in gifted programs. In contrast to IQ tests, which offer a narrow, Western view of intelligence—that is, linguistic and logical–mathematical abilities—MI theory argues for a pluralistic view of intelligence that acknowledges the role of sociocultural influences on the individual. This broader conceptualization is essential in cross-cultural settings where there are likely to be differences in the patterns of strengths across intelligences. For example, Kearins's (1976) research demonstrated the superior spatial abilities of Australian Aboriginal children compared to children of European descent. Similar observations have been made of the superior spatial intelligence of Native American children (Ford, 2003; Maker, 1992). Consequently, we are more likely to recognize the intelligence of culturally diverse students when a pluralistic view of intelligence is applied.

In terms of defining giftedness, there is now a general acceptance in the literature of a broader conceptualization of giftedness (Gallagher, 2003; Shore et al., 1991). Gardner's theory, along with the work of Sternberg (2000) and Perkins (1995), has contributed to this shift in the literature. While the definitions of giftedness have embraced a broader range of domains, many educators view intelligence as one subset of giftedness, which they term "academic giftedness." Hence, narrow definitions of intelligence continue to dominate practice, as the IQ test remains the primary form of identification for many gifted programs (Clark, 1990). For this reason, minority representation in gifted programs is disproportionately low and the development of culture-fair means for the identification of giftedness remains a pressing need. MI theory is a framework that argues for more authentic means of assessment and is consequently suited to the identification of children from diverse backgrounds who may not do well on IQ tests because of language differences. To illustrate this, Gardner's theory has been frequently cited as the basis for several Jacob K. Javits grants, a U.S. program providing funds for research into giftedness in disadvantaged groups (see, e.g., Baum, Owen, & Oreck, 1996; Maker, Nielson, & Rogers, 1994; Plucker, Callahan, & Tomchin, 1996).

Gifted education is often accused of being elitist and it is clear that the underrepresentation of diverse cultural groups has provided some support for such conclusions. However, the cornerstone of gifted education is that provision for gifted students is more a matter of equity than elitism. Gifted education practitioners would argue, then, that what is at stake is an appropriate education that recognizes and responds to the individual differences of all students. MI theory is one tool that can assist in this process. In Australia, it has been a powerful tool for getting teachers who were opposed to gifted education to recognize the need to cater appropriately to the diverse students they teach.

MI theory is now 21 years old and it has been used as a framework for a highly diverse range of applications from preschools through to adult career development, as well as in special education settings, mainstream classrooms, and gifted programs. Despite such widespread practical application, however, the research base is still relatively small.

REVIEW OF GARDNER'S THEORY

Rethinking Intelligence

Gardner's diverse studies of normal and gifted students at Harvard's Project Zero, his work with brain-damaged patients at Boston Veterans

Administration Medical Center and his involvement with the Project on Human Potential, led to the publication of *Frames of Mind* in 1983. In that original publication, Gardner defined intelligence as "the ability to solve problems, or to create products, that are valued within one or more cultural settings" (1983, p. x). The theory has generated a great deal of commentary in the 21 years since its publication and has been warmly embraced by educators.

One of the reasons for the success of MI theory among teachers is that it captures what good teachers have always tried to do—that is, to understand the complex array of abilities in each of their students and develop appropriate programs to nurture those abilities. What has been critical is that the theory honors the diverse ways in which people understand, know, learn, and express their views of the world. It has done so by acknowledging that intelligence is something that is not reified as an immutable thing but is culturally defined and enacted. In *Teaching through the Eight Intelligences* (Vialle & Perry, 2002), I made the following observations about how intelligence was reconstituted from an MI perspective:

- Intelligence is not a single trait as it has been so often conceptualized in the past. The current theories broaden the conception of intelligence, albeit in different ways. This is critical for appreciating the intellectual strengths of culturally diverse students.
- Intelligence is "teachable." Sternberg (1986), for example, has developed a program to teach intelligence called *Applied Intelligence*, while Gardner has focused on the development of creativity in young children through Project Zero initiatives in a variety of educational settings (Krechevsky, 1991; Krechevsky & Gardner, 1990). The ideas of both Gardner and Sternberg have been combined in a program for teaching practical intelligence in the middle years within the school system (Gardner & Krechevsky, 1993).
- Intelligence is culture dependent. Each society—indeed, each cultural group within a society—determines what is intelligent and thus the conception of intelligence will vary over time and space. For example, the ability to locate food sources and navigate a harsh environment was a highly valued form of spatial intelligence in traditional Aboriginal communities. Today, the spatial intelligence of the visual artist is highly regarded.
- Intelligence involves both internal and external factors. The individual's intellectual potential is activated, enhanced, or hindered by interaction with the environment. (Vialle & Perry, 2002, p. 9)

The Eight Intelligences

Gardner's eight intelligences may be described as follows:

- *Linguistic* intelligence is the ability to use language to excite, please, convince, stimulate, or convey information;
- *Logical–mathematical* intelligence is the ability to explore patterns, categories, and relationships by manipulating objects or symbols, and to experiment in a controlled, orderly way;
- *Spatial* intelligence is the ability to perceive and mentally manipulate a form or object, and to perceive and create tension, balance, and composition in a visual or spatial display;
- *Musical* intelligence is the ability to enjoy, perform, or compose a musical piece;
- *Bodily-kinesthetic* intelligence is the ability to use fine and gross motor skills in sports, the performing arts, or arts and crafts production;
- *Intrapersonal* intelligence is the ability to gain access to and understand one's inner feelings, dreams, and ideas;
- *Interpersonal* intelligence is the ability to understand and get along with others; and,
- *Naturalist* intelligence is the ability to recognize and classify species in the natural environment. (Vialle & Perry, 2002, pp. 9–10)

Gardner (1999) also considered the possibility of a ninth intelligence, existential intelligence, which incorporates notions of spirituality along with philosophical contemplation of the nature of existence. However, this candidate intelligence does not meet all his criteria and so he has dismissed it at this point. There is an extensive literature on spiritual intelligence emerging in different disciplines (see, e.g., Sisk & Torrance, 2001; Suhor, 1999; Zohar & Marshall, 2000), nevertheless, that may resolve some of Gardner's concerns in the future.

It is important to note that Gardner viewed each of these intelligences as being relatively independent of each other. In other words, it is possible to have extremely high ability in one intelligence while the remainder of one's intelligences are below average—we might see such a pattern in an Autistic Savant such as Dustin Hoffman's film persona in *Rain Man*. While human beings are not all as extreme as this in their brain organization, we all differ in the combination of strengths and weaknesses across the eight intelligences we possess. In fact, it is precisely the combination of intellectual strengths and weaknesses that make us suited to the particular vocations and avocations that interest us.

The intelligences, then, are a hypothetical construct for how our brains are organized. Whenever we go to perform a task in our world, however, we use a combination of intelligences. Hence, the concert pianist will draw heavily on musical intelligence in performance but will also draw on her intrapersonal intelligence (to feel the emotion and nuances of the piece), her interpersonal intelligence (to communicate those nuances to an audience), her bodily-kinesthetic intelligence (in the fine motor dexterity needed to play the piano) and even her logical–mathematical intelligence (to make sure that she makes a living from it).

Implementation of MI in Schools

The Key School, Indianapolis

In the decade following the publication of *Frames of Mind* (1983), Gardner's theory stimulated a plethora of publications from his collaborators at Project Zero (located at Harvard University) and from educators throughout the United States. One of the early pioneers was the Key School in Indianapolis, which adopted a whole-school approach to MI theory. Established in 1987, the principal, Pat Bolanos, and her staff created an educational program based on their interpretation of MI (Bolanos, 1990). The student intake was deliberately selected by ballot to ensure that it reflected the racial diversity of Indianapolis, with 40% of the students being African American. The school's curriculum utilized a school-wide thematic approach such as Connections, Animal Patterns, or Changes in Time and Space over a 9-week cycle. The students undertook their regular subjects in intact classes and then regrouped into interest pods for special activities related to the theme. Children also worked on an individual project on the theme that could be presented in any form they desired. These presentations were videotaped and retained in the child's portfolio of achievements.

A feature of the Key School was the Flow room. Csikszentmihalyi (1990) described Flow as the state attained when a person applies intense, focused concentration on a task that results in high levels of satisfaction and enjoyment. In Key School's Flow room, students were invited to enjoy any of the wide-ranging games and puzzles available. A Flow-room teacher encouraged the students to reflect on the activities they selected, thereby emphasizing the metacognitive aspects of the learning experience. Assessment and reporting at the Key School were designed to focus on the students' strengths because the teachers believed that this would enhance the students' intrinsic motivation and lead to more successful learning. The reporting forms were based on the different intelligences and included ratings for active or passive participation and intrinsic or extrinsic motivation.

Almost 20 years later, the school is still operating with its MI-based curriculum and its culturally diverse school population. Although formal evaluations of the school's program have not been conducted, the former principal reported that the school ranks well in the state's mandated standardized tests and action research projects conducted at the school reveal a strong link between their curriculum approach and enhanced intrinsic motivation in the students (Bolanos, 1994).

Whole-school Approaches in Australia

Following in the wake of the Key School, other MI schools, classrooms, and projects were established in the United States (see, e.g., Armstrong, 1994; Campbell & Campbell, 1999; Campbell, Campbell, & Dickinson, 1992; Chapman, 1993; Haggerty, 1995; New City School, 1996) and it is now being implemented in some form in most countries throughout the world. Some examples of whole-school approaches in Australia include the Gardner's Patch Preschool in New South Wales, Cook Primary School in Canberra, and Sacred Heart in Sydney's Cabramatta.

The Gardner's Patch Preschool is located in a southern suburb of Wollongong and reflects the ethnic diversity of the city, with 70% of the students' families originating from southern Europe and the Middle East. The center's director and teachers have worked together to provide an educational environment that is organized around learning centers based on the eight intelligences and named after Australian personalities such as Fred Hollows (interpersonal intelligence) and Pro Hart (spatial intelligence). When interviewed about their views on the effectiveness of the MI approach, the teachers at Gardner's Patch reported to me that it had provided them with a sound theoretical framework on which to base an Early Childhood program. They all expressed some initial reservations but as they became familiar with the changes in emphasis, they came to realize that they gained better insights into their culturally diverse children's abilities through the focused observations they conducted.

Cook Primary School is a small school in the suburbs of Canberra that was closed temporarily in 1990 because of declining enrollment. As a result of concerted community action, the school was reopened and Judy Perry was appointed its principal. While reestablishing the school, Perry heard an interview with Howard Gardner on the local radio and was sufficiently stimulated to read everything she could locate on MI theory. In mid-1991, she introduced the theory to her staff and parents at Cook School and proposed that it represented an effective framework for designing a quality curriculum at the school and one that would allow all children to reach their potential. The school's population has a mix of cultural backgrounds, resulting largely from the various embassies and consulates located in Canberra.

By 1993, all the teachers in the school felt that they had assimilated MI into their regular teaching practices and were positive about the model it had provided for them to offer quality teaching and learning programs. They made the shift from being teacher-focused in their planning to a more student-centered approach where they try to cater for the varying interests and talents of their students. In 1994, I interviewed all the teachers individually and they confirmed that it had become natural for them to teach both to and through the intelligences and to recognize different intelligences in the students. One teacher commented: "It's good for seeing children's strengths in different areas. The enthusiasm is higher. It reaches the kids."

In 2000, Cook Primary School produced a videotape designed to showcase the MI approach it has adopted. In the video, staff, students, and parents talk enthusiastically about the difference Cook School's approach has made in their lives. Chief among these comments is the emphasis placed on the opportunities students have to learn in a variety of ways. The premise of the school is that students need to learn how to learn, how to learn in diverse ways, and how to honor and value the different ways of knowing, thinking, and learning evident in different cultures. The community of Cook Primary School believes that MI is a framework that allows them to accomplish these aims.

In contrast to Cook Primary School, Sacred Heart is a large Catholic primary school in Cabramatta, one of the densely populated western suburbs of Sydney. The vast majority of the students who attend the school are from a low socioeconomic background and over 95% are from a non-English-speaking background, predominantly Asian. In the mid-1990s, the principal, Shirley Jackson, introduced MI theory to her staff and suggested that this provided the key to recognize and nurture the abilities of their diverse group of students. Jackson reported to me that the MI approach has been an outstanding success at the school, particularly in terms of the children's academic achievements. She stated that the secondary schools, to which the students progress, had commented favorably on the academic levels and the independence and initiative of the students coming from Sacred Heart (S. Jackson, personal communication, 1996).

Project Spectrum

At the end of the 1980s, Gardner's collaborators at Harvard's Project Zero conducted research through Project Spectrum that sought to test MI theory in an early childhood setting. The researchers devised a number of activities within each of the intelligences and then implemented these with children in a number of preschools. The participating children were observed solving problems and creating products across the intelligences over the course of a year. These observations and assessments formed the basis for a Spectrum report, which indicated each child's individual profile of strengths and weaknesses across the intelligences. This research project demonstrated that children from an early age possessed distinctive intellectual profiles. Furthermore, the study indicated that there was no correlation among the intelligences (Krechevsky, 1991; Krechevsky & Gardner, 1990). Similar findings were evident when the Spectrum approach was replicated in Florida in the Prism study, which focused on children from diverse cultural backgrounds (Vialle, 1993a).

While there are numerous publications on the implementation of MI theory, the majority of these are descriptions of programs from the lesson level to the school organizational level, outlines of teaching strategies, or descriptions of assessment procedures. The articles rest on testimonials of participants rather than engaging in systematic research or evaluation. This is epitomized in the September 1997 (Volume 55, Number 1) issue of the Association for Supervision and Curriculum Development's publication, *Educational Leadership*, in which the majority of articles relate to practical applications of the theory.

MI IN CROSS-CULTURAL CONTEXTS

As indicated previously, MI theory seemed to offer a viable alternative to recognize and nurture the abilities of culturally diverse students. In the remainder of this chapter, I focus on two programs of research and practice that demonstrate the contribution that MI theory can make to the education of culturally diverse students. The first of these is my own research into MI, which is now in its second decade; the second program is the DISCOVER Project, an international program directed by my U.S. colleague, June Maker.

Tuesday's Children: A Study of African American Preschoolers

The Research Approach

My PhD research used MI theory as a framework through which to observe preschoolers from low socioeconomic backgrounds. The study was conceptualized as a means of identifying the abilities of children whose minority status militates against their being identified as gifted when conventional IQ tests are used. My dissertation, *Tuesday's Children: A Study of Five Children Using Multiple Intelligences Theory as a Framework* (Vialle, 1991), describes the intellectual profiles of five African-American children age 3 to 5.

In order to investigate the utility of MI theory as a lens through which to assess the abilities of preschoolers, a two-phase study was undertaken. In the first phase, 60 children in five diverse early childhood settings were selected. Intellectual profiles, based on the children's interactions with activities modeled on the work of Project Spectrum (Krechevsky, 1991), were constructed. From these 60 children, five children were selected for more intensive case studies. In selecting the children, I aimed to maximize the differences among the children—that is, the children seemed to possess different patterns of intellectual strengths and weaknesses; some children were viewed positively by their day-care providers whereas others were regarded negatively; their home environments varied in the degree of supportiveness as perceived by the day-care providers; and one child appeared to have a flat profile (i.e., absence of particular strengths or weaknesses). The five children were observed intensively over the period of a year by the researcher who operated as a participant observer. Observations were conducted at the day-care facility, the home, and other community settings (e.g., church, cinema, zoo, etc.). Additionally, ongoing semi-structured interviews were conducted with the day-care providers, the family caregivers, and the children. Artifacts in the form of drawings and stories (tape-recorded) were also collected and analyzed.

High Spatial Intelligence: The Case of Thomas

The findings of the original PhD research have been published more fully elsewhere (Vialle, 1991, 1993a, 1993b, 1994a, 1994b, 1995). In brief, the case studies confirmed the utility of Gardner's framework for children whose profiles do not stand out in the traditionally valued linguistic and logical–mathematical intelligences to be found in IQ tests. The case of Thomas, an African-American preschooler, illustrates this point.

Thomas was 4 years old when I first met him. His day-care providers described him as a child who would inevitably end up in an emotionally disturbed classroom because of his unruly behavior. I was told Thomas could not concentrate, he did not know his geometric shapes, and that he was practically nonverbal. I noted in my early observations that he was a loner who rarely interacted with the other children or the teachers in the day-care setting. I was surprised, therefore, when Thomas chose to work with me one day when I had brought in a Peg-a-train (a wooden train that dismantled into about 10 pieces). He sat down and before I could give him my well-rehearsed instructions for the activity, he had completely dismantled and reassembled the train without a single false start. I was impressed because I had had a lot more difficulty with the task myself. In my researcher zeal, I was excited to "discover" Thomas's competence in this spatial intelligence task and I resolved to closely observe his artwork. Once again, I was impressed with his eye for detail and focused attention.

On another occasion, Thomas, who had been described as having poor concentration skills, sat with me for 40 minutes while he tackled a complex assembly task. Forty minutes from a 4-year-old cannot be labeled as poor concentration. I also noted that this "nonverbal" child spoke at great length while constructing and drawing. One example I noted as he drew was: "The cat was coming out of the rainbow and saw the monster looking at him." Again, this hardly qualifies as the utterance of a nonverbal child.

Thomas had a fascination with patterns and would often trace out patterns on my clothing as if he were trying to commit them to memory; he would also accurately name all the geometric shapes as he encountered them. However, he rarely demonstrated these skills when called upon to do so. Nevertheless, it is important to note the impact that my positive interactions with him over the course of the year seemed to have on Thomas. His violent outbursts, while not disappearing completely, diminished significantly from a twice-daily average to rare occasions.

Thomas is an important example of a child whose progress through school is likely to be marked by preoccupation with his deficits rather than acknowledgment of his strengths. Yet, my study indicated that when his strengths were acknowledged and used as the starting point, he was able to develop his skills in weaker domains. His language skills, for example, improved dramatically over the course of the study and his confidence was also enhanced.

The key to unlocking Thomas's potential lay in recognizing his superior spatial intelligence, an intelligence that is more highly valued by indigenous cultures (Kearins, 1976; Maker, 1992) and African Americans (Ford, 2003). The implications for the design of school curricula are clear. Educators need to be aware of the salience of different intelligences for different cultural groups and ensure that time is provided for students to develop these intelligences. The salience of spatial intelligence for indigenous and African American cultures is the likely explanation for the success of school programs that emphasize visual arts, such as the Key School in Indianapolis and the DISCOVER programs described later in this chapter.

Lessons Learned: Challenging the Stereotypes

In 1994, I conducted the first of a series of follow-up studies on the children in my PhD research. Thomas had just completed grade 1 and I interviewed his class teacher about his development. The teacher reported that she had been surprised by his performance on the recently completed basic skills tests because his marks were quite high and close to the top marks in the class. She was surprised because she had placed Thomas in the "bottom" ability groups during the year. She explained to me that "his attitude will always do him down. He has a giant chip on his shoulder and doesn't get along with anybody." I was dismayed to learn that this white teacher had failed to recognize the abilities of Thomas because of his underdeveloped interpersonal skills. I am not convinced that she would have made the same judgment if Thomas had been white.

The teachers regarded Thomas and other children in the study as intellectually deficient and yet they possessed outstanding abilities in other intelligences. The assessments that permitted these abilities to be discerned were dynamic in nature: they allowed children to become familiar with the materials; they allowed for the researcher to scaffold their solutions to problems; and they allowed performance across the full range of intelligences rather than filtering all tasks through the child's linguistic competence. Furthermore, the dynamic assessment approach demanded that the teachers develop their observational skills along with a willingness to probe children's solutions.

Dynamic assessment is a concept emanating from the theories of Vygotsky (1978), particularly his concept of the zone of proximal development (ZPD). Based on the belief that children learn best when they are operating beyond the level they can achieve alone through the guidance of a more expert person, Feuerstein, Rand, Hoffman, and Miller (1980) elaborated the principles of dynamic assessment. In the classroom context, dynamic assessment allows educators to shift the emphasis away from the measurement of current performance that may be depressed for a variety of reasons and therefore not accurately reflect the learning capacity of the child. Instead, dynamic assessment focuses on the process of change and, particularly, the joint construction of knowledge and skill in the process of collaboration with an adult or more capable peer (Kirschenbaum, 1998; Roth, 1992). For example, in my research I used a garden sprayer as an assembly task; as the children attempted to take the object apart and reassemble the pieces, I assisted them with verbal prompts such as, "Which piece needs to go on top?" or "Where do you think this tube needs to go?" or nonverbal cues such as passing them the required piece. Furthermore, children would undertake the same activity over the course of the study and improvements in their performance were noted.

What is vital is that teachers adopt an attitude of seeking students' strengths rather than assuming a deficit. Teachers who maintain a narrow perception of intelligence and development will continue to regard children outside the norm as deficient, thereby affecting the quality of their interactions with those students. Conversely, teachers who recognize individual differences are more likely to nurture each child's intellectual development. This is particularly important for children from cultural minorities because their blend of intelligences may not be as evident as those from the mainstream.

MI in Culturally Diverse Australian Classrooms

From 1993, I conducted similar research to my PhD research but located in kindergarten and Year 1 classrooms in Australian schools with high proportions of children from non-English-speaking backgrounds (NESB). Data were initially collected over a 2-year period and involved classroom observations, interviews, and collection of artifacts. Despite the differences between the research samples, the results from this initial Australian study were similar to the findings of my original research study. The following observation of Samuel, a Chinese boy, is illustrative.

The NESB Learner: The Case of Samuel

In mid-May 1994, I observed Samuel, a recent Chinese immigrant, immersed in a rich linguistic environment as he interacted with the teacher, the kindergarten aides, and other children. He demonstrated his understanding of the teacher's instructions as he immediately and accurately completed the tasks required. He also worked cooperatively with other children in the culturally diverse classroom. In all these interactions, Samuel spoke only when directly asked a question but he listened to a wide variety of language types (instructions from the teacher, descriptions of the children's drawing activities, cooperative sharing of puzzle completion, and so on). Samuel was then withdrawn with seven other children for ESL (English as a Second Language) instruction. The ESL teacher was midway through a reconstruction of *Hattie and the Fox* with the group. Each child had a collection of stenciled sheets in which the labels of parts of the body had been removed for the children to complete; the final sheet was given to the children in this lesson. As soon as he received the sheet, Samuel reached for a pencil and started to fill in the missing words until he was instructed to "wait for the other children." The teacher directed the entire session with minimal linguistic instructions: "What part is next?"; "Watch the board," and "Color the fox." All the children in the group had to simultaneously name the part of the fox's body, watch the teacher write the word on the board, and then copy it onto their sheets. In this situation, Samuel was completing tasks well below his capability at a pace that was far too slow for him. Throughout the entire session, Samuel was not required to speak a single word nor was he immersed in a rich linguistic environment—and yet it was his oral language abilities that concerned his kindergarten teacher. This example demonstrates the mismatch that can occur between an NESB child's intellectual needs and the compensatory language program that he or she is given. The problem is exacerbated when the ESL teacher has not been adequately trained to fulfill the demanding role required of him or her.

My observations had revealed that Samuel, like many Asian children, had outstanding strength in logical–mathematical intelligence. Given the teachers' desires to develop his oral English skills, an alternative approach would be to link his logical–mathematical skills to the desired outcome. For example, mathematical problems could be presented as story-problems and Samuel could be encouraged to conduct small research projects (e.g., the number and types of pets owned by the class members) and report the findings verbally.

The Teacher's Role in Developing the Intelligences of Culturally Diverse Students

Since 1994, I have continued to work with teachers, schools, and education systems to implement MI as a key element in the design and delivery of educational programs. This ongoing evaluation and research have clearly demonstrated the need for teachers to be sensitive to the cultural and ethnic diversity of their students. The predominance of white middle-class norms in schools continues to constrain the educational opportunities of children from certain ethnic groups and social classes. In a multicultural society, we can no longer cling to stereotypical attitudes and neglect our responsibilities to promote the opportunities for all students to develop their intelligences, regardless of their cultural background.

Furthermore, the conclusions of the various research projects I conducted underscore the need for teachers to cease using Standard English usage as a de facto measure of intelligence. The analysis of classroom interaction in the Australian classroom research demonstrated a clear mismatch between teachers' stated beliefs regarding intelligence and their classroom behaviors. For example, teachers readily described a wide range of abilities when interviewed about their views of intelligence but within the classroom, these teachers responded to children according to their use of Standard English. As a result, culturally diverse children were less likely to have their abilities recognized because they did not demonstrate high levels of competence in Standard English. Ironically, the data demonstrated that NESB children were given a less rich linguistic environment, less cognitively challenging activities, and fewer opportunities for verbal interaction than their English-speaking-background peers. When assessing the linguistic competence of NESB children, we should pay more attention to their facility in their first language than in Standard English. This will give us a much more accurate view of the child's abilities.

There are three key themes that emerged from the MI research I have conducted. The first relates to the importance of distinguishing among intelligence, domain, and field; the second relates to the importance of dynamic assessment in understanding and extending intelligence; and the third relates to mediation.

Intelligence, Domain, and Field

My research has demonstrated the need to make a distinction among the concepts of intelligence, domain, and field. Without making such a distinction, it is possible to confuse intelligence and domain, and this confusion prevents us from understanding how the intelligences work together. From the MI perspective, intelligence is a psychological construct that hypothesizes how human intelligence has evolved and how it is organized. Each intelligence is discrete and enables us to deal with various aspects of our world. Clearly, there is a significant genetic component in these intelligences. A domain is a cultural invention and represents a collection of human endeavors; examples include quantum physics, detective fiction, and Impressionist painting. While an intelligence is discrete, activities within a domain draw on a combination of intelligences; it is therefore the pattern of intelligences that is important in determining our preferred vocations and avocations. The field represents those people who make up a domain. In the context of children (and many adults), parents, teachers, and peers provide feedback that shapes the way those children view their abilities.

This distinction among intelligence, domain, and field is at the heart of understanding the different emphases that cultural groups place on the intelligences, as well as the different ways in which intelligence may be enacted in different cultures. As indicated previously, Thomas possessed high spatial intelligence, an ability that is valued in his cultural group. Another of my African American case study children, Kayla, demonstrated high levels of musical and bodily-kinesthetic intelligence. When she commenced school, she struggled to learn to read and write, despite the fact that she had a love of story. She would spend hours at home creating elaborate stories, punctuated with her own songs and dance, but at school could not focus on the flashcards her teacher used. Again, musical and bodily-kinesthetic intelligences are valued in Kayla's culture and rather than dismissing their value in the classroom, teachers need to recognize their contribution to the motivation and learning of such students. This means not only providing students with opportunities to develop their musical or bodily-kinesthetic intelligences but also to allow students to demonstrate their understanding of topics through multiple intelligences; in cultural contexts where these intelligences are valued, teachers may also consider introducing new concepts or topics through music or dance.

Dynamic Assessment as an Alternative to IQ Testing

In my work with children and adults, I have realized that IQ assessments do not adequately reflect the breadth of human abilities. This is especially pertinent for cultural minority groups whose dominant intelligences may not fit the Western view of intelligence. What has been important in understanding intelligence in the context of my research studies has been to move away from the snapshot approach of single-instance testing to a dynamic process in which assessors and those being assessed work together over time to develop their intellectual profiles. Through the adoption of this dynamic assessment approach, I discovered that I gained insights into how children learned from interventions and what degree of scaffolding was needed for individual children. These insights were far more important from an educational perspective than the results of any test that may have been utilized.

In the context of culturally diverse classrooms, teachers are more likely to develop the abilities of all their students if they adopt a dynamic approach that is mindful of the different ways in which intelligence may be expressed and understood in different cultural groups. For example, the verbal prompts that teachers provide to scaffold children's learning will be more effective if linked to aspects of the children's culture.

For some cultural groups, particularly indigenous cultures, interpersonal intelligence is highly valued and this also needs to be given attention in classroom organization. For such children, a dynamic assessment approach would mean that their development is assessed within group activities as well as individually. In one of my studies, I observed Paul, a boy from Samoa, who struggled with the majority of classroom tasks and was regularly absent from school. On one occasion, I was working with his class on an MI project, introducing the students to each of the intelligences and asking them to reflect on their own strengths and weaknesses. Paul analyzed himself as being weak at everything. I then asked the class to work in groups to design a theme park that would cater to all the intelligences, which they would present to the rest of the class. In this activity, Paul's outstanding interpersonal intelligence came to the fore as he organized all the other groups in the class, coordinated their efforts, negotiated with the students, and confidently presented the final proposal. The skills he displayed in this activity would not have been evident if he had been given an individual task to complete. While group work is valuable for the learning of all students, it is essential for students whose cultures place high value on the interpersonal.

Mediation of Children's Learning

Finally, the importance of mediation was a key element in my research. For example, I observed the preschoolers but also interacted with them, often enabling them to accomplish tasks they were unable to complete alone. Furthermore, my original PhD research demonstrated that I became a significant person in the children's lives, perhaps illustrated by my being included in a drawing by one child of his family. The rapport that developed between the researcher and the children led to my doctoral supervisor quipping that the key outcome of the study was that "Every child needs a Wilma." Again, while this holds true for all students, it is particularly important in contexts where the teacher and the students do not share the same cultural group.

From a Vygotskian perspective, mediation is at the heart of children's learning, particularly the mastery of higher mental processes (Wertsch, 1985). According to Vygotsky (1978), the most important part of children's psychological development is acquisition of the culture to which they belong and this only occurs through interaction with others. The role of teachers is to create contexts in which children gain mastery over the cultural tools and the key means by which they do this is through mediation. Central to the concept of mediation is intersubjectivity, which is described by Wertsch (1985, 1998) as the establishment of shared understandings between the child and the adult (see also Dixon-Krauss, 1996). Intersubjectivity is an essential step in the process of internalization as the adult gradually removes scaffolding and transfers responsibility to the child (Diaz, Neal, & Amaya-Williams, 1990). Wertsch (1985) argued that language was highly influential in establishing child–adult intersubjectivity. Drawing on these ideas, unless teachers attain shared understanding with their culturally diverse students, their attempts to mediate instruction for such children may not be successful.

DISCOVER: A FRAMEWORK FOR HONORING DIVERSITY

Rethinking Assessment

Professor June Maker at the University of Arizona, like myself, was concerned by the underrepresentation of cultural minority children in programs for the gifted (Maker, 1996). From the early 1990s, she has conducted extensive research on projects that combined MI with various problem-solving approaches. Her initial research in this area involved the development of an assessment process that she called DISCOVER (Maker, 1992, 1993, 1994). Like Project Spectrum and the Prism study, the DISCOVER approach involves the use of culturally appropriate activities including toys and puzzles, such as Tangrams. Maker's approach, however, also incorporates a problem-solving continuum so that the tasks children complete range from simple tasks requiring convergent thinking skills to more complex and open-ended tasks that require divergent thinking skills. Trained observers meticulously record the children's problem-solving skills and behaviors across the intelligences and these observations form the basis for a Strength Profile for each child to guide curriculum development and educational choices.

The creation of the DISCOVER Assessment approach was founded on extensive research focusing on multiple intelligences, problem solving and creativity, and cultural diversity. Drawing on the salience of different intelligences for different cultures, the approach has five components: (1) Spatial Artistic tasks such as Pablo (large, colored cardboard pieces) require the child to create particular items such as an animal as well as a free-choice item; (2) Spatial Analytical tasks such as Tangrams require the child to create increasingly complex geometric figures using puzzle pieces; (3) the Oral Linguistic task involves the child in selecting items from a toy bag and then telling a story about them in their first language; (4) the Logical-Mathematical task is a worksheet with questions such as "Write as many problems as possible that have 10 as the answer"; and (5) the Linguistic writing task asks children to write whatever they choose (Maker et al., 1994). The precise tasks may be modified to suit the cultural groups for which they are used.

Key features of the approach are that it is:

- Nonbiased in its construction and therefore applicable in diverse ethnic, cultural, and linguistic groups;

- Performance-based rather than filtered through language, thereby allowing children to engage in broad-ranging assessments across intelligences;

- Intelligence-fair, which means that children are assessed in the intelligence itself rather than through language, for example;

- Criterion-referenced, which allows observers to note the children's performance against specific problem-solving behaviors rather than ranking them against other children;

- Standardized in its implementation but also allowing flexibility for specific cultural contexts; and,

- Future oriented in its focus on the problem-solving skills needed for success in school and beyond.

Issues of Validity and Reliability

As indicated, the DISCOVER Assessment approach was initially based on extensive research. It has continued to develop and evolve over the last decade, supported by grants from the Office of Bilingual Education and Minority Languages Affairs and the Javits Gifted and Talented Education Program. During that development time, the approach has been used extensively with cross-cultural groups throughout the world. This has included African American, Anglo-American, Navajo, Tohono O'Odham, and Mexican American groups in the United States (Maker et al., 1994), as well as different cultural groups in the Middle East, Europe, and Asia. Research studies have consistently demonstrated that the DISCOVER approach is effective in identifying the abilities of these culturally diverse students (Maker, 1997; Maker et al., 1994; Nielson, 1994; Sarouphim, 1999a, 1999b, 2000).

Maker and her colleagues have also researched the Assessment approach itself, particularly examining its reliability and validity (Griffiths, 1997; Maker, 1997; Sarouphim, 1999a, 1999b, 2000). Studies of the Assessment approach's reliability (Maker, 1997) revealed high levels of interrater reliability (85–100%) in those who were experienced observers compared to lower ratings for observers who were less experienced. Maker (1997) concluded that observers needed to be appropriately trained to conduct the observations reliably.

Research on the theoretical validity of the DISCOVER Assessment approach revealed that, in line with Maker's belief that giftedness is distributed equally across all groups in society, the approach identified high-ability students in numbers that reflected the overall percentages of the students in the general school population (Nielson, 1994; Maker, 1997;

Sarouphim, 1999a, 1999b, 2000). This is particularly pertinent for cultural minorities who are underrepresented when more traditional assessments are implemented. The DISCOVER approach, for example, has been demonstrated to be particularly effective for Navajo and Mexican American populations in the southwest Untied States (Griffiths, 1997; Maker, 1995; Maker et al., 1994; Maker, Rogers, Neilson, & Bauerle, 1996; Sarouphim, 2000).

From Assessment to Curriculum

The principles of the DISCOVER Assessment approach were utilized in the development of a curriculum model (Maker et al., 1994, 1996) that has been implemented in the United States as well as in Saudi Arabia, Egypt, France, England, Thailand, China, Hong Kong, and Taiwan (Maker, 2004). Based on a constructivist approach, the model includes the following components:

- Active, hands-on learning;
- Integration of culture and language, which may involve bilingualism or using aspects of the child's culture in concept learning;
- Group work and provision of choice;
- Learning centers with MI materials such as musical instruments and art materials;
- Interdisciplinary themes;
- Problem-solving tasks that range from closed-ended to open-ended;
- Visual and performing arts;
- Self-selected assessment formats; and,
- Technology integration.

Maker and her colleagues have researched the effectiveness of the DISCOVER Curriculum Model in elementary schools in the United States. Based in four elementary schools over a 3-year period, the method undertaken was to train all teachers in the DISCOVER approach and then subsequently to observe all the teachers in their classrooms. Teachers were rated as either high implementers or low implementers depending on the congruence of their teaching approaches with the DISCOVER approach. Research in the four schools revealed that students who spent all 3 years in classrooms with high implementer teachers showed significant improvements on mandated standardized tests (e.g., the Kentucky Instructional Results Information System and the Commonwealth

Accountability Testing and System) compared to those students in class-rooms with low implementer teachers (Maker, 2004; Maker et al., 1996). What is significant in this research is that the schools were selected because of the high percentages of culturally diverse students, particularly African Americans, Hispanics, and Native Americans, who do not normally perform as well on these standardized instruments.

Another project involving high proportions of Native American and Hispanic students at Pueblo Gardens Elementary School in Arizona revealed that students showed a significant increase in Stanford 9 Achievement Test scores over a 4-year period (from the 20th percentile to the 60th percentile). These remarkable gains have been attributed by the principal to their curriculum, which has included the DISCOVER approach along with an arts program entitled ArtsBuild, a program that also draws on MI theory (C. J. Maker, personal communication, 2004). ArtsBuild involves devoting significant curriculum time to large-scale artistic projects facilitated by specialist visual and performing arts teachers and volunteers. The arts projects emphasize community building and language arts and are based on social studies and science themes. For example, one project involved the creation of a mural at the Tucson Hispanic Chamber of Commerce entitled "Our Community is Cool."

Maker (2004) has emphasized that the DISCOVER Curriculum Model's arts integration is a key to its success, particularly with culturally diverse students. This research has been confirmed by other studies, drawing on DISCOVER principles, that have found significant transfer effects from arts-based curricula to other academic areas. For example, the New York–based Arts Connection project reported that more than half the students in their study increased their achievement scores in reading, while at the same time the school and school district scores decreased (Baum et al., 1996) and this was particularly marked for the cultural minority students (Baum, Owen, & Oreck, 1997).

Maker's DISCOVER Assessment and Curriculum Model is the most comprehensive application of MI theory of which I am aware. Furthermore, the practical implementation has been accompanied by rigorous research that confirms the value of MI in the design and delivery of curricula for widely diverse school populations.

IMPLICATIONS OF OUR MI RESEARCH

Theoretical Implications

The research reported in this chapter has implications for theory related to diverse approaches to teaching and learning, particularly those that argue for a sociocultural approach to defining intelligence and learning potential. Our research has confirmed the importance of culture in conceptualizations of children's abilities, and the subsequent educational approaches that best meet the needs of such students. We have also demonstrated that the social context in which teacher and learner are engaged collaboratively in the design and delivery of educational programs is vital to the educational success of students from diverse cultural groups.

More specifically, our work has strengthened the key premises of Gardner's MI theory, particularly in confirming the relative independence of the intelligences. Future developments that may arise from our research are likely to impact on the organization of the intelligences within the theoretical framework. For example, I am currently researching the developmental trajectory of spiritual intelligence, an intelligence that is particularly pertinent for indigenous cultures, and Maker (personal communication, 2004) is working on delineating subsets of spatial intelligence, particularly artistic expression.

Implications for Practice

In this chapter, I have highlighted cultural minority children with high ability levels who probably would not perform well on an IQ test with its focus on Western forms of linguistic and logical–mathematical intelligences. Thomas had high spatial intelligence, Kayla excelled in musical and bodily-kinesthetic intelligences, and Paul had highly developed interpersonal intelligence. James had high linguistic intelligence, but this was more evident in the oral sphere than the written; and, Samuel had high logical–mathematical intelligence and reasonable linguistic intelligence, which was masked by his quiet classroom demeanor. Classrooms are cross-cultural environments that pose challenges and opportunities to teachers. The challenge is to understand and cater to the cultural diversity in the classroom while the opportunity lies in the enrichment to be gained for all students from valuing and learning from the intellectual strengths of those diverse cultures.

The biggest impact of our research to date, then, is in its implications for practice, particularly in relation to the assessment of giftedness in culturally diverse groups and in the development of appropriate curricula for those students. Our studies demonstrate that the value of MI lies more in its impact on teacher attitude than in quantifiable learning outcomes, although, as reported, Maker has data that demonstrate such academic gains. It is the contention of this chapter that culturally diverse children such as James, Thomas, Kayla, Paul, and Samuel would have their abilities more readily acknowledged and nurtured if teachers adopt a pluralistic view of intelligence such as that proposed by MI theory.

MI theory itself speaks little to how classrooms should be organized, but our work emphasizes the following principles:

- a valuing of diverse ways of thinking and learning
- a student-centered curriculum
- dynamic forms of assessment
- collaborative partnerships among students, teachers, parents and community
- inquiry-based projects

Future Research Agendas

Our research has demonstrated that MI theory is an effective tool in helping shift teachers' views on the nature of intelligence and the individual differences among the students they teach. As a result, teachers are more likely to rethink their curricula to respond to individuals' needs. As one teacher in my research commented, "It makes me aware of what I'm doing. It makes me a better teacher and my students better learners. It's just a different way of thinking about teaching and learning." However, MI is not an educational end in itself and needs to be combined with other complementary approaches to curricula such as Maker's (1994) problem-solving continuum or an arts-based focus (Baum et al., 1996). Future research needs to focus on more rigorously evaluating the various curricula approaches being conducted throughout the world to complement the largely anecdotally based reports that dominate the MI literature.

Recently, I received an email from one of the students in my original research. His name is Andrew and he has just graduated from high school. As a 4-year-old, he had impressed me with his meticulous drawings of cartoon characters. In my conversations with Andrew and his family over the last 13 years, I have been surprised to see that the intellectual profile of Andrew I constructed in 1991 is still reasonably accurate despite the intervening years of education and experience. Most notably, Andrew's burning ambition is to become a cartoonist. This is surprising to me because I would have hypothesized that the intelligences are more open to change over time. It would seem that some longitudinal studies are needed to investigate the mutability of intelligence and the relationships among the intelligences. This research needs to adopt a multidisciplinary approach drawing on neurology, psychology, and sociology to give us a more complete view of this complex construct we know as human ability.

REFERENCES

Armstrong, T. (1994). *Multiple intelligences in the classroom.* Alexandria, VA: ASCD

Au, K. H. (1998). Social constructivism and the school literacy learning of students of diverse backgrounds. *Journal of Literacy Research, 30*(2), 297–319.

Au, K. H., & Mason, J. M. (1981). Social organizational factors in learning to read: The balance of rights hypothesis. *Reading Research Quarterly, 17*(1), 115–152.

Au, K. H., & Mason, J. M. (1983). Cultural congruence in classroom participation structures: Achieving a balance of rights. *Discourse Processes, 6*(2), 145–167.

Baum, S., Owen, S., & Oreck, B. (1996). Talent beyond words: Identification of potential talent in dance and music in elementary students. *Gifted Child Quarterly, 40*(2), 93–101.

Baum, S., Owen, S., & Oreck, B. (1997). Transferring individual self-regulation processes from arts to academics. *Arts Education Policy Review, 98*(4), 32, 39.

Bolanos, P. (1990). Restructuring the curriculum. *Principal, 69*(3), 13–14.

Bolanos, P. (1994). From theory to practice: Indianapolis' Key School applies Howard Gardner's multiple intelligences theory to the classroom. *The School Administrator, 51*(1), 30–31.

Boutte, G. S., & DeFlorimonte, D. (1998). The complexities of valuing cultural differences without overemphasizing them: Taking it to the next level. *Equity and Excellence in Education, 31*(3), 54–62.

Campbell, L., & Campbell, B. (1999). *Multiple intelligences and student achievement: Success stories from six schools.* Alexandria, VA: ASCD.

Campbell, L., Campbell, B., & Dickinson, D. (1992). *Teaching and learning through multiple intelligences.* Seattle, WA: Horizons for Learning.

Chapman, C. (1993). *If the shoe fits.* Melbourne: Hawker Brownlow.

Clark, B. (1990). *Using brain research as the basis for defining, identifying and nurturing giftedness.* Paper presented at NAGC Convention, Little Rock, AK.

Csikszentmihalyi, M. (1990). *Flow: The psychology of optimal experience.* New York: Harper Perennial.

Diaz, R. M., Neal, C. J., & Amaya-Williams, M. (1990). Social origins of self-regulation. In L. C. Moll (Ed.), *Vygotsky and education* (pp. 127–154). Cambridge, UK: Cambridge University Press.

Dixon-Krauss, L. (1996). *Vygotsky in the classroom: Mediated literacy instruction and assessment.* White Plains, NY: Longman.

Feuerstein, R., Rand, Y., Hoffman, M., & Miller, R. (1980). *Instrumental enrichment: an intervention program for cognitive modifiability.* Baltimore: University Park Press.

Ford, D. Y. (2003). Equity and excellence: Culturally diverse students in gifted education. In N. Colangelo & G. A. Davis (Eds.), *Handbook of gifted education* (3rd ed., pp. 506–520). Boston: Allyn & Bacon.

Gallagher, J. J. (2003). Issues and challenges in the education of gifted students. In N. Colangelo & G. A. Davis (Eds.), *Handbook of gifted education* (3rd ed., pp. 11–23). Boston: Allyn & Bacon.

Gardner, H. (1983). *Frames of mind.* New York: Basic Books.

Gardner, H. (1999). *Intelligence reframed.* New York: Basic Books.

Gardner, H. & Krechevsky, M. (1993). Approaching school intelligently: Practical intelligence at the middle school level. In H. Gardner, *Multiple intelligences: The theory in practice* (pp.119–133). New York: Basic Books.

Griffiths, S. (1997). *The comparative validity of assessments based on different theories for the purpose of identifying gifted ethnic minority students.* Unpublished doctoral dissertation, University of Arizona, Tucson, Arizona.

Haggerty, B. (1995). *Nurturing intelligences.* Menlo Pk, CA: Addison-Wesley.

Heath, S.B. (1983). *Ways with words.* Cambridge, UK: Cambridge University Press.

Howitt, D., & Owusu-Bempha, J. (1994). *The racism of psychology: Time for change.* New York: Harvester Wheatsheaf.

Kearins, J. (1976). Skills of desert Aboriginal children. In G. E. Kearney & D. W. McElwain (Eds.), *Aboriginal cognition: Retrospect and prospect* (pp. 199–212). Canberra: Australian Institute of Aboriginal Studies.

Kirschenbaum, R. J. (1998). Dynamic assessment and its use with underserved gifted and talented populations. *Gifted Child Quarterly, 42*(3), 140–147.

Kozol, J. (1991). *Savage inequalities.* New York: Crown.

Kozol, J. (1995). *Amazing grace.* New York: Crown.

Krechevsky, M. (1991). Project Spectrum: An innovative assessment alternative. *Educational Leadership, 48*(5), 43–48.

Krechevsky, M., & Gardner, H. (1990). The emergence and nurturance of multiple intelligences: the Project Spectrum approach. In Howe, M. (Ed.), *Encouraging the development of exceptional skills and talents* (pp. 222–245). Leicester, UK: British Psychological Society.

Ladson-Billings, G. (2001). *Crossing over to canaan: The journey of new teachers in diverse classrooms.* San Francisco: Jossey-Bass.

Maker, C. J. (1992). Intelligence and creativity in multiple intelligences: Identification and development. *Educating able learners: Discovering and nurturing talent, XVII*(4), 12–19.

Maker, C. J. (1993). Creativity, intelligence, and problem-solving: A definition and design for cross-cultural research and measurement related to giftedness. *Gifted Education International, 9*(2), 68–77.

Maker, C. J. (1994). Authentic assessment of problem solving and giftedness in secondary school students. *The Journal of Secondary Gifted Education, 6*(1), 19–26.

Maker, C. J. (1995). Lessons learned from the children. *Understanding Our Gifted, 8*(1), 1, 8–13.

Maker, C. J. (1996). Identification of gifted minority students: A national problem, needed changes and a promising solution. *Gifted Child Quarterly, 40*(1), 41–50.

Maker, C. J. (1997). DISCOVER Problem Solving Assessment *Quest, 8*(1), 3, 5, 7, 9.

Maker, C. J. (2004, May). *Exploring and discovering around the world.* A paper presented at the International Conference of Multiple Intelligences and its

Application and the Third Annual Conference of DISCOVER in China, Beijing.

Maker, C. J., Nielson, A. B., & Rogers, J. A. (1994). Giftedness, diversity, and problem-solving: Multiple intelligences and diversity in educational settings. *Teaching Exceptional Children, 27*(1), 4–19.

Maker, C. J., Rogers, J. A., Nielson, A. B., & Bauerle, P. (1996). Multiple Intelligences, problem solving, and diversity in the general classroom. *Journal for the Education of the Gifted, 19*(4), 437–460.

Mirza, H. (1992). *Young, female and black.* London: Routledge.

New City School. (1996). *Celebrating multiple intelligences: Teaching for success.* Melbourne: Hawker Brownlow Education.

Nielson, A. B. (1994). Traditional identification: Elitist, racist, sexist? New evidence. *CAG Communicator: The Journal of the California Association for the Gifted, 24*(3), 18–19, 26–31.

Pallas, A.M., Natriello, G. & McDill, E.L. (1989). Changing nature of the disadvantaged population: Current dimensions and future trends. *Educational Researcher, 18*(5), 16–22.

Perkins, D. (1995). *Outsmarting IQ: The emerging science of learnable intelligence.* New York: The Free Press.

Pigott, R. L., & Cowen, E. L. (2000). Teacher race, child race, racial congruence, and teacher ratings of children's school adjustment. *Journal of School Psychology, 38*(2), 177–196.

Plucker, J. A., Callahan, C. M., & Tomchin, E. M. (1996). Wherefore art thou, multiple intelligences? Alternative assessments for identifying talent in ethnically diverse and low income students. *Gifted Child Quarterly, 40*(2), 81–92.

Roth, W. (1992). Dynamic and authentic assessment: An approach for assessing cognitive change and learning in authentic settings. *Science Scope, 15*(6), 37–40.

Sarouphim, K. M. (1999a). DISCOVER: A promising alternative assessment for the identification of gifted minorities. *Gifted Child Quarterly, 43*(4), 244–251.

Sarouphim, K. M. (1999b). Discovering multiple intelligences through a performance-based assessment: Consistency with independent ratings. *Exceptional Children, 65*(2), 151–161.

Sarouphim, K. M. (2000). Internal structure of DISCOVER: A performance-based assessment. *Journal for the Education of the Gifted, 23*(3), 314–327.

Scrimsher, S., & Tudge, J. (2003). The teaching/learning relationship in the first years of school: Some revolutionary implications of Vygotsky's theory. *Early Education and Development, 14*(3), 293–312.

Shore, B., Cornell, D., Robinson, A., & Ward, V. (1991). *Recommended practices in gifted education: A critical analysis.* New York: Teachers College Press.

Sisk, D. & Torrance, E. P. (2001). *Spiritual intelligence: Developing a higher consciousness.* New York: Creative Education Foundation.

Sternberg, R. (1986). *Intelligence applied.* San Diego, CA: Harcourt Brace Jovanovich.

Sternberg, R. (2000). Patterns of giftedness: A triarchic analysis. *Roeper Review, 22*, 231–240.

Suhor, C. (1999). Spirituality – Letting it grow in the classroom. *Educational Leadership, 56*(4), 12–16.

Tharp, R. G., & Gallimore, R. (1988). *Rousing minds to life.* New York: Cambridge University Press.

Vialle, W. (1991). *Tuesday's children: A study of five children using multiple intelligences theory as a framework.* Unpublished doctoral dissertation, University of South Florida.

Vialle, W. (1993a). The prism study. In Rosselli, H. & MacLauchlan, G. (Eds.), *Blue printing for the future* (pp. 123–149). Tampa: University of South Florida.

Vialle, W. (1993b). Tuesday's children: Case studies of African-American pre-schoolers. Culture, dominance and control: Indigenous peoples, minorities and education. In *Proceedings of the 21st Annual International Conference of the Australian and New Zealand Comparative and International Education Society* (pp. 35–46). Wollongong:ANZCIES.

Vialle, W. (1994a). Identifying children's diverse strengths: A broader framework for cognitive assessment. In Long, P. (Ed.), *Quality outcomes for all learners* (pp. 90–100). Clifton Hill, Victoria: Australian Association of Special Education Inc.

Vialle, W. (1994b, November). *Racism in the classroom.* A paper presented at the annual conference of the Australian Association for Research in Education, Newcastle.

Vialle, W. (1995). Giftedness in culturally diverse groups: The MI perspective. *Australasian Journal of Gifted Education, 4*(1), 5–11.

Vialle, W., & Perry, J. (2002). *Teaching through the eight intelligences.* Melbourne: Hawker Brownlow Education.

Vygotsky, L. (1978). *Mind in society.* Cambridge, MA: Harvard University Press.

Wellman, D. (1993). *Portraits of white racism.* Cambridge, UK: Cambridge University Press.

Wertsch, J. V. (1985). *Vygotsky and the social formation of mind.* Cambridge, MA: Harvard University Press.

Wertsch, J. V. (1998). *Mind as action.* Oxford, UK: Oxford University Press.

Wetherell, M., & Potter, J. (1992). *Mapping the language of racism.* New York: Harvester Wheatsheaf.

Zohar, D., & Marshall, I. (2000). *SQ—Spiritual intelligence: The ultimate intelligence.* London: Bloomsbury.

CHAPTER 8

INSIDE CULTURE AND CURRICULUM

Religious and Sex Differences among Arabic Students' Perceptions of Personal Development, Health, and Physical Education

Dennis M. McInerney, Martin Dowson, and Alexander Seeshing Yeung

Sociocultural studies in psychology often investigate differences between cultural groups with respect to psychological variables of interest. However, it is also of interest in sociocultural studies to investigate intracultural psychological differences, especially amongst non-Western cultural groups. An examination of intracultural differences can alert researchers and practitioners to within-culture variables that may influence sociocultural differences and dynamics.

Investigations of intracultural differences are of particular interest where a given cultural group exists within a dominant culture, as is the case with non-Western cultural groups existing in Western societies. The

Focus on Curriculum, 199–221
Copyright © 2005 by Information Age Publishing
All rights of reproduction in any form reserved.

reason for this interest is that a deeper understanding of minority cultural groups, including intracultural differences that may exist within these groups, can enhance our understanding of how minority groups "operate" within a dominant culture. Too often, cultural and ethnic groups are stereotyped as homogeneous, even when intracultural differences may be stronger than intercultural differences. Thus, there is a need to develop an understanding of what types of differences may exist within cultural groups in order to understand how they operate in educational and other relevant settings (Gutiérrez & Rogof, 2003; Tucker & Herman, 2002). This understanding should lead to a greater cross-cultural sensitivity in policy, curriculum, and program development and application within majority cultures characterised by diversity. This is an important objective of socio-cultural studies.

The study reported in this chapter investigates intracultural religious and sex differences among students of Arabic-language backgrounds in Australia. These differences were investigated with respect to students' perceptions of physical development, health, and physical education (PDHPE) curricula. The specific aim of the research was to develop a deeper understanding of intracultural differences with respect to PDHPE so that PDHPE policies and programs may be targeted more specifically toward the diverse needs of students from Arabic-language backgrounds. The more general aim of the chapter is to use this research to demonstrate that investigating intracultural differences can lead to the development of sociocultural insights of both theoretical and practical importance and relevance.

PERSONAL DEVELOPMENT, HEALTH, AND PHYSICAL EDUCATION

Many nations are becoming increasingly diverse as a result of voluntary immigration and the international movement of refugees. As a result, school systems that once developed educational programs for relatively homogeneous populations are now confronted with the need to sensitise their programs to the needs and values of students from diverse cultures, language backgrounds, and religions (Kalantzis, Cope, Noble, & Poynting, 1990; McDonald & Fairfax, 1993; McInerney, 1987a, 1987b, 1991; Smolicz, 1995).

One area of education that has proved particularly problematic in this respect is personal development, health, and physical education (see DeSensi, 1994, 1995; Sparks & Wayman, 1993; Swisher & Swisher, 1986; Wessinger, 1994). Specifically, it has been suggested that the values conveyed in school PDHPE programs may substantially conflict with the values emphasized by culturally and religiously diverse family and social groups (King, 1994; Smith, 1991). This, in turn, may have significant implications for student motivation, absenteeism, and achievement in PDHPE studies.

There is some evidence that this conflict may be particularly pro-nounced among Arabic communities (Abdel-Halem, 1989; Ahmed, 1992), particularly those Arabic communities where Islam is the dominant religion (Carroll & Hollinshead; 1993; Kalantzis, et al., 1990; Lindsay, McEwan, & Knight, 1987). In these communities, beliefs and practices relevant to PDHPE may diverge substantially from the teaching practices and content typical of PDHPE curricula. With regard to teaching prac-tices, for example, Islam encourages and recommends physical education and sports (e.g., "Teach your children to run, swim, ride and throw the javelin"; Abdel-Halim, 1989, p. 16). However, there are also many stric-tures on how physical education might be appropriately undertaken (Ahmed, 1992). These strictures include the requirement that boys and girls should be separated for particular activities at the age of puberty, and that under no circumstances should any part of the female body, with the exception of the face and hands, be exposed (Abdel-Halim, 1989). For these reasons, male and female Islamic students who adhere to Islamic teachings should not mix in physical education classes, and girls should not use costumes or uniforms that expose their body (Abdel-Halim, 1989). Moreover, although there are apparently fewer restrictions on boys, shared male showers and common change rooms are not permitted (Abdel-Halim, 1989; Ahmed, 1992).

It is also possible that specific content taught within PDHPE (e.g., dietary habits, personal decision making, drug use and safety, community health, relationship building, parent-craft, sex education and contracep-tion) may impact upon Arabic, and particularly Arabic-Islamic, students' participation in and enjoyment of PDHPE (Carroll & Hollinshead, 1993; Clyne, 1994; Lindsay, et al., 1987; Siraj-Blatchford, 1993; Williams, 1989). In addition, observance of Ramadan, during which fasting is required, may impact substantially upon Islamic students' physical ability (let alone their psychological choice) to participate in physical activity.

Due to these cultural and religious considerations, Arabic-Islamic par-ents expect a general sensitivity to the way PDHPE content is approached and presented, especially with regard to potentially controversial topics and experiences (Abdel-Halim, 1989; Williams, 1989). This expectation is no doubt communicated to their children, and if violated, may compro-mise students' participation in PDHPE activities.

RELIGIOUS DIFFERENCES AMONG CULTURAL GROUPS

Culture and religion are not necessarily convergent with respect to the development of beliefs, values, and practices (McInerney, 1991; McInerney, Davidson, Suliman, & Tremayne, 2000; Sparkes & Wayman, 1993). Thus, the same cultural group may exhibit divergent beliefs and values, and these divergences may be attributable to religion. While a majority of Arabic communities practice the Islamic faith, sizable Christian communities also come from Arabic backgrounds (McInerney et al., 2000). It is possible, then, that religious background may be influential in determining Arabic people's beliefs and values, including in potentially contentious areas such as PDHPE in schools. Despite this, little research has been conducted to verify (or otherwise) the existence of differences in attitudes toward PDHPE, which may be attributable to religion when holding cultural background as a constant. Hence, it may be that conflicts involved in teaching PDHPE that are hypothesized to be related to Arabic culture may in fact be more properly attributed to religious differences among Arabic students. In other words, it may not be valid to talk about "Arabic students" as if they were a homogeneous group with respect to their PDHPE perceptions. Rather, religious differences within Arabic communities may account for quite different perceptions of PDHPE education.

Given this possibility, the study reported in this chapter sought to investigate the perceptions of Arabic students from two different religious groups, Islamic and Catholic, toward PDHPE. Specifically, we suggest that intracultural religious differences may influence Arabic students' attitudes toward PDHPE. If this is shown to be true, it may be possible to use the research to make particular recommendations concerning the structure and teaching of PDHPE, not just for Arabic students as a whole, but for religious subgroups within Arabic student populations.

SEX AND RELIGIOUS DIFFERENCES IN PDHPE PERCEPTIONS

Not only may religious differences among Arabic students account for their differing perceptions of PDHPE, but sex differences both of themselves, and related to religious differences, may also have a profound effect on PDHPE perceptions (Ahmed, 1992; Lindsay et al., 1987; Sanders, 1989). It may be, for example, that Muslim and/or Catholic girls hold very different perceptions toward PDHPE than Muslim and Catholic boys. This may also be the case despite religious differences common to both boys and girls that effect PDHPE perceptions. In fact, we directly hypothesize that Muslim girls (due to the particular strictures placed on them by Islamic teachings) will hold quantifiably different perceptions toward PDHPE than Muslim boys, and different perceptions than Catholic boys and girls. Given this hypothesis, we investigate both religious and sex differences, and the individual and interactive effects these may have on Arabic students' PDHPE perceptions.

PURPOSE AND OBJECTIVES

The purpose of the study reported in this chapter was to investigate intracultural religious and sex differences in Arabic language-background students' perceptions of personal development, health, and physical education. This purpose, as indicated above, is directed toward the broader aim of developing a deeper understanding of how diversity within cultural groups may influence perceptions in at least one important educational context.

The specific objectives of this study were to:

1. validate for Islamic and Catholic students of Arabic background a set of scales that reflect their values and attitudes toward PDHPE;
2. examine group differences (Islamic/Catholic and female/male) in attitudes toward PDHPE based on these scales;
3. identify key variables acting as predictors of interest in, and valuing of, PDHPE among both male and female Islamic and Catholic Arabic students;
4. consider implications of the findings of the study for developing effective educational practices for PDHPE in settings characterized by intracultural religious diversity.

METHOD

Participants and Setting

Four high schools cooperated in this research. The students of one school were male only (a state school), two schools were female only (one state school and one Catholic school), and one school was coeducational (a state school). The schools are located in predominantly Arabic-speaking areas in the southwestern region of Sydney. A sample ($n = 278$) of students from Arabic language backgrounds was selected. For the purposes of this study, students from an Arabic-language background were defined as those whose parents both spoke Arabic (almost all of these were also from Lebanon), and who regularly spoke Arabic at home. Of these students, 125 (85 boys, 40 girls) nominated their religion as Islamic and 153 (35 boys, 118 girls) nominated that their religion was Catholic.

Each of the schools was concerned about a number of PDHPE-related issues including the lack of participation of students in competitive and noncompetitive sports and sports carnivals and the apparent lack of fitness of students. Furthermore, many students appeared to lack interest in the PDHPE program as a whole. Moreover, teachers commented on how difficult it was to design and implement culturally sensitive study programs in PDHPE.

The research setting (geographic, cultural, and educational) is of interest for several reasons. The southwestern area of Sydney is typical of many such areas in major cities in the Western world where a minority cultural group (as far as the city as a whole is concerned) is in fact the dominant cultural group in a particular geographic area of the city. This establishes some interesting sociocultural dynamics that are often acutely experienced in schools (which are, of course, a key societal institution with which all cultural groups must interact). For example, school curricula framed by, and for, the dominant cultural group are not atypically treated with suspicion and even contempt by minority groups (e.g. Hernandez, 1995; Mintz & Yun, 2001; Segarra & Dobles, 1999). Moreover, where these minority groups are predominant (as is the case in "enclave" areas such as that dealt with in this study) they may exert considerable overt pressure to have school curricula modified or even (at least in part) abandoned. Alternatively, these groups may adopt a "silent protest" form of resistance against certain educational activities or curricula areas as whole. The existence of this type of protest, on face value, appeared to be the case in this study with respect to PDHPE programs.

In this context, PDHPE programs represent one point at which culture "clashes" may be particularly pronounced. This is because PDHPE programs, as we have suggested above, may be particularly confronting to certain cultural groups. Despite this confrontation, PDHPE programs (in one form or another) are compulsory in schools across the Western world, not just in Australia. Thus, studies of potential intracultural cultural dynamics that may influence the delivery and acceptance of PDHPE programs may provide important perspectives that are applicable in a wide range of educational settings.

Materials

Measures of Religious Commitment

Students were asked a number of questions in order to ascertain the nature and level of their religious commitment. These questions were important as they provided the opportunity to gather evidence that participants' religious beliefs were reflected in their actual practices, and were not just "nominal" beliefs. Such evidence would provide a basis upon which sensible comparisons between religious groups with respect to PDHPE perceptions may be made.

Specifically, students were first asked how often they practiced their religion (with three response categories provided, i.e., "frequently," "occasionally," and "never"). Participants were then asked (in an open-ended question without response categories) to describe the type of religious practices in which they engaged. After a preliminary qualitative analysis of students' answers to this question, these practices were grouped into three categories: public practices of religion, personal religious devotions, and complying with ethical rules. Next, participants were asked whether their religious practices were important to them (with a "yes," "no," and "don't know" response format provided). Finally, participants were asked (in another open-ended question) why their religious practices were important to them. Answers to this question did not lend themselves to further categorization, and as such were simply tabulated according to the specific answers given.

Main Survey

A survey was constructed to measure relevant dimensions of students' PDHPE perceptions. Descriptions of the six scales and their composite items constructed to measure these dimensions follow.

Perceived parental support. Perceived parental support was inferred from four items asking students if their parents found the student's PDHPE program important, and whether their parents encouraged them in their PDHPE program. The items were coded such that higher scores reflected greater parental support.

Dislike of physical activity and embarrassment. Dislike of, and embarrassment within, physical activities were inferred from three items coded such that higher scores reflected greater dislike or embarrassment.

Mixed-sex activity. Three questions asked students if they believed that their school should encourage mixed-sex PDHPE activities. Higher scores reflected more favorable views toward mixed-sex activities.

Sex education. Four questions asked students whether their school should include sex education topics in PDHPE programs. Higher scores reflected more favorable views toward the inclusion of such topics.

Interest. Four questions asked students to rate their interest in their school's PDHPE program. Higher scores reflected greater interest in the program.

Importance.   Four questions asked if PDHPE was important to students. Higher scores reflected higher perceptions of importance.

All the items in the survey used a 5-point Likert-type scale ranging from 1 (strongly disagree) to 5 (strongly agree).

Administration

The surveys were administered in English, the language of instruction of the students. However, the survey was read aloud to avoid any difficulties students might encounter with the language of the survey.

Statistical Analyses

In cross-cultural research it is essential to demonstrate that the research measures used have cultural validity, and are reliable (Byrne, 1998, 2003). "Cultural validity" refers to the extent to which, particularly self-report measures, are interpreted by different cultural groups in the manner in which they were intended to be interpreted. The same principle applies to intracultural differences (i.e., "Do subgroups within a given cultural group interpret measures in a consistent manner?").

In order to demonstrate the applicability of our scales to the Arabic subgroups (Muslim and Catholic) in our study, we utilized Invariance Tests within a confirmatory factor analysis (CFA) framework. Invariance tests assess the degree to which (in this case) intracultural groups interpret survey items as measuring the same underlying constructs (e.g., parental support, dislike of PDHPE, interest, etc.). Again, it was important to specify the degree of invariance (or otherwise) because it was possible that the Muslim and Catholic subsamples in the study may have interpreted the survey in different ways. If this was the case, then data from the study would be difficult to interpret, and any findings or conclusions based on these interpretations may be compromised.

In order to avoid difficulties associated with unrecognized noninvariance, we first tested whether, in this Arabic setting, the data in the study supported a delineation of the six a priori PDHPE scales described above. Second, we tested whether these scales were invariant across the Muslim and Catholic subgroups. We will not go into substantial detail here regarding how we conducted and measured the accuracy of the invariance tests (for further details, see Byrne, 1998; Mueller, 1996). Briefly, however, we tested a structured sequence of invariant models, which constrained various aspects of the models to be invariant between the Muslim and Catholic subgroups. We then tested the accuracy of each model using various "fit indices." These indices measure the degree to which the data supported the invariant models "imposed" on them. The fit indices are scaled from 0 to 1, with 1 indicating perfect model fit with the data, and 0 indicating perfect misfit with the data. Generally, values over .9 are considered to indicate "good" model fit. We also examined the reliability of each scale using Cronbach's alpha.

Once the properties of the scales across subgroups had been established through the procedures outlined above, a series of structural equation models (SEMs) were used to test relationships between the scales. Specifically, we proposed that Parent Support, Dislike of Physical Activity, Mixed-Sex Activity, and Sex Education would all influence students' interest in, and the importance they ascribed to, PDHPE. For this reason, we tested models where the first four factors (scales) were modeled to "cause" the last two factors. In these models, it was of particular interest to examine the relative strength of the predictors (the first four factors) on the last two factors across the two religious groups. This is because the strength of these predictors may vary across groups, thus revealing some interesting cross-group comparisons. The between-group (Muslim–Catholic) invariance and goodness-of-fit of these models was also tested.

Gender × Religion Differences in PDHPE Perceptions

It was also of interest in this research to determine whether male and female Islamic and Catholic students held different (or similar) perceptions of PDHPE. In other words, while a primary focus of the research was on religious differences among Arabic-language background students, any effect that sex might have on these differences should not be ignored. In order to compare responses by Islamic and Catholic boys and girls for each of the six scales considered here, the responses for each scale were first averaged. Then, a 2 (Religion: Islamic, Catholic) × 2 (Gender) multivariate analysis of variance (MANOVA), and follow-up one-way ANOVAs, was conducted in order to identify any main and interaction effects of religion and gender with respect to PDHPE perceptions.

RESULTS

Frequency, Type, and Importance of Religious Practices

With respect to the frequency of religious practice, 42% of the Islamic students indicated that they practiced their religion frequently, 52% occasionally, and 6% never. The corresponding figures for the Catholic students were 34%, 57%, and 9%. These results suggest that there is a high level of religious commitment within each group, with very few students (less than 10% in each case) indicating that they never actively practiced their religion.

Among the specific religious practices most often cited by the Islamic respondents were:

1. public religious practices (66%) such as visiting Mecca, celebrating Eid, visiting a mosque, and participating in religious festivals;
2. personal religious devotions (61%) such as prayer, fasting, and chants; and
3. complying with ethical rules and regulations (18%), such as not smoking, not drinking, giving money to the poor, and dressing appropriately.

Among the traditions most often cited by the Catholic respondents were:

1. public religious practices (81%) such as attending mass, taking Holy Communion, confession, and religious festivals,
2. personal religious devotions (8%) such as prayer and fasting; and
3. complying with ethical rules and regulations (20%).

These responses are summarized in Figure 8.1.

An interesting feature of these responses is that the level of public religious practice is statistically significantly higher ($\chi^2 = 8.12, p < .005$) and the levels of personal religious devotions ($\chi^2 = 46.55, p < .005$) significantly lower for Catholic students than for Islamic students. In contrast,

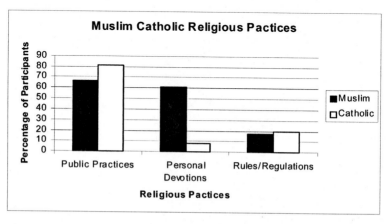

Figure 8.1.   Comparison of Muslim and Catholic religious practices.

very similar proportions of both groups (χ^2 = 1.68, p > .05) reported practicing compliance with ethical rules and regulations.

Eight percent of Islamic students responded that the practices noted were "not important," and 18% did not know or did not respond. Thus, nearly three-quarters of Islamic students responded that their religious practices were important to them.

Among the reasons given by Islamic students for the importance of their religious practices were that they:

1. were in the Koran (3%);
2. expressed intrapersonal religious commitment (46%) (e.g., "I believe in it" or "It's important to me");
3. expressed a recognition of external compulsion (13%) (e.g., "We must be obedient to God"); and
4. expressed a recognition of parental and/or cultural influences (25%) (e.g., "My parents think it's important" or "It's part of our culture").

Thirteen percent of Catholic students responded that religious practices were not important, and 11% did not know or did not respond. Thus, just over three-quarters of Catholic students felt their religious practices were important to them.

Among the reasons given for the importance of Catholic students' religious practices were that they:

1. were in the Bible (15%);
2. expressed intrapersonal religious commitment (20%);
3. reflected external compulsion (3%); and
4. reflected parental and cultural influences (50%).

These results are summarized in Figure 8.2.

These results again suggest interesting differences between the two groups with respect to the reasons given for the importance of religious practices. Specifically, Catholic students emphasized the Bible more than Islamic students emphasized the Koran (χ^2 = 13.37, p > .001). Conversely, Islamic students emphasized intrapersonal (χ^2 = 8.19, p > .005) and external (χ^2 = 5.76, p < .05) reasons for the importance of religious practices more than the Catholic students. Finally, Catholic students emphasized parental and cultural influences on the assigned importance of religious practices more than Islamic students (χ^2 = 19.5, p < .001). Indeed, the finding that the Catholic students emphasized family and cultural reasons for practicing their religion more so than the Islamic stu-

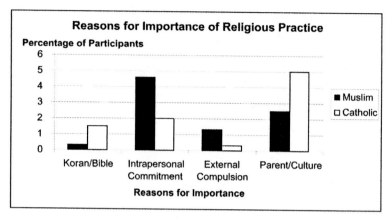

Figure 8.2.   Comparison of Muslim-Catholic reasons for importance of religous practices.

dents is somewhat surprising given the widespread perception that there is a strong link between familial and cultural influences and religious practices within Arabic-Islamic groups.

Psychometric Modeling Results

Alpha reliability estimates for each of the six scales (see Appendix) ranged from .65 to .87 (*Mdn* = .75). Four of the six scales had reliabilities above .70, and of these two had reliabilities above .80.

A full discussion of the measurement and causal models tested in this study is not attempted here. Rather, we report the main features of the modeling processes and refer the reader to McInerney, Dowson, and Yeung (in review) for further details.

Table 8.1 presents a summary of the goodness of fit of the CFA and Causal models tested in the study, the invariance of these models across religious groups, and the null models from which the TLI (Tucker–Lewis Index) and RNI (Relative Noncentrality Index) fit indices are derived.

Table 8.1 indicates that most of the tested models fit the data well (i.e., they displayed fit indices above .90). Where the fit of models was lower than normally accepted (i.e., where fit indices were below .90), we made various modifications to the models in order to improve their fit. Thus, the latter models (reported toward the end of each block of models in Table 8.1) all demonstrated good fit with the data. Taken together, these results demonstrate the robust psychometric properties of the instrument utilized in the study, the validity of the causal models imposed on the

Table 8.1.   Goodness-of-Fit Summary of Models and Path Coefficients

Model	χ^2	df	N	TLI	RNI
1. Null model total sample	2,954.49	231	349		
2. Null model Islamic	1,098.49	231	120		
3. Null model Catholic	1,388.74	231	149		
4. 6 factors, total sample, no CU	539.37	194	349	.8490	.873
5. 6 factors, Islamic, no CU	298.90	194	120	.8560	.879
6. 6 factors, Catholic, no CU	394.21	194	149	.7941	.827
7. 6 factors, total sample, CU	313.97	191	349	.9454	.955
8. 6 factors, Islamic, CU	234.09	191	120	.9399	.950
9. 6 factors, Catholic, CU	276.87	191	149	.9103	.926
10. 2-group Factorial Invariance Models					
a. 6 factors total invariance	713.10	444	269	.8617	.867
b. 6 factors total noninvariance	510.96	382	269	.9230	.936
c. 6 factors, FL invariant	525.44	398	269	.9270	.937
d. 6 factors, FL & FC invariant	557.62	419	269	.9245	.932
11. 2-group Causal Models					
a. Total invariance	713.10	444	269	.8617	.867
b. Total noninvariance	510.96	382	269	.9230	.936
c. FL, R, & U invariant	700.86	436	269	.8614	.869
d. FL, PC, & U invariant	681.52	431	269	.8674	.876
e. FL & U invariant	669.89	423	269	.8669	.878
f. FL, PC, & R invariant	557.62	419	269	.9245	.932
g. FL & R invariant	546.55	411	269	.9248	.933
h. FL & PC invariant	536.16	406	269	.9269	.936
i. FL invariant	525.44	398	269	.9270	.937

Note: TLI, Tucker–Lewis index; RNI, Relative Noncentrality Index. Measurement models were tested with and without correlated uniquenesses (CU). A series of models were tested for invariance of factor loadings (FL), or factor correlations (FC), or path coefficients (PC), or residuals (R), or uniquenesses (U), or a combination of these across groups, but a summary of only the critical models is reported.
* $p < .05$.

data, and the substantial invariance of the instrument and the models across religious groups.

Differential Effects of Features on PDHPE Interest and Importance

Figure 8.3 shows the final model, for both Muslim and Catholic students, relating PDHPE features (Parental Support, Embarrassment, Mixed-Sex

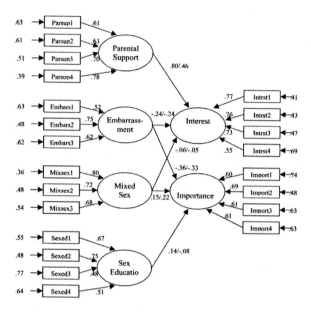

(NB. The structural paths in Figure 8.1 have two coefficients (in the form .xx/.xx). The first coefficient is for the Islamic subsample, and the second coefficient is for the Catholic subsample. All other (measurement) coefficients are for the sample as a whole. The structural paths from Sex Education to Interest (−.04/.02) and Parental Support to Importance (.47/.63) are not shown for the sake of clarity.)

Figure 8.3.   Path model latent PDHPE variables (from Table 8.3).

Activities, and Sex Education) to interest in, and importance ascribed to, PDHPE.

Figure 8.3 shows that Parental Support is strongly and positively related to both PDHPE Interest and Importance for both Muslim and Catholic students. Conversely, Embarrassment is strongly but negatively related to Interest and Importance for both groups. Relationships between Mixed-Sex Activities and Sex Education and PDHPE Interest and Importance are weaker and less consistent for both groups than is the case with Parental Support and Embarrassment. These findings suggest that Parental Support and Embarrassment are the key positive and negative influences, respectively, on both Muslim and Catholic students' PDHPE Interest and Importance.

Religion and Sex Differences

On the basis of the CFAs and reliability analyses, the mean responses of the Islamic and Catholic students with respect to each of the six factors were computed and compared. The means and standard errors of responses by Islamic and Catholic boys and girls are presented in Table 8.2. All standard errors for the means, with the exception of Islamic Females on Mixed Sex Activities, are below 1.00.

In order to test whether any significant differences reflected religious and/or sex differences, a 2 (Religion: Islamic, Catholic) × 2 (Sex) MANOVA was conducted. The analysis found a statistically significant main effect of Religion (F (6, 268) = 5.70, p < .001, effect size = .11); a marginally significant main effect of Sex (F (6, 268) = 2.48, p < .05, effect size = .05); and a statistically significant Religion x Sex interaction effect (F (6, 268) = 2.92, p < .01, effect size = .06).

Decomposition of Main Effects

Univariate F-statistics (in Table 8.2) showed that Catholic students reported higher Perceived Parental Support than Islamic students, were more positive about Mixed-Sex Activity, and were more positive about Sex Education. Conversely, Islamic students had stronger feelings of Disliking Physical Activities and Embarrassment. Differences in interest and perceived importance were statistically nonsignificant. Interestingly, all univariate estimates for the Sex effects were statistically nonsignificant (Table 8.2).

Decomposition of Interaction Effects

Univariate analyses of the statistically significant Religion × Sex effect showed that not only were Islamic students' ratings of Mixed-Sex Activity significantly lower than Catholic students, but that Islamic girls' ratings were significantly lower again. The significant Religion x Sex interaction effect for the Interest factor indicated that Catholic girls reported the highest interest in PDHPE, Catholic boys the lowest interest, with both Islamic sex groups between these two means. Thus, sex differences within the Catholic group are much more pronounced than those in the Islamic group.

Second, in order to compare religious differences in each sex group more closely, MANOVAs were conducted separately for boys and girls. For boys, the MANOVA found statistically significant effects of Religion (F (6, 113) = 2.46, p <.05, effect size = .12). However, univariate F-statistics showed that Catholic boys rated only Perceived Parental Support higher than Islamic boys (F (6, 118) = 4.04, p < .05, effect size = .03). For girls, the MANOVA found statistically significant effects of Religion (F (6, 150) = 6.01, p < .001, effect size = .19). Univariate F-statistics indicated that Islamic girls disliked physical activity and were embarrassed more than Catholic girls (F (1, 155) = 10.25, p < .01, effect sizes = .06). The MANOVAs also indicated that Catholic girls were more positive than

Table 8.2. Means and Standard Deviations of Responses by Islamic and Catholic Boys and Girls and Univariate F-Statistics

| | Islamic | | | | Catholic | | | | Main Effects | | | | Interaction | |
| | Boys (N=85) | | Girls (N=40) | | Boys (N=35) | | Girls (N=117) | | Religion(R) | | Gender(G) | | C x G | |
Variable	M	SE	M	SE	M	SE	M	SE	F(1,273)	E	F(1,273)	E	F(1,273)	E
PARSUP	3.47	(0.91)	3.58	(0.79)	3.83	(0.84)	3.78	(0.73)	6.56*	.02	0.07	.00	0.49	.00
EMBARS	2.26	(0.98)	2.37	(0.89)	2.02	(0.86)	1.90	(0.75)	9.04**	.03	0.00	.00	0.91	.00
MIXSEX	3.89	(0.97)	3.38	(1.23)	3.95	(0.84)	3.99	(0.89)	6.52*	.02	3.20	.01	4.45*	.02
SEXEDU	3.44	(0.70)	3.41	(0.68)	3.62	(0.63)	3.90	(0.51)	15.96***	.06	2.28	.01	3.35	.01
INTRST	3.43	(0.90)	3.33	(0.88)	3.28	(0.97)	3.75	(0.69)	1.52	.01	2.80	.01	6.62*	.02
IMPORT	4.05	(0.81)	3.89	(0.80)	3.94	(0.82)	3.93	(0.77)	0.11	.00	0.64	.00	0.56	.00

Note: $N = 277$. The variables were Perceived parent support (PARSUP), Dislike physical activity and embarrassment (EMBARS), Mixed-sex activity (MIXSEX), Sex education (SEXEDU), Interest (INTRST), and Importance (IMPORT). E, effect size. * $p < .05$. ** $p < .01$. *** $p < .001$. F-statistics are univariate estimates from the 2 (Religion) x 2 (Sex) MANOVA.

Islamic girls toward Mixed-Sex Activity (F (1, 155) = 11.39, $p < .01$, effect size = .07) and Sex Education (Fs (1, 155) = 22.54, $p < .001$, effect size = .13). Catholic girls also showed greater interest (F (1, 155) = 9.84, $p < .01$, effect size = .06).

DISCUSSION

Religion as an Important Intracultural Construct

The levels of reported adherence to religious practices among students in this study, and that fact that approximately three-quarters of both Islamic and Catholic students reported that their religious practices were important to them, suggest that religion is a potentially important construct to consider when investigating Arabic sociocultural dynamics in educational settings. We know from other studies that the reported levels of religious practice among Anglo-Australians (e.g., Kaldor, 1987) is much less than that reported by Arabic students in this study. Thus, it may be that Australian Arabic students, whether they be Islamic or Catholic, are much more religiously committed than the dominant Anglo cultural groups in which they are embedded.

Second, although religion appeared to be an important intracultural construct for Arabic students, the particular type of religion practiced also appeared to differentiate between patterns of students' reported religious practices. Thus, Islamic and Catholic students report different patterns of adherence to particular religious practices. This may be particularly important in educational settings. For example, Islamic-Arabic students' personal religious devotions (prayer, fasting, and chants) may interfere with their participation in educational activities, particularly in the PDHPE domain. Conversely, the relatively low participation of Catholic students in these types of devotions presumably poses little threat to their participation in PDHPE activities. It may not be sufficient, then, to frame educational policy for Arabic students per se. In contrast, it may be necessary to frame policy (at least in PDHPE) for particular religious groups among Arabic students.

Finally, the fact that intrapersonal and parental-cultural reasons, as opposed to external and theological reasons, were provided more often for the importance of religious commitment suggests that students' religious beliefs are embedded in their personal, familial, and cultural identities. This, in turn, suggests that these beliefs are likely to influence students' perceptions.

Implications for PDHPE Curricula

The provision of generalized curricula, and "one-size-fits-all" modes of delivery, is based on the assumption of substantial homogeneity in student populations. However, particularly in potentially sensitive areas such as PDHPE, where pertinent cultural and/or religious values and beliefs may differ markedly within and among groups, this assumption is very questionable.

Using a construct validation approach, this study found both similarities and differences in values and beliefs about PDHPE among Arabic-Islamic and Arabic-Catholic students. In particular, the results showed that Arabic-Islamic and Arabic-Catholic students differed in their perceptions of parental support for PDHPE, their dislike of, and embarrassment in, physical activities, and their attitudes toward mixed-sex activity and sex education. Moreover, for both the Islamic and Catholic groups, perceived parental support and dislike of physical activity and embarrassment had strong impacts on their interest in, and the importance they assigned to, PDHPE.

Each of the schools in the survey indicated that they thought parental support for PDHPE was low, and that there was little interest from parents in students' active involvement in physical activities in school. Supporting this observation, a large number of students in this study also suggested that parental support for PDHPE was low. Also, this study suggests that perceived parental support could be a significant predictor of interest in, and the importance assigned to, PDHPE. Hence, it is probably critical that schools liaise effectively with parents concerning PDHPE programs and their importance. In this way, parents may be able to provide more of the support that underpins student interest in, and valuing of, PDHPE. This may be particularly important for Arabic-Islamic students (especially boys) who, in this study, did not report as much parental support as their Catholic peers.

Disliking physical activity and embarrassment was found to have detrimental impacts on both PDHPE interest and perceived PDHPE importance. This was particularly true among Islamic girls. It is important, therefore, that the implementation of PDHPE curricula be particularly sensitive to sex-based cultural issues (such as dress and public performance) that are likely to be of particular concern to Islamic females. If such an approach was adopted, the participation of Islamic females in PDHPE may be enhanced.

Mixed-sex activity was apparently more acceptable among Arabic-Catholic students than Arabic-Islamic students. However, Islamic girls were even less supportive of mixed-sex activities than Islamic boys. This finding probably reflects values that are emphasized in Islamic communities, in particular those values that relate to appropriate sex roles for females. Conversely, Catholic students' views probably reflect somewhat less stringency concerning female sex roles and, hence, the perceived appropriateness of mixed-sex activities. Whatever the case, the findings concerning mixed-sex activity again highlight the vulnerability of Islamic females with respect to participation in PDHPE.

The main effect of religion on sex education was (statistically) the most significant effect in the research, with Catholic students (regardless of sex, which is interesting in itself) reporting being much more supportive of sex education than Islamic students. It might have been expected, for example, that Arabic girls regardless of religion would be more sensitive to sex education than Arabic boys of either religious background (implying that there would either be a main effect of sex, or perhaps interaction effect, for sex education). Alongside the strength of the main effect of religion, the fact that neither of these latter effects was significant suggests that religion in and of itself is a particularly important determinant of differences in attitudes to sex education.

The strength and specificity of the main effect of religion on sex education suggests the possibility that both the content of sex education within PDHPE curricula, and the perceived inappropriateness of the ways in which such content is presented (as judged by Islamic values), may contribute to the more negative perceptions of sex education among Islamic students. Hence, if sex education is to be taught in Arabic-Islamic religious contexts, both the content and the modes of delivery of that content may need to be particularly sensitive to concerns those Islamic students of both sexes may hold with respect to that education.

Interestingly, Islamic and Catholic students did not differ in their interest in, and perceived importance assigned to, PDHPE. This finding is somewhat surprising given the differences expressed in specific areas of the PDHPE program. However, this finding does offer hope that PDHPE programs may capitalize on the relative homogeneity of students' interest in, and valuing of, PDHPE. In other words, religious differences do not necessarily mean that students will express differential interest in, and value for, PDHPE, despite the fact that interreligious experiences and perceptions toward PDHPE may differ markedly in particular areas of the PDHPE program.

Finally, the two specific hypotheses (i.e., that intracultural religious differences would effect PDHPE perceptions, and that Islamic females may differ substantially from Islamic males and Catholic males and females in their perceptions of PDHPE) were both supported by the research. This support again serves to highlight the potential inappropriateness of treating Arabic students as an undifferentiated group with respect to PDHPE perceptions, and the particular sensitivity Muslim females may have to

PDHPE content and delivery issues. Both these points deserve further attention by PDHPE researchers and practitioners.

WIDER IMPLICATIONS FOR
SOCIOCULTURAL UNDERSTANDINGS

In order to better understand sociocultural dynamics, it is often important and informative to understand within-culture dynamics. In this study, for example, an understanding of the religious and sex dynamics operating within one cultural group may lead to a greater appreciation of how that cultural group perceives (and, thus, potentially reacts to) an important but often contentious area of education. Conversely, without such intracultural understandings, sociocultural dynamics may be difficult to understand. For example, again in the context of this study, if it is not understood that particular religious or sex groups among Arabic students may perceive PDHPE in different ways, then educators may be perplexed why the same PDHPE program "works" in one Arabic-student setting but not in another.

It is important that those working in diverse sociocultural settings (such as educators from dominant cultural groups working in schools with significant "minority" populations) have a well-developed understanding of salient intracultural factors that may impact upon the delivery of relevant policies and programs. It is also important for researchers to understand that studies that include an examination of intracultural factors may provide a more nuanced understanding of the cultural groups under consideration, as well as potentially leading to more accurate predictions concerning the ways in which cultural groups, and subgroups within them, may act and react in given situations. In other words, the specificity of sociocultural studies may be enhanced through an improved understanding of important intracultural variability.

APPENDIX

Item   Perceived Parental Support (PARSUP): 4 items $\alpha = .87$

1   My father encourages me to learn all that I can from the PDHPE program.

2   My mother encourages me to learn all that I can from the PDHPE program.

3   My father thinks the PDHPE program is important to my health and development.

4   My mother thinks the PDHPE program is important to my health and development.

Disliking Physical Activity and Embarrassment (EMBARS): 3 items $\alpha = .65$

1   I am embarrassed changing into PE and sports clothes at school.
2   My parents do not like me doing physical activities.
3   I do not like doing physical activities, such as athletics.

Mixed-Sex Activities (MIXSEX): 3 items $\alpha = .79$

1   PDHPE activities should include mixed groups of boys and girls.
2   Schools should facilitate the mixing of boys and girls in social settings.
3   PE activities should be taught separately for boys and girls.

Sex Education: 4 items $\alpha = .68$

1   The personal development and health subjects should include sex education.
2   The personal development and health subjects should include birth control education.
3   The personal development and health subjects should include AIDS education.
4   The personal development and health subjects should include topics such as dating.

Interest (INTRST): 4 items $\alpha = .81$

1   The PDHPE program at school interests me.
2   I like PDHPE classes.
3   I like what is taught in the PDHPE program.
4   Most of my friends find PDHPE interesting.

Importance (IMPORT): 4 items $\alpha = .71$

1   If I participate in organized sports at school I am more likely to be healthier.
2   Sports are important to me.
3   People who participate in sports and exercise get more out of life than those who don't.
4   Leisure activities such as swimming and running are important to me.

REFERENCES

Abdel-Halem, A. (1989). *Meeting needs of Islamic students in the Australian education system*. Sydney: Research Project.

Ahmed, J. (1992, October). *Sports and recreation issues.* Paper presented at the National Islamic Women Conference, Sydney.

Byrne, B. M. (1998). *Structural equation modeling with LISREL, PRELIS, and SIMPLIS: Basic concepts, applications, and programming.* Mahwah, NJ: Erlbaum.

Byrne, B. M. (2003). Testing for equivalent self-concept measurement across culture. Issues, caveats, and application. In H. W. Marsh, R. G. Craven, & D. M. McInerney (Eds.), *International advances in self research* (Vol. 1). Greenwich, CT: Information Age.

Carroll, B., & Hollinshead, G. (1993). Ethnicity and conflict in physical education. *British Educational Research Journal. 19,* 59–76.

Clyne, I. (1994). Beyond bay 13. *Aussie Sport Action. 5,* 5–9.

DeSensi, J. (1994). Multiculturalism as an issue in sport management. *Journal of Sport Management, 8,* 63–74.

DeSensi, J. (1995). Understanding multiculturalism and valuing diversity: A theoretical perspective. *Quest. 47,* 34–43.

Gutiérrez, K. D., & Rogoff, B. (2003) Cultural ways of learning: Individual traits or repertoires of practice. *Educational Researcher, 32,* 19–25.

Hernandez, A. E. (1995). Do role models influence self-efficacy and aspirations in Mexican American at-risk females? *Hispanic Journal of Behavioral Sciences, 17,* 256–263.

Kalantzis, M., Cope, B., Noble, G., & Poynting, S. (1990). *Cultures of schooling.* London: Falmer Press.

Kaldor, P. (1987). *Who goes where and who doesn't care.* Sydney: Lancer.

King, S. (1994). Winning the race against racism. *Journal of Physical Education, Recreation and Dance. 65,* 69–74.

Lindsay, K., McEwan, S., & Knight, J. (1987). Islamic principles and physical education. *Unicorn. 13,* 75–78.

McDonald, J. M., & Fairfax, J. L. (1993). Meeting the needs of a multicultural society. Implications for professional preparation programs. *Journal of Physical Education, Recreation and Dance,* pp. 77–79.

McInerney, D. M. (1987a). The need for the continuing education of teachers: a multicultural perspective. *Journal of Intercultural Studies, 8,* 45–54.

McInerney, D. M. (1987b). Teacher attitudes towards multicultural curriculum development. *Australian Journal of Education, 31,* 129–144.

McInerney, D. M. (1991). Key determinants of motivation of urban and rural nontraditional Aboriginal students in school settings: Recommendations for educational change. *Australian Journal of Education, 35,* 154–174.

McInerney, D. M., Davidson, N., Suliman, R., & Tremayne, B. (2000). Personal Development, Health and Physical Education in context: Muslim and Catholic perspectives. *Australian Journal of Education, 44,* 26–42.

McInerney, D.M., & Dowson, M., & Yeung, A. S. (in review). Religious and sex differences in Arabic students' perceptions of PDHPE: Muslim and Catholic perspectives. *Journal of Cross-Cultural Psychology.*

Mintz, E., & Yun, J.T. (2001). *The complex world of teaching. Perspectives from theory and practice.* Cambridge, MA: Harvard Educational Review.

Mueller, R. O. (1996). *Basic principles of structural equation modelling.* New York: Springer-Verlag.

Sanders, C. (1989). Educating Saeeda. *New Statesman and Society, 2,* 25.

Segarra, J. A., & Dobles, R. (1999). *Learning as a political act.* Cambridge, MA: Harvard Educational Review.

Siraj-Blatchford, I. (1993). Ethnicity and conflict in physical education: a critique of Carroll and Hollinshead's case study. *British Educational Research Journal, 19,* 77–82.

Smith, Y. (1991). Issues and strategies for working with multicultural athletes. *Journal of Physical Education, Recreation and Dance, 62,* 39–44.

Smolicz, J. (1995). The emergence of Australia as a multicultural nation. An international perspective. *Journal of Intercultural Studies, 16,* 3–23.

Sparkes, W. G., & Wayman, L. L. (1993). Multicultural understanding in physical education: A comparison of urban and rural perspectives. *Physical Educator, 50,* 58–68.

Swisher, K., & Swisher, C. (1986). A multicultural physical education approach. An attitude. *Journal of Physical Education, Recreation and Dance, 57,* 35–39.

Tucker, C. M., & Herman, K. C. (2002) Using culturally sensitive theories and research to meet the academic needs of low-income African American children. *American Psychologist, 57,* 762–773.

Wessinger, N. (1994). Celebrating our differences. *Journal of Physical Education, Recreation and Dance, 65,* 69–74.

Williams, A. (1989). Physical education in a multicultural context. In A. Williams (Ed.), *Issues in physical education for the primary years* (pp. 160–172). London: Falmer Press.

CHAPTER 9

THE INTERACTION OF TYPE OF RELIGIOUS EDUCATION AND SOCIOCULTURAL CONTEXTS

Implications for Motivation and Learning

Martin Dowson

Religious education (RE) in school settings has, in many social and cultural contexts, a long and not uncontroversial history (Burgess, 1996; Haakedal, 2000; Johnson, 1993). Essentially, controversy concerning religious education in schools has centered on whether religious education has any place in schools at all, and if so, in what form and under what constraints. Responses to this controversy range from the very positive to the very negative, with many "shades of gray" in between. What is striking from a cross-social and cross-cultural perspective, however, is the differing reactions to broadly the same type of religious education in various sociocultural contexts. For example, in some contexts (e.g., Greece and Iran) single-faith religious education (i.e., religious education from one particular faith perspective) is cherished and protected by society as a whole--and secured and developed through state legislation and educational support. In other contexts, however, single-faith religious education is specifically

Focus on Curriculum, 223–238
Copyright © 2005 by Information Age Publishing
All rights of reproduction in any form reserved.

legislated out of formal state-school curricula (e.g., in Australia and many other Western nations, although notably not in the United Kingdom) and, in some cases, out of state schools altogether (e.g., the United States). Conversely, multifaith religious education (i.e., education that recognizes many faith perspectives) is valued in some settings, tolerated in others, and actively opposed in the remainder.

The complexity of reactions to religious education in diverse social and cultural settings makes it difficult to ascertain: (1) the status of religious education in general, and (2) the particular place of religious education in any given social or cultural setting. Put as a question: "Is religious education viewed (or to be viewed) as 'good' or 'bad,' and what circumstances and considerations inform this judgment?" A central thesis of this chapter is that the interaction between the *type* of religious education in question and the *nature* of the sociocultural context in which that religious education is embedded determines how that religious education is viewed and whether or not it may be acceptable in state schools.

In addition, exploring the interaction of RE type and sociocultural context is not just an esoteric question of interested scholars of religious education. Rather, this interaction has substantial implications for the way in which students may respond to RE in a given context (e.g., Arai, 1996). Thus, issues of motivation and learning are substantially related to the interaction of RE type and sociocultural context. To complicate matters, however, family religious orientation, and the three-way interaction between family religious orientation, RE type, and sociocultural context, must also be taken into account when making judgments concerning students' motivation toward, and learning from, RE (Baston & Ventis, 1982).

Given this introduction, the specific purposes of this chapter are to: (1) develop a framework for understanding religious education in diverse social and cultural contexts, and (2) explore some implications of this framework for student motivation and learning with respect to RE. The broader purpose for developing this framework is to systematically conceptualize the contexts and content of RE in a way that will assist RE practitioners to understand the links between the sociocultural contexts (i.e., family and society), the epistemological content (reflected in RE Type), and the motivational impact of RE in their particular settings. Understanding these links may, in turn, contribute to a broader perspective on RE in general, and on motivation and learning within RE in particular.

THE FRAMEWORK

The framework proposed in this chapter draws upon, but extends and refines, existing frameworks such as those proposed by Hull (2001) and

Grimmitt (2000). The framework consists of three interrelated elements: the wider sociocultural context, the type of religious education, and the religious orientation of the family.

The Sociocultural Context of RE

For the purposes of this chapter, the broader sociocultural context of RE (what might be called the "religious context") is defined as the social and cultural attitudes toward religion in general that are embodied in social practice, societal institutions, and legal frameworks. In particular, two dimensions of this context are considered important: formal recognition (or otherwise) by the state of a particular religion or religions, and the dominance (or otherwise) of a particular religion in a particular sociocultural context. Recognition (or not) by the state of a particular religion is an important consideration because it determines whether the resources of the state will be directed toward supporting a religion and the activities of that religion, including religious education. Obviously, if the resources of the state support the RE activities of a particular religion, the effectiveness, or at least pervasiveness, of that RE will be enhanced.

With respect to the second dimension, religious "dominance" is important because it acts as a measure of the influence of a religion within a particular society. Religious dominance typically, but not necessarily, means that a religion is the largest religion in terms of its actual or nominal adherents. More importantly, however, religious dominance means that beliefs, and often the institutions, associated with a particular religion exert the predominant religious influence on the societies in which they are embedded. So, for example, a nation or society may be called a "Christian nation/society" or a "Muslim nation/society" if these religions exert the most profound religious influence in the nation or society in question. Dominance may also apply to particular branches of a religion. Thus, for example, a society may be not just "Christian," but predominantly Catholic, Protestant, or Orthodox.

Importantly, the interaction of the two dimensions determines the nature of religious context within which RE is embedded. This interaction is represented in Table 9.1.

Table 9.1.   Interaction of Dimensions Affecting Religious Context

Socially/Culturally Dominant Religion	State-Sanctioned/State-Supported Religion	
	Yes	*No*
Yes	Monoreligious	Secular traditional
No	Multireligious	Secular pluralistic

Table 9.1 indicates that there are four general religious contexts in which RE may reside: monoreligious, multireligious, secular traditional, and secular pluralistic. These religious contexts may be amalgamated into two broader types of context: formal-religious and secular. For the purposes of this chapter, formal-religious contexts are defined as those with a state-sanctioned or state-supported religion. Monoreligious contexts are those in which the state religion and the dominant religion are one and the same. For example, Greece is considered a monoreligious context because Greek Orthodoxy is both the state and the dominant religion. Similarly, in Iran, Islam is both the state-sanctioned and the dominant religion. Multireligious contexts are those where the state-sanctioned or supported religion is not the dominant religion. For example, in England, the Church of England is explicitly recognized in legal frameworks and broadly Protestant beliefs are taught in public schools through state-supported curricula. However, English society is generally considered to be a multifaith society, with many non-Christian religions and non-Protestant Christian religions substantially represented in English society.

Secular contexts are those in which there is no state religion. Secular-traditional contexts are those in which, for historical reasons, there is a dominant religion that is not recognized formally by the state. This is the case, for example, in the United States and many other Western nations, where most people report their religious affiliation as Christian, but where there is an explicit separation of church and state in legislative and constitutional frameworks. Similar patterns are evident in Turkey and Indonesia, where Islam is the dominant religion, but the state is constituted in secular terms. Finally, secular contexts, in which there is not a single dominant religion, are labeled secular-pluralistic. In the Western context, France (despite its sizeable Catholic and Lutheran populations) is a good example of secular-pluralistic society. In the East, China, with its explicitly atheistic constitution but its social mix of Buddhism, Confucianism, and various "primal" (e.g., Animist) religions, is perhaps a good example. India, too, has very large Hindu, Muslim, and Buddhist populations, but has a secular constitution.

Defining Religious Education

The first element of the RE framework is the religious context in which RE is situated. Four general contexts, with examples of each, are defined above. The second element of the framework is type of religious education. Based on Hull (2001), the following section identifies three types of religious education: learning for religion, learning about religion, and learning from religion. This nomenclature of religious education types is very useful when taking a broad sociocultural perspective. This is because the nomenclature is largely *content free* (i.e., it does not depend on the particular teachings of any religion as they might be embedded in RE). Rather, the nomenclature focuses on the *purposes* of religious education. This shift of emphasis is important because it frees the analysis of RE from the tricky (and some say impossible) task of effectively delineating between specific religious beliefs. In contrast, the purposes of RE may be relatively easily defined, as well as broadly applied to any RE setting.

Type 1 Religious Education: Learning for Religion

Learning for religion describes the approach where (a) a single religious tradition is taught, (b) by "believers" of that religion, and (c) the aim of religious instruction is to promote belief in, or strengthen commitment to, the particular religion (e.g., Digiovanni, 1992). Thus, this type of religious instruction may be broadly defined as any educative activity that teaches the beliefs of *a particular* religion for the primary purpose of inspiring commitment to that religion (e.g., Foster, 1997). Type 1 religious education is typically used to educate children and adolescents in the religious beliefs of their guardians. Another purpose of this type of religious education is to educate new adherents to a religion in the "ways" of that religion. The form (pedagogy) and content (curriculum) of Type 1 RE is usually controlled by the teacher and/or the teacher's religious "superiors." Thus, in school settings, control over the form and content of Type 1 RE is not usually exercised by state education systems, although this is not universally true. For example, in England, a broadly Protestant religious education syllabus is managed by the state education system.

A variation of Type 1 RE is that which seeks to examine various religions, but from the point of view of one religion. Such an approach is common, for example, in the Christian schools developing in many Western countries. These schools also seek to examine content areas other than directly religious areas (e.g., mainstream curricula areas such as mathematics or the sciences) from "a Christian perspective" (e.g., Edlin, 1999). Whether examining religious or nonreligious content, however, the approach is aimed at developing the Christian faith of students. Hence, the classification of this variation within Type 1 RE.

Type 2 Religious Education: Learning about Religion

Learning about religion (Type 2 RE) describes the approach where religious beliefs, and religions in general, are studied and taught with the stated aim of informing students about religion, rather than inspiring commitment to any particular religion (or even toward religious commitment in general) (e.g., Haakaedal, 2000; Melchert, 1995). Type 2 RE is commonly known as *religious studies, studies of religion,* or *comparative studies of religion,* depending on the context. In Australia, the distinction between *special* (Type 1) and *general* (Type 2) religious education is also used. Unlike Type 1 RE, Type 2 RE is typically taught by the regular classroom teacher, from a state-designed (or at least state-sanctioned) curriculum, with students of many faiths, or no faith, present in the one classroom. "Studies of Religion," for example, is a designated secondary school subject in Australia, the United Kingdom, and several other countries.

A central distinction between Type 1 and Type 2 RE is that Type 1 RE teaches religion and religious belief from a religious perspective, whereas Type 2 teaches religions and religious belief from a nonreligious perspective. This nonreligious perspective typically involves the use of the social sciences (e.g., anthropology, sociology, psychology, and history), in preference to (or to the exclusion of) the "spiritual sciences" (e.g., theology and the philosophy of religion). One disadvantage of this approach, however, is that it reifies religious content, and hence may contribute little to students' moral or spiritual development.

Type 3 Religious Education: Learning from Religion

The exclusiveness of Type 1 RE and the reified nature of Type 2 RE have, at least in the eyes of some authors, proven to be significant impediments to the effectiveness of both (Hull, 2001). Type 1 RE has the advantage of directly addressing the moral and spiritual development of students, but does so in a way that often (although not exclusively) precludes the involvement of nonreligious students and the development of dialogue between faiths. Type 2 RE is open to all, but deals with religious content largely or only on an intellectual level, rather than on a personal or existential level (e.g., Miedema, 1995).

For this reason, a third alterative (Type 3 RE) has recently been proposed. This alternative may be called "learning *from* religion" (Hull, 2001; see also Scheiner, Spinder, Taylor, & Westerman, 2002). In Type 3 RE, students learn about religion in much the same way as they do in Type 2 RE. However, unlike Type 2 RE, Type 3 RE encourages students to respond to the content of RE on a personal level, but in ways that do not necessarily imply religious commitment or belief. Thus, Type 3 RE is distinguishable from Type 2 RE because it encourages personal responses, and from Type 1 RE because these responses are not necessarily faith-based. For example, having studied a series of religions, students might be asked what these religions may contribute to their understanding of themselves, to their sense of relatedness to others, or to their conception of social, political, or environmental issues. These reflections, however, do not necessarily imply or require specific belief in any particular religion.

Type 3 RE is related to a philosophical view (not unsupported by the literature; e.g., Ginsburg, & Hanson, 1986; Jackson, Boostrom, & Hansen, 1993; Scheiner et al., 2002), which suggests that religious belief and involvement, or at the very least an openness to religious reflection, may exert a positive influence on students' morality, behavioral standards, social participation and, not least for schools, academic achievement. Moreover, these benefits appear to accrue across the range of religious beliefs. Thus, the beneficial effects of religion do not appear to be confined to any one religion or denomination. As such, "encountering" religion and religious belief in schools is seen as an important step in developing socially responsible and equipped adults. A central question in Type 3 RE, then, concerns the extent to which students may benefit in both an academic and a personal sense from the comparative study of religions. This distinguishes the projected outcomes from Type 3 RE from the spiritual benefits said to accrue from the "passionate" study of one religion (as in Type 1 RE), or the academic benefits said to accrue from the "dispassionate" study of many religions (as in Type 2 RE).

Table 9.2 summarizes the main features of each of the types of RE described above.

Table 9.2.   Types of Religious Education

	Type 1 *Education for* *Religion*	Type 2 *Education about* *Religion*	Type 3 *Education from* *Religion*
Aim	To make new believers (evangelism) and educate existing believers (discipleship)	To educate all students about the content of multiple religions (i.e., to inform)	To allow students to understand and develop personal responses to the content of multiple religions
Faith Perspective	Single faith	Multiple faith	Multiple faith
Teacher	Adherent to the faith	Regular classroom teacher	Regular classroom teacher
Students	Believers (or at least potential believers)	All students	All students
Desired Response	Religious belief and commitment	Understanding and empathy	Understanding and personal reflection

Interaction of Religious Context and Religious Education Type

The sections above have identified four broad religious contexts and three types of RE. The specification of these contexts and types is of interest in itself--not least because it provides some clarity to an understanding of RE in diverse contexts. However, more importantly, the interaction of these contexts and types determines the degree of acceptability of the particular type of RE in a given context. How this interaction may work in each of the four religious contexts is discussed below.

Monoreligious Contexts

In monoreligious contexts, Type 1 RE of the dominant religion would seem to represent a "natural" sociocultural fit. So, for example, Type 1 Islamic RE taught in schools in an Islamic country would be completely congruent with the wider sociocultural context. However, Type 1 RE of other than the dominant religion may be outright rejected, or at least actively discouraged. Thus, the status of Type 1 RE of other than the dominant religion would be expected to be tenuous in monoreligious contexts.

Education about religion (Type 2 RE) represents a less natural fit in monoreligious contexts. It may be that Type 2 RE is interpreted as a useful adjunct to Type 1 RE in certain contexts (i.e., the study of religions other than the dominant religion may be seen to facilitate comparisons and contrasts, which serve to highlight the unique benefits of the dominant religion). Conversely, it may be that Type 2 RE is considered a threat to the dominant religious beliefs of the wider monoreligious society. Thus, in many Islamic countries, teaching about other religions is forbidden in schools, and often forbidden or at least severely discouraged in other contexts as well.

Finally, in monoreligious contexts, learning from religion (Type 3 RE) may be problematic. This is because Type 3 RE not only studies other religions, but actively encourages positive personal and existential engagement with those religions. This type of religious engagement is unlikely to be welcome in monoreligious contexts, which affirm the preeminent religious efficacy and authority of one particular religion.

Multireligious Contexts

In multireligious contexts, the status of Type 1 RE of the same type as the state religion is essentially the same as it is in monoreligious contexts (i.e., it will be most likely supported and sanctioned by the state). In contrast, Type 1 RE derived from religions other than the state-sanctioned religion may have a firmer footing in multireligious than monoreligious contexts. This is because religions other than the state-sanctioned religion are well represented in the society at large, and would be expected to seek the opportunity to provide Type 1 RE in schools. Also, in multireligious contexts, the religious authorities of the state-supported religion may have less social power, if it was their mind to exercise it, to dissuade the state from allowing the presence of Type 1 RE of non-state-supported types.

Type 2 RE might be expected to be accepted or rejected for much the same reasons in multireligious contexts as in monoreligious contexts. The difference in multireligious contexts is that acceptance of Type 2 RE might be more certain. This is because the social need to understand many religions would be perhaps more obvious in multireligious contexts. For similar reasons, Type 3 RE might stand a greater chance of acceptance in multireligious settings. However, it may still be the case that the presence of a state-supported religion precludes acceptance of Type 3 RE in state schools on the same grounds as outlined with respect to monoreligious contexts.

Secular-Traditional Contexts

In secular-traditional contexts, Type 1 RE may be rejected on the basis of the secularity of the society (as is the case in the United States), accepted into the formal curriculum of state schools on the basis of the social-religious traditions of the society (as is the case in Germany), or accepted into the informal (adjunct) curriculum of state schools on the basis that equal access is given to all religions. The latter is the case in Australia, for example.

Type 2 RE may be accepted in secular-traditionalist contexts on the basis of the secularity of the context (i.e., Type 2 RE represents a nonreligious approach to the study of religion). This is the case in many Western nations, where Studies of Religion (Comparative Religions) in school are common. However, it may also be that Type 2 RE encounters anywhere from minimal to substantial opposition from the traditionally dominant religion, particularly if the traditionally dominant religion views Type 2 RE as a threat to its social, if not legislative, authority.

Similarly, Type 3 RE may be accepted on the basis of the secularity of the secular-traditional context. However, it is perhaps more likely that Type 3 RE will be opposed by the dominant religious tradition because it implies that religions other than the dominant religion may contribute to the spiritual and existential well-being of students. Indeed, in many secular-traditional contexts, the dominant religion has established parallel educational systems because it perceives secular educational systems to be overly influenced by religious and philosophical perspectives other than that of the dominant religion. Thus, in Australia, New Zealand, the United States, and other secular-traditional contexts, Christian schools have arisen with the explicit intention of effectively forming a monoreligious school culture within the broader secular-traditional societal setting. In this monoreligious school culture, Type 3 RE is rejected in much the same way as it would be in a monoreligious societal context.

Secular-Pluralistic Societies

The status of Type 1 RE in secular-pluralistic contexts is similar to that in secular-traditional contexts. The main difference is the absence of a dominant religion whose Type 1 RE may be accepted on the basis of social-religious tradition. The other two alternatives--outright rejection or acceptance on the basis of religious equality--remain the same. Type 2 RE will be very likely accepted, and quite possibly advocated, in secular-pluralistic contexts. Moreover, the lack of a dominant religion means that Type 2 RE cannot threaten the religious hegemony of any particular religion, because such hegemony does not exist in the first place. Similarly, Type 3 RE may be accepted on the basis that it contributes to a socially valued understanding of multiple religions. The personal and existential responses encouraged by Type 3 RE may also be acceptable because no particular faith response is either required or encouraged.

Revisiting Type 1 RE in Secular-Traditional and Secular-Pluralistic Contexts

The introduction to this chapter noted that RE in schools has often attracted controversy. The discussion above indicated that such controversy may arise in any religious context with respect to more than one type of RE. However, the status of Type 1 RE in secular contexts (of either the traditional or pluralistic type) has perhaps been most controversial. For this reason, the role of Type 1 RE in a secular setting is explored a little further below.

Type 1 religious education in state schools (as opposed to that in church/religious schools or nonschool settings) is often challenged in secular societies. When this is the case, two reactions are commonly observed. First, Type 1 religious education may be abandoned altogether, and the state education system may become completely secular. This reaction draws, not least, on the psychology of Freud (1927) and the philosophy of Dewey (1934), which suggest that all religious education (but particularly Type 1) represents irrational indoctrination and, as such, religious education has no place in secular schools. In France, for example, the state recognizes no religion and, almost exclusively, does not fund religious education in public schools. Similarly, in the United States, Type 1 religious education is banned in public schools, but Type 2 may be acceptable if all religions are treated as equally valid.

A second reaction is where Type 1 RE continues in state schools, but where children from various faiths are educated in separate classroom settings and receive instruction from a representative of each faith. This view is based on the philosophy that religious beliefs (rightly or wrongly) are held by members of society (in this case, particularly parents). So, educating children in specific religious beliefs is a legitimate part of the school's teaching role *in loci parentis*. In Australia, for example, Special Religious Education (commonly designated "Scripture") is taught in schools, by adherents of particular religions, to children whose parents wish them to be religiously educated. Nonparticipation in Scripture is also an option.

MOTIVATION AND LEARNING AT THE INTERSECTION OF RELIGIOUS EDUCATION CONTEXT AND TYPE

Earlier it was suggested that students' motivation and learning may be analyzed at the intersection of RE contexts and types. This perspective is based on two interrelated assumptions. The first assumption is that students will be most motivated in school settings that broadly reflect their own sociocultural experiences. This assumption is based on a strong tradition of sociocultural theory and research, reflected in many different theoretical conceptualizations (e.g., Kozulin, 1990; Martin, Nelson, & Tobach, 1995; Moll, 1990). In general terms, sociocultural theory suggests that when students experience in school settings the same language structures, cultural symbols, patterns of thought and social interaction they have internalized from their primary sociocultural background (i.e., their family), then they are likely to experience in those school settings strong positive affect, enhanced cognition, a sense of belonging, and other positive intrapsychic experiences (Forman, Minick, & Stone, 1993; Kozulin, 1990). These experiences in turn will lead to positive motivation, learning, and social relationships in the school settings in question.

The second assumption is that the sociocultural context of a student's home and that of the school and/or society at large may, or may not, be congruent (for an example relating to literacy, see Gallimore & Goldenberg, 1993). With respect to this second assumption, for example, it is possible that in a monoreligious or secular-traditional sociocultural context a student's family may hold, or not hold, to the dominant religious belief of the society at large. Somewhat differently, in a multireligious or secular-pluralistic context, a family may hold strongly to a particular religious belief system, and may believe that the rest of the society should hold the beliefs of the family as well.

The immediate importance of the second assumption is that the beliefs of a family and the beliefs of a school (as representative of the wider sociocultural religious context) may be either congruent or incongruent. In the case of congruence, a family's religious beliefs will support and reinforce the religious beliefs of the wider society reflected in the RE approach of the school. This support and reinforcement will, in turn, lead to enhanced student motivation and learning in the school's RE program. In the case of incongruence, the family's religious beliefs may at least counter, if not actively undermine, the beliefs of the wider society reflected in the RE approach of the school. In this case, it is quite likely that student motivation and learning in the school's RE program will be compromised.

All the Pieces of the Jigsaw: Religious Context, Family Religious Orientation, RE Type, and Motivation

Earlier it was demonstrated that the four religious contexts and three types of RE may interact to influence the degree of *social acceptability* of any given form of RE in a given sociocultural context. This framework is also useful for examining issues of motivation and learning from a sociocultural perspective. This utility arises because sociocultural approaches to learning and achievement, at least from a Vygotskian perspective, emphasize ways in which features of the social context come to be internalized by the individual (McCaslin, 2004; Wertsch & Stone, 1985). Thus, the individual, in a way, assimilates the features of the social and cultural settings in which they are situated. This includes the religious parameters of the sociocultural context. The complicating factor here is that students are, effectively, located in at least two religious contexts, which may differentially impact the way students internalize religious beliefs. These contexts are the family and the wider religious context of the society (i.e., monoreligious, multireligious, secular-traditional, or secular-pluralistic). For the sake of simplicity, I will assume that the religious orientation of the family is in fact the religious orientation of the student. This will not be true in all cases. However, there is substantial research support that suggests that students will often adopt the religious orientations of their families (Swatos & Kvisto, 1998).

The point here is that when students' family religious orientations are congruent with the religious status of the society as a whole, then students' reactions to a given type of RE are likely to be similar to that of the society as a whole. Moreover, students' reactions include their motivational reactions based on their cognitive evaluations of the RE situation. This perspective on student motivation is, as indicated above, congruent with Vygotskian sociocultural theory, which suggests that the source of individual motivation is located in the sociocultural interactions that students observe, and in which they participate (McCaslin, 2004). Take the example of a student who comes from a monoreligious family background in a monoreligious sociocultural context, where the religion of the family and the wider context are the same. If the student experiences Type 1 RE of "their" religion, it is quite likely that the student will experience this RE as a positive, motivating experience. This motivation arises because the societal, family, and educational contexts all converge on one set of religious beliefs. Moreover, these religious beliefs will have already been internalized to some extent by the student (not least through the religious language and symbols used within the student's religious family background). Thus, the RE context presents the student with beliefs that they already call their own, to some extent at least, and with language and symbolic structures familiar to the students that mediate the communication of these religious beliefs. Similarly, if a student comes from a secular religious family background in a secular society (of either the traditional or pluralistic type), they are likely to respond favorably to Type 2 or Type 3 RE.

The examples above illustrate motivational processes that occur when family, social context, and RE type coincide. Perhaps the more interesting affects occur, however, when family and wider religious context are incongruent. For example, students from monoreligious family backgrounds may be unhappy with Type 2 or Type 3 RE, quite probably reflecting the attitudes of their families. This unhappiness may be exacerbated in secular societies, especially of the pluralistic type, which the family (and so the student) may already see as threatening to their beliefs. This underlying tension between the beliefs of the wider society and the beliefs of the family, coupled with the specific tension between the beliefs of the family and the Type of RE being taught in schools, would be expected to result in lowered student motivation and learning in the RE situation in question. Similarly, students raised in a secular family who live in mono- or multireligious society that includes Type 1 RE as part of the formal school curriculum, are likely to be less motivated than students from the religion associated with the type of RE in question. Again, this decrement in motivation occurs because, in this case, the secular student will most likely not have internalized the beliefs and language structures embodied in the Type 1 RE under consideration.

At least two important points arise from the above discussion. The first point is that the three-way interaction between family–religious orientation, sociocultural context, and religious type determines, at least to some extent, but quite probably to a large extent, the motivational reactions of the student to RE. The second point is that this three-way interaction may be decomposed into three two-way interactions: the interaction between sociocultural context and RE type (as explored above), the interaction between family context and wider sociocultural context, and the interaction between family and type of RE. Each of these interactions are important for determining students' motivational reactions to RE. One way of characterizing these two-way interactions is that (a) the interaction between sociocultural context and type of RE determines *what* type of RE will, at least potentially, be taught in school; (b) the interaction between family and sociocultural context will determine the perceived religious *status* of the student (e.g., as part of a religious majority, a religious minority, etc.); and (c) the interaction between family religious background and RE type will determine the student's immediate *reaction* to the RE involved. Thus, student motivation is determined at the intersection of type of RE allowed in schools, perceived family status with respect to religion, and the student's immediate reaction to the actual RE encountered.

Another example may help further illustrate the two-way interactions described above. Take the example of a Muslim student (i.e., a student from a Muslim family who ascribes to their family's Islamic faith), living in a Western secular-traditional context dominated by Christian beliefs, who encounters Type 3 RE in school. First, this student will be aware that they come from a religious (and social) minority. This minority status may cause the student to be uneasy, perhaps even suspicious, of any RE taught outside the context of their family and/or Islamic religious community. Moreover, Type 3 RE, although acceptable in the wider society and, hence, in the school, in and of itself may be offensive to the student who may believe that their religion is the only true religion. Thus, teaching other religions is tantamount to teaching falsehood. In this situation, it is very unlikely that the student will be motivated toward their RE studies, and may even seek to withdraw from these studies, perhaps with the support of their family. The point here is not so much to precisely predict what will happen with respect to student motivation in any given RE context. Rather, it is to point out that, from a sociocultural perspective, three of the central parameters in the RE motivation equation are family, society, and type of RE, and that the ways these parameters interact will substantially determine the strength of students' motivation and learning in RE contexts.

SUMMARY AND CONCLUSION

This chapter provided an integrated sociocultural framework for analyzing religious education. The framework first identified four types of religious context (monoreligious, multireligious, secular-traditional, and secular-pluralistic) and three types of RE (education for, about, and from religion). The framework then identified how the interaction between religious context and RE type may influence the social acceptability of a given form of RE in a given context. The framework also introduced the additional complication of family religious orientation, and whether or not this orientation is congruent or incongruent with the religious orientation of the wider society. Finally, the three-way interaction (and associated two-way interactions) of family religious orientation, social-religious context, and type of RE were said to profoundly influence students' motivation and learning in RE settings.

One of the central values of the framework is that it helps explain both the place of RE in a given religious context and the reactions of student in RE settings. In this way, the framework links processes at the social level with processes at the family-individual level, including psychological processes associated with motivation, learning, and achievement. In this sense, the framework reflects Vygotsky's "mind in society" (see Gallimore & Tharp, 1990) perspective, and to the extent that it does, represents an authentic sociocultural framework for religious education.

REFERENCES

Arai, J. (1996). Religious education in Christ with culture from a Japanese perspective. *Religious Education, 91*, 222–237.

Baston, C. D., & Ventis, W. L. (1982). *The religious experience: A social-psychological perspective*. New York: Oxford University Press.

Burgess, H. (1996). *Models of religious education*. Wheaton, IL: Victor Books.

Dewey, J. (1934). *A common faith*. New Haven, CT: Yale University Press.

Digiovanni, C. (Ed.). (1992). *The philosophy of Catholic education*. Ottowa, ON, Canada: Novalis.

Edlin, R. J. (1999). *The cause of Christian education* (3rd ed.). Sydney: National Institute for Christian Education.

Forman, E. A., Minick, N., & Stone, C.A. (Eds.). (1993). *Contexts for learning: Sociocultural dynamics in children's development*. New York: Oxford University Press.

Foster, C. R. (1997). Teaching for belief: Power and pedagogical practice. *Religious Education, 92*(2), 270–284.

Freud, S. (1927). The nature of an illusion. *Standard Edition, 21*, 5–56.

Gallimore, R., & Goldenberg, C. (1993). Activity settings of early literacy: Home and school factors in children's emergent literacy. In E. A. Forman, N. Minick, & C. A. Stone (Eds.), *Contexts for learning: Sociocultural dynamics in children's development* (pp. 315–335). New York: Oxford University Press.

Gallimore, R., & Tharp, R. (1990). Teaching mind in society: Teaching, schooling, and literate discourse. In L. C. Moll (Ed.), *Vygotsky and education: Instructional implications of sociohistorical psychology* (pp. 175–205). New York: Cambridge University Press.

Ginsburg, A., & Hanson, S. (1986). *Gaining ground: Values and high school success.* Washington, DC: U.S. Department of Education.

Grimmitt, M. H. (Ed.). (2000). *Pedagogies of religious education.* Great Wakering, UK: McCrimmons.

Haakedal, E. (2000). From Lutheran catechism to world religions and humanism: Dilemmas and middle ways through the story of Norwegian religious education. *British Journal of Religious Education, 23*(2), 88–97.

Hull, J. M. (2001). The contribution of religious education to religious freedom: A global perspective. In Z. Caldwell (Ed.), *Religious education in schools: Ideas and experiences from around the world,* (pp. 1–8). Oxford, UK: International Association for Religious Freedom.

Jackson, P., Boostrom, R., & Hansen, D. (1993). *The moral life of schools.* San Francisco: Jossey-Bass.

Johnson S. (1993). Reshaping religious and theological education in the 1990s--toward a critical pluralism. *Religious Education, 88*(3), 335–349.

Kozulin, A. (1990). *Vygotsky's psychology: A biography of ideas.* Brighton, UK: Harvester Wheatsheaf.

Martin, L. M. W., Nelson, K., & E. Tobach. E. (Eds.) (1995). *Sociocultural psychology: Theory and practice of doing and knowing.* New York: Cambridge University Press.

McCaslin, M. (2004). Coregulation of opportunity, activity and identity in student motivation: Elaborations on Vygotskian themes. In D. M. McInerney & S. Van Etten (Eds.), *Big theories revisited* (pp. 249–274). Greenwich, CT: Information Age.

Melchert, C. (1995). Pluralistic religion education in a postmodern world. *Religious Education, 90,* 346–359.

Miedema, S. (1995). The quest for religious experience in education. *Religious Education, 90,* 399–410.

Moll, L.C. (Ed.). (1990). *Vygotsky and education: Instructional implications of sociohistorical psychology.* New York: Cambridge University Press.

Scheiner, P., Spinder, H., Taylor, J., & Westerman, W. (2002). *Committed to Europe's future. Contributions from education and religious education.* Munster, Germany: Comenius Institute.

Swatos, W. H., & Kvisto, P. (Eds.). (1998). *Encyclopedia of religion and society.* Walnut Creek, CA: Altamira.

Wertsch, J. V., & Stone, C. A. (1985). The concept of internalization in Vygotsky's account of the genesis of higher mental functions. In J. V. Wertsch (Ed.), *Culture, communication, and cognition: Vygotskian perspectives* (pp. 162–179). New York: Cambridge University Press.

CHAPTER 10

LANGUAGE PROFICIENCY AND SCHOOL ACHIEVEMENT AMONG STUDENTS FROM MIGRANT FAMILIES IN AUSTRALIA

Rosemary Suliman

THE LANGUAGE SITUATION IN AUSTRALIA

Australia is a country of great cultural and linguistic diversity where a significant number of its people use languages other than English (LOTE) daily, and have cultural values and traditions different from those of Anglo-Celtic-Australians. The 2001 census indicates that 23.8% of Australia's population were first-generation immigrants, while another 18.8% were second-generation immigrants who had at least one first-generation immigrant parent.

Sydney has the highest percentage of first-generation immigrants of any capital city in Australia (34.5%) with another one-fifth of the total population of Sydney being second-generation immigrants. This means that one in every two Sydney residents is a first- or second-generation

Focus on Curriculum, 239–252
Copyright © 2005 by Information Age Publishing
All rights of reproduction in any form reserved.

immigrant. These immigrants come from over 180 birthplaces. Although the highest percent of Sydney immigrants are from the United Kingdom and are English speaking, about one half of Sydney's immigrants are from non-English-speaking countries (Ethnic Affairs Commission of NSW, 1998; cited in Poynting, Noble, & Tabar, 1999). These people have come to Australia with their unique cultures, customs, diverse traditions, and languages.

Most immigrants widely use their migrant language at home, in social situations, and at work (Lo Bianco, 1987). Despite this affinity to their migrant language, English is still the lingua franca for migrants (Clyne, 2003). English is the national and dominant language in Australia, and the language necessary to achieve mainstream success in most areas. In the government sector, for example, English is essential. Also, any involvement in the political scene requires a confident grasp of the English language, as English is the language of both politics and Australian law (Lo Bianco, 1987).

English is also the dominant language of education. All levels of education are conducted in English. At the primary level, children are tested with respect to their English literacy and competency, and at the secondary level all school examinations are in English only. Similarly, at the tertiary level, except in language subjects, all lectures and assessments are conducted in English. Therefore, without a certain degree of competency in English, it is difficult for students to achieve high results at any educational level. This is particularly the case in subjects in the humanities, which require the reading of complex texts in English, and which are usually assessed through students' written work in English.

In brief, English is the primary and dominant language of mainstream Australian culture. All Australian citizens, regardless of their ethnic background, have to achieve adequate proficiency in English in order to function effectively in educational, social, and occupational settings. To be without English is to be without the means of participating effectively in public life.

Language Policies

Attitudes and policies toward migrants and migrant languages in Australia have changed over the years. These changes can be traced from policies of 'assimilation' to "integration" to "multiculturalism." Up until the 1960s, the policy theme of assimilation dictated that different cultural groups participate in the nation's social, economic, and political institutions as "Australians" (albeit "new Australians"). By the mid-1960s it became evident that assimilation was not working because it was difficult (or impossible) for many immigrants to shed their specific cultural traditions. As a result, a policy of integration (the "melting pot" philosophy) emerged. Integration was criticized, however, for not respecting or celebrating cultural diversity sufficiently. As a result of these criticisms, integration was followed by "multiculturalism" in the 1970s. Multiculturalism developed in the hope of achieving a culturally and politically diverse yet united nation. The notion of multiculturalism brought with it a recognition and celebration of cultural diversity and multiple cultural identities.

Despite a commitment to multiculturalism, lack of English proficiency was nevertheless considered a primary disadvantage for migrants. As a result of this recognition, attempts at achieving social justice through language development programs were made (Clyne & Kipp, 1997). The 1980s brought with it the development of Australia's first National Policy on Languages, which recognized that English is the national language of Australia, but that alongside English the Australian community regularly used a wide range of languages other than English (Lo Bianco, 1987). In 1991, the Australian Language Policy was succeeded by "Australia's Language and Literacy Policy" (ALLP). The guiding principle of the ALLP is to "address the place of Australian English, the role and importance of indigenous Australian languages and community languages other than English, and the need for widespread and equitably available public language services" (Dawkins, 1991, p.7).

Language Choice

Regardless of the status of government policies, the fact remains that in many migrant homes the use of two languages is unavoidable, one language being the mother language of the migrant family and the other being English. Thus, for many migrant children growing up in Australia, "bilingualism" is not a choice but a necessity. This form of bilingualism is referred to by Fishman (1985) as "folk bilingualism" or "bilingualism by necessity."

The coexistence of two languages in the home and community creates the possibility of a language conflict, especially for the young children of migrants, who have to either choose between the two languages or combine both. For these children, both languages are important. Their home language is their parents' language and, as such, is an essential element in communication with members of the family and the family's community. At the same time, gaining a native-like proficiency in the dominant language (English) is also very important. Given this potential conflict, three questions arise:

1. How proficient are the bilingual children of migrant families in their home language?

2. How proficient are these children in English?

3. What are the implications of 1 and 2 for bilingual students' school achievement?

These questions will be addressed in this chapter by examining the results of a study conducted to examine the school achievement and language proficiency of a group of students from Lebanese-background (LB) families in southwestern Sydney. Specifically, this study explored the correlation between language proficiency and school achievement. The study will be placed in the context of other research, which discusses the potential positive and negative effects of bilingualism on students' overall language development and school achievement.

THE STUDY

In order to assess the proficiency of students in their home language and in English, the study examines the language use and language proficiency of the students described below. Some previous research has employed language use (i.e., the use of a migrant language spoken in the home as a proxy for "ethnic" status) while ignoring language proficiency. There is an assumption in this line of thinking that speaking a language at home implies proficiency in that language (Sturman, 1997). However, more recent research suggests that using a particular language at home does not necessarily imply proficiency in that language. This is the case with many children of migrants who speak their mother language at home but are not very proficient in it. Conversely, they are more proficient in English, although it is not the language used at home. Therefore, language use and language proficiency are not one and the same thing.

In this study, "language use" refers to the extent to which students use each of the two languages at home with different interlocutors, while "language proficiency" is used to refer to two aspects of language: (a) how well students perceive themselves as speakers, readers, and writers of each of the two languages; and (b) how confident students feel in speaking, reading, and writing the two languages.

The school achievement of the students was assessed through results of their Year 10 School Certificate (Suliman, 2001). These results indicated that in the key subject areas of the Year 10 School Certificate (English, science, and mathematics) there was a high concentration of students in the two bottom grades and a low concentration in the two top grades. A comparison of the results of the Lebanese background (LB) and non-Lebanese-background students (i.e., English-background, Chinese-background and Vietnamese-background groups) indicated that the percentage of LB students in the lowest grade was higher than for any of the other three groups (Suliman, 2001).

As well as reporting on students' language use and language proficiency in Arabic and English, this chapter discusses the relationship between the two languages, and between each language and students' school achievement.

Participants

Participants in this study were a total of 135 Lebanese-background students in three state high schools in southwestern Sydney: one school was male only, one school was female only, and one school was coeducational. All schools are closely located to each other and are classified as socioeconomically disadvantaged. Most of the parents of the students at the school were first-generation immigrants, with only 11.8% of fathers and 14.4% of mothers born in Australia. Although this study examined all students in Year 9 in the three schools, the main focus of this study was the LB students. This is primarily because the LB students have been identified as underachievers (Horvath, 1980; Suliman, 2001), yet no previous studies have investigated the factors behind the underachievement of this group of students.

Instruments

A survey instrument (Suliman, 2001) consisting of 148 items was designed to elicit information about various aspects of the linguistic status of students.

Language use at home. Language use refers to the extent to which students use each of the two languages at home (English and Arabic) with different interlocutors (mother, father, and siblings). Language use was assessed using questions such as "Which language is spoken most at home by your mother when she speaks with you?" These questions were answered on a 3-point scale (1 = English; 2 = Arabic; 3 = Mixed).

"Mixed" language in this context refers to the use of both languages in the same discourse, and even in the same sentence or phrase (Clyne, 1991; Goebel, Nelde, Stary, & Wolck, 1996). Although there are differences between the spoken and written forms of Arabic (dialect vs. the standard form of the language) (Holes, 1995; Mansouri, 1999), the term

"Arabic" in this study refers to both the spoken and the written forms of the language.

Students were also asked about the importance of speaking Arabic and English at home and about their perception of their parents' attitude toward the speaking of Arabic and English at home. This perceived importance was assessed by statements such as: "Speaking Arabic at home is important to me/to my father/to my mother," etc. Responses to these statements were measured on a 5-point scale (1 = strongly agree; 2 = agree; 3 = not sure; 4 = disagree; 5 = strongly disagree).

Students' perceived proficiency in speaking, reading, and writing Arabic and English. Perceived language proficiency was measured by three sets of questions:

(a) The first set of questions addressed how often Arabic or English was used by students in speaking, reading, and writing. These questions were answered on a 5-point scale (1 = all the time; 2 = often; 3 = rarely; 4 = sometimes; 5 = never).

(b) The second set of questions addressed how well students perceived themselves as speakers, readers, and writers of the language. These questions were measured using a 5-point scale (1 = very well; 2 = well; 3 = not well; 4 = badly; 5 = very badly).

(c) The third set of questions addressed how confident students felt in speaking, reading, and writing the language. These questions were answered using a 4-point scale (1 = very confident; 2 = confident; 3 = a little confident; 4 = not confident at all).

RESULTS

The original research reports and discusses the results of the study in great detail and the statistical tables relating to the results discussed below are presented in Suliman (2001). This chapter focuses on the major outcomes that address the research questions posed at the beginning of the chapter.

Language Use at Home

An important and sometimes confusing question upon which migrant families have to decide is what language to use at home when communicating with each other. The results of this study indicate that among the LB students, the language used mostly with parents is neither Arabic nor English exclusively but the "mixed" language, followed by Arabic, then

English. With siblings, English is the language most in use by students, followed by "mixed," then Arabic. In the case of parents, Arabic is the language used most by parents with each other, followed by "mixed," and lastly English.

Another important aspect of language use at home is how parents and students feel about the use of Arabic and English at home. For example, do parents and students consider speaking Arabic at home important and is speaking English at home as important as speaking Arabic? Students perceived that their parents put more importance on speaking Arabic at home than on speaking English, but students themselves see the importance of using both languages at home. Students' perceptions are that 80.7% of mothers and 84.3% of fathers "strongly agree" or "agree" that speaking Arabic at home is "very important," in comparison to only 28.9% of mothers and 26.1% of fathers who "strongly agree" or "agree" that speaking English at home is "very important." Among the students themselves, 78.3% see that speaking Arabic at home is very important and 58.4% perceive speaking English at home as being very important. Students perceive that for both students and parents, speaking Arabic at home is more important than speaking English. Students perceive, however, that there is an uncertainty among parents about the importance of speaking English at home: according to student beliefs, about one third of their parents are not sure that speaking English at home is important.

Students' Perceived Proficiency in Speaking, Reading and Writing Arabic and English

How often are Arabic and English used by students in speaking, reading, and writing? Results indicate that students frequently use both English and Arabic in speaking. Almost all students (98.5%) use English in speaking "all the time" or "often" and a large majority (75.4%) use Arabic in the same way. In reading and writing, English is by far the language predominantly used by students. Students' use of Arabic in reading and writing is much less than in speaking. More than one-third of students never use Arabic in reading and writing.

With respect to perceived ability and confidence in Arabic language use, more than half the students reported that they can read and write Arabic, but of those more than 40% reported that they read and write Arabic "badly" or "very badly." Predictably, more than half the students reported little or no confidence in Arabic reading and writing. Students perceive themselves as being better in English than in Arabic with respect to all three areas of language use (speaking, reading, and writing). The great majority (96.3%, 96.2%, and 96.4%, respectively) of students reported that they can speak, read, and write English "very well" or "well" and have confidence in speaking, reading, and writing English.

On the whole, students have a very low perception of their bilingualism; only a small percentage (ranging from 6.7% to 9.6%) perceived themselves as being able and confident in speaking, reading, and writing both languages.

RELATIONSHIP BETWEEN PERCEIVED PROFICIENCY IN ARABIC AND ENGLISH

Correlation analyzes indicated that there is a high correlation between language skills within each language (i.e., English speaking is significantly correlated with English reading and English writing and English reading and English writing are highly correlated with each other). Similarly, Arabic speaking is significantly correlated with Arabic reading and Arabic writing and Arabic reading is significantly correlated with Arabic writing.

However, in general, there is no significant positive correlation across skills in the two languages. The only significant correlation between skills across the two languages is a negative one between English speaking and Arabic speaking (i.e., students who consider themselves fluent in speaking English do not consider themselves fluent in speaking Arabic).

RELATIONSHIP BETWEEN STUDENTS' PROFICIENCY IN ARABIC AND ENGLISH AND THEIR SCHOOL ACHIEVEMENT

Results indicated that there is a significant negative correlation between students' self-assessment of their proficiency in Arabic reading and their English and science grades. This means that those students who perceive themselves as being proficient in reading Arabic are typically not high achievers in English and science. In contrast, there is a significant positive correlation between students' perceived proficiency in English reading and writing and students' achievement grades in English and science (i.e., those students who perceived themselves to be proficient in reading and writing English are typically higher achievers in English and science).

To sum up, the important findings of this study are:

1. Among students and parents, there is a high use of "mixed" language at home;
2. There is an uncertainty as to which language to use at home, and although parents appear to have stronger feelings toward the use of Arabic at home, students see both languages as being important;

3. Students' perceived proficiency in speaking, reading, and writing Arabic is weaker than it is in English;

4. Students' perceived proficiency in speaking Arabic is much stronger than in reading and writing;

5. Students have a low perception of their bilingualism; being proficient in one language means feeling less proficient in the other language;

6. There is high correlation of language skills within languages, but no positive correlation of language skills across the two languages;

7. There is a negative correlation between perceived Arabic reading proficiency and students' School Certificate results for English and science;

8. There is a high positive correlation between perceived English proficiency and students' School Certificate results for English and science.

DISCUSSION

This study indicates that, in Arabic, students perceive themselves to be far more proficient in speaking than in reading and writing, with approximately one-third of students never using Arabic in reading or writing. Moreover, of those who use Arabic, about one-third rated themselves as reading and writing Arabic "very badly" or "badly," and as not being confident "at all" in the use of Arabic.

The majority of students rated themselves as being stronger in English than in Arabic with respect to all three areas of speaking, reading, and writing. Therefore, English appears to be the students' stronger language. However, these students' academic achievement in English, as indicated by their Year 10 School Certificate results, suggest that a high majority of LB students are achieving in the lower grades for English (and other subject areas). Therefore, in English, which is students' perceived better language, their actual proficiency is below the average of all students.

An important question that arises here is: what are the implications of this low proficiency in English (in particular) on students' school achievement? Studies by Cummins (e.g., 1976, 1979, 1981, 1984, 1992, 1996), which examine the relationship between language proficiency and school achievement, suggest that bilingualism may contribute positively to the cognitive and educational development of children and to their school achievement. Cummins's "Threshold Hypothesis," however, suggests that there may be "threshold levels of linguistic proficiency bilingual children must attain in order to avoid cognitive deficits and allow the potentially beneficial aspects of becoming bilingual to influence cognitive growth" (1976, p. 107). This hypothesis assumes that for bilingualism to have a positive cognitive effect, children must attain a certain minimum threshold level of proficiency in both languages. If bilingual children attain only a very low level of proficiency in one or both of their languages, their long-term interaction with their academic environment through these languages is likely to be impoverished.

Cummins (1984) also makes a distinction between "surface, conversational proficiency" in a language, and "cognitive, academic" aspects of language proficiency. Cummins suggests that "conversational fluency" in a language is not related to academic and cognitive performance, but that there is a strong relationship between academic aspects of proficiency in a language and school achievement. The level of cognitive and academic proficiency in a language is therefore important in determining school achievement.

Cummins's research findings and hypothesis suggest that LB students' poor proficiency in Arabic and English in this study may represent a major problem for their achievement. These students may not have the level of cognitive and academic proficiency in Arabic or English to enable their bilingualism to have a positive effect on their school achievement. This may explain these students' relatively low School Certificate results.

Lambert (1978) points out that bilingualism yields negative results when a child's first language (L1) is neglected and replaced by a dominant and more prestigious second language (L2). In this case, there occurs "subtractive bilingualism" (i.e., L1 is subtracted and replaced by L2). Students who experience "subtractive bilingualism" do not gain native-like proficiency in either L1 or L2. Therefore, to gain advantage from bilingualism, children's two languages need to be developed. The lack of perceived proficiency in reading and writing in Arabic among students in this study indicates that these students' first language may have been neglected, and therefore that their overall language development may have been handicapped. This in turn may account further for these students poorer school achievement.

The widespread use of the "mixed" mode of Arabic and English may also be a matter of concern, as it could be hindering the development of both Arabic and English as independent languages. This may result in two half-developed languages. For example, when students speak at home, how extensively and how well is Arabic used? When parents do use Arabic with their children, do they use Arabic in "decontextualized" situations to discuss abstract concepts and ideas and therefore give the language scope to develop, or is the language used only to speak about concrete topics? Duquette (1991) refers to two levels of language: "contextualized" and "decontextualized" language. Contextualized language depends on physical cues such as gestures, intonation, and other concrete characteristics of face-to-face communication, whereas decontextualized language is more abstract and independent of the communicative context. As students progress in school, they need more abstract, decontextualized language. A high level of literacy (decontextualized skill) in the first language is more closely related to development of literacy in the second language than is contextualized proficiency in the language (Garcia, 1994).

Although the present research does not investigate this particular area, previous studies indicate that students' speech in Arabic may be limited to basic conversations, and that students find it difficult to discuss any abstract topic in Arabic. One could, therefore, hypothesize that the Arabic language of the present students is limited to speaking about "contextualized" situations. This hypothesis may help explain the negative correlation between proficiency in Arabic reading and school achievement in English and science. It may be that students' proficiency in reading Arabic is not at an academic level sufficient to allow it to have a positive effect on reading English and on achievement in English.

More generally, this study suggests that it is not the existence of another language that presents a problem to children of migrants, as has been assumed for many years, but rather the low level of proficiency in the two languages that is a mitigating factor. Thus, when considering ways of improving the English proficiency and wider school achievement of students who use another language alongside English, it is very important to consider ways of developing students' proficiency in their home language. Thus, schools and curricula may need to look at ways of specifically addressing the bilingual competency of students by considering programs that aim at developing students' proficiency in their home language (Skutnabb-Kangas & Cummins, 1988). Allied to this, teachers also need to accept and value students' mother language.

There are difficulties with these suggestions for schools and teachers, however. In Australian schools, for example, students and parents do not usually have a choice about language instruction in schools, and classes are usually made up of multilingual and multicultural groups of students alongside students whose language-at-home is English. Moreover, bilingual teachers are not usually readily available. Similar problems are faced when looking for bilingual materials, which are very rare and typically do not comply with Australian curriculum standards. However, the biggest obstacle to implementing effective bilingual programs in Australian schools is an administrative one. Australian school students come from a wide range of linguistic and cultural backgrounds, and schools have difficulty deciding which languages to introduce into the school curriculum. Even in schools where there is a clearly predominant migrant group of students (e.g., Lebanese or Vietnamese), there are usually 5–10 other groups or individual students from diverse language backgrounds. Offering bilingual classes to some students in their home language and not to others, then, becomes an equity issue.

In Australia, and perhaps elsewhere, the only schools that can relatively easily incorporate bilingual approaches to education are private schools run by specific language or religious groups (e.g. Greek, Coptic, Melkite, Maronite, and Islamic schools). In these schools, students tend to come from relatively homogeneous bilingual backgrounds. For example, most students in a typical Melkite school are from a Lebanese- or Arabic-speaking background, and parents have made a choice to enroll their children in the school because they want them to learn the Arabic language. In such a case, the school is not faced with the problem of having to choose a language of instruction. Moreover, because in these schools bilingualism is limited to one pair of languages (Arabic and English), finding suitable bilingual-trained teachers is a generally easier task, and these teachers typically produce their own bilingual teaching materials relatively easily.

Despite the fact that these private schools are in a very privileged position to incorporate effective bilingual programs, there is still a certain lack of direction and uncertainty as to how to facilitate this implementation. The uncertainty is attributable to the dilemma concerning whether instruction should be first in L1 followed by L2, in L2 assisted by L1, or in the two languages taught simultaneously. Over the years private schools have experimented with various models. However, there has been no formal evaluation of the outcomes of the different models used in these schools. Such an evaluation would be important to further support the case for the development of students' first language alongside English, and could be the subject for future research.

CONCLUSION

Bilingualism may well promote academic development and achievement. However, a certain level of proficiency and certain patterns of language use (e.g., decontextualized use) are required for bilingualism to make a positive contribution. The evidence of the study reported in this chapter is that Lebanese-background students do not have high levels of proficiency in either Arabic or English. This lower proficiency may well be a contributing factor to these students' relatively lower academic achievement. In order to counter the effects of this lower proficiency, effective bilingual programs may need to be implemented in schools. However, there are structural reasons why, in most Australian school settings, bilingual programs may be difficult to implement. For this reason, the language development and subsequent academic achievement of LB students will probably remain a significant education problem for the foreseeable future.

REFERENCES

Clyne, M. (2003). *Dynamics of language contact. English and immigrant languages.* Cambridge, UK: Cambridge University Press.

Clyne, M., & Kipp, S. (1997). *Language maintenance in multicultural Australia.* Report to the Department of Immigration and Multicultural Affairs.

Cummins, J. (1976). The influence of bilingualism on cognitive growth: A synthesis of research findings and explanatory hypotheses. *Working Papers on Bilingualism, 9,* 1–43.

Cummins, J. (1979). Linguistic interdependence and the educational development of bilingual children. *Review of Educational Research, 49,* 222–251.

Cummins, J. (1981). *Bilingualism and minority language children. Language and literacy series.* Toronto: OISE Press.

Cummins, J. (1984). *Bilingualism and special education: Issues in assessment and pedagogy.* Clevendon, UK: Multilingual Matters.

Cummins, J. (1991). Interdependence of first- and second-language proficiency in bilingual children. In E. Bialystok (Ed.), *Language proficiency in bilingual children* (pp. 70-89). New York: Cambridge University Press.

Cummins, J. (1996). Bilingual education: What does the research say? In J. Cummins (Ed.), *Negotiating identities: Education for empowerment in a diverse society* (pp. 97–133). Ontario: California Association for Bilingual Education.

Dawkins, J. (1991). *Australia's language: The Australian language and literacy policy.* Canberra: Australian Government Publishing Service.

Duquette, G. (1991). Cultural processing and minority language children with needs and special needs. In G. Duquette & I. Malave (Eds.), *Language, culture and cognition* (p. 69). Philadelphia: Multilingual Matters.

Fishman, J.A. (1985). *The rise and fall of the ethnic revival: Perspectives on language and ethnicity.* Berlin: Mouton.

Garcia, E. (1994). *Understanding and meeting the challenge of student cultural diversity.* Boston: Houghton Mifflin.

Holes, C. (1995). *Modern Arabic: Structures, functions and varieties.* London: Longman Linguistics Library.

Horvath, B. (1980). *The education of migrant children: A language planning perspective.* Canberra: Australian Government Publishing Service.

Lambert, W. E. (1978). Cognitive and socio-cultural consequences of bilingualism. *Canadian Modern Language Review, 34,* 537–547.

Lo Bianco, J. (1987). *National policy on languages.* Canberra: Australian Government Publishing Service.

Lo Bianco, J. (1997). *National literacy policy.* Canberra: Australian Government Publishing Service.

Mansouri, F. (1999). The Acquisition of Arabic as a second language: From theory to practice (*ASLA Australian studies in language acquisition*, No. 7). Sydney: LARC University of Western Sydney.

Poynting, S., Noble, G., & Tabar, P. (1999). Intersections of masculinity and ethnicity: a study of male Lebanese immigrant youth in western Sydney. *Race, Ethnicity and Eduction, 2*(1), 59–77.

Skutnabb-Kangas, T., & Cummins, J. (1988). *Minority education: From shame to struggle. Multilingualism and the education of minority children*. Clevedon, UK: Multilingual Matters.

Sturman, A. (1997). *Social justice in education* (Australian Education Review, No. 40). Melbourne: ACER, Victoria.

Suliman, R (2001). *The motivational and linguistic context of the school achievement of Lebanese-background students in high achools in south-western Sydney*. Unpublished doctoral dissertation, University of Western Sydney.

CHAPTER 11

AMAZING SPACE

Reading Life in the Literature Classroom

William McGinley, Jennifer A. Whitcomb, and Sarah M. Zerwin

The Education of Little Tree, by Forest Carter, was first published in 1976. "A tender reminiscence of the author's boyhood makes a case for the natural approach to life.... A memorable reading experience ... poignant, happy, warm, and filled with love and respect for the Indian way of life" was one of several of very complimentary comments that appeared on the book jacket when it was first published. Today, the story is perhaps best known for the literary controversy that was produced some years later when it was revealed that Forest Carter was plainly not of American Indian ancestry as he and the book's publishers had led so many trusting readers to believe. Not only was Carter not an American Indian, but he was rumored to have had connections to white supremacist groups and to have worked as a speech writer for George Wallace during some of his darker days as the Governor of Alabama. In short, the book is not the autobiographical account of a Native child's life that it was once considered to be. Needless to say, it quickly disappeared from the "nonfiction" best-seller list of the *New York Times* before reappearing a few books further down on the list in the "fiction" column.

Focus on Curriculum, 253–272
Copyright © 2005 by Information Age Publishing
All rights of reproduction in any form reserved.

This controversy aside, and with sincere consideration for those whose experience of reading the story was perhaps forever changed, we hope to coax the readers of this chapter into taking one last look at a passage or two from *The Education of Little Tree*—not for the account of Native American life that it promises to provide, but for the depiction of story reading and the ways of talking about literature that its characters sometimes practice in the "classroom" they called their home. In beginning with this passage, we hope to explore and raise questions about certain long-standing disciplinary beliefs and assumptions about the nature of literature study in the English language curriculum.

GRANPA AND SHAKESPEARE

The book, set in the 1930s, tells the story of Little Tree, a 5-year-old orphan boy who is adopted by his Cherokee grandmother and half-Cherokee grandfather. Living in the Appalachian mountains of Tennessee during the Great Depression, Little Tree learns about the social injustice and prejudice that many American Indians experienced, as well as the cruelty of an American educational system that sought to assimilate Native people into mainstream cultural life at almost any cost. Against this cultural grain, Little Tree's grandparents teach him about his own cultural history and important Native social and cultural traditions. They also teach him how to read and, in so doing, about the possibilities, both real and imagined, that stories of many kinds offer for looking carefully at one's life and world. As the tale goes, every Saturday and Sunday night Granma would read to Little Tree and Granpa by the light of a coal oil lamp. Among the many books that Granma read, the works of Shakespeare were a clear favorite, often provoking Granpa into a state of downright moral indignation or confusion as he found himself drawn into the motives and misfortunes of so many "living" characters. Little Tree described an instance of one night's reading:

> Granpa taken the side of Julius Caesar in his killing. He said he couldn't put his stamp on everything Mr. Caesar done—and, in fact, had no way of knowing all he had done—but he said that was the low-downest bunch he'd ever heard of, Brutus and all the others, the way they went slipping up on a feller, outnumbering him and stabbing him to death. He said if they had a difference with Mr. Caesar, they'd ought to be made theirselves known and settled it square out. He got so het up about it that Granma had to quiet him down. She said we was, all present, in support of Mr. Caesar at his killing, so there wasn't anybody for him to argue with, and anyhow, it happened so long ago, she doubted if anything could be done about it now. (p. 15)

As Little Tree's account of one night's reading makes clear, Granpa's way of reading and responding to *Julius Caesar* is not exactly what many of us interested in teaching English might consider to be a reaction worthy of such an esteemed work of art. This literary "fact of life," a truth that is often thought to be self-evident by the brokers of literature curriculums in schools across the country, is one that has never failed to generate discussion among students in our own education courses that focus on the teaching of English and literature. For approximately 10 years we have been asking both practicing and prospective English teachers to respond to Granpa's remarks. Our approach to engaging our students in conversations about valued and less valued ways of examining literature has always been straightforward. We typically began class by simply presenting Granpa's response to the "evening's reading" along with an invitation to share opinions about the kind of reader he appeared to be (i.e., academic, sophisticated, educated, uneducated, etc.). Finally, we requested that our students provide reasons for their specific view(s).

Throughout the years, we have never had more than a handful of students in any one class say anything complimentary about the reaction and the apparent moral evaluation in which Granpa engaged in response to the circumstances surrounding Caesar's death. Needless to say, this has been disappointing for several reasons, the most obvious having to do with our expectations regarding the insight, be it personal, social, or political, that literature and an education in the humanities might offer individuals from all walks of life.

Although we have no way of knowing for certain what Granpa may have meant by the recommendation that Brutus and Caesar should have "settled it square out," the vast majority of our students respond to the entire episode with a kind of well-mannered academic disdain, citing most often Granpa's unsophisticated analysis, and on occasion, his obvious "pedestrian" approach to the writing of a great author. Seldom has anyone made note of the rather obvious moral attention that Granpa devotes to Caesar's demise. Interestingly, the moral nature of this attention seems to arise from a set of values about how one should handle conflict in the world at large. To the contrary, in response to our questions about the content of Granpa's interpretation or the appropriateness of his everyday language as a way to talk about literature in school, the answer has always been a plain-spoken "amusing, a little interesting, but it doesn't quite measure up."

As former teachers of English ourselves, it is not our intention to diminish or dismiss the voices of practicing or preservice teachers who are skeptical about the educational value of exploring literature in Granpa's more colloquial or "less than literary" manner in a school classroom. Rather, we embrace Grandpa's approach to *Julius Caesar* for the questions about literature reading that it invites us to pose. Why do we read and talk about stories in school? What kinds of knowledge, insight, or understanding should develop from our conversations with such books? What ways of investigating stories, songs, novels, poems, and plays are valuable and productive for young readers who are learning not only how to read and discuss books, but also how to live in the world? These are questions with which we are all familiar, yet when looking for answers, we too often rely upon the received wisdom or conventional mind of our discipline to direct us.

We begin with Granpa and Shakespeare as an invitation to think carefully about some of the taken-for-granted instructional beliefs of the English teaching "establishment" that touch secondary English teachers everywhere. As has been the case for us as former English teachers, and now as teachers of English teachers, we are interested in why Granpa's everyday words and interpretations, or the language of other readers inclined to a similar sort of everyday, life-based analysis, don't quite measure up to the standard of what counts as meaningful, academic literature content. We wish to do so because we take seriously the relatively small number of English education students in our courses over the years who approach reading literature with this more expansive view of what counts as a worthwhile exploration of a story, poem, or play in a school literature classroom. Specifically, we want to examine what Granpa and other readers like him have to offer us as we contemplate our professional responsibilities and possibilities as readers and teachers of stories. Why would so many of the prospective and practicing teachers in our classes dismiss his everyday language and interpretive focus as inappropriate to the study of literature and the life it represents? How might we encourage our students to broaden their view, and by so doing, broaden the participation and engagement of their students?

Back to the Future: Granpa and the Academic Literary Infrastructure

It has always seemed to us that Grandpa's way of reading and thinking about *Julius Caesar* stands in contrast to more formally inscribed and officially accepted ways of "doing English" (Applebee, 1993, 1996; Simon, 2001) in classrooms. However, it also makes us wonder how literature reading in school might build upon his sense of liveliness, moral inquiry, spirited analysis, and plain old everyday irreverence. Fortunately, these habits of mind are not unique to the fictional reading practices of Granpa, Granma, and Little Tree. Nor is the inclination to use stories in such life-informing ways confined only to those stories that appear in printed books. From the hybrid street-based literature "curriculum" of the work-ing-class men and women of 19th-century England (Willinsky, 1991) to the vernacular expressions of hope and struggle implicit in the literature of the blues in early 20th-century North America (e.g., Baker, 1984; Mur-ray, 1974) to the personally and socially transformative literacy practices of women's literary societies of the progressive era (e.g., Blair, 1980; Long, 1992; Martin, 1987), readers (and writers) have lived out an engaged and vital literacy.

In *The Triumph of Literature and the Fate of Literacy,* John Willinsky (1991) provides a stirring account of the drama and history of literature reading practices among working class people in 19th-century England. In a les-son about reading, most informative for the living manifestations of liter-ature use that it provides, Willinsky describes an everyday communal literary culture that was vital, engaging, inquisitive, and sensational—aimed steadfastly at the improvement of personal, social, and political life. A mix of street and lecture hall, cafe and classroom, poster and poetry, this was a literature or literacy that cultivated a "sense of moral agency, fearless inquiry, self-initiated discovery, and creative irreverence" (p. 50). This account is, in itself, a history lesson worth remembering for all of us, one that we might not only take to heart, but also take into our English classrooms and into the daily teaching practices that we seek to develop. To do otherwise is perhaps to risk losing an audience for stories, poems, and plays in the life beyond school. In looking back to accounts of this period, Willinsky describes the literary landscape:

> Wherever a few workers began to gather for a smoke, coffee, or ale, an orga-nization of educational and political concerns formed.... men, women, and children took what limited time was available to them and thronged to pub-lic libraries, reading rooms, book clubs, Sunday schools, discussion circles, female societies, workingmen's clubs, and literary societies. An array of con-tentious books and periodical literature were read aloud, discussed and freely circulated. (p. 21)

Perhaps, in the same way that Bakhtin (1981), a Russian literary critic, describes the diversity of social speech types that inhabited the public spaces, streets, and cities during the Middle Ages and the Renaissance, the style and content of literature study in school might take something from the lively play of "languages" that challenged accepted literary prac-tices of the time. As he writes,

> on the lower level, on the stages of local fairs and at buffoon spectacles, the heteroglossia of the clown sounded forth, ridiculing all "languages" and dia-lects: there developed the literature of the *fabliaux* and *Schwanke* of street songs, folksayings, anecdotes, where there was no language-center at all,

where there was to be found lively play with the "languages" of poets, scholars, monks, knights, and others, where all "languages" were masks and where no language could claim to be an authentic, incontestable face. (p. 273)

Still, even as the reader-based approaches of the past few decades (e.g., Beach, 1990; Galda & Beach, 2001; Purves, Soter, & Rogers, 1995; Rosenblatt, 1978; Sumara, 2002; Wilhem, 1995) seem to offer the possibility of the lively mix of the "languages" that might build on literature's personal and democratic functions, such approaches remain on the instructional edge of many English classrooms where formal, primarily text-centered, analytical literary talk and interpretation still play a dominate role in the instructional day (Applebee, 1993, 1996).

As it turns out, the inclination to view so-called "everyday" or "street" ways of responding and interpreting as descendent or inadequate to the task of examining literature and its lessons in school is relatively common among the professional English teaching community. Not surprisingly, the origin of at least part of this inclination can be traced both to the world of corporate book publishing, as well as to various circles of academic literary influence. In her studies of book clubs and popular reading, for example, Elizabeth Long (1993) has argued for the need to recognize some of the ways that cultural and institutional authorities (e.g., universities, college professors, book critics) shape reading practices both in and out of school by officially prescribing what books are worth reading as well as how to read and study them:

> this authoritative framing has effects on what kinds of books are published, reviewed, and kept in circulation in libraries, classrooms and the marketplace, while legitimating, as well, certain kinds of literary values and correlative modes of reading. Academics tend to repress consideration of variety in reading practices due to our assumptions that everyone reads (or ought to) as we do professionally, privileging the cognitive, ideational, and analytic mode. (p. 192)

Such a view, Long goes on to make clear, "inevitably brings into view both the commercial underside of literature and the scholar's position of authority within the world of reading" both in and out of school (p. 192). It is a world, we might imagine, where readers inclined to take up more colloquial or perhaps even morally-centered conversations and interpretations might have difficulty finding an appropriate moment to speak. That these academic and commercial positions on reading have influenced the teaching of secondary school English in significant ways is beyond doubt.

One can find personal, commercial, and research-based examples that speak to the relative prevalence of predominately text-centered, analytical approaches to literature instruction. In her recent book entitled *Moral Questions in the Classroom*, Katherine Simon (2001) began with a story about her early years as a high school English teacher. Her account calls attention to the tendency within the English teaching community for studying literature's aesthetic and structural features in the face of what are often obvious and more readily available opportunities to engage students in reading life and the world to which a text refers. As she recalled the events of one particular day in her English classroom,

> I asked my students to memorize and recite some lines from Macbeth. On the day the assignment was due, one of the students called out the following lines from her seat:
>
> > Life's but a walking shadow, a poor player
> > That struts and frets his hour upon the stage
> > And then is heard no more. It is a tale
> > Told by an idiot, full of sound and fury
> > Signifying nothing.
>
> I then did what I understood to be my job as an English teacher: I helped the students understand the definitions of the words, "struts," "frets," and "signifying." I asked them to comment on the central metaphor, in which life is compared to an actor. We pounded out the rhythm on our desks, noting that the first, fourth, and fifth lines do not fall neatly into iambic pentameter and discussing why Shakespeare might have departed from the norm for these....
>
> Neither I nor my students, however, thought to discuss the heart of the passage, the real question being raised here: does life have meaning? I knew that English teachers were supposed to teach about figures of speech and vocabulary, and I knew how to do that. I was neither equipped nor expected to explore questions about what it means to be human. (p. 1)

So, as Simon laments, that day's discussion of Shakespeare focused regrettably on the play's external structures and literary features rather than on its existential core. In so doing, the lesson disregarded the very aspects of the play that might have held most interest for the literature students in her classroom. As she wonders, "Does life have meaning?"

Although most would agree that instructional decisions such as those Simon describes are a matter of individual choice, it is also clear from her remarks that no instructional decision or teaching choice is entirely one's own. The instructional choices she makes in this instance seem to arise anonymously from nowhere and yet from everywhere, simultaneously. For many of us, it is as if such ideas about teaching literature reside in the air we breathe or in the words that surround our heads as it were, the voices of former teachers, textbook authors, inservice presenters, college professors, and so on (Lortie, 1975). Indeed, it is important to keep in mind that words and ideas about teaching literature or other subjects have particular social and historical moorings that render some ways of reading and exploring books more "natural" or "desirable" than others. As teachers, we read stories and teach stories within an institutional context or within particular communities of practice (Wenger, 1999; Wertsch, 1998). In so doing, we are often left to imagine instructional possibilities within, or according to, existing traditions, teaching frameworks, standards, and received guidelines that the discipline of English makes available to us—some of which are more well known and accepted than others (e.g., Hunter, 1982; Morgan, 1990).

In relation to Simon's account of teaching, Robert Coles (1989) recounts his experience with an English teacher at Henry Grady High School in Atlanta who expressed similar questions and concerns about what counts as legitimate or acceptable literature instruction, as well as her professional identity as an English teacher. The students were reading "O Yes," by Tillie Olson (1977), a story that explores the developing racial awareness of a black girl and a white girl who were friends in childhood but seem destined to be drawn apart by separate social worlds. Rather than begin the conversation with the usual text-centered analysis questions, the teacher "decided to be less the teacher than usual. . .and ask the students what they thought" (quoted in Coles, 1989, p. 96). In this case, being "less the teacher" was connected to a professional sense or assumption that such open invitations to give personal opinions on the meaning or life-informing aspects of a text was a disciplinary taboo. As she gave her reaction to the discussion that took place in class,

> It was the most dramatic class I've ever taught, and the most emotional one.... They kept asking them [questions] one after the other.... I think I feared that the class was getting too upset.... And the truth—well, it was I who was upset.... I thought I'd failed, because I was afraid someone might say this was no longer an English class in a high school, but some kind of group therapy going on, and so we were way off target—not doing what we were supposed to be doing. (p. 57)

From the critic to the classroom teacher, from the book review to the worksheet, ways of reading and interpreting stories, songs, novels, poems, and plays have always been nested within a larger literary-pedagogical discursive framework, "which itself embodies an ensemble of norms, practices, and institutional conditions" (Morgan, 1990, p. 329) by which we teach. In this Atlanta classroom, as in others like it, the perceived boundaries of acceptable literature instruction had been crossed with important consequences for the possible roles and identities an English teacher might assume. As Gee (2000) has explained, people (and teachers) are identified as being particular kinds of individuals through their uses of particular kinds of language. Language, and more specifically the language of literature instruction, *acquires* those who speak it. Such languages prescribe the instructional norms and values that teachers/speakers embody in their daily classroom practices.

Though Granpa read and discussed books in the comfort of his own home, we have suggested that responses like his and other similarly personal explorations continue to occupy a place on the instructional fringe of literature classrooms. This is a territory somewhat outside the more official literary reading practices embodied in Simon's (2001) instruction as noted above, and it is the very terrain that caused an English teacher in Atlanta to question her professional practices around the teaching of a Tillie Olson story because the students talked too much about moral and social issues in the world. We have also suggested that the English teaching community could benefit from thinking about the social and historical origin of the instructional ideas they develop so that we might continue to imagine new possibilities for the teaching of literature.

As Simon (2001) makes clear, her own instructional choices were rooted in the disciplinary assumptions and intellectual ancestry of what she understood to be the responsibilities of a high school English teacher. As she reflects, "I then did what I understood to be my job as an English teacher" (p. 1). In relation to this point, we might ask whose version of a literature teacher did she find herself becoming, and what were the consequences of reading and exploring literature in the way that she described? Doubtless, behind each and every instructional choice we make, the discipline of English, with its accepted and authorized approaches to teaching literature, speaks to us and through us—often with consequences for the fate of reading in the life beyond school. As John Willinsky (1991) cautions,

> The considerable amounts of time spent in high school classrooms discussing the ill-fated faults of tragic characters [or iambic pentameter] add little to students' understanding of how writing [or literature] operates not only on the page but in the world.... The irony, however, is not that this prevailing triumph of literature does not seem to prepare students adequately to deal with their literate lives; it is that this triumph fails to ensure a widespread audience for literature in the life after school.... The shame is that the one power of literature that perhaps can be said to be felt by all students is its use to grade and sort them on the school and standardized examinations. (p. 5)

Indeed, knowledge about how one ought to read a story is expressed and experienced in a wide range of settings, including, but certainly not limited to, the school classroom. From an Oprah Winfrey book club discussion to the *New York Times Review of Books*, from national teaching standards to academic research journals and textbooks, select ways of reading literature are produced and deemed to be more or less appropriate, tasteful, refined, or official than others. As Robert Morgan (1990) made clear, "legitimate" reading "always shifts in concert with the changing nature of institutional arrangements and the dominate social discourses of a period" (p. 328). To talk about *literature reading* or reading of any kind is always to tell a particular social, institutional, and historical tale (Wenger, 1999; Wertsch, 1998).

What's more, uncertainties about the social nature of literature reading, or literacy more generally, lead not only to a rather hegemonic picture of reading as a solitary act involving a book and an autonomous reader, but also to the general suppression of the many ways that reading books are socially framed and produced within specific contexts or settings (e.g., Fish, 1980; Hunter, 1982; Long, 1992). By failing to acknowledge the socially contingent and situated quality of such activities, these uncertainties allow some ways of reading (and writing) to achieve an official or "universal" status while rendering other approaches descendent, invisible, or simply not worth the effort (e.g., Greenfield, 1983).

In conceptualizing reading as a social or discursive practice, we distance ourselves from many of the pedagogical models or academic English traditions that rank ways of reading literature as more or less "sophisticated," "tasteful," or "refined." Indeed, there are instructional problems and implications for the fate of literature reading that are associated with the tendency to fashion the academic reader, deliberately or not, as a cultural elite—a distinguished reading superior, who in his or her almost exclusive preference for the "scholarly," ends up denying the commonplace. One such problem is that literature, or art more broadly conceived, ends up legitimating the very social and economic differences it was imagined to perhaps mitigate. In *Distinction: A Social Critique of Judgment and Taste*, Pierre Bourdieu (1984) touches on this very point:

> The denial of lower, coarse, vulgar, venal, servile—in a word, natural— enjoyment, which constitutes the sacred sphere of culture, implies an affirmation of the superiority of those who can be satisfied with the sublimated, refined, disinterested, gratuitous, distinguished pleasures forever closed to the profane. That is why art and cultural consumption are predisposed, consciously and deliberately or not, to fulfill a social function of legitimating social differences. (p. 7)

An additional problem associated with the status given to academic, text-centered reading practices is that the kinds of conversation Simon (2001) regrettably missed or that which the teacher in Atlanta was fearful are often given a descendent status—one without academic merit and likely to be labeled "group therapy" or "touchy-feely."

This is strange, and it also sells literature reading short for its potential to engage students in explorations of how stories reach out into our lives and our world, refashioning some part of that world in its own images. Additionally, the exclusive analytical study of literary elements, aesthetic devices, abstract themes, period histories, and the lives of authors forestalls the possibility that literature's worth might also be tested *outside* the classroom for its potential to generate moral deliberation, critical and democratic debate, personal and social reflection, and pleasure. In thinking about stories, Coles (1989) carefully notes that "a story is not an idea, though there are most certainly ideas in stories; that reading a story is not like memorizing facts" (p. 127). As creatures of words, language, and symbols of all kinds, we have a strong capacity to abstract and reconstruct elements of knowledge in verbal and written form. Still, we need not apply ourselves in only that way. What's more, he adds,

> We have memories; we have feelings. We reach out to others. We have the responsiveness that one sees in preliterate infants who cry when others cry, smile when others smile, frown when others frown.... That side of ourselves is not set apart from our intellect. In order to respond [to stories] one remembers, one notices, then one makes connections—engaging the thinking mind as well as what is called one's emotional side. (p. 128)

A Brief Story Reading Reminder

As Coles suggests, the English classroom is a place where students should be encouraged to read with both their heart and mind, so to speak. It is this quality of human reading that we wish to more fully acknowledge and explore as an essential component of the process of literature instruction. However, as the physician and American poet William Carlos Williams once noted, people can, as he put it, "talk a big line" and "come out badly wanting in their actions." In other words, talking about the value of "heart and mind reading," as we refer to it, is easier than actually practicing it in a classroom. What's more, this is not a style of reading that has been enthusiastically received by the traditional English teaching community (Applebee, 1996). Nevertheless, stories do matter in ways that exceed their usefulness in the study of literary elements or textual aesthetics. For example, in the closing pages of his essay *The Story That Saved Life*, Kim Stafford (1991) reminds us of the storied nature of our lives—the way narratives of human experience help to "rescue" and therefore save us, others, and our understanding of the world in which we live. The sort of "saving" Stafford describes isn't of the dramatic or heroic sort, but a kind of incremental recuperation or mending that often takes place without much notice in the course of daily life:

A story saves a life a little at a time by making us see and hear and taste our lives and dreams more deeply. A story does not rescue life at the end, heroically, but along the road, continually. I do not make the story; the story makes me. (p. 28)

As Coles (1989) makes clear, stories and the lives of the characters they portray can provide the basis for moral analysis because their struggles and joys of these characters become part of our own mental life in a way that only story can make possible:

[T]he whole point is not "solutions" or "resolutions" but a broadening and even a heightening of our struggles—with new protagonists and antagonists introduced, with new sources of concern or apprehension, or hope, as one's mental life accommodates itself into a series of arrivals: guests who have a way of staying, but not necessarily staying put. (p. 129)

These "guests," or the characters whose intentions, motivations, and inner lives are made available to us in literature, provide the basis for helping readers of all ages to explore moral and ethical dilemmas or conflicts of many kinds. Indeed, the act of listening, reading, or responding to the stories of others can have important consequences for the ways in which we think about our own lives because the indirections and vicissitudes that are part of a story and the lives of its characters become our own. A story's power and emotion requires our own involvement in the thoughts, feelings, desires, and fears of its characters.

This potential for stories to engage readers in an exploration of human possibilities or in another's vision is nicely illustrated in a passage from the novel *Black Boy* by Richard Wright (1937). In this excerpt, Wright recounts the feelings he experienced as a young boy while listening to a story as read to him by his teacher Ella:

She whispered to me the story ... and I ceased to see the porch, the sunshine, her face, everything. As her words fell upon my new ears, I endowed them with a reality that welled up from somewhere within me. The tale made the world around me be, throb, live. As she spoke, reality changed, the look of things altered, and the world became peopled with magical presences. My sense of life deepened and the feel of things was different somehow. Enchanted and enthralled, I stopped her constantly to ask for details. My imagination blazed. The sensations the story aroused in me were never to leave me. When she was about to finish, when my imagination was keenest, when I was lost in the world around me, Granny stepped briskly onto the porch. (p. 47)

Wright's passage endows the experience of story reading with a certain life-informing energy and significance. Such power, Bruner (1986) has suggested, is at least partially dependent upon the quality of a given story. In other words, the plights of characters must be rendered in such a way that their experiences can be "rewritten" through a reader's own "play of imagination" (p. 35).

A novel, explains Nussbaum (1991), is also a "morally controversial form" that provides readers with other ways of imagining and participating in social life. Specifically, she emphasizes the important role that literature plays in the development of the literary imagination by portraying possibilities for human life and choice that are in effect the reader's own to seize, or in some cases, resist. In contrast to the factual, detached imagination of economic science, literature also has the capacity to engage readers in the cultivation of "fancy" or the "metaphorical imagination." Fancy, Nussbaum explains, is literature's name for "the capacity to see one thing as another—to go beyond the limits of the facts and see more than the direct-sense perception of things" (p. 900). But this too, she writes, is preparation for moral activities of many kinds in life. As she tells us,

> The man in the moon, the cow with the crumpled horn, the little star—in all these cases the child fancies that a form, which perception presents to it as a simple physical object, has a complex inner life, in some ways mysterious, in some ways analogous to its own. To see moon craters as a face, to speak to a star, to tell a story about a cow—these are things that the factual detached imagination of economic science is unwilling to do. But there is as the novel says, a charity in this willingness to go beyond the evidence. And this charity is a preparation for the greater charities of life. (p. 900)

HYBRID DISCOURSE, CARNIVAL, AND TALK IN THE LITERATURE CLASSROOM

The stories our own work leads us to tell are about the kinds of possibilities or "greater charities of life" we make available to students when they enter into engagements with stories. We are certainly not alone in our interest or enthusiasm for approaches to instruction that build on the life-informing possibilities of such reading. Alternative approaches have been explored recently in the work of Athanases (1998); Bennion (2002); Binger (2002); Gere, Fairbanks, Howes, Roop, and Schaafsma (1992); McGinley & Kamberelis (1997); Moller & Allen (2000), Wilhelm (1997); and Wolf and Heath (1992), to name just a few. In building upon this and other related work, the possibility of heart and mind reading is also rooted in a specific theoretical approach to classroom language and talk. Such an approach understands how the authoritative languages of school literature discussion and exploration might unfold in conjunction with more expressive forms of talk as well as with discursively diverse approaches to interpretation. What's more, such an approach to literature study actively *promotes* this sort of hybrid discursive practice as an important part of producing vital and engaged literary conversations. In developing more engaging discussion practices, one could argue that literacy researchers have borrowed a little from the street and lecture hall, the cafe and classroom, and the poster and poetry sensibilities that once characterized the literacy practices of the 19th-century working-class men and women of England. In relation to this point, we believe that literature classrooms that value the sort of hybrid discourse practices that develop when a diverse collection of speech genres are permitted provide an avenue for active and accessible literature communities that engage students in examining both text and life.

The notion of speech genres (Bakhtin, 1986) is an important component in understanding how such cross-discursive or hybrid discussions/explorations might take place in an English classroom. According to Bakhtin, a speech genre is defined in terms of the specific values, beliefs, social rules, and ways of speaking, writing, and reading that particular communities of language users practice within particular social contexts. Like other discourse communities, literature conversations have their own unique set of values, norms, and rules for participation. Although we often traffic in a number of different social contexts in a given day, each with their own somewhat distinct and requisite ways of using language, we are seldom fully conscious of the specific conventions that different social settings require. According to Young (1999), "Speech genres are internalized within social institutions such as school and become part of their organizational structures" (p. 248). As such, these genres inscribe and codify the ideology, beliefs, and norms of a given institution as they are rehearsed in their respective classrooms, conference rooms, or production room floors.

In exploring some of the possibilities that might be connected with broadening the range of speech genres that classrooms make available to readers and writers, Kamberelis (2002) notes that when the authoritative languages or the "externally persuasive discourse" of specific academic disciplines occupy the discursive center of a classroom, they are often poorly understood or assimilated by students in only a superficial manner. However, when the authoritative discursive practices of particular school disciplines and classrooms interface with "other internally persuasive discourses [they] constitute what seem to be 'natural' ways of thinking, talking, and acting, ... flexible enough to adapt to the ever-changing contexts of our lives" (p. 87). According to Kamberelis, these ways of thinking, talking, and acting "are fertile spaces for cultivating learning, where learning is viewed not as the simple acquisition of knowledge but as the construction and reconstruction of new identities by fusing authoritative and internally persuasive discourses" (p. 120).

For our purposes, engaging literature solely according to the languages and literary codes of the professional English student does little to engage younger, less "skilled" readers in activities that speak to their hearts and minds in meaningful ways. This discursive uniformity requires that adolescent readers must always adapt and find access to the literary life of a classroom through a somewhat limited set of possible student roles or expressive choices. This is not to say that both externally and internally persuasive discourses are incompatible. To the contrary, the relationship between these two kinds of discourse creates a dialogic tension that is highly important to learning:

> The tension between authoritative and internally persuasive discourses is the engine of development for both individuals and social formations. Hybrid discourse practices exploit this tension by linking authoritative and internally persuasive discourses in various relations of contiguity and interpenetration. These linkages can exert powerful and pervasive effects on developing classroom (micro)cultures and on students' (and teachers') ongoing thinking and social practice. (Kamberelis, 2002, p. 87)

Our desire to think about literature classrooms as places of discursive diversity versus uniformity is also inspired by Bakhtin's (1973) theory of carnival. Specifically, Bakhtin describes carnival as both a public social occasion, as well as a state of mind in which less enfranchised citizens of the Middle Ages participated. During this period, carnival embodied an attitude of liberation, equality, caricature, and sacrilege. Social hierarchies were suspended and public officials were ridiculed. Laughter, offensiveness, and public drunkenness momentarily liberated the lower classes (Fiske, 1989; Gardiner, 1992) from an otherwise harsh existence.

In a recent year-long study of the discussion practices of adolescents, Young (1998) drew upon Bakhtin's notion of carnival as a metaphor for examining and encouraging "active, free, playful, and familiar participation among young people who are usually separated by hierarchical positions" (p. 249). In contrast to conventional wisdom about what counts as productive discussion behavior, Young found that meaningful discussion could also take place "amidst the chaos" of Read and Talk Clubs where "numerous overlapping" conversations about text took place (p. 260). As she explained further,

> The notion of carnival with its irreverence, celebration, and disdain for traditional hierarchies and social order created a way for me to critique, displace, and destabilize the institutional boundaries inherent in speech genres

of adolescent text-based discussions [traditionally associated with school].
(p. 250)

Though it is not our intention to try to recreate the street-based literacy practices of 19th-century England or the irreverence of Bakhtin's carnival, we do believe there are some "literacy lessons" for literature teachers in each of these contexts. As educators of prospective and practicing English teachers, our interest in Granpa and Shakespeare, street literacies, the moral dimensions of stories, hybrid discourse practices, and the metaphor of carnival originates with the desire to assist young readers in making connections between text and life. This possibility is in some sense dependent upon our students' sense of literacy and literature's history, as well as their knowledge of how ways of talking in a classroom influence the manner in which stories are interpreted—or even what it means to "interpret." As internally persuasive discourse or everyday ways of talking and thinking are rooted in the vernacular cultural practices and associated speech genres of adolescent readers, they offer the possibility of increasing the likelihood that adolescent readers might find literature more meaningful and accessible (e.g., Alvermann et al., 1998). These ways with words develop from adolescents' experientially-based understandings and local knowledge of world and the community where they reside. As with all forms of vernacular knowledge, their words and their ways of thinking and valuing grow out of local settings and everyday forms of cultural and family life. These are the speech genres or social languages that are used in the settings where survival is most contested—where the exigencies of lived life are encountered and interpreted on a daily basis. It makes sense that students should be encouraged, at least in part, to draw on these same social languages in interpreting literature.

IMAGINING HEART AND MIND READING

As a story of literature reading in school classrooms, this paper is a collection of related tales of literacy and literature across time, people, and place. We began with the story of Granpa and the "living" account of reading and responding to literature that he offered to both beginning and practicing teachers of English. Specifically, we selected Granpa's "reading" story in order to introduce some of the possibilities for moral reasoning and insight that particular approaches to text might make available. We also hoped to foreshadow the notion that reading both text and life were perhaps linked to particular ways of talking and interacting—that reading in this way might require something other than an academically-styled literary conversation. We wanted to raise questions about some of the taken-for-granted approaches to reading and examining literature that often go unexamined within the discipline of English. Specifically, we asked our readers to consider carefully their reasons for teaching stories, novels, poems, and plays in school with an eye for identifying the kinds of insight about self and world that such reading might engender.

In encouraging this sort of (re)considering, we provided stories of literacy and literature from both the past and present, in and out of school. These accounts juxtaposed a vital, 19th-century communal literary culture aimed steadfastly at the improvement of personal, social, and political life with the culture of two contemporary English classrooms where the value of moral, social, and political discussions were either not considered or not considered appropriate teaching practice. In each case, we drew attention to the teacher's discomfort with such conversations because they seemed to be in violation of long-standing disciplinary conventions in English. In making sense of this problem, we noted that teachers never teach "alone," above or beyond the influence of their particular institutional moorings or disciplinary conventions. Deciding what counts as legitimate book reading, like legitimate book teaching, is always a social, institutional, and historical process. Different approaches to text result in different consequences for readers and for what it means to read literature in particular settings. We noted that uncertainties about the social nature of literature reading, or literacy more broadly, can lead to the conclusion that some ways of reading and examining books are in fact "mo better," as Spike Lee might say.

We also wanted to remind readers that stories do matter in ways that exceed their usefulness in the study of textual aesthetics or as a vehicle for teaching reading comprehension and other related language skills. Our disciplinary inclination to read and study literature in "intellectual" ways need not preclude the possibility that we engage our emotional side as well.

Finally, we asked that teachers think about the language they use in order to engage young people in examining literature. Of fundamental importance here is the idea that the way we talk about stories is perhaps connected to the kinds of understanding students acquire from texts. Reading life through text and text through life, engaging stories in ways that encourage or lead to moral deliberation and reflection, thoughtful critique of everyday social and community life, and careful reflection on matters of personal importance and experience requires a language rooted in the lived lives and local knowledge of its readers. If this sort of language is to be cultivated as part of literature discussions, it will require a broader perspective regarding *what counts* as academically acceptable and productive classroom literacy practices associated with literature reading. In other words, as the primary focus of literature study shifts to include the study of life as an equal partner with the study of text, then such study will require a *life language* in all its rich, improbable, and unpredictable forms or genres. The classrooms where text and life are examined will, by necessity, be discursively diverse learning environments. They will combine the best of the street and lecture hall, the café and classroom in helping young students to learn that it is possible to read with one's heart and mind. In so doing, teachers will contribute to the development of readers' "literary imaginations," or their ability to "see" another's vision of the world. In encouraging this disposition to see beyond the evidence, we nourish a certain construal of the world that enables readers to contemplate possibilities for human life and choice in ways they would not have previously imagined had they not read (Nussbaum, 1991).

REFERENCES

Alverman, D. E., Hinch, K. A., Moore, D. W. , Phelps, S. F. & Waff, D. R. (1998). The literacies in adolescents lives. Mahwah, NJ: Erlbaum.

Applebee, A. (1993). *Literature in the secondary school: Studies of curriculum and instruction in the United States.* Urbana, IL: NCTE.

Applebee, A. (1996). *Curriculum as conversation: Transforming traditions of teaching and learning.* Chicago: University of Chicago Press.

Athanases, S. (1998). Diverse learners, diverse texts: Exploring identity and difference through literary encounters. *Journal of Literacy Research, 30,* 273–296.

Baker, H. (1984). *Blues. ideology. and Afro-American Literature: A vernacular theory.* Chicago: University of Chicago Press.

Bakhtin, M. M. (1981). *The dialogic imagination.* Austin: University of Texas Press.

Bakhtin, M. M. (1986). *The problem with speech genres* (V. W. Megee, Trans.). In C. Emerson & M. Holquist (Eds.), *Speech genres and other late essays* (pp. 60–102). Austin: University of Texas Press.

Beach, R. (1990). The creative development of meaning: Using autobiographical experiences to interpret literature. In D. Bogdan & S. B. Straw (Eds.), *Beyond communication: Reading comprehension and criticism* (pp. 211–235). Portsmouth, NH: Boynton/Cook.

Binger, M. J. (2002). From Archetypes to xenophobia: World Literature is the "rite" stuff. *English Journal, 91,* 40–45.

Bennion, J. (2002). Austen's granddaughter: Louise Plummer (re)defines romance. *English Journal, 91,* 44–50.

Blair, K. J. (1980). *The clubwoman as feminist: True womanhood redefined, 1868–1914.* New York: Holmes & Meier.

Bourdieu, P. (1984). *Distinction: A social critique of the judgment of taste* (R. Nice, Trans.). Cambridge, MA: Harvard University Press.

Bruner, J. (1986). *Actual minds, possible worlds.* Cambridge, MA: Harvard University Press.

Carter, F. (1976). *The education of Little Tree*. Albuquerque: University of New Mexico Press.

Coles, R. (1989). *The call of stories: Teaching and the moral imagination*. Boston: Houghton Mifflin.

Fish, S. (1980). *Is there a text in this class? The authority of interpretive communities*. Cambridge, MA: Harvard University Press.

Fiske, J. (1989). *Understanding popular culture*. Boston: Unwin Hyman.

Galda, L., & Beach, R. (2001). Theory and research into practice: Response to literature as a cultural activity. *Reading Research Quarterly, 36*, 64–73.

Gardiner, M. (1992). *The dialogics of critique*. New York: Routledge.

Gee, J. (2000). Discourse and sociocultural studies in reading. In M. L. Kamil, P. D. Mosenthal, P. D. Pearson, & R. Barr (Eds.), *Handbook on reading research* (Vol. 3, pp. 225–246). Mahwah, NJ: Erlbaum.

Gere, A. R., Fairbanks, C., Howes, A., Roop, L., & Schaafsma, D. (1992). *Language and reflection: An integrated approach to teaching English*. New York: Macmillan.

Greenfield, C. (1983). On readers, readerships and reading practices. *Southern Review, 16*(1) 121–142.

Hunter, I. (1982). The concept of context and the problem of reading. *Southern Review, 15*, 80–91.

Kamberelis, G. (2002). Producing heteroglossic classroom (micro)cultures through hydrid discourse practice. *Linguistics and Education, 12*, 85–125.

Long, E. (1993). Textual interpretation as collective action. In J. Boyarin (Ed.), *The ethnography of reading* (pp. 180-211). Berkeley: University of California Press.

Lortie, D. (1975). *Schoolteacher*. Chicago: University of Chicago Press.

Martin, T. P. (1987). *The sound of our own voices: Women's study clubs, 1860–1910*. Boston: Beacon Press.

McGinley, W., & Kamberelis, G. (1997). Maniac Magee and Ragtime Tumpie: Children negotiating self and world through reading and writing. *Research in the Teaching of English, 30*, 75–113.

Moller, K., & Allen, J. (2000). Connecting, reading, and searching for safer places: Students respond to Mildred Taylor's *The Friendship*. *Journal of Literracy Research, 32*, 145–186.

Morgan, R. (1990). Reading a discursive practice: The politics and history of reading. In D. Bogdan & S. B. Straw (Eds.), *Beyond communication: Reading comprehension and criticism*. Portsmouth, NH: Heinemann.

Murray, A. (1973). *The hero and the blues*. New York: Vintage Books.

Nussbaum, M. C. (1991). The literary imagination in public life. *New Literary History, 22*, 877–910.

Olson, T. (1977). *Tell me a riddle*. New York: Bantam.

Purves, A., Soter, A., & Rogers, T. (1995). *How porcupines make love: Readers, texts, cultures in the response-based literature classroom*. New York: Longman.

Rosenblatt, L. M. (1978). *The reader, the text, the poem*. Carbondale: Southern Illinois University Press.

Simon, K. (2001). *Moral questions in the classroom: How kids get to think deeply about real life and their schoolwork*. New Haven, CT: Yale University Press.

Stafford, K. (1991). The story that saved life. In C. Witherell & N. Noddings (Eds.), *Stories lives tell: Narrative and dialogue in education* (pp. 15–28). New York: Teachers College Press.

Sumara, D. (2002). *Why reading literature in school still matters*. Mahwah, NJ: Erlbaum.

Wenger, E. (1999). *Communities of practice: Learning, meaning, and identity*. New York: Cambridge University Press.

Wertsch, J. (1999). *Mind as action*. New York: Oxford University Press.

Wilhem, J. (1995). *You gotta be the book*. New York: Teacher's College Press.

Willinsky, J. (1991). *The triumph of literature and the fate of literacy: English in the secondary school curriculum*. New York: Teacher College Press.

Wolf, S. A., & Heath, S. B. (1992). *The braid of literature*. Cambridge, MA: Harvard University Press.

Wright, R. (1937). *Black boy*. New York: Harper & Row.

Young, J. P. (1998). Discussion as a practice of carnival. In D. Alvermann, K. Hinchman, S. Phelps, D. Wolf, & D. Moore (Eds.), *Reconceptualizing the literacies in adolescents' lives*. Mahwah, NJ: Erlbaum.

PART II

POSTSCHOOL CURRICULUM

CHAPTER 12

UNDERSTANDING STUDENT DIVERSITY AND THE FACTORS THAT INFLUENCE ACADEMIC SUCCESS AT UNIVERSITY

A Preliminary Study

Lorelle J. Burton, David Dowling, Marilyn Dorman, and Lyn Brodie

The contemporary university campus in Australia today is culturally and demographically diverse. Look around any campus and you will find an amazingly diverse group of people. Mixing with fresh-faced teenagers straight from high school are students from across the age spectrum, who bring with them a vastly different range of life experiences. You will also find students from many different countries, some with Western cultures similar to Australia, and others with markedly different cultures. There are also many students whose faces you cannot see; those studying in the distance modes, sometimes overseas and in countries where languages other than English are dominant. Academic staff members also bring a

Focus on Curriculum, 275–298
Copyright © 2005 by Information Age Publishing
All rights of reproduction in any form reserved.

diverse mix of cultural, educational, professional, and life experiences to the learning environment.

For teachers, this diversity highlights the need to take a fresh look at the learning environment they provide and how it caters for vast differences in backgrounds, abilities, skills, and learning styles. Students have always had individual differences in learning preferences and strategies, influenced by sociocultural factors such as ethnicity, culture, educational background, gender, geographical location, and socioeconomic status. The more culturally homogenous student bodies of the past tended to mask this fact. However, the increasing diversity of today's students has brought those differences more clearly into focus. So too has the increase in off-campus—sometimes even offshore—enrollments. Educators therefore need to respond to diversity in abilities, experiences, and learning strategies if they are to support students to become confident, self-directed, and independent learners (Venter, 2003). The challenge, then, is how to achieve that goal. What are the individual and sociocultural factors that influence how individual students perform? How can teachers recognize the impact those factors can have on student learning? What changes can be made to the teaching and learning environments they provide to cater for these factors and ensure that all students have the optimum chance to succeed?

This chapter describes how a research team from the University of Southern Queensland (USQ) has taken up this challenge. We are studying a group of first-year engineering students to identify the key individual differences and sociocultural factors that influence their academic performance. Three main factors of individual differences are being examined:

1. Learning styles: The way people prefer to learn. Some people respond to verbal instructions, some to visual material, while others learn by a practical demonstration of the topic.

2. Cognitive abilities: People's levels of verbal abilities and spatial abilities.

3. Personality traits: The Big Five factors (Costa & McCrae, 1992) of personality (openness to experience, conscientiousness, extraversion, agreeableness, and neuroticism/emotional stability) and other constructs such as self-efficacy, proactive attitudes, and proactive coping styles.

It is important to remember that these individual differences do not develop in isolation from sociocultural influences. In fact, sociocultural factors can have a direct influence on how those individual differences develop. Ayre and Nafalski (2000) indicated that students' learning styles are formed by a combination of inherited personality characteristics, their cultural backgrounds, and the ways they have been encouraged to learn in their previous educational institutions. Thus, knowledge of a student's sociocultural background often provides great insight into their learning profile. Our research project breaks new ground because it examines the interrelationship between all the different variables that impact on student performance. Most past research has focused on individual variables in isolation.

With that in mind, we have developed a battery of tests to develop a "learning profile" for each student, identifying their individual differences for a range of variables relating to learning styles, cognitive abilities, and personality traits. In the longer term, our project involves tracking the academic performance of these students through to completion of their degree, then analyzing the results to identify correlations between the key individual differences variables and academic success. This will help identify both potential predictors of success and failure, as well as correlations between those variables and sociocultural influences.

The benefits of this testing process are numerous. Every participant receives personalized feedback on their "learning profile," increasing self-awareness of their learning styles and abilities. The results also provide teachers with greater knowledge of the differences within the student cohort, so they can start adjusting their curriculum and methodologies to take these variables into account. Research supports the conclusion that "students who have knowledge of their individual learning preferences, who have been taught to use a variety of strategies consistent with this learning preference, and who have teachers who accommodated the preferences by adapting teaching strategies have made statistically significant increases in academic achievement" (Sarasin, 1999, p. 8). As Burke Guild (2001) urged, educators need a deeper understanding of the sociocultural influences on learning to inform their teaching and avoid a superficial response to student diversity. Finally, close inspection of the results and other key demographic data will enable staff to identify students who are most at risk of failing or withdrawing from their course.

Program-specific data are required because the profile of "at-risk" students varies between programs and institutions (Walstab, Golding, Teese, Charlton, & Polesel, 2001). Research at Edith Cowan University identified multiple "higher risk" categories of students, including students in isolated regions, particularly Aboriginal students, students from a low socioeconomic background, commencing nonschool leavers, and distance students (Attrition Working Party, 1998, as cited in Walstab et al., 2001). According to Shuman and colleagues (2002), roughly 50% of students who start engineering leave before receiving their degree. Half of this attrition occurs during the first year. Our research project will help to identify the individual differences factors that might place students at risk of failure—and, more importantly, alert teachers to ways to adjust methodologies to cater to these individual differences. This will include techniques to cater for sociocultural diversity in terms of cultural norms and expectations, geographical locations, self-efficacies, individual learning preferences, languages spoken, and ability levels.

DIVERSITY—THE NEW FACE OF THE STUDENT POPULATIONS AT AUSTRALIAN UNIVERSITIES

Australia had an estimated 303,324 international students in 2003, up 11% from 2002 (Department of Education, Science, and Training [DEST], 2004b). The DEST (2004a) report showed that international students are increasing in number and diversity—including what they study and by what mode—while "domestic" Australian groups tend to be more stable in course choices and numbers. More than three-quarters of Australia's international students come from Asia. However, in the 2002–2003 period, there was a significant increase in intake from the Middle East, Africa, North America, and Europe. In 2002, most international students (66%) lived in Australia while studying. They were typically younger than domestic students, while international students living overseas tended to be older.

PROFILES OF THE USQ STUDENT POPULATION

Approximately 75% of USQ students are off-campus. Of those studying full time on-campus at USQ, about half come from the Toowoomba region, 30% from elsewhere in Queensland, 8% from overseas, and 5% from interstate. In 2002 approximately 80% of the commencing Australian students were from rural areas, 12% from urban areas, and 4% from isolated areas. Sixty one percent were female, and only 1% identified themselves as Indigenous. The students came from 25 countries. Most (65%) were under 20 years old when they started, 20% were age 20–24, 6% were 25–29, 4% were 30–34, and 5% were 35 years or older. Approximately 99% of the students came from an English-speaking background. Finally, 44% of the commencing students came directly from high school and a further 12% one year after high school (University of Southern Queensland, 2003).

The Faculty of Engineering and Surveying offers 4-year bachelor degrees, 3-year technology degrees, and 2-year associate degree programs in both engineering and spatial science. More than 2,700 students enrolled in engineering programs in 2004, with approximately 75%

studying by the distance mode. The diversity of the enrolled student body mirrors that of the University as a whole.

SOCIOCULTURAL FACTORS

A main aim of this study was to establish whether any of the sociocultural differences identified within the student body has a significant impact on success. Consider all these variables in relation to the following scenarios: A mature-age student granted block exemptions for courses previously completed in a Middle Eastern university and studying by the distance mode while still residing in his home country; a 21-year-old Malaysian student who has just completed her first degree in her home country and has traveled to Australia to undertake a higher degree; an 18-year-old male school-leaver about to begin his first degree at a metropolitan university, far from his home in rural New South Wales, away from family and friends, and the first person in his family to undertake higher education studies; or a 35-year-old male engineering technician working in a remote mining town studying by the distance mode to become a professional engineer.

What do they all have in common? Each will undergo several stages of adjustment as they adapt to the university culture, learn what is expected of them, learn to manage their time, and develop necessary support networks. Students with more than one of the "at-risk" factors mentioned earlier, and those students whose first language is not English, may take longer to adjust and may feel socially isolated.

Devlin (2003) referred to the challenges of learning the "unfamiliar and unwritten rules" of university study, and recommended that for first-year students in particular, social connections at university can contribute to academic success. Clulow and Brennan (1996, as cited in Lawrence, 2003) highlighted the value to students of appropriate and varied social interaction. This contact, coupled with motivation to seek help, are significant factors in students' acculturation, and ultimately in their success at university. However, Volet and Ang (1998) observed that where different cultural groups are involved, especially where negative cultural stereotypes exist, interaction between groups might be difficult.

Increasingly, the roles of educators as primary knowledge sources are being challenged and renegotiated. Students are now encouraged to play a greater role in knowledge creation and sharing. However, such interactions are generally conducted in English, are facilitated by the norms of the dominant culture, and are based heavily on the teacher's own learning experiences. Furthermore, where students are not "literate" in the host culture's idioms, contextual subtleties, and mores, they can struggle to interpret expectations. These students may take longer to understand and respond to course requirements (Pincas, 2001).

Cooperative behavior is particularly important in some engineering courses that are designed around a problem-based learning approach, requiring teamwork and peer support. Ryan and Hellmundt (2003) reported on the value of educators using the cultural diversity of classes to help students view issues from multiple perspectives, and to help them broaden their cultural knowledge, or "cultural intelligence" (Peterson, 2004). However, fitting into this scenario can be difficult for students from another culture. Parsons and Dowling (2004) argued that international students coming to Australian universities need greater support in adjusting to a different teaching and learning paradigm.

Thus, the challenge for teachers in today's tertiary education sector is delivering a learning environment that is inclusive and caters to the increasing diversity among student populations. Adopting one teaching style is no longer sufficient. But acknowledging diversity is one thing, and achieving inclusiveness is another. To make effective adjustments to their methodologies, teachers need to better understand exactly what it is about individual students that can make the difference between success and failure.

The lack of female participation in engineering is a sociocultural factor worthy of examination. Engineering remains one of the few professions where women have not achieved greater equality with men (Department of Employment, Training, and Youth Affairs [DETYA], 1999). Women make up just 5% of engineers and 14% of engineering students in Australia (Institution of Engineers Australia, 1996). Just 7% of engineering students at USQ are women. The domination of the engineering profession by men and the consequent image of engineering as masculine have helped to keep many women out of engineering (Beder, 1998). So too has the fact that women believe their priority values are not being adequately reflected in engineering work and learning environments, which put high value on objectivity and disconnection from human and social concerns (Burrowes, 2001).

Interestingly, engineering has attracted many high-achieving women, despite the barriers. These are often women who have been through an unconscious and systematic "toughening" and "weeding out" in both their school system and their community. Girls studying math and physics (not traditional subjects for girls) take them due to real passion, commitment, and talent. Thus, women proceeding to engineering can be academically superior to their male colleagues. This phenomenon of women being "top of the class" may have been detrimental to the overall long-term promotion of women entering the engineering profession. Consequently, it has been difficult for engineering faculties to accept that changes still need to occur to support the increased participation of women.

INDIVIDUAL DIFFERENCES FACTORS

The three categories of individual differences variables of interest in the current research project are: learning styles, cognitive ability (including spatial and verbal abilities), and personality traits.

Learning Styles

Learning style can be defined as the way in which individuals most efficiently and effectively perceive, process, store, and recall what they are attempting to learn (James & Gardner, 1995). Researchers such as Zhenhui (2001) and Peacock (2001) highlighted the value of matching teaching and learning styles. As the first year of study is typically where expectations, values, study habits, and support networks are established, it is critical that educators consider these variables in the design and teaching of courses.

Learning styles can be categorized in a number of ways: for example, the preferred mode for receiving information (reading, writing, listening); the preferred way of processing information (active, sequential, intuitive); and the preferred environment (alone, in groups, at home) for learning. Consequently, many learning style models, and associated test instruments, have been developed to gain an understanding of student learning preferences.

Learning style is strongly influenced by life, societal, and educational experiences (Ayre & Nafalski, 2000; Felder & Soloman, 2003; McInerney & McInerney, 2002; Sarasin, 1999). People's learning style preferences change over time as they learn from their experiences and adopt strategies that are likely to be successful (Dunn, 1990). Adaptability is especially important when students move from course to course, experiencing diverse approaches to teaching, as well as for their professional needs and for life-long learning contexts that are continually changing.

Research suggests that students who actively engage in their learning are more likely to succeed (Blackmore, 1996; Hartman, 1995). However, to engage students, academics must first understand learning styles and how they can influence a student's performance (Birkey & Rodman, 1995; Hartman, 1995). Academics must also know and understand their own learning style (Sarasin, 1999) so they are aware of how these may influence their teaching styles. Felder and Soloman (2003) highlighted two important issues. First, the data do not indicate how well an individual learns. Second, when planning teaching strategies, the data for a group (such as a class) are more useful than that for individuals. However, individual feedback is important for students to self-manage their own learning environments.

According to Dunn (1990), students improve their academic performance when they understand their own learning preferences and when teachers adapt their practices to accommodate different preferences. Thus, students need to acquire this metacognitive knowledge—an understanding of their own motivations, beliefs, attitudes, learning preferences, and responses to different teaching strategies—to succeed (Hacker, 1998; Thomas, 2002).

However, there are two perspectives to consider. Teachers also need to adapt their approaches to cater to these different learning preferences. This can be difficult, and mismatches may exist between the learning styles of students and their teachers (Fowler, Campbell, McGill, & Roy, 2003; Montgomery, 1995). For example, Fowler and colleagues (2003) found that many engineering students were sensors, had a strong visual preference, and were global learners. Despite this, most lectures are delivered verbally and teaching materials are sequentially focused. Thus, teaching practices need to acknowledge that no single approach is best for all students.

Cognitive Abilities

It is generally accepted that human intelligence does not consist of one factor alone but a number of cognitive abilities that together form our overall intellectual capacity. Cognitive abilities can be thought of as people's capacity to solve problems and understand concepts. A number of specific and separate cognitive abilities can be identified, including verbal and spatial abilities. Verbal abilities involve the ability to understand linkages between words and process information presented in word form. Spatial abilities involve the ability to visualize and mentally manipulate shapes. Past research has shown verbal and spatial abilities may be significant predictors of academic success (Rothstein & Paunonen, 1994). One could speculate that people from different cultural groups will be stronger or weaker on specific dimensions. For example, indigenous students might be strong on the spatial dimension because they are taught to track game from a very early age (Eckermann, 1995). In contrast, black South African students are reported to have low spatial ability when compared to other South African students (Potter & van der Merwe, 2003). Work by Dyson (2002) suggested, though, that perceived weaknesses in one context may be strengths in another. She cited work by O'Donoghue (1992), which indicates that computer-based learning, with colorful illustrative elements, and interactivity may appeal to indigenous visual–spatial strengths.

Spatial Ability

Navigating a car through a strange city is an example of spatial ability. The navigator must be able to visualize the information from the map and relate it to the real world in real time. Spatial ability involves the ability to "generate, retain, and manipulate abstract visual images" (Lohman, 1979, p. 116). Spatial ability tests require the examinee to mentally handle and transform complex images.

A number of sociocultural factors can influence spatial ability: age, experience, childhood environment, culture, and gender. Men generally have higher levels of spatial ability (Magin & Churches, 1996) and show superiority in tests of spatial rotation performance (Poltrock & Agnoli, 1986). Some authors have suggested that this is due to environmental reasons. Different socialization practices and cultural expectations mean boys are much more likely than girls to engage in activities and experiences that promote the development of spatial abilities (Magin & Churches, 1996). Factors such as handedness, use of video games, parents' experience with technology, geometry courses undertaken, technical education, sports played, and play with construction toys, can all play a role as well (Kosslyn et al., 2002; Miller & Boud, 1996; Strong & Smith, 2002).

Considerable research has found spatial abilities are critical for success in graphics and engineering (Magin & Churches, 1996; Sorby & Baartmans, 1996), even scoring a higher correlation than results on verbal or intelligence tests (McGee, 1979, as cited in Strong & Smith, 2002). First-year engineering students with poor spatial ability are more likely to fail graphics courses and drop out. For this reason many engineering schools around the world test the spatial ability of their first-year cohort and provide intervention programs to enhance these skills (Gradinscak & Lewis, 1995; Leopold, Gorska, & Sorby, 2001; Magin & Churches, 1996; Medina, Gerson, & Sorby, 1998; Skorupan, 1998). Such testing at the University of Witwatersrand in South Africa resulted in a dramatic improvement in student pass rates in first-year engineering graphics courses (Potter & van der Merwe, 2003).

Spatial ability tests were included in this project to identify "at-risk" students and correlations with sociocultural features. Interestingly, Potter and van der Merwe (2003) did identify the impact of political and sociocultural factors in their initial data, with the pass rate for African students at 20%, compared to 64% for all engineering students.

Verbal Ability

Language is the way we communicate, how we represent our ideas and convey them to others. People high in verbal abilities can rapidly convert physical representations into a conceptual meaning, and quickly perform mental scanning and simple computation tasks (Hunt, Lunneborg, & Lewis, 1975). Verbal abilities are typically measured by tasks requiring the demonstration of accumulated knowledge, such as vocabulary or reading tests (Sternberg, 1986).

Verbal ability is known to be a predictor of success in academic settings (Driskell, Hogur, Salsa, & Hoskin, 1994). Dawson and Conti-Bekkers (2002) cited language difficulties as one of the key adjustment issues for international students, along with unfamiliarity with the new education system, homesickness, and isolation. Language can also be an issue for indigenous students, with Zeegers, Muir, and Lin (2003) reporting up to 250 languages and 700 dialect groups among indigenous Australians. Pidgin and other informal versions of English add to the complexity.

Verbal skills are clearly relevant in the engineering profession. Graduates are expected to communicate technical information simply and clearly; use appropriate formats for technical memos, letters, and reports; and communicate within team environments. Given its importance, this study included verbal ability as a key variable in the test battery.

Personality Traits

Personality traits are the typical thoughts and feelings that individuals have in response to specific situations. A common taxonomy classifies personality traits in terms of the "Big Five" factors (Costa & McCrae, 1992; Farmer, Jarvis, Berent, & Corbett, 2001; Goldberg, 1993). These broad domains "provide a global indication of the individual differences in patterns of interpersonal relationships and experiential style" (Albion, 2000, p. 9) and are considered comprehensive descriptors of personality (Rottinghaus, Lindley, Green, & Borgen, 2002). The Big Five are measures of: Extraversion, a person's interest in interactions with others and levels of sociability; Agreeableness, cooperation versus competition; Conscientiousness, self-control and need for achievement; Neuroticism versus Emotional stability; and Openness to Experience, preference for familiar versus novel experience (Costa & McCrae, 1992).

Researchers using personality type indicators have found that engineers do tend to have more reflective and introverted personality traits (Macdaid, McCaulley, & Kainz, 1986), with some minor variations depending on their field of engineering (Johnson & Singh, 1998). It will be interesting as part of the current research project to examine whether engineering students of different sociocultural backgrounds show different dominant personality traits.

Apart from personality traits, other individual differences variables can determine how people respond to specific situations. These include self-efficacy, proactive attitudes, and proactive coping.

Self-efficacy, Proactive Attitude, and Coping Style

Self-efficacy refers to a person's optimistic belief in their ability to cope with a variety of stressful or challenging situations (Bandura, 1977; Schwarzer, 1993). The scholastic and emotional stressors of first-year tertiary study can be very difficult. Students with high self-efficacy have confidence in their ability to cope, and a sense of personal competence to deal effectively with a variety of demanding situations (Schwarzer, 1993). Proactive attitude refers to people's belief that there are many opportunities available in order to make self and environmental improvements (Schwarzer, 1999). The student high in proactive coping believes that sufficient resources exist to succeed, including external resources such as study materials and internal resources such as intelligence, courage, and strength (Schwarzer, 1999).

All of these constructs hold great promise in determining which individual differences factors are most important to academic success.

PERFORMANCE OUTCOMES

The grade point averages (GPAs) the participants achieved in their first-semester courses were used as an overall measure of their academic success. To this end, data on the grades the students achieved in their first-semester courses were also obtained. These courses dealt with communication (ENG1001), problem solving (ENG1101), graphics and design (ENG1100), mechanical engineering materials (MEC1201), and foundation mathematics (MAT1100).

THE CURRENT STUDY

Participants

This study gathered data by putting a total of 132 first-year engineering students (17 females and 115 males) at USQ through a battery of tests designed to identify key individual differences variables. All were volunteers and studying on-campus at the time of testing. Complete data were obtained from 66 students (13 females and 53 males), with a mean age of

20.15 years ($SD = 4.99$). The mean age of the females was 18.15 years ($SD = 2.51$) and of the males was 21.96 years ($SD = 6.51$). Most had not previously studied engineering or surveying. All but five students spoke English as their first language, with six other languages spoken across the sample.

Measures

Cognitive Ability Tests

The reference tests were mostly selected from the Ekstrom, French, Harman, and Dermen (1976) kit, except where otherwise indicated. The dependent variable for each test was the total number correct. Verbal ability was measured by three verbal tests: Scrambled Words, Hidden Words, and Incomplete Words.

Three tests were included to measure each of the following three major spatial abilities: Visualization, Spatial Relations, and Spatial Scanning. Visualization reflects the ability to apprehend a spatial form and rotate it in two or three dimensions before matching it with another spatial form. Visualization ability was measured by the following tests: Paper Form Board, Paper Folding, and Surface Development. Spatial Relations reflects the ability to perceive an object from different positions, and was measured by the following tests: Card Rotations, Cube Comparisons, and Spatial Relations (Thurstone & Thurstone, 1965). Spatial Scanning reflects the ability to mentally scan a map or object and find a path or connection between two points, when speed is a factor. Spatial Scanning ability was measured by the following three mental scanning tests: Maze Tracing Speed, Choosing a Path, and Map Planning.

Personality Variables

The self-report survey asked for demographic information on gender, age, language, nation of origin, handedness (i.e., left or right), field of study, and experience. Other questions measured personality, self-efficacy, proactive attitude, and proactive coping, each using a 5-point Likert scale.

The short version of the International Personality Item Pool questionnaire (Goldberg, 1999) was used to measure the Big Five factors of personality. Ten items were included to measure each personality factor. Negatively phrased items were reverse scored, and a total score was computed for each personality factor: Extraversion, Agreeableness, Conscientiousness, Neuroticism/Emotional Stability, and Openness to Experience.

The revised General Self-Efficacy scale (Schwarzer & Jerusalem, 2000) was designed to assess the self-efficacy of the students. The Proactive Attitude scale (Schwarzer, 1999) comprises eight items that measure a person's belief in various facets such as resourcefulness, responsibility, values, and vision. The Proactive Coping scale (Greenglass, Schwarzer, & Taubert, 1999) is a 14-item scale designed to measure a person's ability to commit to, and engage in, an autonomous and self-directed setting.

Learning Styles

The Index of Learning Styles (Felder & Solomon, 2003) is a 44-item self-report questionnaire used to identify preferred learning styles. It assesses student preferences in modal perception and information processing, with the results being presented on four bipolar scales: processing, perception, input, and understanding (see Felder & Solomon, 2003). Individual preferences are indicated for each of the four dimensions of learning: active versus reflective (e.g., retain information best when they discuss or apply it vs. make time in study to think quietly on new material); sensing versus intuitive (e.g., use specific examples of abstract principles and find practical, real-world applications vs. enjoy innovation and discovering relationships between ideas); visual versus verbal (e.g., remember best information that is presented visually, including pictures, diagrams, flow charts, and demonstrations vs. gain understanding through using words, either written or spoken explanations); and sequential versus global (e.g., relate new topics to things previously learned and to the course as a whole vs. skim a chapter for an entire overview before studying the content in greater detail).

Fleming's (2001) VARK is a 13-item questionnaire designed to measure an individuals' preference for the intake and output of information based on four different modes: visual (e.g., replace words with pictures, symbols, and diagrams), aural (e.g., explain ideas to others and read notes and answers out loud), reading/writing (e.g., use definitions and rewrite notes and ideas into other words), and kinesthetic (e.g., use practical examples and a hands-on approach to engage all of your senses). Scores are calculated on each mode and participants may have a preference for one mode or for a number of modalities (i.e., multimodal).

Procedure

The individual differences and sociocultural factors examined in this chapter were completed as part of a large-scale longitudinal study currently in progress at USQ. Only those measures relevant to the current research topic will be analyzed here.

The total testing time was about 2.5 to 3 hours, broken into two 1-hour test sessions and a take-home self-report survey. The first session involved the timed verbal ability tests and the first half of the spatial ability tests. The second session included the second half of the spatial ability tests. A maximum of 25 people were present in either test session. At the end of the second test session, participants were each given the self-report survey to complete in their own time. They were required to return the completed survey in a sealed envelope within one week. Testing was carried out over a 4-week period. Participants who completed the full battery of tests received feedback on their verbal and spatial ability levels, personality traits, and preferred learning styles. While some staff from the Faculty also volunteered to participate, their data are incomplete and not available for inclusion at the time of publication.

Results and Discussion

The results confirmed our initial thoughts that individual differences in cognitive abilities, learning styles, and personality variables play a role in academic success. They also confirmed the considerable influence that sociocultural factors can have on student performance. The results are only preliminary at this stage, and we need to track students' performance across a 4-year period to identify the best predictors of success, particularly in relation to identifying exactly which sociocultural influences can have the greatest impact.

As shown in Table 12.1, both verbal and spatial abilities were related to success in students' first semester of tertiary study. Verbal abilities were particularly important to those courses that required the reporting of solutions in clear and precise English (i.e., ENG1001 and ENG1100). While all spatial ability tests were associated with success, the three visualization tests strongly related to final grades in the mechanical engineering materials course (i.e., MEC1201), which requires students to use their visualization skills to understand molecular structures, spatial relationships, and to carry out mental manipulations and rotations. A multiple regression analysis, with the cognitive ability tests as the predictor variables, showed the Paper Form Board test to be the best predictor of success in this course $F(12, 44) = 2.45$, $p < .05$, with a standardized beta weight of .753. If these strong correlations are verified in future testing they may prove to be the critical predictors of student success in their overall program.

The present results also support the findings of other researchers, with students showing the following learning preferences: active rather than reflective, sensory rather than intuitive, and visual rather than verbal (see Fowler et al., 2003; Montgomery, 1995). However, the students showed no clear preference for either global or sequential learning styles. Our results

Table 12.1 Correlation Matrix: Verbal Ability, Spatial Ability, and Personality Measures Correlated against GPA and First-Year Engineering Course Results

	ENG1001	ENG1100	ENG1101	MAT1100	MEC1201	GPA
Verbal Ability						
Scrambled Words	.42**	.49**	.22*	.12	.12	.24**
Hidden Words	.42**	.57**	.22*	.32*	.21	.21**
Incomplete Words	.40**	.22	.24*	.28*	.28*	.27**
Spatial Relations Ability						
Card Rotations	.14	.07	.08	.19	.09	.18
Cube Comparisons	.26*	.27*	.19	.24*	.22*	.21
Spatial Relations	.16	.16	.20	.17	.13	.23*
Visualization Ability						
Paper Form Board	.43**	.09	.19	.16	.55**	.19
Paper Folding	.29*	.32*	.26*	.27*	.32*	.29**
Surface Development	.36*	.37*	.26*	.36*	.34*	.35**
Spatial Scanning Ability						
Maze Tracing Speed	.20	.03	.18	.16	.27*	.25*
Choosing a Path	.36*	.05	.16	.23*	.25*	.07
Map Planning	.55**	.09	.23*	.26*	.18	.33**
Personality Traits						
Self-Efficacy	.10	.24*	.23*	.23*	.31*	.33**
Proactive Attitude	.08	.28*	.33*	.11	.25*	.33**
Proactive Coping	.00	.41**	.29*	−.03	.13	.24*
Extraversion	.10	.24*	.26*	.11	.19	.31**
Agreeableness	.14	.09	.22*	.06	.32*	.26*
Conscientiousness	.07	.03	.16	.20	.21	.21
Neuroticism	.17	.21	.20	.41**	.32*	.20
Openness	.01	.19	.06	.19	.02	−.02

Note: ENG1001 is a basic communications and report writing course; ENG1100 is a first-year graphics course; ENG1101 is a first-year problem-solving course; MAT1100 is a foundation mathematics course; and MEC1201 is a first-year course in mechanical engineering materials. GPA is the final grade point average.
$*p < .05. **p < .01.$

therefore indicate that students prefer to learn in a variety of ways and that teaching practices should be inclusive enough to accommodate these preferences. Teaching methods, materials, and resources should cater to as many of the learning preferences of the group as possible to help maximize the learning potential of each student (Sarasin, 1999). Helping students to better understand their own learning styles and abilities on key skills indicators (e.g., verbal and spatial abilities for engineering students), is likely to increase their motivation and confidence in their ability to succeed.

As expected, self-efficacy, proactive attitude, and proactive coping traits were each shown to be important to academic success. Self-confidence helps empower students to manage their learning environment, regardless of the course of study. Students high in these self-regulatory traits also do well in courses where they must work in teams, as they need to collaborate with others to complete the task. It will be interesting to also investigate the importance of these traits to students learning via distance education.

The on-campus student sample scored highest on the Agreeableness personality trait ($M = 38.13$, $SD = 5.48$)—being sympathetic, trusting, cooperative, modest, and straightforward—and this was related to success in the problem-solving course. This makes sense as students were required to consult and collaborate with others, to evaluate the contribution of peers, and to acknowledge and respond positively to diversity in team situations as part of the assessment in this course. A multiple regression analysis, with the eight personality traits as the predictor variables, showed Extraversion to predict overall academic success (GPA), $F (8, 67) = 2.64$, $p < .05$, with a standardized beta weight of .249. However, further testing is required to establish the significance of these initial findings.

The results indicate that the small proportion of females studying engineering were highly successful in their studies, even outperforming their male counterparts in two final course grades. They also scored better than males on a test of verbal ability and on the proactive attitude measure and matched results in terms of spatial abilities. While the proportion of women in the course was relatively small, these data indicate that there is no underlying gender difference that would prevent women performing at the same level as men in engineering studies.

This study has reinforced that students do have different approaches to study and that there are some key indicators that can be used as predictors of success. By completing tests that examine individual learning-style preferences, cognitive abilities, and personality traits, students can become empowered to manage their own learning. That is particularly important at the first-year level, where students are still trying to find their feet in an unfamiliar environment. Following initial successes in making those adjustments, their confidence grows and they begin to take ownership of their learning. Individual feedback for students on test results is therefore crucial.

Teaching staff can use the results from the learning styles inventories to inform them about the most effective ways to deliver their courses to that group. In a tertiary setting where there are large numbers of students, and where lecturers are not aware of the learning styles of individual students, they should cater to as many of the learning preferences of the group as possible. To this end, the university will need to provide appropriate training and resources to staff to enable them to develop appropriate teaching and learning environments. Staff will also be encouraged to complete the testing program so that they have a sound understanding of the characteristics of the student cohorts and the implications that will have for their teaching.

The Importance of Examining Sociocultural Influences

As discussed earlier, this study is breaking new ground because of the way it is examining the interrelationship of individual differences in cognitive abilities, learning styles, and personality variables. Sociocultural factors can be shown to have a considerable influence on those variables, and therefore, on academic success. Greater understanding of a student's sociocultural background can often place individual variables in a context that enables educators to better meet their needs. The influence of sociocultural factors is best illustrated by three case studies of participants drawn from this study.

Case Study 1

This student is a 19-year-old-male enrolled in the Electrical and Electronic Engineering major of the Bachelor of Engineering degree. He formerly lived in rural Queensland and relocated to Toowoomba to live on-campus. At the end of his first semester of tertiary study, his GPA was 2.75, indicating that he failed two of his four foundation courses and was therefore at risk of dropping out. Why might this student be failing in his first year of study? He showed a strong preference for learning in the visual mode, and in contrast with the majority of students, showed a preference for reflective rather than active learning approaches. His performance on the cognitive ability tests indicated that he has average verbal ability and that he has above-average spatial ability. One would therefore assume that lack of cognitive ability is not an adequate explanation for his lack of success.

A partial explanation for why this student is failing may come from an analysis of his personality data in conjunction with his social background. His results indicate that he possessed no dominant trait of personality, with Emotional Stability and Openness to Experience being his equal highest scores (32). His scores on the Extraversion, Agreeableness, and Conscientiousness traits were all between one and two standard deviations below their average means, respectively. These results therefore indicate that he is an Introvert, and so would most likely not "stand out" in a class or seek help from others, especially in those courses where teamwork was vital to success. He was of average self-efficacy, and scored below average on the proactive attitude and proactive coping personality traits. It is unlikely that he would be a self-directed learner and thus highly probable that he would need assistance in adapting to his new study environment away from home. As noted by Devlin (2003), a lack of social support in his new home and study environment appears to be contributing to his academic failure. He may not have family and friends close by, so is struggling to adjust to the new demands of tertiary study.

Case Study 2

This is a 25-year-old-male enrolled in the Environmental Engineering major in the Bachelor of Engineering Technology degree. He was born in Sudan, and lived there for 13 years before moving to Kenya, where he lived for 10 years. He currently lives on-campus in Toowoomba. His GPA in his first semester of tertiary study was 4.17. Why is this student successful, despite being a nonschool leaver and a risk candidate for attrition? His performance on the cognitive ability tests indicated that he was of low average verbal ability and below average in spatial ability. However, these results may reflect his cultural background, particularly as English is not his first language. It is reasonable to expect that he would find the course content somewhat challenging, yet he is passing and meeting the challenges of adapting to his new educational environment. He showed strongest preferences for learning in the visual mode and by reading and writing, and was clearly able to adjust to the demands of tertiary study.

Another possible explanation is provided through consideration of his cultural background in combination with his personality results. His dominant personality trait was Conscientiousness, indicating that he worked extra hard to ensure he met the course objectives. He was also an Extravert who could easily adapt to the more active learning environment typically found in Western classrooms. He scored average on the self-efficacy, proactive attitude, and proactive coping measures. These results therefore indicate that he is a self-directed learner who has a sense of self-competence and can develop effective strategies to cope with the scholastic and emotional stressors of first-year tertiary study.

Case Study 3

This is an 18-year-old-female school leaver enrolled in a combined Bachelor of Engineering (Mechanical) and Bachelor of Science (Mathematics) degree. She was born in Australia and has English as her first language. At the end of her first semester of tertiary study, her GPA was 6.20, indicating a high achievement level. Why is this female student so successful? Her performance on the cognitive ability tests indicated that she was of average verbal ability and above average in spatial ability. These abilities were evidenced by a strong preference for learning in the visual mode. Therefore, given that spatial abilities have been shown to be predictive of success in engineering courses (Magin & Churches, 1996; Sorby & Baartmans, 1996), it is not surprising that she is passing such courses at a very high standard. Second, her personality results indicated that she is an Extravert, and that she scored high on the Agreeableness trait, making it relatively easy for her to get along with others and to work in a team. She also scored above average on the self-efficacy, proactive attitude, and proactive coping measures. These results therefore indicate that she is a self-directed learner who has a strong sense of self-competence and is willing to undertake behaviors to help her achieve her realistic, yet high learning goals.

Overall, the females in this sample achieved better academic results than the males, indicating that engineering does indeed attract high-achieving women who self-select into this field of study. It is therefore highly likely that this female will continue to be highly successful in her studies and to even "out-rank" her male counterparts.

FUTURE RESEARCH DIRECTIONS

The full benefits of this study will occur as the students are tracked through their 4-year degree. However, the initial results are being used to inform a review of the engineering programs at USQ starting in January 2005. The Faculty is considering a core skills course that all students will undertake, regardless of the amount of advanced standing they may receive. This course would, first, inform students of their individual differences, strengths, weaknesses, and gaps in their knowledge and experience, and then, second, provide them with the opportunities and resources to acquire the knowledge and skills needed to succeed in their chosen program. Further testing of USQ students in different study modes is planned, and comparisons on these variables may shed light on other sociocultural variables, such as cultural differences, gender, age, and previous study experience. Further investigation of these variables is timely, as the engineering profession is one that operates globally, and has made concerted attempts to attract more women.

ACKNOWLEDGMENTS

We would like to acknowledge and thank Kristine Dun for her work as a research assistant. She helped compile the data file for the current analyses and develop the feedback sheets for all participants. We would also like to thank the Faculty of Engineering and Surveying for providing the seed funding required for the first phase of testing.

REFERENCES

Albion, M. J. (2000). Developing and validating a model of career decision making. Unpublished doctoral dissertation, University of Southern Queensland, Toowoomba, Australia.

Ayre, M., & Nafalski, A. (2000, October). *Recognising diverse learning styles in teaching and assessment of electronic engineering.* Paper presented at the international conference Frontiers in Education: Building on a Century of Progress in Engineering Education, Kansas City, MS.

Bandura, A. (1977). Self-efficacy: Toward a unifying theory of behavioural change. *Psychological Review, 84,* 191–215.

Beder, S. (1998). *The new engineer: Management and professional responsibility in a changing world.* Sydney, Australia: Macmillan Education.

Birkey, R., & Rodman, J. (1995). *Adult learning styles and preference for technology programs.* Paper presented at the Lifelong Learning conference of Innovations in Higher Education, Technology and Workplace Literacy, California. Available online at http://www.nu.edu/nuri/llconf/conf1995/birkey.html

Blackmore, J. (1996). *Pedagogy: Learning styles.* Available online at http://cyg.net/~jblackmo/diglib/style-a.html

Burke Guild, P. (2001). *Diversity, learning style, and culture.* Available online at http://www.newhorizons.org/strategies/styles/guild.htm

Burrowes, G. (2001). *Gender dynamics in an engineering classroom: Engineering students' perspectives.* Unpublished master of philosophy dissertation, University of Newcastle, Sydney, Australia. Available online at http:// www.newcastle.edu.au/services/library/adt/uploads/approved/adt-NNCU20021210.142001/public/02chapter.pdf

Costa, P. T. J., & McCrae, R. R. (1992). *Revised NEO Personality Inventory (NEO-PI-R) and NEO Five Factor Inventory (NEO-FFI): Professional manual.* Odessa, FL: Psychological Assessment Resources.

Dawson, J., & Conti-Bekkers, G. (2002). *Supporting international students' transitional adjustment strategies.* Proceedings from Teaching and Learning Forum 2002. Available online at http://lsn.curtin.edu.au/tlf/tlf2002/dawson.html

Department of Education, Science, and Training. (2004a). *International higher education students. How do they differ from other higher education students?* (Strategic Analysis and Evaluation Group Research Note No. 2). Available online at http://www.dest.gov.au/research/publications/research_notes/2.htm

Department of Education, Science, and Training. (2004b, March 9*). International student numbers.* Media release by Dr Brendan Nelson, Australian Government Minister for Education Science and Training, MIN 638/04. Available online at http://www.dest.gov.au/Ministers/Media/Nelson/2004/03/n638040304.asp

Department of Employment, Training, and Youth Affairs. (1999). *Women in engineering statistics*. Canberra, Australia: DETYA.

Devlin, M. (2003, February 12). Making the leap to uni life. *The Age*. Available online at http://www.theage.com.au/articles/2003/02/12/1044927657355.html

Driskell, J. E., Hogur, J., Salsa, E., & Hoskin, B. (1994). Cognitive and personality predictors of training performance. *Military Psychology, 6*, 31–46.

Dunn, R. (1990). Rita Dunn answers questions on learning styles. *Educational Leadership, 48*, 15–19.

Dyson, L. E. (2002). Design for a culturally affirming indigenous computer literacy course. In A. Williamson, C. Gunn, A. Young, & T. Clear (Eds.), *Winds of change in the sea of learning: Proceedings of the 19th annual conference of the Australasian Society for Computers in Learning in Tertiary Education* (pp. 185–194). Available online at http://www-staffit.uts.edu.au/~laurel/Publications/Publications.htm

Eckermann, A. K. (1995). *Introduction to traditional Aboriginal societies*. Armidale, Australia: University of New England Press.

Ekstrom, R. B., French, J. W., Harman, H. H., & Dermen, D. (1976). *Manual for kit of factor-referenced cognitive tests*. Princeton, NJ: Educational Testing Service.

Farmer, R. F., Jarvis, L. L., Berent, M. K., & Corbett, A. (2001). Contributions to global self-esteem: The role of importance attached to self-concepts associated with the five-factor model. *Journal of Research in Personality, 35*, 483–499.

Felder, R. M., & Soloman, B. A. (2003). *Index of learning styles questionnaire*. Available onlineat http://www.engr.ncsu.edu/learningstyles/ilsweb.html

Fleming, N. D. (2001). *VARK: A guide to learning styles*. Available online at http://www.vark-learn.com/english/index.asp

Fowler, L., Campbell, V., McGill, D., & Roy, G. (2003, September). *An innovative approach to teaching first year programming supported by learning style investigation*. Paper presented at the conference Engineering Education for a Sustainable Future, RMIT University, Melbourne, Australia.

Goldberg, L. R. (1993). The structure of phenotypic traits. *American Psychologist, 78*, 26–34.

Goldberg, L. R. (1999). A broad-bandwidth, public domain, personality inventory measuring the lower-level facets of several five-factor models. *Personality Psychology in Europe, 7*, 7–28.

Gradinscak, Z., & Lewis, W. P. (1995). *An evaluation of curriculum changes in engineering graphics*. Paper presented at the International Conference on Design and Technology, Loughborough University of Technology, Loughborough.

Greenglass, E., Schwarzer, R., & Taubert, S. (1999). *Proactive Coping Scale*. Available online at http://www.fu-berlin.de/gesund/skalen/Language

Hacker, D. J. (1998). Definitions and empirical foundations. In D. J. Hacker, J. Dunlosky, & A. C. Graesser (Eds.), *Metacognition in educational theory and practice* (pp. 1–23). Mahwah, NJ: Erlbaum.

Hartman, V. F. (1995). Teaching and learning style preferences: Transitions through technology. *The Victorian Curriculum and Assessment Authority Journal, 9*, 18–20. Available online at http://www.so.cc.va.us/vcca/hart1.htm

Hunt, E., Lunneborg, C., & Lewis, J. (1975). What does it mean to be high verbal? *Cognitive Psychology, 7*, 194–227.

Institution of Engineers Australia. (1996). *Changing the culture: Engineering education into the future*. Canberra, Australia: IEAust.

James, W. B., & Gardner, D. L. (1995). Learning styles: Implications for distance learning. *New Directions for Adult and Continuing Education, 67,* 19–32.

Johnson, H. M., & Singh, A. (1998). The personality of civil engineers. *Journal of Management in Engineering, 14,* 45–56.

Kosslyn, S. M., Cacioppo, J. T., Davidson, R. J., Hugdahl, K., Lovallo, W. R., Spiegel, D., & Rose, R. (2002). Bridging psychology and biology: The analysis of individuals in groups. *American Psychologist, 57,* 341–351.

Lawrence, J. (2003). The "deficit-discourse" shift: University teachers and their role in helping first year students persevere and succeed in the new university culture. Available online at   http://ultibase.rmit.edu.au/Articles/march03/lawrence1.htm

Leopold, C., Gorska, R., & Sorby, S. (2001). International experiences in developing the spatial visualisation abilities of engineering students. *Journal of Geometry and Graphics, 5,* 81–91.

Lohman, D. F. (1979). *Spatial ability: A review and reanalysis of the correlational literature* (Technical Report No. 8). Palo Alfo, CA: Stanford University, School of Education, Aptitude Research Project.

Macdaid, G. P., McCaulley, M. H., & Kainz, R. I. (1986). *Atlas of type tables*. Gainsville, FL: Centre for Application of Psychological Type.

Magin, D., & Churches, A. (1996, December). *Gender differences in spatial abilities of entering first year students: What should be done?* Paper presented at the 8th AAEE Annual Convention and Conference, Sydney, Australia.

McInerney, D. M., & McInerney, V. (2002). *Educational psychology: Constucting learning* (3rd ed.). Sydney, Australia: Prentice Hall.

Medina, A. C., Gerson, H. B. P., & Sorby, S. A. (1998). *Identifying gender differences in the 3-D visualisation skills of engineering students in Brazil and in the United States*. Paper presented at the International Conference on Engineering Education, Rio de Janeiro.

Miller, N., & Boud, D. (1996). Animating learning from experience. In D. Boud & N. Miller (Eds.), *Working with experience: Animating learning* (pp. 3–13). London: Routledge.

Montgomery, S. M. (1995). *Addressing diverse learning styles through the use of multimedia*. Available online at http://fie.engrng.pitt.edu/fie95/3a2/3a22/3a22.htm

O'Donoghue, R. R. (1992). Why the Aboriginal child succeeds at the computer. *The Aboriginal Child at School, 20,* 48–52.

Parsons, D., & Dowling, D. (2004, September). *Teaching engineering to South-East Asian students*. Proceedings from the Australian Association for Engineering Education Conference, Toowoomba, Queensland, Australia.

Peacock, M. (2001). Match or mismatch? Learning styles and teaching styles in EFL. *International Journal of Applied Linguistics, 11,* 1–20.

Peterson, B. (2004). *Cultural intelligence: A guide to working with people from other cultures*. Maine, WI: Intercultural Press.

Pincas, A. (2001). Culture, cognition and communication in global education. *Distance Education, 22,* 30–51.

Poltrock, S. E., & Agnoli, F. (1986). Are spatial visualisation ability and visual imagery ability equivalent? In R. J. Sternberg (Ed.), *Advances in the psychology of human intelligence: Volume 3* (pp. 255–296). Hillsdale, NJ: Lawrence Erlbaum.

Potter, C., & van der Merwe, E. (2003). Perception, imagery, visualisation and engineering graphics. *European Journal of Engineering Education, 281,* 117–133.

Rothstein, M. G., & Paunonen, S. V. (1994). Personality and cognitive ability predictors of performance in graduate school. *Journal of Educational Psychologist, 86,* 516–531.

Rottinghaus, P. J., Lindley, L. D., Green, M. A., & Borgen, F. H. (2002). Educational aspirations: The contribution of personality, self-efficacy, and interests. *Journal of Vocational Behaviour, 61,* 1–19.

Ryan, J. & Hellmundt, S. (2003). *Excellence through diversity: Internationalism of curriculum and pedagogy.* Paper presented at the 17th IDP Australian International Education Conference. Available online at http:// www.idp.com/17aiec/ selectedpapers/Ryan%20-%Excellence%20through%20diversity%2024-10-03.pdf

Sarasin, L. C. (1999). *Learning style perspectives: Impact in the classroom.* Madison, WI: Atwood.

Schwarzer, R. (1993). *General perceived self-efficacy in 14 cultures.* Available online at http://www.fu-berlin.de/gesund/skalen/Language

Schwarzer, R. (1999). *Proactive attitude scale.* Available online at http://www.fu-berlin.de/gesund/skalen/Language

Schwarzer, R., & Jerusalem, J. (2000). *General perceived self-efficacy scale.* Available online at http://www.fu-berlin.de/gesund/skalen/Language

Shuman, L. J., Atman, C. J., Eschenback, E. A., Evans, D. L., Felder, R. M., Imbrie, P. K., McGourty, J., Miller, R. L., Smith, K. A., Soulsby, E. P., Waller, A. A., & Yokomoto, C. F. (2002). *The future of engineering education.* Proceedings of the 32nd ASEE/IEEE Frontiers in Education Conference (pp. T4A-1–T4A-14).

Skorupan, C. (1998). The effect of spatial experience on engineering students' visualisation abilities. *The Penn State Behrend Psychology Journal, 2,* 45–50.

Sorby, S. A., & Baartmans, B. G. (1996). A course for the development of 3-D spatial visualisation skills. *Engineering Design Graphics Journal, 60,* 13–20.

Sternberg, R. J. (1986). *Intelligence applied: Understanding and increasing your intellectual skills.* New York: Harcourt Brace.

Strong, S., & Smith, R. (2002). Spatial visualisation: Fundamentals and trends in engineering graphics. *Journal of Industrial Technology, 18,* 1–6.

Thomas, G. P. (2002). The social mediation of metacognition. In D. M. McInerney & S. Van Etten (Eds.), *Sociocultural influences on motivation and learning* (pp. 225–247). Greenwich, CT: Information Age.

Thurstone, L. L., & Thurstone, T. G. (1965). *Primary mental abilities.* Chicago: Science Research Associates.

University of Southern Queensland. (2003). *Annual report, book 1.* Toowoomba, Australia: Author.

Venter, K. (2003). Coping with isolation: The role of culture in adult distance learners' use of surrogates. *Open Learning, 18,* 271–287.

Volet, S. E., & Ang, G. (1998). Culturally mixed groups on international campuses: An opportunity for intercultural learning. *Higher Education Research and Development, 17,* 5–23.

Walstab, A., Golding, B., Teese, R., Charlton, M., & Polesel, J. (2001). *Attrition and wastage in tertiary education.* Canberra, Australia: Lifelong Learning Network.

Zeegers, M., Muir, W., & Lin, Z. (2003). The primacy of the mother tongue: Aboriginal literacy and non-standard English. *The Australian Journal of Indigenous Education, 32,* 51–60.

Zhenhui, R. (2001). Matching teaching styles with learning styles in East Asian contexts. *The Internet TESL Journal, 7.* Available online at http://iteslj.org/Techniques/Zhenhui-TeachingStyles.html

CHAPTER 13

RETHINKING RESISTANCE IN MULTICULTURAL TEACHER EDUCATION

Reflection and Miseducation

Katherine Richardson Bruna

I was very open in the beginning of the discussion and after our teacher did that and didn't listen, I kind of hunched over and was doodling in my book and I totally turned off because I figured if she didn't want to hear anything I had to say, I wasn't going to listen to anything she had to say.

Two weeks into the Cultural Diversity course required of all teacher candidates at her institution, Yvonne has made a conscious decision to "turn off." The multicultural teacher education literature describes her decision as one of resistance. Such resistance, the literature explains, is to be expected from Yvonne. As a "white, Anglo-Saxon, lower or middle-class female who has grown up in a suburban or rural area ... is monolingual in English ... and has attended a local college or university close to her home" (Wideen, Mayer-Smith, & Moon, 1998, p. 140), Yvonne is the "typical" candidate for teacher education. Yvonne knows little about the

Focus on Curriculum, 299–326
Copyright © 2005 by Information Age Publishing
All rights of reproduction in any form reserved.

history and cultural practices of racial/ethnic groups different than her own (Bennett, Niggle, & Stage, 1989; Moultry, 1988; Wahab, 1989; Wayson, 1988) and her unsophisticated understanding of the social hierarchy and its effects makes it easy for her to take an individualistic view of school failure (Avery & Walker, 1993; Paine, 1989). Because of this profile, she is likely to resist learning about diversity, the scholars say, on "pedagogical change" and/or "ideological change" grounds (Rodriguez, 1998, pp. 1017–1018). Yvonne is likely to oppose the student-centered, constructivist approaches to teaching and learning advocated by diversity-oriented teacher educators, as well as the premise that using such approaches should be part of a broader struggle for social justice in U.S. schools and society. In other words, as a "typical" teacher candidate, Yvonne is predisposed to resistance before the Cultural Diversity course even begins. Her decision to "turn off" comes as no surprise. It is, after all, just evidence that Yvonne really *does* lack the multicultural understandings that courses like Cultural Diversity were designed to provide. This is the story the multicultural teacher education literature tells us about Yvonne.

I will interrupt this story by telling a different story about Yvonne. The story I tell is grounded in a 3-year ethnographic study I undertook before I became a multicultural teacher educator, one that takes on more and more relevance as I consider my own teaching experiences with white teachers. The story I tell is about how "typical" teacher candidates, like Yvonne, resist learning about diversity not necessarily because they have a natural predisposition to oppose movements for pedagogical and ideological change, but because they oppose their own construction as a "particular human kind for pedagogical intervention" (Popkewitz, 2004, p. 4); that is, they oppose being inscribed with the "white racist" identity upon which courses like Cultural Diversity and, in fact, the entire field of multicultural education, relies. Resistance, then, is not best understood through an individualistic lens that locates the source of opposition in the teacher candidate merely on account of her bodily and social identity (Ferguson, 1996, p. 115), but by acknowledging how her bodily and social identity affects pedagogical relations. What is needed is a socially constructed understanding of resistance, one that locates the source of opposition in the interaction between the teacher candidate's self-perception as a "good white" (Thompson, 2003, p. 8) and the teacher educator's inscription of her as a "bad white." Rethinking resistance this way challenges assumptions of its absolute inevitability by creating space for transformed pedagogical relations. Transformed pedagogical relations will move us away from reinforcing a purposeless sense of whiteness among teacher candidates and instead toward encouraging a purposeful sense of white antiracism. These will motivate, not alienate, the "typical" teacher in preparing her for work in culturally and linguistically diverse settings and by so doing most effectively accomplish the important goal of multicultural teacher education.

I begin by providing a broad overview of the field of multicultural teacher education. I describe the development within the field of the focus on white teacher identity and how that constitutes the "typical" white teacher as "a particular human kind for pedagogical intervention" (Popkewitz, 2004, p. 4). I do this within the context of differentiating between the *fact* and *force* of the "cultural mismatch" rhetoric that dominates the field of multicultural teacher education. I suggest that this rhetoric serves as an "inscription device" (Popkewitz, 2004, p. 4) to reinforce the whiteness-oppression equation (Howard, 2000, p. 111). It is this equation, I argue, that generates pedagogical relations that lead to experiences that Dewey termed "miseducative"; these are experiences that have "the effect of arresting or distorting the growth of further experience" (1938, p. 25). Resistance, such as Yvonne's decision to turn off, I suggest, is evidence of such arrest and distortion. I then turn my attention specifically to the use of critical reflection in multicultural teacher education as an example of a miseducative "pedagogical intervention" because of its investment in the identity of the "typical" white teacher as a "particular human kind." I also discuss how the use of critical reflection is part of a larger reflective turn in teacher professionalization that reflects modern economies of power (Foucault, 1982, p. 210). Resistance, I suggest, is best understood as opposition to this modern power economy. It does not reside within the individual teacher candidate, but is socially constructed out of pedagogical relations influenced by broader theoretical and historical currents.

To ground my discussion within the practice of multicultural teacher education, I relate an incident involving Yvonne, the "typical" teacher candidate who has decided to "turn off," another teacher candidate, Theresa, and their teacher educator, Ellen. I relate this incident as a "snapshot" of socially constructed resistance. It is one of many such incidences that I documented as part of my research on life in a multicultural teacher education classroom. While the data I collected comes from only one classroom and thus could be unrepresentative of more widespread practice, the literature, as I will explain, shows us that this is not the case. In addition, in presentations I have given at state, national, and international conferences, snapshots such as the one I share here find great resonance with experiences of the multicultural teacher education audience. For these reasons, I am convinced that it is a valid or trustworthy (Denzin & Lincoln, 1998, p. 287) indication of the phenomenon of white teacher resistance and that from my analysis generalizations can be made to other (though admittedly not all) multicultural teacher education settings.

The importance of my discussion, however, rests in a different kind of validity, what Lather calls "catalytic validity" (1991, p. 68). I hope my discussion will serve as a catalyst for further examination of the theory and practice of multicultural teacher education so that we can counter miseducative approaches with educative ones. To this end, I outline one such alternative I am implementing in my own work with white teacher candidates. The goal of my approach is to take a different point of departure to white teacher identity, one formed not around a purposeless sense of whiteness but around a purposeful sense of white antiracism, and in this way permit "typical" teacher candidates to discover aspects of themselves too readily withheld by the cultural mismatch framework. This point of departure is necessary, I assert, if we are to build genuine capacity among white teacher candidates for effective work with culturally and linguistically diverse students. Right now, as I will show, the current conception and practice of multicultural teacher education works against this very goal.

MISEDUCATION: THE FORCE OF CULTURAL MISMATCH IN MULTICULTURAL TEACHER EDUCATION

The field of multicultural teacher education concerns the work of equipping teacher candidates with both the cultural skills needed to work effectively with diverse youth as well the cultural knowledge of diverse group histories needed to teach about the experiences and contributions of individuals often underrepresented in Eurocentric school curricula. It regards such preparation as a fundamental feature of school reform oriented toward embracing and enacting the pluralist ideals of democracy (Nieto, 2004, pp. 436–437). In the United States, the history of multicultural teacher education is inextricably linked to the civil rights struggles among underrepresented groups both for the *recognition* of their histories and experiences and a *redistribution* of the social and economic resources kept from them as a result of institutionalized racism in social policy and practice (Fraser, 1998, p. 2). While multicultural teacher education today has expanded to include attention not only to race, but to the interrelated causes of sexism, classism, homophobia, and able-bodyism, race remains a central component of theory and practice. How best to prepare white teachers for work with students of color has steadily been the subject of research and debate. Increasingly, the debate revolves around the extent to which multicultural teacher education is predicated upon and invokes the very kind of racialized intergroup dynamics that the broader social movement for multiculturalism tries to problematize (Goldberg, 1996; Gordon & Newfield, 1996; Kincheloe & Steinberg, 1997; McLaren, 1997).

This, as Gonzales and Cauce (1995, pp. 140–141) astutely point out, is the paradox of multicultural education: "How does one recognize ethnic differences and support ethnicity as an important dimension of self-definition without paradoxically encouraging group divisions and intergroup tensions that often result when ethnic categories are emphasized?"

This emphasis on racial categorization is most salient in the discourse of cultural mismatch that underlies many understandings of and approaches to multicultural teacher education. The cultural mismatch discourse points to the "gap" between the white teacher and her "Other" students of color. Gomez (1994) refers to cultural mismatch when she writes that the "race, social class … and language backgrounds of prospective teachers affects their attitudes toward 'Others,' their willingness to live and be part of communities with 'Others,' to teach 'Others,' and to expect that 'Others' can learn" (pp. 320–321). In this way, cultural mismatch is a discourse that aligns the white teacher with racism (conscious or not) so that the main task of multicultural teacher education becomes that of having the white teacher confront her "white racism" (Sleeter, 1994) by making meaning of her "whiteness" (McIntyre, 1997).

The *fact* of cultural mismatch in the United States is absolutely uncontroversial: 87% of public school teachers are white and experience significantly higher socioeconomic outlooks than do their students of color who comprise, in some schools and districts, a majority of the student population (Choy, Henke, Alt, Hedrick, & Bobbitt, 1993; Council of Economic Advisors, 1998). The *force* of cultural mismatch, the effect it has in shaping approaches and pedagogical relations in multicultural teacher education, however, merits examination.

A proliferation of articles attests to the prevalence of the cultural mismatch theme in multicultural teacher education and its accompanying spotlight on the white teacher. Articles with titles like *Preparing Teachers to Work with Culturally Diverse Students* (Burstein & Cabello, 1989), *Educating Teachers for Cultural Diversity* (Zeichner, 1992), *Preparing Teachers for Cultural Diversity* (Cannella & Reiff, 1994), and *How Preservice Teachers Think about Cultural Diversity* (Smith, Moallem, & Sherrill, 1997) proclaim, though not explicitly, that the goal of multicultural teacher education is to teach the white teacher to teach the diverse "Other." They do that by describing the negative attributes white teacher candidates, like Yvonne, bring with them to their programs of preparation, characteristics that it is the task of multicultural teacher education to disrupt and alter. Zeichner (1992) has organized the techniques that multicultural teacher educators use to accomplish this task into five domains: autobiography, attitude change, field experience, cultural knowledge, and instructional strategies. While all of these techniques are important to the work of multicultural teacher education, attitude change frequently surfaces as the most central feature of approaches to addressing and redressing the racism of the white teacher candidate.

A "BOOT CAMP" APPROACH TO ATTITUDE CHANGE

An example of an attitude-change approach can be seen in Berlak & Moyenda's (2001) description of their "boot camp" activity. Berlak's description of the objective of her course reveals the force of cultural mismatch:

> [I wanted my students] to destabilize ideas they had been incorporating throughout their lives (and were continuing to incorporate daily) and to experience any significant changes in their views of and relationships to the children, parents, and teachers they would be working with who have identities different from their own. (p. 48)

To achieve this objective, Berlak organized opportunities for her students to "engage in deeply personal self-explorations" (p. 48). One of these opportunities involved Moyenda, an African American woman with a self-described "black attitude" problem, and the role-plays she had designed to illustrate the "worst-case scenario of an elementary classroom experience" (p. 52). These role-plays, thoughtfully described as coming out of Moyenda's own teaching experience, were intended to target issues Moyenda has been affecting the educational experiences of black children—parental violence, emotional distress, and drugs and alcohol (p. 55). In enacting the scenarios provided by Moyenda, teacher candidates were provided with scripts featuring a character overview. The overview for the student character of LaTipha, for example, describes her as "a ten-year-old African American female who reads at the second grade level. She is big and loud and capable of getting the entire class's attention.... Her mom is mentally ill, drug-addicted, alcoholic, and angry" (pp. 56–57). The teacher candidates play out these roles in interaction with a peer who has volunteered to play the role of teacher.

In writing about the activity, Moyenda notes that the teacher candidates were "obsessesd with their disruptive roles" (p. 60) and that the role-play resulted, as she had hoped it would, in "chaos." Then a "heated argument" ensues between Moyenda and the white actor-teacher as he challenges the realism of the scenario. She counters, "Well, I've seen it happen many times in the school where I teach. Especially in the classrooms of white teachers. It's based on my experience. I don't know where you've been teaching..." (p. 61). Moyenda goes on to tell the teacher candidates that many white teachers don't understand children who have experienced violence. In response to this, Moyenda tells us that a white teacher candidate begins to cry. She has taken exception to Moyenda's assumption that "there is no alcoholism and violence in white middle-class homes" (p. 61). This is Moyenda's response to that student:

> If what I say to you doesn't apply to you, it doesn't apply. But I'll say this: If I can make you cry by making an off-the-cuff comment, you're in even bigger trouble when you get into a classroom and school filled with people like me. (p. 61)

Berlak and Moyenda's (2001) approach exemplifies the force of cultural mismatch in multicultural teacher education and the miseducation of the white teacher candidate. Intent on a goal of attitude change that is based on the presumption of absolute difference between the experience of black children and those of the white teacher candidates, a white teacher's attempt to challenge that presumption by pointing out a place of similarity between the black–white experience (childhood exposure to alcohol-based violence) is dismissed, first, as a legitimate conceptual challenge ("If what I say to you doesn't apply to you, it doesn't apply") and, second, used as an opportunity to inscribe the teacher candidate's white identity against Moyenda's black identity ("you're in even bigger trouble when you get into a classroom and school filled with people like me"). The time devoted to student reflection after the role-play is not used as an opportunity for genuine dialogue on a provocative classroom activity. Instead, it is used to point out how the teacher candidates are, as Moyenda later describes them, "silly/dangerous white people" (p. 136). In this way, reflection is used to construct the white teacher candidate as a "particular human kind for pedagogical intervention" and, in effect, justify the cultural mismatch framework. Here, the teacher candidate's challenge to the cultural mismatch framework is turned against her and used by Moyenda as indisputable evidence of her inability to teach the "Other."

Pedagogical relations like these contribute to the miseducation of the white teacher in multicultural teacher education. "A [miseducative] experience," Dewey pointed out, "may be such as to engender callousness; it may produce lack of sensitivity and of responsiveness [such that] the possibilities of having richer experience in the future are restricted" (pp. 25–26). Miseducative outcomes occur in multicultural teacher education when, within a cultural mismatch frame, the white teacher candidate and the "Other" are continuously and categorically set against each other in such a way that the white teacher's identity is always and necessarily viewed first and foremost as a racist one. Taking this perspective on the education of the white teacher candidate does not and will not promote positive attitudes and dispositions toward teaching in culturally and linguistically diverse settings, nor promote continued interest in learning about cultural and linguistic difference. It is, quite simply, a demotivating perspective. How the use of reflection can contribute to the miseducation of the white teacher is thus an important element to consider when understanding motivational influences on the white teacher in multicultural teacher education.

REFLECTION OR REGULATION?

One of the first to write extensively about the role of reflection in teacher education was Dewey (1933). Dewey was worried about passive, technical models of teacher education and argued for a reflective model because he thought it best suited to the nature of a democracy and its requirement for active-thinking citizenship. He wanted teachers to think for themselves and contextualize instructional methods in light of specific goals or "purposes." Reflective thought, he wrote, "enables us to direct our activities with foresight and to plan according to the ends-in-view, or purposes of which we are aware" (p. 17). To this end, Dewey called for inquiry-oriented approaches to teaching and teacher education, approaches that would lead, he argued, to "intelligent action."

Dewey was writing during a time in which, as Popkewitz (1991) describes, changes in social organization had led to changes in social regulation requiring a "self" capable of "self"-management (p. 223). In Europe, a shift had occurred in the 17th–19th centuries away from the religious tradition of a stable social order organized around an unquestioning relationship to God and King (the Classical Age), to the age of social reform spurred by the rise of scientific and analytic thinking (the Enlightenment). The promise of modernity had given people more control over their social conditions, but what this meant in actuality was a different kind of social control over the people, a situation described by Foucault (1982, p. 210) as a "new economy of power." In the modern social order, knowledge of "self"—one's body and mind—was to be organized and supervised by an increasingly professionalized and disciplined social body (Popkewitz, 1991, p. 39). The social science of psychology, for example, constituted a new way of organizing, supervising, wielding power over the individual in that "the individual's innermost thoughts were made the focus of the experts' gaze" (p. 39). The relationship between "self"-management and social power was hidden, however, and instead the teachings of psychology were normalized as a means by which the characteristics of individuals or groups of individuals could be legitimately described and adjusted (Popkewitz, 1991, p. 39). In 20th-century America, the influence of psychology was seen in how the purposes and procedures of modern schooling became inherently supervisorial:

[E]xposure of the individual to public scrutiny was integral to the new peda-gogies. There were conceptions of correct information (learning), attitudes (socialization), deviance (backward and disadvantaged), sexuality, domestic-ity, as well as measures of competence and incompetence. Through a combi-nation of hierarchical observations and normalizing judgments, all human characteristics became potential categories of observation and social admin-istration. (Popkewitz, 1991, p. 41)

These changes in schools affected the nature of professionalization in education. A focus on the character of the students became paralleled by a focus on the character of the teacher and her "specific attitudes of intel-lectual discipline and self-possession" (Popkewitz, 1991, p. 68). We see this focus in Dewey's prescription of the properties of inquiry-oriented reflection: through its use, he wanted teachers to achieve a "self" charac-terized by orderly, consecutive, appropriate, and logical thinking (1933, p. 30).

Today's postmodern writers on the role of reflection in teaching and teacher reflection value other "attitudes of intellectual discipline and self-possession," but they nonetheless rest on the same premise of a "self" capable of "self"-management. To Kincheloe (1991), for example, it is not the intelligence of the reflection that matters, but its ethical and polit-ical nature. He wants reflection to help teachers develop "selves" commit-ted to critical action research, "selves" dedicated to uncovering the ideology of society through the ideology of schools and, importantly, through the ideology of their own personal and professional practice. The questions he wants teacher candidates to ask themselves in this project of "self" formation in multicultural teacher education reflect a goal of edu-cational equity:

Do I unconsciously respond to the children of the dispossessed differently than I do the children of privilege?; Do I condemn the children of the dis-possessed with low expectation?; Do I operate with a different set of rules for students of different status backgrounds?; Do I respect the form of knowledge (subjugate knowledge) that many of my students bring to school or do I equate education with the eradication of such ways of knowing? (p. 103)

The emancipatory ends of these questions, however, do not free them from their "power effects" in the multicultural teacher education class-room (Popkewitz, 1991, p. 222). There they are intended to produce "desire, dispositions, and sensitivities" by "rules, standards, and styles of reasoning" that help define "categories of good/bad and envision possibil-ities" (p. 223). In this way, they produce a particular kind of "self"-knowl-edge that is important to the very conceptualization of multicultural teacher education. A critically reflective "self," the multicultural teacher education literature claims, is more likely to teach in culturally appropriate ways and to shift blame for school failure away from students and toward the instructional situation itself (Kleinfeld & Noordhoff, 1988, as cited in Zeichner, 1992, p. 73). Critical reflection, it is argued, enables teacher candidates to see how their views influence instruction and then ultimately how the instruction they provide, or the manner in which they provide it, may not be in the best interest of their students.

But the multicultural teacher education literature is full of accounts of resistance to critical reflection. Allard and Cooper (1997) explain that teacher candidates come to feel that their own voices are being drowned out by well-intentioned but overzealous teacher educators (as cited in Wideen et al., p. 148). Zeichner (1993, p. 14) and Boyd, Boll, Brawner, and Villaume (1998, p. 68) also document this outcome by describing how their students felt critical content was forced upon them in their reflection-oriented programs. Accounts like these have led to recognition of the need to reconsider the criteria for critical reflection so that it is not confused for indoctrination (Valli, 1997).

THE RESEARCH

I had the opportunity to explore these issues during the 3 years that I observed and interviewed teacher candidates in a required Cultural Diversity course at a large research university in Northern California (Richardson Bruna, 2002). I examined the experiences of 27 teachers in that course and those of the one teacher educator. The following "snapshot" and its discussion draws largely from data I collected the first year of that study from my initial cohort of 10 teacher participants. Eight of these participants were white, one African American, and one Mexican American. I performed 10 2-hour observations of the Cultural Diversity class, and 10 90-minute interviews, one with each of the participants. I also interviewed the teacher educator, the director of teacher education in the program, and collected course-related documents. My intention was to capture the "radical contextuality" of the multicultural teacher education site, particularly the white teachers' resistance. By "radical contextuality" Grossberg (1997) explains:

> An event or practice (even a text) does not exist apart from the forces of the context that constitute it as what it is. Obviously context is not merely background but the very conditions of the possibility of something. (p. 255)

Drawing on multicultural teacher education and other scholarly literature, as I've done in the previous section, and using the scene that follows, my purpose is to show the "very conditions of the possibility" of white teacher resistance, particularly how individualistic understandings of resistance (pedagogical or ideological) miss important elements of the teacher candidates' experience. A socially constructed framework of resistance, one that takes into consideration how the teacher educators' response to her students is one organized by a cultural mismatch framework invested in identifying "a particular human kind for pedagogical intervention," is one of these conditions necessary to fully understand resistance and demotivation in multicultural teacher education.

In my research (Richardson Bruna, 2002), I account for context by nesting the practice of the multicultural teacher educator within four "layers": the first layer is the history and literature of multicultural teacher education; the second layer is the program in which she taught; the third is her own educational biography; and the fourth is her practice in the classroom. Because I have already described earlier in this chapter, in a condensed way, the history and literature of multicultural teacher education (the first of my layers), the section that follows will very briefly provide some basic background information about the second and third layers (who the multicultural teacher educator is and what the program is like in which she teaches) while strategically focusing on the fourth layer (her classroom practice). In this section, I tell the story of Yvonne and her teacher and their socially constructed resistance.

Yvonne's teacher in the Cultural Diversity class was Ellen. Ellen was a white, middle-class woman who attended a racially mixed high school in a major California city during the Civil Rights era. She related the stories she told of her own schooling experiences to a journey toward cultural exploration and social consciousness informed by extensive experience as an elementary teacher in bilingual, bicultural California elementary schools. Underlying Ellen's use of critical reflection was her belief that teacher candidates came to the Cultural Diversity class with negative assumptions about difference that it was her responsibility to get them to rethink. The force of cultural mismatch shapes her goals for the course. As Ellen said:

> I would hope that the student teachers would start to rethink some of the assumptions that they've had all their lives, some beliefs that they've had about people that are different from them, some stereotypes.... They need to start looking at what these cultures have to offer us and what the kids bring to class with them, the knowledge that they bring to class, and respect that, and use that in their classrooms. So I really need for them to reflect on their beliefs and assumptions, and to start looking through a different lens.

In this quote, Ellen expresses several ideas that characterize the force of cultural mismatch on multicultural teacher education (that her students have negative images of communities of color, that they lack respect for "Other" cultures and knowledge systems, that it is her job as a multicultural teacher educator to challenge these images, etc.). Importantly, one of these ideas is that reflection is the way to mount this challenge.

Her interest in reflection was one endorsed program-wide. Reflection was one of four practitioner roles that the program emphasized in its preparation of teachers (the others were collaboration, investigation, and advocacy). Reflection was supposed to be infused into all of the teacher candidates' coursework and accomplish the mission of the program—to prepare teachers for culturally and linguistically diverse classrooms. Program documents attest to this mission. They state:

> [Our] program aims to prepare teachers who can collaborate with parents and colleagues to create learning environments that integrate the language and culture of the home and the school, and who can reflect and investigate the efficacy of that learning environment for all students, but particularly for culturally and linguistically diverse students.

Note that the administrative language of the program description (and in fact of teacher licensure in general) takes these students' culturally and linguistically diverse identities for granted as a natural social category and does not press for clarity into the historical, economic, and political processes that define difference to begin with (Popkewitz, 1991). Thus, the goal of reflection in the program was cast, again in cultural mismatch terms, as one of preparing the nonproblematized white teacher to teach the nonproblematized "Other."

Importantly, in my discussion of the scene that follows I am not making the argument that white teachers are not racist or do not possess white privilege. I am making another argument entirely. I am suggesting that Ellen, in enacting the cultural mismatch rhetoric of the multicultural teacher education literature and of the program in which she taught, played an important role in triggering resistance and that this resistance was then used to reinscribe racist and privileged identities on white teachers. This phenomenon has not been sufficiently understood by multicultural teacher education scholars, especially the role it plays in the miseducation and demotivation of the white teacher.

"It Takes Drive and Determination": A Snapshot of Socially Constructed Resistance

Yvonne is a white, upper-middle-class, monolingual English-speaking student teacher in her early 20s who has decided to teach because she enjoys working with children. She grew up not far away from the university she now attends. Although she describes her community as racist, pointing out that African American drivers were routinely stopped by the police, Yvonne claims her family did not share racist views. She says, for example, that her mother refused to allow her to go to birthday parties to which the only African American girl in her class was not invited. Because of her perceived color-blind upbringing, it is hard for Yvonne to reconcile the attention given to racial difference in the Cultural Diversity class. Yvonne sees "kindergartners as kindergartners." She insists she was taught that "people are people and it doesn't matter what they look like." Because of her race, class, and language status, as well as her cultural insulation, Yvonne fits the profile of the "typical" teacher education candidate. It is students like Yvonne for whom multicultural teacher education is intended.

But by the second week of the Cultural Diversity course, Yvonne has consciously decided to "turn off." In response to being asked by Ellen to reflect, Yvonne shared her thinking with the class. Now she is frustrated, even angry, at Ellen and has decided she *wasn't going to listen to anything she [Ellen] had to say.* The multicultural teacher education literature tells us her decision is one of resistance—that she is reacting out of opposition to ideas of pedagogical or ideological change. Yvonne's resistance is better understood, however, by examining the pedagogical relations surrounding her act of reflection. Rather than attributing Yvonne's resistance to her identity as a "typical" teacher education candidate, I believe we should be attributing Yvonne's resistance to Ellen's inscription of her as a "particular human kind for pedagogical intervention"—a white racist teacher. This inscription leads Ellen to make a couple of decisions and it is these decisions that create the "very conditions of the possibility" of Yvonne's resistance.

Ellen begins the session that week by putting on the overhead projector a figure from the chapters the teachers had been assigned and asking them to discuss its representation of the "referent ethniclass" (Spindler & Spindler, 1990, p. 33). The figure is a grid with class status indicated on one axis and ethnicity on the other. In the center, where upper- and lower-middle class intersect with Protestant, European nonethnic, is a box marked "referent ethniclass." This is bordered by the word *mainstream*. Ellen asks the teachers to reflect on themselves in relation to the figure. "If you're not already in the box," she asks, "then how do you get there?"

In response to this request to reflect, Yvonne shares an anecdote. She tells a story of a man who lives in her neighborhood. It is a rags-to-riches tale of his struggle with poverty and drugs and of the teacher who turned his life around. It is meant to speak to the meritocratic ideal, to prove her point that people can, if they work hard enough, break through social barriers and get into "the box." The story concludes with Yvonne saying,

"It takes drive and determination to get yourself into that box; it doesn't just depend on race and socioeconomic status." Yvonne's story is a supreme example of what Frankenberg (1993) calls "color-and-power evasive thinking" (p. 140):

> We are all the same under the skin ... culturally we are converging ... materially, we have the same chances in U.S. society; and ...—the sting in the tail—any failure to achieve is therefore the fault of people of color themselves. (p. 14)

The "sting in the tail" of Yvonne's story ("it takes *drive and determination* to get yourself into that box" so if you don't get into the box you are not driven or determined *enough*) does not fall on deaf ears. Using language that captures the confrontational nature of the exchange with Yvonne that followed, Ellen said in a later interview, "Theresa jumped her shit for that."

Theresa is an African American woman in her late 30s. She comes from a lower working class family and lived in a neighborhood, not too far from Yvonne's, that she described as "pretty diverse ... until a lot of the Mexicans and whites moved out." She in no uncertain terms describes her education as "crappy" and points to having only one African American teacher in her whole PK–12 education. This lack of African American teachers is her primary motivation for going into teaching.

Theresa responds to Yvonne's story by telling the class about the racism she has experienced. She relates her own anecdote, a story about her husband, who is Nigerian, and his hesitation to drive her Mercedes because of an incident in which he was almost taken to jail merely for having expired tags. She makes it clear that her story of racial profiling (the kind, ironically, that Yvonne says was routine in her neighborhood) is an example of how institutionalized racism *does* exist, and by framing it that way, poses a strong challenge to Yvonne's reflection.

This exchange between Yvonne and Theresa leads to a heated discussion that stood out vividly in the memories of the teacher candidates I interviewed. They referred to the discussion using terms such as "fighting" and "blaming," and emphasized its racialized nature:

> We had one case where an African American and also an Anglo ... the African American woman was talking about how she [the Anglo woman (Yvonne)] would never be to where you know she [the African American woman (Theresa)] had been, you know, and it just, it just got really like, almost like they were fighting back and forth.

> Literally, there were people crying in there. [Yvonne's story] triggered other people to talk and it was just like this domino effect.... There was a lot of

blaming going on, at least that's the perception that people had, that "you white people did this" and stuff like that.

What was the multicultural teacher educator's role in the exchange? Ellen handled the exchange, she told me, by "letting it go." She explained, "My whole participation in that discussion was that I sat down and let it go. I don't even remember responding to her [Yvonne]." Ellen didn't let it turn into a "brawl," she said, but she did not intervene to facilitate the way in which Yvonne's anecdote was taken up by Theresa, nor did she mediate the racialized tension that developed in the classroom as a result of the "fighting" and "blaming" that ensued. Her decision to not intervene or mediate was motivated, as she described it, by a desire to "give voice" to Theresa, to provide institutional space for Theresa to tell her story of racism. As she explained, "If these students [she means students of color] had *had* voice to begin with, this [she means accounts of racism, like Teresa's] wouldn't have been news."

Yvonne, however, interprets Ellen's "giving" voice as, essentially, "taking" hers away. She sees Ellen's nonparticipation as evidence that Ellen is "not listening" and so decides, as she says, to "totally turn off":

> I was very open in the beginning of the discussion and after our teacher did that and didn't listen, I kind of hunched over and was doodling in my book and I totally turned off because I figured if she didn't want to hear anything I had to say, I wasn't going to listen to anything she had to say.

Two weeks after this incident, Yvonne goes to see Ellen during office hours, in her words, to ask her what the "goals" for the class are. While talking with Ellen, Yvonne makes the assertion that there was reverse discrimination operating in the course. Yvonne told me:

> I felt like the white people in the class were getting discriminated against purely because they were white, because of the way the discussions would go. So I went and asked [Ellen] what her goals were so that I could have a better outlook for the class, so I could know going in that she wasn't just going to get all over the white people in the class.

Yvonne has taken it upon herself to approach Ellen about how she is feeling in the Cultural Diversity class. Wanting to know what Ellen's goals are so she "could have a better outlook for the class" indicates that her experience in the course has been a demotivating one. Yvonne is telling Ellen quite clearly that she objects to being "a particular human kind for pedagogical intervention" ("so I could know going in that she wasn't going to get all over the white people in the class"). She is resisting the inscription of her white racist identity in the cultural mismatch framework.

Ellen has an intensely negative response to Yvonne's continued resistance. Importantly, she minimizes her own role, delegitimizing Yvonne's claim that she was not being listened to. She attributes it instead directly to Yvonne and her "petty and immature" ["silly/dangerous white people"] way of thinking. In an interview, Ellen told me:

> It's a way of not dealing. It's an out. An easy out. I also think it is petty and immature thinking that some people never outgrow. "Well, I'm being discriminated against." "It's my turn at the tether ball," you know? I think that's how some people view things.

Yvonne's decision to turn off was echoed in the decisions I heard from other teacher candidates about their choosing not to speak in the Cultural Diversity class. They considered the class "uncomfortable" because of a fear that they would say something, like Yvonne, perceived as offensive by Ellen or their peers. The following quote shows how their decision not to speak is linked to their awareness that they have been inscribed as a "particular human kind," that they, as this teacher candidate says, "come from this kind of background so [are] not qualified."

> I'm not even going to open my mouth in this class because I'm not going to open myself up to someone turning around and saying, "Well, God, you come from this kind of background so you're not qualified."

Statements like this were a response to what happened to Yvonne and other teachers in the Cultural Diversity course. Talking about an exchange with Ellen during the fourth week of class, another "typical" teacher candidate, Elizabeth, said she was "traumatized" by Ellen's response to her reflection, that she felt like she was "kicked back down." Teachers expressed a well-grounded fear in the Cultural Diversity class that with speaking came a risk. Yvonne and Elizabeth's "beating," so called by their peers, served as an example for the other teacher candidates of what might happen when one shared a reflection of which Ellen or their peers disapproved.

Discipline, Not Dialogue: The Contradiction of Critical Reflection

About the contradiction between the emancipatory philosophy of critical education and its authoritarian implementation, Boler (1998) writes:

Critical pedagogues' disciplining of their own and other bodies in pedagogical events is, of course, no less a form of policing than many of the authoritarian practices they seek to overturn... . Thus, there will be moments of ambivalence and duplicity in any pedagogical event, including those in which there was an expressed commitment to overturning racist, sexist, and classist practice. (p. 228)

In Ellen's classroom, reflection was not used as an opportunity to explore alternative points of view, but to reinscribe the whiteness of the white teacher. Whether or not they shared their reflections with the whole group, white teachers felt rebuked for their whiteness. In this way, by risking speaking or maintaining false silence to spare the risk, reflection resulted in teaching teachers to self-police (Boler, 1998, p. 31).

When Yvonne told her rags-to-riches story, she felt that Ellen didn't listen because she didn't agree with Yvonne's point of view. Yvonne's perception was that she was silenced, punished, for an unpopular opinion. Ellen's perspective on the incident supports this. She said she had hoped the critique of Yvonne's story would come from the teachers and, with Teresa's "jumping her shit," it did. This is the kind of "ambivalence and duplicity" that Boler is referring to in the pedagogical event. Ellen wanted to critique Yvonne, but felt that to do so would conflict with the sense of "dialogue" she wanted to create. When Teresa critiqued Yvonne, Ellen was able to feel like she was being a critical educator by letting the "dialogue" happen. In fact, she wasn't really interested in exploring what Yvonne had to say. The thinking behind Yvonne's story was never addressed; instead, Yvonne was talked down, made to feel bad for sharing it. In this way, emotional disciplining is a very real outcome of reflective activity in multicultural teacher education. Reflection, if it doesn't take an appropriate form, as Yvonne's meritocratic story didn't, can be punitive. This punishment serves as a model to others who would dare repeat the offending behavior, so it is not surprising that other teacher candidates made conscious decisions to withdraw their participation in the course. To reflect "[politically] incorrectly" was emotionally dangerous.

That these teachers needed and wanted more leeway than Ellen allowed them was evident from comments on her student evaluations. Students felt she had an "agenda," that she "didn't allow all students to be heard," and that they would have liked a "wider forum to discuss the issues." These comments make it quite clear that the students didn't perceive reflection as a form of "deeply personal self-exploration," but, instead, as Popkewitz (1991) suggests, a form of regulation.

To their credit, some multicultural teacher educators have theorized from the contradictions of their teaching. Ahlquist (1991) discusses her struggle with power and resistance in the multicultural course she taught. She writes about how she came to see that "the manner in which [she] presented [her] views intimidated several students. They did not view [her] approach as an invitation to dialogue; instead, sides were taken and lines were drawn" (p. 163). Cochran-Smith (1995) also reflects on what she sees as the central tension in multicultural teacher education, "the tension between inviting students to formulate new and perhaps disconcerting insights, on the one hand, and, on the other, using the power of one's position as a professor to impose those perspectives" (p. 561). And MacGillivray (1997) attempts to "explore the way [her] unconscious biases/expectations sabotaged [her] conscious attempts to change the traditional power structures created in college classrooms" (p. 471) by examining points of contact with various students in her teacher education reading course and disclosing the tacit rules she used for limiting the interaction. Accounts like these (see Ellsworth, 1992; Gore, 1992; Kramer-Dahl, 1996; and Lather, 1991, for more critiques) support a continued interrogation of reflection as it is implemented in multicultural teacher education. This is in keeping with the suggestions made by Wideen and colleagues (1998) in their review of the literature on learning to teach:

> Research, whether on multicultural teacher education or on teacher education in general, must take a more holistic and critical approach to interrogate and challenge the structures, approaches, and mythology of teacher education. (p. 169)

Putting "Education" Back in Multicultural Teacher Education

One mythology of multicultural teacher education is that our white teacher candidates are best served by seeing them first and foremost as white. I believe this mythology is one of convenience: seeing them this way makes it easy for us to dismiss their challenges to the social justice agenda as evidence of white racism, rather than simply as questions that it is our job to help them answer. Taking the second perspective is a lot harder than taking the first. It means staying with your students even when you don't agree with them, helping them clarify their thinking by insisting they provide evidence and encouraging them to analyze what effect their thinking has on the world. Taking the second perspective means, in essence, actually *teaching*.

When Yvonne shared her reflection, Ellen responded not by holding up Yvonne's tale as the example of meritocratic thinking that it was. Doing so would have allowed her to create pedagogical space to expose its assumptions. Instead it was something she regarded as "silly/dangerous" and, using Theresa as a shield, readily dismissed.

Multicultural teacher educators know that white people evade engagement with their whiteness as a location of racial privilege (Frankenberg, 1999, p. 19). Why then are we so surprised when our students reveal their whiteness? Isn't this what we should expect? This is what the literature tells us to expect; in fact, the whole field is organized around the task of exposing whiteness. Yet we continue to feel inconvenienced by reflections like Yvonne's and hold such reflections against her. This is because we look at our students through a cultural mismatch framework. The goal of confirming the reality of racist identities among our teachers—"there you have it; I see you are indeed a 'typical' white teacher"—has misplaced the goal of affirming the possibility of their antiracism. This seems antithetical to what we know about learning. Learning does not happen by continually hammering on about what one does *not* know, but instead by providing opportunities for participation in a community of knowers. These opportunities are appropriate to the development of the learner, understanding that, with support, there will be movement from the periphery of the target community to the center (Lave & Wenger, 1991). Importantly, the provision of learning opportunities takes place with the assumption that the learner can eventually become a knower. For multicultural teacher education, this would mean providing opportunities for students to not only examine their whiteness, but to see themselves as potential antiracist whites.

There was general confusion among the teachers I interviewed about what being white meant in the multicultural agenda. They talked about feeling guilty, victimized, scorned by students' parents, lumped together, and excluded. In the following quote, a student gestures toward a meaning of multicultural education that might include an understanding of what it feels like to be white in a multicultural world:

> I always feel in classes where we're talking about appreciating different cultures and things, I feel left out. Like, I don't have a culture. It's like white, upper-middle class, your parents aren't divorced ... basically that puts me in the ... I felt put in the category of "you're not interesting." Like, "you've had it too good to be interesting and we don't want to talk about that kind of stuff."... But then I think too part of [multicultural education] might be what it's like to be the white kid in a group of people where you feel like everyone else has this big culture and you don't. Like I don't know if anyone's written a story like that. But I think that's part of it too.

White teacher candidates desperately want to have "a story" in the multicultural education curriculum. They want to have a story that is not entirely predetermined by what whiteness has meant in the past, but one that discusses what whiteness means in the present and what it might mean in the future. This is different than whites claiming victimization (Kincheloe & Steinberg, 1998, pp. 14–16). This is about extending some of the key truths of critical multiculturalism—the dynamism of identity and meaning, and the recognition of the multifaceted nature of power—to whites. To lock these students into "typical" teacher candidate roles and not understand how they are making sense of their identity (or perhaps even changing their identity) is to not do the very work that is the foundation of critical multiculturalism. As Howard (1999) says, the analytical approach of whiteness-equals-oppression "will merely serve to alienate white educators rather than inspire them to become co-responsible for positive change" (p. 111). He writes:

> If Whiteness is theorized to be synonymous with oppression, then how do we provide White educators with a positive racial identity and include them in the work of social transformation?... Our attempts to dismantle dominance and oppression must follow a path other than that of either vilifying or obliterating Whiteness. Just as African-Americans have challenged the negative associations of "Blackness" and chosen to recast their identity in their own positive image, so Whites need to acknowledge and work through the negative historical implications of "Whiteness" and create for ourselves a transformed identity as White people committed to equity and social change. Our goal is to neither deify nor denigrate Whiteness, but to defuse its destructive power. To teach my White students and my own children that they are "not White" is to do them a disservice. To teach them that there are different ways of being White, and they have a *choice* as White people to become champions of justice and social healing, is to provide them a positive direction for growth and to grant them the dignity of their own being. The question then becomes, how do we balance critique of white identity with care for our students' struggle with that white identity and respect for the visions they might have for their identity? (pp. 111–112)

Goldstein (2002, pp. 117–145) is clear to differentiate the kind of care Howard is talking about from simplistic ideas about "gentle smiles and warm hugs." She insists that caring needs to be viewed as a moral and intellectual relation, a conscious and deliberate part of the pedagogical process. What we need are caring multicultural teacher education classrooms that allow and, in fact, encourage white teachers to explore their perspectives, classrooms in which these perspectives are not taken as wholesale evidence of cultural insularity, of political disengagement, of undeniable proof of an unexamined racist self. To have these classrooms requires multicultural teacher educators to distance themselves from the cultural mismatch approaches to the education of the white teacher that make that unexamined racist self the default identity of all white teacher candidates. Unless we can do that, we will be predisposed to hear through a negative filter everything our white students say, to attribute an idealized immunity to our teachers of color, to create, in effect, divisions in our classrooms that override the tidy rhetoric about creating dialogue across difference. In essence, white teacher candidates need to be granted the right to Gordon's "complex personhood" (1994, pp. 4–5). They need to be given permission to name "the psyche of whiteness," which Frankenberg (1997) describes as one of "guilt," "shame," "entitlement," and "exculpation," while also being given permission to claim their "interconnectedness," their "interdependency," their "dependent co-arising" as human beings on this planet (p. 24). Frankenberg, about the work she has done on whiteness, says quite simply, "I have always found it hard to set aside the fundamental goodness of all living beings" (p. 24). What does it mean to extend to white teachers the capacity for fundamental goodness? Among other things, it means seeing more in them than just a "particular human kind for pedagogical intervention."

Toward a Pedagogy of White Antiracism

In her ethnography of white racial identity among high school students, Perry (2002) explores what she calls the "mutability and multiplicity of white identities" and argues that "contradictions not be seen as nefarious, but as potential inlets for nurturing antiracism" (p. 3). In describing one of her interviewees, she writes:

> I believe that when Melissa revealed to me the "devil" in her, she was not hiding anything or looking to be absolved so that she could continue benefiting from white privilege guilt-free. She was asking for help in somehow controlling if not eradicating that part of her that she abhorred, a part she obtained by virtue of living in a structurally white-dominant society but that was by no means dominating her consciousness. If we reduce Melissa to that "devil" in her, then we lose the opportunity to nurture and bring to the foreground her antiracism. Our analytical foci may need to be less on what makes white people "racist" and more on what makes them actively non- or antiracist. (p. 192)

What was notably missing from the Cultural Diversity class was precisely this—an analytical focus that would allow Ellen to regard her white students in the antiracist light that Perry is suggesting. Because of cultural mismatch, identity was seen as a fixed object to be manipulated rather than a dynamic process to be explored. This resulted, I argue, in resistance among the white teacher candidates, resistance reflecting an overwhelming and demotivating lack of purpose.

Let's say that Melissa, the young white woman whom Perry discusses, has enrolled in a teacher education program where she will be required to take a Cultural Diversity course. If that program and/or the instructor of that course adopts a cultural mismatch approach to her preparation, reducing her, as Perry (2002) says, "to that [racist] 'devil' in her," then Melissa's desire "for help in somehow controlling if not eradicating that part of her that she abhorred" will not be filled. She may then give up that desire and think there is no place for her in the multicultural agenda.

Multicultural teacher education can, however, nurture Melissa's desire to have a positive, antiracist, white teaching identity, through a critical literacy approach. In this model, students learn to deconstruct and reconstruct social text (including their own white identities) as a means of articulating emergent critical practice. This approach is "critical *literacy*" because it helps teachers see the social world as a text that can, like any other, be read—deconstructed, then reconstructed—so that a new meaning emerges (Kelly, 1997). Teachers learn to read how the meaning of difference itself is produced and reproduced in schooling, even in their own classroom practice, so that difference begins to be understood as a social process, not as an inevitable part of the social order. Importantly, for white teachers, this enables an emphasis on moving toward a positive, antiracist, white teaching identity.

What does critical literacy look like in a multicultural teacher education classroom? I suggest that, at its core, critical literacy is an instructional strategy that uses a set of questions to probe thinking about educational philosophy, policy, and practice so that otherwise hidden assumptions, or "theories," are made visible and accessible for analysis and action. Drawing on the feminist theorizing model of Bunch (1998, pp. 16–17) and the discussion of Kirk and Okazawa-Rey (1998, pp. 7–11), I propose that the questions that constitute a critical literacy of difference in multicultural teacher education be conceived of in four clusters: *description* questions (those concerned with documenting how difference exists in schools and society as academic, social, political, and economic disparity); *analysis* questions (those concerned with exploring, from a historical and contemporary perspective, what educational philosophies, policies, and practices cause these disparities to exist); *vision* questions (those concerned with determining what are the desirable academic, social, political, and economic alternatives to these disparities), and *strategy* questions (those concerned with planning for professional actions that promote equitable academic, social, political, and economic outcomes). Multicultural teacher educators can use these clusters of questions to get their students to think about or "read" their thinking.

For example, when a teacher candidate, like Yvonne, tells a rags-to-riches story that downplays the role of sociocultural factors in academic and socioeconomic success or failure, the multicultural teacher educator can acknowledge the student's contribution by using the story as an invitation for further discussion. She can point out that, while meritocratic stories of overcoming-all-odds do exist, what the educational research tells us about dropout rates is very different. "*Who is most at-risk for dropping out?*" she can ask, in this way getting the students to *describe* what disparities exist. Once the existence of disparities is established, she can next ask "*How would the ideal of meritocracy explain these disproportionate dropout rates?*" This question requires the students to *analyze* the effect of meritocratic thinking on the world. Since, in a meritocratic system, reward is based on individual talent and/or effort, this way of thinking has the effect of explaining disproportionate school failure in terms of the inadequacies of the student and his community. *What does it mean in the world to say that some groups don't do well because they are stupid or lazy?* It means, for instance, that smartness and motivation are purely genetic traits and it also means there must be enough jobs, and equal access to those jobs, for all these genetically selected motivated and smart people. *Does this way of thinking about the world fit with what we know about the world?* If it doesn't, then it's not an adequate theory. *If it's not an adequate theory, then what purposes and whose purposes does it serve? What might be a better theory? Is a theory that accounts for how structures in our society, like schools, and practices within them, like tracking, work to withhold success from certain groups speak more accurately to what we know about the world?* With questions like these, the teacher educator moves the students to a deeper level of understanding and enhances their ability to see inequities as socially constructed, not as just "the way things are."

Once teacher candidates are at this deeper level, the teacher educator can continue by encouraging them to *envision* alternative scenarios. She can ask, "*What would we like to see happen with dropout rates?*" Would we feel better in a world where we saw that students from different groups were at equal risk of dropping out or would we feel better in a world where dropouts didn't exist? These questions take them to the final cluster of critical literacy questions, those that prompt them to *plan* for what would need to happen in society, in schools, in their practice, to bring the alternative scenario into being. "*What would we like to see ourselves doing for the children in our classrooms to reduce their risk of dropping out?*" Addressing questions at this planning level is where the really critical work of multicultural teacher education as a process of professional preparation begins. And it is here where reflection, as a tool to help teacher candidates clarify and target instructional decisions and behavior, finds a most appropriate place in the multicultural teacher education curriculum. Reflection at the planning level channels the new knowledge created at the description, analysis, and vision levels into a plan for personal and professional practice. Reflection here is liberating and purposeful, not oppressive and purposeless, because it recognizes in each and every teacher a capacity for intelligent *and* ethical-political action. As one of my white students remarked to me, "It's made me think clear out of my bones." This is the kind of deep thinking we withhold from "typical" teacher candidates like Yvonne when we are duplicitous about our use of reflection, summarily dismissing their beliefs before allowing them a chance to explore for themselves the effects of those beliefs on the teaching, learning, living world.

CONCLUSION

The story I told here counters the one told of white teacher resistance in multicultural teacher education. It suggests that we are missing out on an important aspect of the white teachers' experience in multicultural teacher education by understanding resistance through an individualistic rather than a socially constructed lens. By focusing on resistance as something the teacher candidate brings with her into the multicultural teacher education classroom, we gain *political* advantage. We can foreground the "typical" teacher candidate's white racist identity and maintain a focus on the whiteness-equals-oppression equation that is the enduring legacy of colonialism at home as well as abroad (Carlson, 1997). By focusing on resistance as something constructed out of interactions in the classroom, we gain *pedagogical* advantage. We can examine the miseducative effects of reflection, theorize about its influence on motivation in multicultural teacher education, and design alternative approaches that, by promoting the possibility of a positive antiracist white identity, keep them "turned on." This must be an essential feature of teaching white teachers about cultural and linguistic diversity.

But regardless of our understanding of resistance and despite our emancipatory goals, reflection serves as a mechanism of regulation in the multicultural teacher education classroom. It is intimately tied to power relations in modern schooling and teacher professionalization because once something is created as an attribute or behavior of desired student or teacher performance, it is open to inspection and control (Popkewitz, 1993, p. 207). With states proposing amendments to add cultural competency to teaching standards and to specify, in administrative and homogenizing language, what teachers must be able to "know, understand, and appreciate" about the students they teach (Capellaro, 2004, p. 26), we will need to weigh our interest in promoting change in the "typical" white teacher candidate against the implications of using reflection to teach to this administrative, homogenous outcome. It will become more urgent than ever to detangle the promise from the peril of reflection in multicultural teacher education.

REFERENCES

Alhquist, R. (1991). Position and imposition: Power relations in a multicultural foundations class. *Journal of Negro Education*, *60*, 158–169.

Allard, A., & Cooper, M. (1997). *"Too much talk, not enough action": An investigation of fourth year teacher education students' responses to issues of gender in the teacher education curriculum.* Paper presented at the annual meeting of the American Education Research Association, Chicago.

Avery, P. G., & Walker, C. (1993). Prospective teachers' perceptions of ethnic and gender differences in academic achievement. *Journal of Teacher Education*, *44*(2), 27–37.

Bennett, C. Niggle, T., & Stage, F. (1989). *Preservice multicultural teacher education: Predictors of student readiness.* Paper presented at the annual meeting of the American Education Research Association, San Francisco.

Berlak, A., & Moyenda, S. (2001). *Taking it personally: Racism in the classroom from kindergarten to college.* Philadelphia: Temple University Press

Boler, M. (1998). *Feeling power: Emotions and education.* New York: Routledge

Boyd, P. C., Boll, M., Brawner, L., & Villaume, S. K. (1998). Becoming reflective professionals: An exploration of preservice teacher's [sic] struggles as they translate language and literacy theory into practice. *Action in Teacher Education*, *XIX*(4), 61–75.

Bunch, C. (1998). Not by degrees: Feminist theory and education. In G. Kirk & M. Okazawa-Rey (Eds.), *Women's lives: Multicultural perspectives* (pp. 14–17). Mountain View, CA: Mayfield.

Burstein, N. D., & Cabello, B. (1989, September-October). Preparing teachers to work with culturally diverse students: A teacher education model. *Journal of Teacher Education*, pp. 9–16.

Cannella, G. S., & Reiff, J. C. (1994). Preparing teachers for cultural diversity: Constructivist orientations. *Action in Teacher Education*, *XVI*(3), 37–45.

Cappellaro, C. (2004, Spring). Closing the gap: How educators and policymakers can tackle the achievement gap (an interview with Ohio State Senator C. J. Prentiss). *Rethinking Schools*, pp. 25–26.

Carlson, D. (1997). Stories of colonial and postcolonial education. In M. Fine, L. Weis, L. C. Powell, & L. M. Wong (Eds.), *Off white: Readings on race, power, and society.* New York: Routledge.

Choy, S. P., Henke, R. R., Alt, M. N., Hedrick, E. A., & Bobbitt, S. A. (1993). *Schools and staffing in the United States: A statistical profile, 1990–91.* Berkeley: MPR Associates.

Cochran-Smith, M. (1995). Color blindness and basket making are not the answers: Confronting the dilemmas of race, culture, and language diversity in teacher education. *American Educational Research Journal*, *32*(3), 493–522.

Council of Economic Advisors for the President's Initiative on Race. (1998). *Changing America: Indicators of social and economic well-being by race and Hispanic origin*. Washington, DC: Author.

Denzin, N. K., & Lincoln, Y. S. (1998). *The landscape of qualitative research: Theories and issues*. Thousand Oaks, CA: Sage.

Dewey, J. (1933). *How we think*. Chicago: Henry Regnery.

Ellsworth, E. (1992). "Why doesn't this feel empowering?" Working through the repressive myths of critical pedagogy. In C. Luke & J. Gore (Eds.), *Feminisms and critical pedagogy* (pp. 90–110). New York: Routledge.

Ferguson, A. (1996). Can I choose who I am? And how would that empower me? Gender, race, Identities, and the self. In A. Garry & M. Pearsall (Eds.), *Women, knowledge, and reality: Explorations in feminist philosophy* (pp. 108–126). New York: Routledge.

Focault, M. (1982). The subject and the power. In H. L. Dreyfus & P. Rainbow (Eds.), Michel Foucault: Beyond structuralism and hermeneutics (pp. 208-226). Chicago: University of Chicago.

Frankenberg, R. (1997). The mirage of an unmarked whiteness. From an early version of a manuscript later published in B. B. Rasmussen, I. J. Nexica, E. Klinenberg, & M. Wray (Eds.), *The making and unmaking of whiteness* (pp. 72–96). Durham, NC: Duke University Press.

Frankenberg, R. (1993). *White women, race matters: The social construction of whiteness*. Minneapolis: University of Minnesota.

Fraser, N. (1998). *Social justice in the age of identity politics: Redistribution, recognition, and participation*. Unpublished manuscript.

Goldberg, D.T. (1996). *Multiculturalism: A critical reader*. Cambridge, MA: Blackwell.

Goldstein, L. S. (2002). *Reclaiming caring in teaching and teacher education*. New York: Peter Lang.

Gomez, M. L. (1994). Teacher education reform and prospective teachers' perspectives on teaching "other peoples'" children. *Teaching and Teacher Education, 10*(3), 319–334.

Gonzales, N. A., & Cauce, A. M. (1995). Edthnic identity and multicultural competence: Dilemmas and challenges for minority youth. In W. D. Hawley & A. W. Jackson (Eds.), *Toward a common destiny: Improving race and ethnic relations in America* (pp. 131-162). San Francisco: Jossey-Bass.

Gordon, A. F. (1994). *Ghostly matters: Haunting and the sociological imagination*. Minneapolis: University of Minnesota.

Gordon, A. F., & Newfield, C. (1996). *Mapping multiculturalism*. Minneapolis: University of Minnesota.

Gore, J. M. (1992). What we can do for you! What *can* "we" do for "you"?: Struggling over empowerment in critical and feminist pedagogy. In C. Luke & J. Gore (Eds.), *Feminisms and critical pedagogy* (pp. 54–73). New York: Routledge.

Grossberg, L. (1997). *Bringing it all back home: Essays on cultural studies*. Durham, NC: Duke University.

Howard, G. (2000). Reflections on the 'white movement' in multicultural education. *Educational Researcher, 29*(9), 21–23.

Howard, G. (1999). *We can't teach what we don't know: White teachers, multiracial schools*. New York: Teachers College Press.

Kelly, U. A. (1997). *Schooling desire: Literacy, cultural politics, and pedagogy*. New York: Routledge.

Kincheloe, J. L., & Steinberg, S. R. (1997). *Changing multiculturalism*. Philadelphia: Open University Press.

Kincheloe, J. L. (1991). *Teachers as researchers: Qualitative inquiry as a path to empowerment*. New York: Falmer Press.

Kirk. G., & Okazawa-Rey, M. (Eds.). (1998). Theory and theorizing: Integrative frameworks for understanding. In *Women's lives: Multicultural perspectives* (pp. 7–14). Mountain View, CA: Mayfield.

Kramer-Dahl, A. 1996). Reconsidering the notions of voice and experience in critical pedagogy. In C. Luke (Ed.), *Feminisms and pedagogies of everyday life* (pp. 242–262). Albany: State University of New York Press.

Lather, P. (1991). *Getting smart: Feminist research and pedagogy with/in the postmodern*. New York: Routledge.

Lave, J., & Wenger, E. (1991). *Situated learning: Legitimate peripheral participation*. New York: Cambridge University Press.

MacGillivray, L. (1997). Do what I say, not what I do: An instructor rethinks her own teaching and research. *Curriculum Inquiry, 27*(4), 469–488.

McIntyre, A. (1997). *Making meaning of whiteness: Exploring racial identity with white teachers*. Albany: State University of New York.

McLaren, P. (1997). *Revolutionary multiculturalism: Pedagogies of dissent for the new millenium*. Boulder, CO: Westview Press.

Moultry, M. (1988). *Multicultural education among seniors in the College of Education at Ohio State University*. Paper presented at the meeting of the American Educational Research Association, New Orleans, LA.

Nieto, S. (1994, Spring). Affirmation, solidarity, and critque: Moving beyond tolerance in multicultural education. *Multicultural Education*.

Paine, L. (1989). *Orientation towards diversity: What do prospective teachers bring?* (Research Report 89-90). East Lansing, MI: National Center for Research on Teacher Education.

Perry, P. (2002). *Shades of white: White kids and racial identities in high school*. Durham, NC: Duke University Press.

Popkewitz, T.S. (1991). *A political sociology of educational reform: Power/knowledge in teaching, teacher education, and research*. New York: Teachers College.

Popkewitz, T. S. (Ed.). (1993). U.S. teacher education reforms: Regulatory practices of the state, university, and research. In *Changing patterns of power: Social regulation and teacher educational reform* (pp. 263-301). Albany: State University of New York Press.

Popkewitz, T. S. (2004). The alchemy of the mathematics curriculum: Inscriptions and the fabrication of the child. *American Educational Research Journal, 41*(1), 3–34.

Reyes, B. (2001). *A portrait of race and ethnicity in California: An assessment of social and economic well-being*. San Francisco: Public Policy Institute of California.

Richardson Bruna, K. (2002). *Manufacturing dissent: The new economy of power relations in multicultural teacher education.* Unpublished doctoral dissertation, University of California, Davis.

Rodriguez, A. J. (1998). Strategies for counterresistance: Toward sociotransoformative constructivism and learning to teach science for diversity and for understanding. *Journal of Research in Science Teaching, 36*(6), 589–622.

Sleeter, C. E. (1994, Spring). White racism. *Multicultural Education,* pp. 5-8.

Smith, R., Moallem, M., & Sherril, D. (1997, Spring). How preservice teachers think about cultural diversity: A closer look at factors which influence their beliefs towards equality. *Educational Foundations,* pp. 41–61.

Spindler, G., & Spindler, L. (1990). *The American cultural dialogue and its transmission.* Bristol, PA: The Falmer Press.

Thompson, A. (2003). Tiffany, friend of people of color: White investments in antiracism. *Qualitative Studies in Education 16*(1), 7–29.

Valli, L. (1994). Listening to other voices: A description of teacher education in the United States. *Peabody Journal of Education, 72*(1), 67–88.

Wahab, Z. (1989). *The melting pot revisited.* Paper presented at the annual conference of the Oregon Multicultural Association, Salem, OR.

Wayson, W. (1988). *Multicultural education among seniors in the College of Education at Ohio State University.* Paper presented at the meeting of the American Educational Research Association, New Orleans, LA.

Wideen, M., Mayer-Smith, J., & Moon, B. (1998). A critical analysis of the research on learning to teach: making the case for an ecological perspective on inquiry. *Review of Educational Research, 68*(2), 130–178.

Zeichner, K. M. (1992) *Educating teachers for cultural diversity.* East Lansing, MI: National Center for Research on Teacher Learning.

CHAPTER 14

PASIFIKA AUSTRALIA

Culturally Responsive Curriculum and Teaching

Mike Horsley and Richard Walker

CASE STUDY: VILIAMI

I am 15 years old and my name is Viliami. I was born in Tonga and did the first 3 years of primary school there. School was alright and not far from my home. I learned English at school but only during English lessons, and the teacher only spoke English during the lessons. We read books and did spelling tests every day. After the English class we only spoke Tongan.

In June 1997 my family moved to Australia, and after a week I enrolled at a primary school. I enjoyed the school very much because the school had more books and games than the one in Tonga. I also enjoyed watching children's programs on television after school.

The uniforms were nice too and I had to wear shoes every day. The only thing I found difficult was that I had to speak English all the time. There were other Tongan kids at school. Some of them spoke English most of the time and some spoke Tongan as well as English. I was put into an ESL class to learn English. It was not much different from what I did in Tonga except that I did not have someone to talk to in Tongan, so I tried to speak English

---

Focus on Curriculum, 327–351
Copyright © 2005 by Information Age Publishing
All rights of reproduction in any form reserved.

all the time. One thing that helped my learning of the language was that I had a very good friend at school. His parents are from Italy but they have been in Australia for a long time and he spoke English very well. He helped me a lot to practice my English and we visited each other's homes to play and watch television all the time. At the end of the year, I could speak and write English better.

Now I am at high school. My dad is very strict about doing my homework and attending school. I never miss school except when I am sick. Even in my last year in primary school I was not allowed to go with my friends to the shopping center except when accompanied by one of my parents. I am allowed to go on my own now. Every night I have to finish my schoolwork before I do anything else. Going to school is the most important thing in my family. With school so important, truanting from school never crosses my mind. We attend church on Sunday but sometimes we miss church and attend my rugby league match. I play for the junior rugby league club in our area.

At my high school it is a different story. I go to a boys high school now and there are a number of Tongan students there. My first year at high school was good but most of the Tongan students were not interested in schooling and they truanted a lot. All the time they tried to make me join the Tongan gang at school, which ruled the playground. They did not care whether they did well in their studies or not. They would stay at home, roam around at the shopping center, or come to school and do nothing except disturb the class. Most of the Tongan students were not serious with their study but the school tolerated them because they were good football players. Their parents are just as strict as mine so I don't know why they are not punished. I think their parents don't know what is happening at school.

In my second year I started to hang out with these boys after school and that was when I really get into trouble with my dad. I got a belting now and then but I knew that no matter what, my parents would not allow me to leave school early or not to finish year 12. The peer pressure to do what my friends did was growing stronger, as most of them started to leave school as they turned 15. With most of my friends not attending school, the time I hung out with them affected my study very much. I did not concentrate as much as I should on my schoolwork. When we did attend class as a group we liked to help each other with all our work and homework but our teachers often said that we should do things on our own. As one of the oldest in my group my friends often ask me to do some of their work for them.

Now I am in Year 10 and I am doing well in Art and all my teachers are encouraging me to pursue a career in graphic design. My parents are so strict that I cannot risk truanting and being belted every time. My father comes around to the school every week and asks all my teachers for a progress report. Either my father or mother attend parent's meeting and interviews every time. My mother has helped our class every year on the school multicultural day festival and every one of my friends and teachers liked her. My friends have finally realized that my parents are so strict that they have started to be very careful about going around with me because all of us at any time would get a belting from my dad if he finds me with them doing something wrong.

Even when I leave school my parents will still be just as strict with me and will expect me to live at home. They will probably let me bring my girlfriend home but they will probably be strict with her too. That is what Tongan parents are like. You are not allowed to cuddle or kiss, especially in front of the family. Even when I get married they may expect me to stay at home.

Because I am the eldest son I will gradually be expected to take over responsibility for the family if my father is not there. One of my friends already has to take that responsibility all the time because his father had died. Probably I will still be treated as a kid when my father is around until I am 60! But I hope to be in charge of my family long before that.

PASIFIKA MIGRATION INTO AUSTRALIA

Polynesian (Pasifika) Australians of Samoan, Tongan, Maori, Niuean, Cook Island, and Fijian heritage are a growing and identifiable cultural group in New South Wales schools. In certain parts of Sydney, this group is the fastest-growing minority cultural group. Already in a number of the school districts in the South Western and Western parts of Sydney, Samoan and Tongan are the dominant non-English-speaking background (NESB) languages. In some school districts, secondary schools, and their associated feeder schools, Tongan enrollments increased by 62% between 1994 and 2000 and Samoan enrollments grew by over 97 % for the same period. Enrollments in the secondary schools of the Penrith, Blacktown, and Mt. Druitt school districts have increased representation for students of Tongan, Samoan, and Fijian origin (Carauana, 2001).

The fast growth of these communities has been relatively unanticipated. According to Va'a (2001), Samoan migration to Australia generally began in a substantial way only within the last 15 years. Although Tongan and Fijian migration began earlier, large-scale immigration from these communities has only been a recent phenomenon. The majority of Tongan and Samoan migrants usually arrive after an extended residence in New Zealand. Many are bicultural with extended experience in the New Zealand school system. Anecdotal evidence, however, suggests that newer migrants are increasingly arriving from the homeland under the family reunion categories of the Australian immigration system. Furthermore, studies of Samoans and Tongans living in Australia show that Pasifika Australians carry, conserve, and reproduce the cultural constructs of the traditional society, albeit with modifications necessitated by the Australian context. In a study of Samoan immigrants in Canterbury Bankstown, Va'a concluded that Samoan immigrants place great emphasis on maintaining their Samoan way of life (*fa'a samoa*) and assert that Samoan culture is faithfully maintained in Australia. As well, Samoans continue to form a tight-knit group characterized by strong membership ties, extensive gift-giving, and extensive participation in social networks that ritually observe life-cycle events (*fa'alavelave – exchange*). Va'a's research showed that in the area of the family, there are conflicts between parents and children over discipline and the degree of parental control over children's lives, and that parents fear a loss of control over their children. Many first-generation migrants feel that some of their values and relationships have been turned upside down.

OUTCOMES FOR PACIFIC ISLAND (PASIFIKA) STUDENTS

The Viliami case study, written jointly by a Tongan student and his father, illustrates many of the problems students of Polynesian background (Pasifika) face in the Australian school system. They are overrepresented in terms of suspensions, expulsions, and discontinuance compared to other identifiable cultural groups (Hutakau, 1999). Retention rates for Polynesian students into senior high school and higher education are low. Furthermore, anecdotal evidence also suggests that the academic achievement of Polynesian students is poor. Unfortunately, owing to the nature of the data collection process, quantitative data concerning the academic performance of Polynesian Australian students (Pasifika) in the school system is not available. National tests of basic skills do not identify the ethnic origin of students participating in these assessment processes that measure student performance. State examinations, such as the Higher School Certificate and the School Certificate test, and language tests such as the English Literacy and Language Assessment tests in NSW, also do not identify ethnic origin. Research data from other Pacific countries does, however, indicate the poor academic performance of Polynesian students. New Zealand data demonstrates that students of Pacific and Maori background perform significantly less well at both the School Certificate and University Entrance level (New Zealand Qualification Authority, 2002), while data from the United States indicate high levels of failure and underachievement among Samoan students in U.S. schools. This research suggested that the high failure rate of Samoan students in U.S. schools was due to a number of factors, chief amongst them being inadequate study skills, lack of proficiency in English, limited culturally specific counselling, and students' lack of realistic or concrete ideas about the operation of schools and colleges. According to Saleeby, these deficiencies had to be surmounted before Samoan students could improve their performances in U.S. schools and colleges The poor academic outcomes of (Pasifika) students are likely to be linked to low levels of retention in the educational system. Australian research (Lowe, Sawyer, Wood, Newman, & Buchanan, 1997), undertaken on the school retention of Cook Island students, identified three main categories of schooling difficulties experienced: (1) teachers and methods of teaching, (2) literacy, and (3) racism. Lowe and colleagues (1997) concluded that the feelings of Cook Island students about specific subjects were often linked to the attitude of the teacher. When students were asked for suggestions for overcoming their difficulties, most of their suggestions included improving the communication channels between students and teachers such as "Teachers should relax," "Seniors need more freedom," "Teachers should talk to us more," "We need more direction." Not surprisingly, the research showed that teachers had little knowledge of the student home culture and most could not actively distinguish between Cook Island students and other Pacific Island students in general. "There was a general culture of seeing Pacific Island students as a group, unless there had been some necessity to seek out a particular student's background." Teachers also felt that Pacific Islanders generally were low achievers in the school. "Islander kids seem to experience the problems of being late, lack of attendance and truancy. They often do not have the equipment and are not prepared for class. Islanders may lose their belongings, textbooks, bags. Because of their cultural influence and communal lifestyle everything is shared" (Lowe et al., 1997).

The available research also suggests that there is considerable variation between the perceptions of Polynesian parents and their children and the perceptions of teachers. In their research in New Zealand, Bishop, Tiakiwai, Richardson, and Berryman (2002) found a mismatch between the perceptions of Maori and other Polynesian parents and students and teachers. Similarly, Lowe and colleagues (1997) found that parents of Cook Island students expressed concern that their children were experiencing difficulties and consequently leaving school with limited career opportunities, while teachers did not express such concerns. Students identified a number of concerns, such as racism, lack of family support, and unrealistic parental expectations, in relation to their difficulties in staying on at school.

CULTURALLY RESPONSIVE TEACHING

The rapid growth in the numbers of Pasifika students and the disadvantage and difficulty they are experiencing in the school system has created a need to develop culturally responsive teaching that is based on an analysis of Pasifika conceptions of knowledge and pedagogy.

Culturally responsive teaching has come to refer to the way that teachers acknowledge the primary role of culture in teaching and learning. As a result of this acknowledgment, teachers then seek to understand the culture of the students and adapt and modify curriculum and teaching as a result of these understandings. The predominant approach to culturally responsive teaching is the "listen to culture" approach (Bishop & Glynn, 1999; Macfarlane, 2004) where teachers recognize the role of culture in "shaping knowledge bases and pedagogies within educational programs" (Macfarlane, 2004, p. 17). As a result, teachers develop cultural knowledge approaches where teaching strategies are based on aspects of the underlying culture of the students. This approach has also been developed by Osborne (2001), who stresses that teachers must acknowledge students' prior cultural experiences to foster cultural identity. From the perspective of culturally responsive teaching, it is important to both spell out the cultural assumptions on which the class operates and then to incorporate aspects of the students' cultural traditions and knowledge in its operation. Sociocultural approaches to learning emphasize processes such as scaffolding, the role of language and social context, recognition of prior learning, and cognitive apprenticeship by expert others as vital determinants in learning and development. Application of this approach to education emphasizes the role of students' prior learning as they approach new authentic learning tasks. A vital aspect of the teacher's role is to build a bridge between the students' existing knowledge and the knowledge the student is to create by operating within the child's zone of proximal development. This approach to planning learning requires that teachers understand the students' non-school cultural life and background and use this knowledge in developing and interpreting curriculum and in planning teaching and learning. This culturally responsive approach to learning requires more attention to be paid to students' non-school life and the cultural knowledge they bring to the classroom. The development of the Pasifika education projects and teacher education courses described later in this chapter applied sociocultural learning principles in the design of experiences and instruction for Pasifika students and opportunities to engage in cultural learning and reflection for teachers.The implications for teaching and learning of the sociocultural approach have been to validate, value, and incorporate elements of Pasifika culture and worldviews into curriculum and pedagogy, and to develop elements of biculturalism in teachers. The research of Bishop and colleagues (2002) and Macfarlane (2004) has stressed that Pasifika students recognize that the quality of classroom relationships and the use of culturally appropriate pedagogy are vital factors in Pasifika student engagement in school.

PASIFIKA AUSTRALIA: CONCEPTIONS OF KNOWLEDGE

Attempts to understand the educational difficulties of Polynesian students require understandings of Polynesian culture and of traditional Polynesian views of the nature and purpose of education. This understanding has been assisted in more recent years by the development of vigorous indigenous education research movements, which have studied the traditional educational ideas of Fijians (Bakalevu, 2003; Nabobo, 2003), Cook Islanders (Mokoroa, 2003), and Samoans (Buatava, 2003). In particular, Helu-Thaman's (1988, 2003) research has shown that traditional epistemology and educational ideas shape and construct Polynesian identity, culture, and being.

Pasifika learners experience life through a much broader and tighter social kinship network, based on the extended family system, than learners from Western societies. In Pasifika cultures, a person's life force is fostered through tradition-based knowledge, use of language, and contributions to the family. The family (*aiga* in Samoan) is the cultural base of life. Development of the individual's life force (*mauli*) and presence and power (*mana*) serves the family and contributes to the development of the community. Learners develop in cultural environments (e.g., Maori *whanau*) that foster working cooperatively for a common family purpose that anchors traditional cultural identity. The most important cultural environment is the kinship group (*aiga*, the extended family), and a person's rank within this group and clan. The school and community and then the world constitute other important environments. According to Hawaiian (Native Hawaiian Education Council, 2002) conceptions of the development of the life force:

> The body contains three umbilical chords (Hawaiian piko): the spiritual connection found at the head; the inherited/family connection found at the navel; and the creative/inventive connection found below the navel at the ma'i. Maintaining our connections enables us to understand the knowledge of the past as a foundation for the present to continue our legacy and further develop it for future generations. Our sense of spirituality, family, place and legacy are maintained and perpetuated through these connections.

In Pasifika cultures, these connections are fostered by integrity (e.g., *pono* in Maori), fairness (Maori *tika*), and love and inclusiveness (Maori *aroha*). Within extended families, relationships are conducted to maximize the impact of extended family commitment, connectedness, and purpose. As a result, Pacific island learners value *aroha* (love and a sense of security) highly, both in family and school life. Family ties and *aroha* are exceedingly strong, even among distant relatives. The extended family, with its close and connected personal relationships, plays the prominent role in the life of the South Pacific islanders. Within the extended family, *aroha* (love and security in togetherness) is often expressed in terms of good personal relationships, with close relationship ties more important than other life goals. In education close relationships between the learner and the teacher, personal trust, respect and loyalty is referred to as the spirit of *aroha* (Samoan *alofa*, Tongan, *ofa*, and Hawaiian *aloha*).

Although loosely translated as love, *aroha* more reflects "the embodiment of all the best attributes of one's concern for the welfare of a fellow human being and for satisfying personal relationships" (Native Hawaiian Education Council, 2002, p. 2). The emotional ties of *aroha* between children and their parents extend to and incorporate relatives (of the extended family) and people who are closely associated with the family, such as teachers (Tongan, *fakiako*). Learning occurs within the cultural environment of *aroha*, *honua*, and *mana*. Relationships and the quality of relationships were seen as the key processes in the way that learning and development occurs. Learning includes emotional and moral support connected by *aroha*. These cultural conceptions based on traditional family relationships are important for understanding the education of Pasifika Australia students. In particular, these cultural conceptions focus thinking on the importance of classroom relationships. Since relationships depend on cultural and social frames, reflecting on pedagogy and curriculum requires reflection on the social construction of Polynesian Australian (Pasifika) learners. Pasifika learners are constructed through the strength of their polynesian socialization. This socialization is based on three foundational educational concepts, "namely '*ako*' (learning, teaching/co-learning), '*ilo*' (knowledge) and '*poto*' or wisdom" (Vaioleti, 2001). Helu-Thaman (1988, 2003) describes *ako* as a lifelong, continuous process, a precondition to gaining knowledge, *ilo*, and becoming *poto* or wise. Pasifika students' personhood and identities are expressed and located by their role and relationships to and with the family and their role in the wider extended family. Education in this cultural context means the seeking of *ilo* or knowledge through study, observation, and practice. If knowledge, *ilo*, is used by learners to assist the community and family, then the education and the person gaining it is seen to have achieved *poto*, or wisdom. Appropriate personal relationships are integral to *ako*, *ilo*, and *poto* and not separate from them.

Also integral to Pacific Island cultures is the assumption that every member must learn their role in the community. Education is expected to assist learners to learn this role and their attendant responsibilities to the wider family, community, and society. *Poto* in particular relates to wisdom that acts to benefit the wider family and the learner's role in it. In addition, these roles were mostly learned by observation with the guidance of an expert (a relation or member of their community). Meleisea and

Schoeffel (1996) note that "Polynesians ... are conditioned from early childhood to learn passively, primarily by careful observation and listening, reinforced by admonition so that they become sensitised to other people at an early age."

Traditional Pasifika education systems featured a holistic and enactive approach to learning and development (Helu-Thaman, 2003). In this approach the role of the teacher focused on providing a role model featuring compassion and love; the role of knowledge was to gain wisdom for the benefit of the family and community; the aim of learning was to enable the learner to meet their role obligations to the family and duties to their community; and through collaboration respond to the directions of senior family members possessing high rank. The holistic approach to learning also emphasized the primacy of the affective domain of learning, as *ofa* and *aroha* (love and compassion) are essential to learning and development for the extended family context. Socialization in this culture creates learners who value

- cooperating in learning tasks, even assessment
- sharing knowledge, resources, and learning materials
- obligations to help each other
- communal approaches to learning
- responsibilities to assist younger, less knowledgeable students
- friendly personal relationships as a key to playing one's role as a teacher and learner

These traditional indigenous educational ideas remain at the core of the culture and learning of Pacific Islanders, even in the Australian school context. Traditional epistemology and educational ideas shape and construct their identity, culture, and being. Western curriculum and education systems, which neglect these values, relationships, social practices, and understandings, ignore the entire purpose (or end) of education. The implications of indigenous education ideas for curriculum and pedagogy have been further spelled out by Taufe'ulungaki (cited in Helu-Thaman, 2003):

Teachers must capitalise on the wealth of experience, knowledge and skills the children bring with them from their home cultures to the learning process, and deliberately use those values, beliefs, world views, knowledge, speech rules and learning systems to organise their classrooms, communicate with and teach their students.

Helu-Thaman (2003) has argued that a cultural gap has arisen in the education of Pasifika students. This cultural gap has been described as the cultural distance between the culture of the classroom and the home. It refers to the processes of exclusion of the culture and nonschool lives of students from the curriculum and pedagogy of what happens in school. Secondary teachers in particular see the schooling process as one of teaching their subject and maximizing the academic outcomes of their students. Outcomes are demonstrated through assessment processes that bear no relationship to the Pasifika Australian cultural context of the young people who are their students.

Teachers' practices, shaped by an unquestioning of the hegemonic cultural perspective, will provide explanations for school failure by students from diverse cultural backgrounds in terms of intrinsic deficiencies, of the individual, the cultural group, or in terms of the failings of the family from which the student comes. These explanations reflect a deficit view of the contribution of cultural diversity to students' lack of achievement in school (Connell, 1993; Sturman, 1997). Such a view is characterized by beliefs that "Cultural differences are problems rather than resources for learning, pupil performance is the result of the two primary factors of pupil psychology and family socialization, and that cultural background is largely determinant of school achievement and future socioeconomic standing" (Florio-Ruane, 2001, p. 8).

For teachers to overcome this cultural gap, what is needed in pedagogy and curriculum are knowledge and experiences that enable teachers to deconstruct their taken-for-granted understandings of schools and cultural diversity. Shifting educational practice so teachers are able to work in cooperation and with their Pasifika Australian school communities presents a challenge to curriculum developers and teachers.

Some educators have attempted to develop curricula and experiences that are aimed at disrupting teachers' taken-for-granted cultural assumptions. McIntyre (2002) writes of disrupting the "dysconscious racism," where teacher perspectives about teaching and multicultural education are challenged to go beyond the economy of the stereotype. This chapter now describes curriculum and pedagogy projects that have forged links with communities, schools, community leaders, teacher educators, students, and preservice teachers. These projects operate with an awareness of the necessity to create in teachers the skills to exercise a critical "cultural imagination" (Florio-Ruane, 2001). The focus has been on creating links with the Pasifika communities to develop both culturally responsive curriculum and pedagogy and critically reflective practices for teachers and to reconnect Polynesian Australian students with their current and future teachers. This reconnection has been forged in a context that values and supports the Pasifika students' culture through the development of the cultural knowledge of their current and future teachers.

CULTURALLY RESPONSIVE EDUCATION PROJECTS

The South Pacific Island Research Group at the University of Sydney have conducted a number of investigations, in consultation with the associated Pasifika communities, concerning the difficulties Pasifika students express about their education in Australia. Pasifika student forums have identified a number of issues relating to pedagogy and curriculum that constrain their learning. Consequently, a variety of culturally responsive curriculum and teaching projects have been implemented with Pasifika students to attempt to overcome or ameliorate these difficulties. Special literacy programs have been developed by schools in partnership with the South Pacific Island Education Group, based on *fa'a samoa* and other Pasifika ways of interacting with the community. Transition programs have also been developed, using a Pasifika family model to link primary and secondary curriculum and teaching in more culturally responsive ways. As well, for many years the Pasifika communities have managed homework and study centers at the University of Sydney based on appropriate cultural models of engagement with the curriculum. Finally, the South Pacific Island Research Group has researched the operation of a tertiary awareness program for Pasifika students that links curriculum study at school with curriculum in tertiary institutions in more culturally appropriate ways.

These projects demonstrate how alignment between current curriculum and teaching can be created with the culture of Pasifika students. The lack of this alignment is a major problem for Pasifika students, their teachers, and the school systems in which they study, and has lead to significant problems concerning the achievement of Pasifika students. The chapter presents research on culturally responsive teaching and research projects, which attempted to create alignments between the expectations of Pasifika parents and students, their teachers, and the curriculum and teaching of schools. These projects have been researched to provide insights into the design of culturally responsive learning environments for Pasifika students.

The first research project discussed below examines the operation of homework and study learning centers for Pasifika students in Sydney. The second research project examines transition programs designed to encourage Pasifika students to continue attending school and attend higher education institutions. These transition projects had two components: transition from secondary school to post-compulsory education and transition from primary to secondary school. The third research project concerns Pasifika students expressing their difficulties and perceptions of schooling to preservice teachers and current teachers. This research was conducted at Pasifika student forums. The fourth research project explores how preservice teachers and current teachers develop cultural reflection as they learn more about the culture of Pasifika students and families through assisting with the homework study centers, the transition projects, and in the Pasifika student forums.

RESEARCH PROJECT 1: HOMEWORK AND STUDY LEARNING CENTERS

The study centers for Polynesian Australian (Pasifika) students and their parents were originally established in 1994 and operated in a number of government schools. In 1996 they were relocated to the University of Sydney. Since 2004 the homework center has operated from Canterbury Girls High (a government school in the southwestern suburbs of Sydney). Over 700 Pasifika primary, secondary, and tertiary students have attended these centers.

The management and operation of these centers was shared between the University of Sydney preservice teachers undertaking culturally responsive teaching courses and the Tongan, Niuean, Fijian, and Samoan Polynesian community groups. The after-school study center was culturally connected. Parents and communities were encouraged to bring their children for coaching, study and homework assistance, which also allowed preservice teachers and current teachers attending to discuss educational issues with parents, community leaders, and students.

The study centers were advertised and organized through community institutions (community radio and TV in Sydney, and church groups). They operated with culturally sensitive and appropriate pedagogy, as preservice teachers and current teachers worked as tutors and established positive relationships with students and parents. The opportunity to support parental engagement was further facilitated by cultural visits with families attending the centers and participating in community events, which provided links to family and community networks.

The centers were operated in a Pasifika culturally responsive manner. They operated in the evening so that parents could attend. Parent groups organized communally to provide transport for the students. Students had the opportunity to return home immediately after school to eat and complete their chores for the family before attending the homework study center. During the operation of the homework centers, parents formed culturally appropriate communication circles and discussed communal tasks. Community advisors and workers from the Pasifka leadership groups (e.g., Samoan Advisory Council) took the opportunity to discuss educational issues with the parents or provide advice on issues raised by the parents. Once a month, parent education courses were conducted.

Tutors from the university had the opportunity to speak to parents about their children's education.

Each homework session commenced with a culturally responsive and formal welcome. Pasifika students were encouraged to bring homework, study, and complete assessment tasks. Tutors assisted in the planning and completion of these tasks. Pasifika students were also shown how to obtain assistance and ask for directions, especially in the completion of school assessment tasks. In addition, tutors were trained to identify Pasifika students' cultural cues and provide assistance and help in accordance with Pasifika behavioral norms.

Research on the Study Centers

Since 1994 data have been collected on the homework and study needs of students attending the center. Data have been collected on the topics and subjects that students have identified as needing assistance with. Data have also been collected on parents' perceptions of the educational needs of their children (for those parents who attend the center). Approximately 75% of the students who attended the centers were secondary students. 25% of the secondary students attending were in stage 6 (preliminary and higher school certificate) completing the senior school qualification. 25% of the students were from primary schools.

Common to all the students is the need to successfully complete school-mandated assessment tasks. In New South Wales, the Higher School Certificate (exit secondary school qualification) requires both external public examination and the completion of school-based assessment tasks to achieve the standards established by the New South Wales Board of Studies. One of the major changes in schooling since the establishment of the centers in 1994 has been change in the ways that schools assess students. Increasingly, assessment tasks set by schools and teachers contribute to students' results and grades and assess a wider range of learning outcomes than previously tested by examinations. As a result, more than 75% of homework study center time concerns assisting students to interpret, plan, and complete school-based assessment tasks. Pasifika students often need assistance in understanding and interpreting course outcomes, planning appropriate responses to assessment tasks, researching and locating appropriate knowledge sources, and preparing responses in the correct language genre. Students identify language forms and text types for different subjects as one of their main needs for assistance. Since school performance is increasingly influenced by the scores obtained on assessment tasks, attendance at the homework study center improves school results relatively rapidly.

The homework study centers also provide computer and Internet access, which students are assisted to use to research responses to assessment tasks. Since Pasifika students normally reflect low socioeconomic-status families, evaluation of the centers has shown that these facilities are much appreciated by students and parents.

Data have also been collected on topics and subjects that students have identified they need as requiring assistance with. Mathematics and English dominate homework and study time for students not completing assessment tasks.

RESEARCH PROJECT 2: TRANSITION PROGRAMS

These transition programs had two components; transition from secondary school to post-compulsory education (transition study A) and transition from primary to secondary school (transition study B).

Transition Study A: Secondary to Post-Compulsory Education

A key feature of Pasifika Australian education has been the low participation of Pacific Islanders in further and higher education. Typically those Pasifika students participating in universities and TAFE are students on scholarship from their country of origin rather than local Pasifika students who are migrants or the children of migrants.

Community concern about the lack of participation of its young people in further education lead to meetings between the communities and the Faculty of Education and Social Work at the University of Sydney. As a result, the **Tertiary Awareness Program for Pacific Island Students (TAPA)** was introduced in 1996. Since then, TAPA programs have been conducted with some 15 schools involving over 275 South Pacific Islander (Pasifika) students. The program is jointly developed and managed by the Faculty of Education and Social Work, the schools to which the Pasifika students belong, preservice teachers undertaking courses in culturally responsive teaching, and representatives from the Pasifika communities (especially Tongan and Samoan).

Pasifika students visit the university for the day where an orientation to the features and life of the university is the focus. During the program, mentors from preservice teacher education programs are assigned to small groups of Pasifika students. These mentors and the Pasifika students develop warm, friendly (*aroha*) relationships and have the opportunity to share experiences and future plans. The intended outcomes are to build the Pasifika students' knowledge and awareness of post-school education and inform them of pathways into higher education. Support for the process of decision making and expanding the framework on which choices about staying on at school and further education are an objective. Pasifika students also have the opportunity to enter a writing competition about continuing their studies post school, and have the opportunity to discuss their future plans with their groups and mentors.

The TAPA program is culturally sensitive and designed to build on the cultural foundations and background of the Pasifika Australian school students. The program includes participation by relevant community role models who discuss their post-compulsory education experiences. The TAPA program includes parent and community members on the university visit. It uses vernacular and first language as well as English in presentations and discussions. The TAPA program follows a narrative structure in its organization, and uses Polynesian patterns of community support and of greeting rituals to provide a secure and comfortable environment that helps to create a cultural continuity for the Pasifika school students. For almost all these students this is their first contact with a university and their initial visit to a post-compulsory campus.

THE TAPA SURVEY AND EVALUATION

At the end of the TAPA program at the university, the teachers of the Pasifika students conduct an evaluation and survey to evaluate the TAPA program, identify its impact, and gather data on Pasifika students' knowledge of post-compulsory education.

The survey gathers data on Pasifika students' post-school intentions, interest in higher education, perceived difficulties in gaining higher education entry requirements, encouragement received through the TAPA program, and links between school and post-school options and evaluation of the TAPA program. Similar survey data have been collected between 1998 and 2004 from six schools. The results from these surveys are discussed below.

Pasifika students' responses to the survey indicate that the TAPA visit has a significant impact on their thinking about school and post-compulsory school options. Eighty percent of the students indicate that they intend to continue in school to the Higher School Certificate (the exit school qualification at year 12 in New South Wales). After the TAPA experience 80% of the Pasifika students also report that they are now considering post-compulsory school options such as University or Technical and Further Education (TAFE). Survey questions on the difficulties of securing higher education places and how to maximize their opportunities showed that Pasifika students' understanding of the success factors in achieving higher education entry standards had also increased significantly. Student comments include

> "I have enjoyed the TAPA day at Uni very much, because it has given me positive views of uni and has encouraged me to set my goals and achieve."
> "Especially coming from a Pacific Island background it teaches me to be a lot more positive at school."
> "This has shown me that I can do something with my life."
> "I heard Mr Sei and Mr Huatukau say that we are the new generation and we have to take care of mum and dad and our families."

After the TAPA Program

Teacher evaluations show that Pasifika students return to school with a renewed enthusiasm to support each other as they negotiate relationships with teachers back at their school. The structural arrangements of the school and classroom, however, make the process a challenging one. Follow-up evaluations reveal that students still have scant knowledge of the pathways to further education and the requirements to enter particular employment domains. Students were generally aware of the importance of "exam marks, assessment, and studying" as factors that might frustrate their ability to participate in further education. Anecdotal evidence collected from the schools that have participated in the program indicate that up to 40% of the students access post-compulsory school options, a significant improvement on current Pasifika access. Schools increasingly apply to join the TAPA program to improve both the motivation of the students in school and their intention to undertake post school study.

TRANSITION STUDY B:
PRIMARY TO SECONDARY EDUCATION

The South Pacific Island Education group at the University of Sydney comprises a loose network of schools, teachers, and communities and is linked through the homework study centers. In 2002–2004, the group attempted some primary to secondary transition education projects designed to improve the transition of Pasifika students from primary to secondary school. This project arose from analysis of difficulties that Pasifika students had expressed about the difficulties they faced when entering secondary school. These identified problems included unclear behavior norms, lack of a friendly relationship with teachers for students new to secondary classrooms, and lack of academic skills in the new secondary school environment.

A two-school primary-secondary school transition project (Campsie Primary and Canterbury Girls) was developed to improve transition for Pasifika students. This project put Pasifika primary students together with Pasifika secondary students at the university. The transition project used a cultural *aiga* (family) frame to structure the day. Each secondary student played the role of brother or sister for primary students. The secondary students conducted a reading program based on a cultural narrative and including Samoan, Tongan, Fijian, and Maori legends and stories. The project was based around the concepts of rank and family, a significant aspect of Pasifika cultures. Secondary students accepted responsibility for the younger students and provided both guidance and direction, both in the transition project and in the wider community. They also conducted discussions on attending secondary school for the primary students and also conducted a writing competition in English and vernaculars. After returning to school, a literacy unit on TAPA has been developed by the primary teachers to build on the links to secondary schooling made by the transition project.

Student data have been collected from the primary school writing competition. Analysis of the student writing revealed how Pasifika students reflected *ako*, *ilo*, and *poto*. Many of the responses of the primary students discussed their new secondary "friends" as new family members (e.g., brothers and sisters from the secondary school), despite the fact that they were not biologically related. The primary students' writing also included a variety of vernacular terms and some of the conversations were in vernacular. The primary students' writing also discussed how information can be gathered from secondary students acting as brother and sisters. Many of the responses also alluded to working together in family groups to overcome any perceived difficulties. These responses reflect the culture of the students and the way the transition day echoed and affirmed this culture in an Australian context.

RESEARCH PROJECT 3: PASIFIKA STUDENTS' PERCEPTIONS OF SCHOOL AND EDUCATION

This section provides results from an analysis of what Pasifika students are saying about their schooling and the relations between school and the culture of their community and home. The context for the collection of the data has been through a course within a preservice teacher education program conducted at Sydney University. This course required preservice teachers in training to engage with the Pasifika community in various school and community settings. These settings included student forums specifically designed for the young Pasifika people to speak out and the homework study centers (already described) where students, parents and community workers were interviewed and participated in focus groups.

The research held to the principle of "self-determination of the participants," which characterizes the work of Bishop with Maori communities in New Zealand (Bishop et al., 2001). This approach provides for the participants to collaboratively construct their stories in culturally appropriate ways. The research seeks to affirm the cultural preferences, practices, and aspirations of the Pasifika Australia community. The research reflects and is dependent "on establishing strong relationships with the community so that students and parents speak openly and honestly" (Prestidge, 2002, p. 4). Between 1996 and 2002 a number of youth conferences were held for school students of Samoan, Fijian, Cook Island, and Tongan background. These conferences were typically of one-day duration and provided a context for students to talk to and with the leaders of their communities about issues of concern to the young people. Their discussions around the experience of life and schooling in Sydney reveal the cultural complexity of negotiating successfully participation in an educational system that seems unresponsive to their needs. The experiences and stories of the school students was recorded and subsequently analyzed.

Results: Pasifika Australia Students Perceptions of Education

In these youth conferences, Samoan young people recognized the strong hierarchical structures within their community and the significant obligatory roles that exist as part of their relationships with chief, church pastor, and, more broadly, elders of the community. While these relationships are valued, they were not seen to be appropriate to the Australian context. The cultural conflict "pushes kids to become separated from their parents." The young people felt that their parents should "adjust to Australian society." The obligatory demands by the church for financial support created conflict for the limited funds that working class-and welfare-dependent families have at their disposal. The adolescents reported that the positive valuing of the traditional Samoan body image "large and fat" created a tension, "a sense of shame," in a dominant culture where thin is beautiful. Young people also expressed a consciousness of the lack of experience of their parents of Australian schools and the education system. They reported that they keep from their parents aspects of their school life, because the task of explanation is too difficult ("they wouldn't understand"). The gap between the knowledge of their parents and their own experience about school was seen as too great. The students reported that they perceived that their parents were critical of the liberal and questionable teaching methods that seemed to characterize Australian schools. Often their parents had no experience of the Australian school context and rarely had any contact with the school.

At school, teachers were perceived as being uninterested and lacking understanding of the world of the students from Samoan and Tongan communities. Subsequently, when students have problems at school they feel that they do not have the skills to cross the cultural divide between themselves and their teachers. Asking for help with academic work or with the personal relationships needed to successfully negotiate school was seen as a difficult task.

The sense of frustration and alienation was just as strong when school counselors were encountered. These "specialist" personnel were seen not to have cultural understandings ("they're not interested in us," "they don't know the Samoan way fa'a samoa"). School counselors were seen to be part of the system, siding with the school and consequently unable to serve the interests of students.

Samoan Australian students reported that "academic study is not part of what happens at home." Parents "do not have the skills" and understandings to "help their children." However, the young people recognized that their parents wanted them to benefit from schooling: "Our parents want us to be good and to work hard so that we can get a good job." "But our parents do not know our schools." The relationship between school and vocation was broadly understood by parents but parents rarely have access to the cultural knowledge that characterized the students' schools. The cultural knowledge of the community was not accessed by the teachers and the school, as teachers were frequently seen to denigrate the students' community and cultural ways.

RESEARCH PROJECT 4: DEVELOPING CULTURALLY RESPONSIVE TEACHERS AND STUDENT TEACHERS

Culturally responsive pedagogy requires the development of awarenesses, understandings, and practices that legitimize Pasifika identity and culture in the context of Australian society. For preservice and current teachers, this means coming to see another culture positively, and viewing it from the lens of possibility, as a source of new learning. Deep cultural learning is only derived through serious engagement with Pasifika communities. Serious engagement requires considerable interaction with the community, in this case provided by visits to homes, churches, and community, and long-term connections with families and students *outside the school*. Through activities in homework centers, student forums, and discussions in community contexts, work with parents and community groups, current and preservice teachers came to learn about other cultures in depth and explore the links between culture, behavior, and learning in its cultural and social context.

The culturally responsive teaching projects discussed so far depend on developing critically reflective teachers. Reflective teachers develop skills in critiquing their pedagogy during and after their teaching (Hatton & Smith, 1995) and evaluating their teaching practices with a view to improvement. Furthermore, "to engage in critical reflection requires a moving beyond the acquisition of new knowledge and understanding, into questioning [of] existing assumptions, values, and perspectives" (Cranton, 1996, p. 8). Becoming culturally critically reflective is an exercise in critical reflection where cultural assumptions, values, and perspectives are critiqued, compared, and evaluated.

Developing culturally critical reflection requires a number of reflective elements and processes that are held to be central to critical reflection (Imel, 1998). These include being aware of the cultural contexts of schooling and learning; critiquing teaching and learning situations from diverse cultural reference points; analyzing the cultural assumptions held in given teaching situations; reviewing one's own cultural assumptions by being questioning and skeptical; and speculating on more culturally appropriate and sensitive teaching and learning behaviors (Brookfield, 1988).

Participants in the culturally responsive projects described previously tutored and coached in the home study centers where they had the opportunity to interact with the Pasifika students' parents; participated in community events and interacted widely with community members; conducted tertiary awareness days for Pasifika students and community members at the university; and were exposed to Polynesian community leaders and speakers during seminars at the university.

At the conclusion of these projects, future and current teachers were asked to briefly evaluate the projects and reflect on their own teacher cultural learnings. A sample of these evaluations and reflections were analyzed to identify the type of reflection that teachers involved had made. The analysis involved exploring the culturally critical reflection of the teachers' and preservice teachers' writing. In particular, their culturally critical reflective writing focused on speculation about appropriate teacher behavior and pedagogy in the context of reviewing cultural assumptions. Such writing evidenced theorizing about the best ways to plan, program, and organize teaching and learning on the basis of reflecting about new cultural learning they had made.

The results of the study revealed that most of the current and future teachers' reflection was not culturally critically reflective. Although most of the respondents' writing included references to vernacular terms such as *Fa'afetai mo fou a'oa'oga, tofa soifua* and *fa'a samoa*, which are essential in developing cultural awareness of Polynesian Australians, it was only culturally descriptive. An example of culturally descriptive writing included:

> The interview with Tongan parents have given me some understanding about Tongan culture both in Tonga and how it has changed in Australia. The parents were very warm and friendly. The reasons that most Tongans came to Australia are to look for jobs and to give their children a better education and life.

Only 20% of the reflective writing attempted to explain educational phenomena from a cultural perspective. This type of reflective writing shows that the writers are engaged in a dialogue with culture and they develop new ways of explaining events and seeing pedagogic situations. An example of this type of reflective writing included:

> The information I collected about Western Samoa not only provided me with a sound background of what the climate, crops, wealth, politics, and village life included, but it also highlighted the hierarchical structure of Samoan villages—who serves who. I hope to use the knowledge gained from my reading as a reference point for storytelling and a way to explain ideas clearer either for the parents or the children.

Only 10% of reflective writing could be classed as critically culturally responsive and reflective where current and preservice teachers synthesized their new cultural knowledge and used it to speculate on how they could improve their teaching by more appropriate and culturally sensitive pedagogy. This writing locates pedagogy in a cultural frame. Another aspect of such reflective writing is its affirmation. Such writing not only values another culture, it also frames it in the context of empowerment both for the teacher (in their speculative and planned action) but also for the Pasifika student group. An example of such writing included:

> I feel it would be useful to talk at length with parents about their role in supporting their children in further education (or possible careers), enabling them to feel a sense of real collaboration and guidance concerning their children's lives at school and beyond. I think the students would appreciate some advice and discussion on what they could achieve and pursue. We as a group could provide some assistance and support to the parents and students in determining and acting upon any ideas they have for education, training, and employment in the future, it may strengthen all of our positions.

Culturally responsive teaching requires that teachers are able to view their pedagogy and curriculum from another cultural frame and augment their approach by "listening to culture" and learning from it.

There is a lack of alignment between the cultural assumptions, knowledge, and learning of Pasifika students and the mainstream learning environments in which they are educated. The homework centers, transition programs, and student forums described in the chapter attempted to create learning environments that are in alignment with the Pasifika students' approaches to learning. They were culturally responsive because they used knowledge of the students' culture in the design of their curriculum and pedagogy. They empowered the students and their communities through inclusion and affirmation and reduced the cultural gap between the students' school and nonschool lives.

Despite the success of these culturally responsive projects described in the first three research projects, the data in study 4 show that attempting to assist teachers and preservice teachers to become more culturally responsive in their teaching is problematic. Very few teachers are able to use their knowledge of another culture to critically reflect on the culture of the classroom and to redesign such a culture to be more affording to Pasifika students and their communities.

CONCLUSION

Viliami: The Case Study Revisited

After sitting with my dad to write the case study at the start of this chapter, a lot of new things happened to me at school and home. The head of student welfare at my school spoke to my father about using the time he spent on disciplining me better. My dad now drives me to an Islander after-school study center, where I get help in doing my English, math, and science school assessment tasks.

My marks are getting better and this makes my father happier with me. I am in a new gang. My art teacher has decided to create a lunchtime art group for the students interested in making a graphic arts advertisement for the school. She asked me to bring some of my friends from my group. Only four came, but I am the oldest and biggest and am now the group leader. We are working on a school video for Tongan, Fijian, and Samoan parents to help them understand what we do at school. I videoed my father asking questions about the school. Since then some other parents from my Samoan and Tongan group and the church leaders from our church have visited the school and spoken to the principal.

My teachers treat me differently, they have changed the way they speak to me. They don't argue with me like before but use more body language and talk to me more about things I know about. One teacher said malololelei (hello in Tongan) to me yesterday, it made me happy and I sang in class. The school has a picolo (Pacific Island Community Liason Officer). It's hard to skip school as he knows where we used to hang out.

We visited the university and met some new university friends who treated us like brothers and sisters. We had a welcoming ceremony and looked at the uni. I'ts so big, I'd never been there before. I think I want to be an art teacher now—but I will have to study hard and be brave by studying to help achieve my goals. Then I will be able to help my mum and dad and family properly.

What has been demonstrated here for Viliami is true for many of the students who have been involved in the culturally responsive education programs at the University of Sydney. Attendance at the homework centers has improved students' performances in school assessment tasks. They have provided an opportunity for Pasifika parents to contribute to their children's education. Parents appreciate the culturally responsive manner in which the centers operate, and as a result were keen to attend and discuss educational issues with other Pasifika parents.

Pasifika students attending the TAPA program identify more post school options that influence their motivation and goal-setting in considering continuing further study. Teachers and students attending the Pasifika student forums gain access to new cultural knowledge that can be used to affirm the cultural identity of the Pasifika students in the Australian school content. In Viliami's story noted above, his teachers have developed a culturally responsive approach to curriculum, pedagogy and behavior management. However, the research discussed in this chapter does not lead to uniformly positive expectations that teachers will be able to develop culturally responsive approaches.

REFERENCES

Bakalevu, S. (2003). Ways of mathematising in Fijian society. In K. H. Thaman (Ed.), *Educational ideas from Oceania: Selected readings* (pp. 101-107). Suva: The University of the South Pacific Institute of Education.

Bishop, R., & Glynn, T. (1999) *Culture counts: Changing power relationships in education*. Palmerston North: Dunmore Press.

Bishop, R., Glynn, T., Berryman, M., McKinley, E., Devine, N., & Richardson, C. (June 2001) *The experience of Maori children in year 9 and 10 classroom: The scope exercise*. Unpublished paper presented to the Research Division of the Ministry of Education, New Zealand.

Bishop, R., Tiakiwai, S., Richardson, C., & Berryman, M. (April, 2002) *The experience of year 9 and 10 Maori students in mainstream classrooms: Milestones Report no. 2*. Unpublished report to the Ministry of Education, New Zealand.

Brookfield, S. D. (1995) *Becoming a critically reflective teacher.* San Francisco: Jossey-Bass

Buatava, B. (2003). Samoan educational ideas. In K. H. Thaman (Ed.), *Educational ideas from Oceania: Selected readings* (pp. 47-65). Suva: The University of the South Pacific Institute of Education.

Carauana, M. (2001) *Tongan, Samoan and Fijian students enrolment, community information.* Blacktown District Office, Department of Education and Training.

Connell, R. (1993) *Schools and social justice.* Montreal: Our/Schools Our Selves Education Foundation.

Cranton, P. (1996) *Professional development as transformative learning: New perspectives for teachers of adults.* San Francisco: Jossey-Bass.

Florio-Ruane, S. (2001). *Teacher education and the cultural imagination.* Mahwah, NJ: Erlbaum.

Hatton, N., & Smith, D. (1995). Reflection in teacher education: Towards definition and implementation. *Teaching and Teacher Education, 10,* 33-49.

Helu- Thaman, K. (1988). *Ako and Faiako: Educational concepts, cultural values and teachers' role perception in Tonga.* Unpublished doctoral thesis, University of the South Pacific:Suva.

Helu-Thaman, K. (Ed.). (2003). *Educational ideas from Oceania: Selected readings.* Suva, Fiji: Institute of Education.

Hutakau, I. (1999). *A multicultural approach to learning, community information.* Blacktown District Office, Department of Education and Training, Australia.

Imel, S. (1996). Summing up: themes and issues related to learning. In S. Imel (Ed.), *Learning in groups: Exploring fundamental principles, new uses, and emerging opportunities.* San Francisco: Jossey-Bass.

Lowe, K., Sawyer, W., Wood, H., Newman, S., & Buchanan, J. (1997). *Retaining Cook Island students in secondary school.* Research report, University of Western Sydney.

Macfarlane, A. (2004). *Kia hiwa ra! Listen to culture—Maori students' plea to educators.* Wellington: New Zealand Council for Educational Research.

McIntyre, A. (2002). Exploring whiteness and multicultural education with prospective teachers, *Curriculum Inquiry, 32*(1), 31-50.

Meleisea, M., & Schoeffel, P. (1996, February). *Pacific Island Polynesian attitudes to child training and discipline in New Zealand: Some policy implications for social welfare and education.* Paper presented at the National Symposium on Pacific Islands Learning, Auckland.

Mokoroa, V. (2003). INdigenous education in Atiu (Cook Islands). In K. H. Thaman (Ed.), *Educational ideas from Oceania: Selected readings* (pp. 79-84). Suva: The University of the South Pacific Institute of Education.

Native Hawaiian Education Council. (2002). *Na Honua Mauli Ola: Hawaii guidelines for a culturally healthy and responsive learning environment.* Honolulu, HI: Author.

Nabobo, U. (2003). Indigenous Fijian educational ideas. In K. H. Thaman (Ed.), *Educational ideas from Oceania: Selected readings* (pp. 85-93). Suva: The University of the South Pacific Institute of Education.

New Zealand Qualifications Authority. (2002). *Secondary qualifications statistics 2001.*Wellington: Author.

Osborne, B. (Ed.). (2001). *Teaching diversity and democracy.* Melbourne, Australia: Common Ground.

Prestidge, B. (2002, December). *Educating new teachers for Culturally complex classrooms: The New Zealand setting.* Unpublished paper presented at "Advance Teacher Education: Our Work, Our Research," University of Sydney and Waikato University.

Sturman, A. (1997). *Social justice in education.* Melbourne: ACER.

Va'a, L. F. (2001). *"Saili Matagi"—Samoan migrants in Australia.* Fiji: Institute of Pacific Studies, University of the South Pacific.

Vaioleti, T. (2001, April). *We left our island, people and our culture to educate our children in New Zealand.* Paper presented at Educating Pasefika Positively, Waikato.

Vygotsky, L. (1978). *Mind in society: The development of higher mental processes.* Cambridge, MA: Harvard University Press.

CHAPTER 15

CREATING COMMUNITY AND BECOMING A MEMBER OF AN URBAN TEACHER EDUCATION PROGRAM

Michelle Kelly and William Buxton

My undergraduate career commenced in the fall of 1998, as I became a part of the C.U.R.E. (Cortland's Urban Recruitment of Educators) program. C.U.R.E. is a merit-based scholarship awarded annually to 10–12 high school graduates choosing to dedicate the next 6 years of their lives to becoming a professional in urban education. At the age of 17, I was presented with this opportunity and humbly accepted the offer to attend State University of New York (SUNY) College at Cortland. In doing so I was provided with a plan. I did not have to think about what I wanted to do when I grew up anymore. Financial decisions were taken out of the equation. The only "small" decision I had to make was whether or not I wanted to teach. Sure, why not. It all seemed right.

Fortunately, the education I received through the C.U.R.E. program proved beneficial. I was immersed in urban experiences from day one, and as a result, uncovered my passion for learning. This discovery sparked an energy that provoked change, uncovering paths that led me to a cross-cultural experience later in my undergraduate career. In my junior year I made the decision to carry out my preservice teaching requirements both domestically in New York City and internationally in London, England....

Focus on Curriculum, 353–376

When I finally looked at [my experience] for what it was and [what I] had grown to be, I was living and teaching in a public school in Brooklyn, New York.

The Longfellow School, or PS 94 as it is more commonly known, where I teach, is a part of one of the most diverse public school systems in the nation: the New York City Public School system. The demographics of the elementary school are ... approximately 65% Latino, 30% Chinese American, and about 5% Arabic. Talk about cultural barriers—I was as much a foreigner to these streets as to any London market or square. I remember my first walk to the school. Coming off the R train onto 4th Avenue and 52nd Street, into a neighborhood I knew nothing about, I was intimidated by its appearance. Halfway up the block I made up my mind: there was no way I was taking a job teaching in this neighborhood. Coming up the stairs in the building's main entrance I asked myself, "What are you doing?" The crime scene tape and handgun reward poster made quite an impression. Needless to say, I went through with the interview and accepted a position as a third-grade teacher. Now, almost 2 years later, I've come to understand the use of the yellow tape as a lack of a better means to rope off construction. It fazes no one familiar to the school community, nor does the NYPD handgun poster on the security desk, as it can be seen in many respected institutions around the city's "less-fortunate" neighborhoods. Had I gone with my initial reaction and dismissed the opportunity due to my unfamiliarity with the surroundings, I would have missed out on being a part of a prosperous school community.

When you are not comfortable with something, you might say, "Give it time." That is what everyone said to me during my first month of teaching. Time seemed to be the answer for everything. It would help me to get used to the public transit system and the neighborhoods it toured. It would allow me to arrange and rearrange my classroom until things felt right. It would bring familiarity to my colleagues and the administration, and it would eventually aid in building the relationships between the children and me. I think my most memorable sign of progress was when Samantha, a Puerto Rican student of mine, clarified the confusion of my skin color for the class in saying, "You're not white, Ms. Gomez. You're just really light-skinned." This gave me the green light to pursue an open discussion of race, culture, and difference that was, shall I say, soaked up by the children. This discussion forum, rooted in respect and understanding, is what upholds our community. It puts forth a feeling of comfort and openness that is conducive to all of our learning.

After time healed the initial shock of my introduction to this culture, I continually worked to enrich this transition by getting to know the neighborhood. Spending time at the local park, bodegas, restaurants, tamale stands, and avenue shops helped me to familiarize myself with the dynamics of the people. I learned more about who they were, where they were from, and what they did. Eventually, I began to recognize faces and exchange greetings. I began to feel comfortable in my new neighborhood. The people would no longer watch me walk up the streets and wonder what I was doing there. "Hola maestra," some would say. As their child's teacher, I was welcomed and accepted as part of the community. (female, elementary school teacher)

In this vignette, a C.U.R.E. graduate describes her own evolution in becoming a member of a community and the recognition that becoming a member is an ongoing process. She talks of being a "newcomer" in unfamiliar and seemingly threatening surroundings to moving to "old-timer" status as a recognized and respected member of the community. The C.U.R.E. program was founded on the belief that preservice teachers need to be apprenticed into their professional communities and the contexts in which those are located. A goal, then, of C.U.R.E. is to help participants create their own understanding of a particular kind of community. Such a process involves the development of awareness and knowledge of the sociocultural context in which they live and work and, as such, they are always evolving in their roles as members of particular communities.

The undergraduate students who participate in C.U.R.E. must apply to the program and are selected through an application and interview process. In return for scholarship support, students commit to teaching for at least 2 years after they graduate from college in a high-need urban school in New York State. The program that students complete is based on the premise that teaching in high-need urban schools is a compelling and challenging professional position.

Data for this chapter were gathered as part of an ongoing evaluation of the C.U.R.E. program. There were multiple purposes in collecting this data: (1) establish a database necessary for grant reports supporting the program and applying for additional grant support, (2) establish the effectiveness of the program to the college, and (3) establish effectiveness for professional dissemination. A sociocultural theoretical framework guided the collection of data. Sociocultural research assumes that human actions are culturally mediated, historically developing, and occur in practical activity (Cole, 1990). The data presented in this chapter focus on the final two assumptions (historical development and practical activity). Students were tracked over a 6-year period from their first semester in college through 2 years after graduation while they were teaching in urban schools. In addition to tracking students, a history of the beginning of the C.U.R.E. program provides additional data for understanding the current place of the program. Practical activity is provided for C.U.R.E. students through ongoing placement in urban schools that begins in their first semester in college. This placement provides students with opportunities to become new participants in the practice of teaching throughout their college careers.

METHODS

Data were collected through a variety of sources. Classroom observations, student reflection papers, and interviews with school personnel provide data for analyzing student performance and attitudes about urban schools. Student papers were collected as part of classroom assignments. Photocopies of papers were saved for research purposes with the consent of students. Exit interviews were conducted with graduating seniors to evaluate the program and for research purposes. Again, students were advised of the purposes of the interviews and gave their consent. The college president, campus administrators, and staff who were founding members of the C.U.R.E. Advisory Committee consented to interviews to document the history of the C.U.R.E. program as well as to gain a perspective on the role of the program in the college at large. Naturalistic enquiry methods were used to gain additional information providing context and details to the research. Informal conversations with C.U.R.E. students and C.U.R.E. Advisory Committee members provided a valuable source of supplementary information.

The Need for Urban Teacher Education Programs

The Urban Teacher Collaborative found that students who attend inner-city schools have only a 50% chance of being taught by a qualified teacher, despite the argument of the National Commission on Teaching and America's Schools (1997) that the most important strategies for achieving our nation's educational goals are effective recruiting, preparing, and supporting excellent teachers—regardless of the context in which they teach. C.U.R.E. addresses two fundamental issues in educational reform: (1) the lack of students of color in higher education and subsequently in teacher education programs, and (2) the lack of qualified teachers prepared for urban contexts.

In the fall of 1997, SUNY Cortland's former President Judson Taylor put into place an idea that developed into the C.U.R.E. program. Taylor had spent 20 years of his career in higher education working in urban contexts in the Los Angeles area as an educational psychologist. New York State's urban schools were in dire straits. Newly certified teachers were unwilling to take positions in New York City and the State handed out thousands of temporary teaching licenses to uncertified teachers each year to fill the City's need for teachers. SUNY Cortland was graduating more certified teachers each year than any other college or university in

New York State. For that reason, Taylor believed that as a state institution SUNY Cortland had a responsibility to prepare teachers for work in areas where they were needed most: high-need urban schools, particularly New York City. Out of Taylor's own previous experience in Los Angeles and his commitment to meeting the needs of New York State's urban school districts came the C.U.R.E. program.

In addition, Taylor recognized the critical shortage of teachers of color in New York State and across the nation. To this end he envisioned a scholarship program to support future teachers from underrepresented groups in their teacher preparation majors. Such a program would serve two purposes: (1) it would help to increase diversity in the teaching ranks, and (2) it would increase diversity of the student body at SUNY Cortland.

Taylor and then Vice President of Institutional Advancement Jim Boyle worked through former local State Assembly representative Marty Luster to secure scholarships with a grant from an anonymous private foundation. These funds were supplemented with financial support from the College Foundation at SUNY Cortland. A working committee of administrators and professional staff representing a wide array of departments on campus worked to recruit and interview 12 finalists for the new 4-year, fully paid scholarship. In addition, a faculty line was created in the Education Department for an Assistant Professor of Urban Education and, one of the authors, Michelle Kelly, was hired in that position for the fall of 1998.

By fall 1998, the C.U.R.E. program was up and running with 11 scholarship recipients, a faculty coordinator, a campus-wide advisory committee, and an introductory course in urban education. Since that time C.U.R.E. has grown to combine creative recruitment, focused mentoring of undergraduates and new graduates, leadership opportunities, culturally relevant courses in urban and multicultural education, and field experiences in urban schools, which has resulted in program success with an 85% retention rate.

The program consists of the following four goals:

- Increase the number of qualified ethnic minority students likely to commit to a career in urban teaching.
- Support students' retention and graduation with scholarships, high-quality mentoring, and leadership opportunities.
- Ensure high-quality pre-professional preparation with coursework and seminars focusing on urban and multicultural education, methods courses incorporating New York State teaching and learning standards, and field experiences in New York State high-need urban schools.

- Support new teacher retention for 2 years following graduation; and maintain and develop partnerships to sustain and expand program success.

The rest of this chapter lays out the process of the C.U.R.E. program's development through the first 6 years of operation and the philosophical rationale that guides the program. In particular, we focus on the aspects of the program that deal with the process of community-building and becoming a member of a particular community.

Program Rationale

Because SUNY Cortland has many existing programs in teacher education, there is a legitimate question as to why it is necessary to create a separate program for urban education. Why are the existing programs not sufficient for preparing teachers for urban areas? Haberman (1996) and Bartoli (2001) argue that urban teaching is a specialized field that is not adequately addressed in typical teacher preparation programs. Haberman critiques universal approaches to teacher education that assume the same program can prepare teachers for high-income, low-income, rural, suburban, and urban schools. In particular, Haberman argues that teacher education programs in this country do not examine social models of learning and development. As a consequence, teacher education programs are dominated by individualistic models that eventually place responsibility for failure on the very people schools are supposed to be helping: in this case, the children attending urban schools.

Sociocultural interpretations of Vygotsky's theory (Lave, 1996; Lave & Wenger, 1991; Moll, 2000; Rogoff, 1994) provide both a theoretical justification for a localized approach to teacher education and help to explain much of the successes achieved at this point in the C.U.R.E. program. Gutierrez and Stone (2000) make the argument for localized knowledge of schools when they say:

> The significance of developing a deep understanding of schools and their social organization is that it can inform policies and practices of urban education. Although there is much to be learned from research that has helped to locate educational problems in the larger social context, educators also need research methodologies and theoretical frames that provide the possibility of more local explanations for the dilemmas and problems facing urban education. Situated understandings of education provide insight into the cognitive and social consequences of educational policies and practices. (p. 150)

In developing C.U.R.E., the work of activity theory (Leont'ev, 1981) provides a lens for examining the situated and purposeful nature of activity in schools. Drawing on Gutierrez and Stone, activity is defined as "a social practice that includes the norms, values, division of labor, and goals of the community" (p. 151). One implication of a sociocultural perspective is that learning is a process of becoming a community member (Lave, 1996; Lave & Wenger, 1991; Rogoff, 1994; Rogoff, Mistry, Goncu, & Mosier, 1993).

Using activity- and community-building as a basis for an urban education program presents some obvious difficulties in a rural setting like Cortland. Moll (2000) presents a way out of this dilemma, however, by arguing that any community is largely an imagined state. All of us define a community based on our historical experiences with different communities. These experiences include not just lived experiences, but experiences derived from various media (e.g., print, television, and cinema). That communities are largely imagined represents an opportunity for educators. "That all communities will remain to a large extent imagined communities is probably unavoidable, but educators can help to deliberately, intentionally determine how they are defined or imagined" (Moll, 2000, p. 264). The challenge for the coordinator of C.U.R.E. was to develop activities that created an imagined community that envisioned urban education and teaching in urban schools in a positive and fulfilling manner. Because communities are constantly recreated by novices or new members to the communities (Lave & Wenger, 1991), much of the evidence for the success of the activities we report will come from the words of the student members of the C.U.R.E. community.

Conceptualizing C.U.R.E. as a community extends to the campus-wide support it receives. People from across campus have come together to form the C.U.R.E. Advisory Committee. They serve as advocates and spokespersons for the program. In 2003 Lois Weiner, an urban teacher educator and author of several books and numerous articles related to urban teacher education, visited the campus to spend time with the people involved in the C.U.R.E. program. She noted that C.U.R.E. was successful in creating an urban teacher education program in a fairly rural environment and that the C.U.R.E. Advisory Committee constituted an unusual coalition:

> C.U.R.E. is a program that is well conceived and well organized, and is an example of how a university that is geographically removed from urban centers can nonetheless develop a fine program of urban teacher education. C.U.R.E.'s development over the past years relied on the support of many different players in the university, people who are not often brought together in collaboration about teacher education, and this collaboration is by itself worthy of commendation. That the collaboration occurred to nur-

ture a program of urban teacher education is all the more remarkable. The result of the cooperation and support present in the institution is evident in the high quality of the students who are in C.U.R.E. (L. Weiner, personal communication, 2003)

The following sections examine specific components of the C.U.R.E. program and the role they play in creating the sort of imagined community that views the educational process as one that provides both social and emotional support for achieving success. Throughout the C.U.R.E. program the goal is one of building community, and this effort begins with the recruiting process.

Recruitment and Acceptance

Potential C.U.R.E. applicants learn about the program in a variety of ways: through mailings to high school guidance counselors and individual students, college fairs, campus presentations during visits to the college, high school visits by the C.U.R.E. coordinator and C.U.R.E. students, personalized recruiting, and word of mouth. The latter becomes increasingly effective as the number of participants in the program and graduates of it grows. During the most recent recruiting season, two of the 11 finalists learned about the program through current participants, one from a former participant, and one from a high school teacher whose son is a graduate of the program. Annual mass mailings sent to over 500 New York State high school guidance counselors who work with seniors aspiring to college have proven to be a costly and highly ineffective form of recruitment. There has never been more than one finalist in a year that learned about the program from a high school guidance counselor and in some years no finalist learned about the program through that avenue. Thus, the most effective recruiting method includes a personal touch of some sort: directly meeting prospective candidates at their high schools or when the candidate comes to the college campus, personal phone calls, and recommendations from current and former C.U.R.E. scholars.

During the entire recruitment process, a primary effort continues to focus on establishing a personal connection with potential applicants. Follow-up then becomes important. Sending an email, a letter, or making a phone call to them within a few days of meeting, then maintaining that connection. Many female students from New York City high schools who have shown an interest in the program end up not applying. If these female students do apply and are selected as finalists, they do not attend the interview day activities at SUNY Cortland. In all such cases, these young women have been the children of working-poor to working-class immigrants, particularly from Mexico or Central or South American countries. In one case, a female student from New York City visited the school in the fall on a college-sponsored bus trip and met with the C.U.R.E. coordinator. She was unable to attend the Interview Day so the coordinator interviewed her over the phone. After being offered the scholarship, she too had to decline, even after the coordinator and a college financial aid officer called her mother to explain the opportunity and scholarship and emailed her information. In the end, the applicant told the coordinator, "I can't. My mother thinks I'm too little to go away." This response reflects what most parents felt. Their daughters, usually the first in the family to be headed to college and often the first to graduate from high school, could live at home and commute to a college in the city, usually in the same borough where they lived, but it was too much to move away from the family home to attend college.

This issue has been the major struggle in recruiting students from New York City, given that the majority of students in teacher education programs, especially elementary programs, are female. One solution, which has been a challenge to carry out, is getting potential students' families to visit the College for C.U.R.E.'s annual Interview Day in the spring. Some parents or guardians are not physically able to make the trip or are not able to take a day off work without the consequences of losing a much-needed day's pay. Those who do make the trip, and who have concerns about sending their daughters away to college or having their child teach in an urban school, always have their fears allayed during this visit. Several parents, who came in with concerns, have left the interview day telling the coordinator that they feel positive about the program and everyone they met and they felt like their child was "leaving one family for another." These comments demonstrate the importance of maintaining C.U.R.E. as not just an academic program, but a program that shows the same commitment to its members as a family. While academic preparation and support are necessary for success in college, the experiences gained from C.U.R.E. suggest that enrolling in college, particularly one geographically distant from other family members, and then succeeding in college represents a social commitment by entire families and frequently a change in identity for the student.

Because of the importance of social interaction, the C.U.R.E. interview day is very important to the finalists and their families. Each spring C.U.R.E. finalists and their families are invited to spend a day at SUNY Cortland to learn more about the C.U.R.E. Scholarship Program, meet current students, the faculty, staff, and administrators who support the program, tour the campus, and interview for the scholarship. The day begins with a buffet lunch and welcomes from the coordinator, the President, and Provost. Families appreciate that the two top college administrators take the time to welcome them and join them for lunch. Each family is seated at a separate table for lunch and joined by at least one current C.U.R.E. student and a member of the campus-wide C.U.R.E. Advisory Committee. Following lunch is an overview of the C.U.R.E. program with most of the information shared by current C.U.R.E. students. The campus tour is led by teams of C.U.R.E. students, and they show families their dorm rooms and share honestly about their experiences with the program and at SUNY Cortland. All current C.U.R.E. students are invited to participate in the interview day process and share their perspectives, and usually a dozen or more choose to do so. Many look forward to the event and begin asking about it as soon as they return to campus for the start of spring semester. First-year students, in particular, look forward to the event after having experienced it as an outsider the previous year and now are eager to share an insider perspective. The opportunity for finalists and families to meet and interact informally with everyone from current students to faculty to upper-level administrators is an important step in establishing the feeling that C.U.R.E. is a cohesive community.

The interview session is divided into two parts. During the first half-hour, each finalist is interviewed individually by one or two members of the C.U.R.E. Advisory Committee using a standard set of questions designed to learn about their leadership experiences. After this question-and-answer session with the finalist is concluded, the finalist's family is invited to join the interview session for the second half hour as an opportunity to raise any questions that they may not have been comfortable asking in front of the large group. It is important for the families to be included in all parts of the process for everyone to feel a part of the C.U.R.E. community.

The recruitment process, culminating with the interview day, is the beginning of building a sense of community with potential newcomers in the C.U.R.E. program and to let their families know that their children will become part of a supportive and nurturing community. In addition, C.U.R.E. wants families to know that they need not be alienated during their children's college experience. They are encouraged to maintain connections with the program coordinator and other faculty and staff associated with the program.

Once students have been offered and accept the C.U.R.E. Scholarship and commit to the program, they return to campus with their families for a summer orientation. Throughout this process, the focus remains community-building. The coordinator arranges for all new C.U.R.E. students to attend the same all-college first-year orientation. This large group orientation of a hundred or more freshmen organizes students into smaller groups for its duration, and all new C.U.R.E. students are placed in a group together so that they can begin to get to know each other. The all-college orientation begins late morning on the first day and runs through lunch on the second day.

The second day blends the general campus orientation and the C.U.R.E. orientation. In contrast to the large general campus orientation, the C.U.R.E. orientation offers a small group experience just for its new students and families. The program coordinator and a returning C.U.R.E. student meet the freshmen in the morning to guide them through the course registration process. Then C.U.R.E. students, their families, and the C.U.R.E. faculty and staff meet for an informal lunch in one of the school's cafeterias. After lunch the formal activities of the C.U.R.E. orientation begin. After formal introductions and ice-breaker activities, new students and any of their siblings who are in attendance spend the afternoon participating in team-building exercises with C.U.R.E. faculty, staff, and a few upper-division C.U.R.E. students who have returned specifically to participate in the orientation. Parents and other family members—aunts and grandparents have sometimes attended—meet with several C.U.R.E. Advisory Committee members for a session on sending a child off to college. As SUNY Cortland is a predominantly white institution, the leaders of this session speak honestly about the cultural conflicts the new students may experience and discuss support measures. Late in the afternoon, everyone comes together to meet and talk with an experienced urban educator, who shares his or her experiences with the entire group and answers questions. Finally, the group reviews the expectations of the program and everyone packs up for the trip home with plans to meet again as a group during the fall semester's Parents' Weekend. New students and family members consistently leave this event feeling positive about the program and looking forward to returning in the fall.

The summer orientation has been crucial for beginning to build a sense of community for both students and family members to begin to make a true commitment to the program. When students return in the fall, they have already formed a bond with other C.U.R.E. students, faculty, and staff on campus. They are not coming in as strangers to one another. The relationships among the new students will continue to grow as they take an urban education course together in the fall, taught by the C.U.R.E. coordinator, and participate in monthly events with other C.U.R.E. students.

PREPARING SUCCESSFUL URBAN TEACHERS: ACADEMICS AND COMMUNITY BUILDING

Support for C.U.R.E. Scholars

I have had a lot of support, from the students, from the faculty; from the people I know who have been very supportive. I don't think they [students not in C.U.R.E.] get that [support].... I think that would be one of the main things, support, and really getting a grasp of what urban education is really all about.

... When I came to Cortland, the people on the committee were just so friendly.... My sister went to a very big private college, and when she came here one day—I had some kind of C.U.R.E. celebration—we got to sit down with President Taylor, and when she left she said, "Oh my gosh, I love your school. My school was never like this. They are so nice here. They know you." The President knew us. I see him walk in the door and see his wife; I go over to give him a hug. People very rarely get the opportunity to do that. (senior female, Childhood Education major)

Another student offers her view of the support C.U.R.E. offers:

One of the strengths I see is that I have a major support system. To this day I still have an outstanding relationship with him [referring to a member of the C.U.R.E. Advisory Committee who she met during her interview before freshman year]. I see him in the halls, or at lunch, and he always says hello, and it's nice to have a smiling face from an administrative position. And a lot of my friends are like, "Wow! Who's that?"

... Also the academic support and the ability to communicate with peo-ple in high places. You know, like the President. The functions that we get to go to, a special orientation, we get to visit schools in an urban setting, and we also get to take an urban education class right out of the gate, you know most students don't get to take any education classes until their junior year. So that kind of sets us up for what we are going to do and it lets us know if we really want to do it. (senior female, Childhood Education major)

Given the high initial dropout rate for teachers in urban schools and the reticence of beginning teachers to teach in urban areas, an immediate challenge facing C.U.R.E. is graduating students who are both prepared for urban teaching and eager to face the challenges of urban teaching. C.U.R.E. draws heavily on the work of Vygotsky and current interpreta-tions of Vygotsky (Lave & Wenger, 1991; Rogoff, 1994; Wells, 2000; Wertsch, 1990) in designing a program for meeting this challenge. Peer and faculty/staff mentors support students' transition to college and their academic success. Scholars meet weekly with a member of the C.U.R.E. staff to evaluate academic progress and needs. Program coordinators pro-vide academic, social, and pre-professional advisement throughout the 4-year degree program and for the first 2 years of teaching. An all-college advisory committee meets monthly to review student progress and address ways SUNY Cortland can support retention and graduation.

The success of this support is evident in exit interviews and class papers as C.U.R.E. students bring up the importance of knowing they are a part of a larger community of faculty, administrators, and peers who provide support and guidance throughout their college careers and beyond. One of the most common themes in exit interviews of graduating C.U.R.E. students was the importance of ongoing interactions with faculty, staff, and administrators (exit interviews, May 2002). The following interview with a graduating senior illustrates the value students placed on their interactions with faculty and administrators:

> I interacted a lot more with professors, and I think that is really good. C.U.R.E. made that easier.... I've gotten to know [the President] through C.U.R.E. Also, my other professors. I've told them about the C.U.R.E. program, they've showed interest. I've written about C.U.R.E. in papers and they've asked me about the whole program. It helped me form relationships outside of the classroom with other professors. (female, Childhood Education major)

Through a combination of selected coursework, peer and faculty mentoring, participation in monthly C.U.R.E. meetings, and social gatherings, C.U.R.E. students are invited to become members of a community that values urban schools and urban teaching as a profession. Students come into this community by engaging in dialogic enquiry (Wells, 2000) throughout the coursework that is specific to C.U.R.E., but community building and dialogic enquiry extend beyond coursework. As is indicated by the quotes that opened this section, some of the most important parts of the community building involve formal and informal activities outside of the classroom by the C.U.R.E. coordinator, the C.U.R.E. Advisory Committee, and many other members of the Cortland Campus (exit interviews, May 2002). The many components of the support offered directly relate to the academic achievement of the C.U.R.E. students.

Academic Achievement

Academic achievement and learning is the heart and soul of the program. Ladson-Billings (2001, p. 78) writes, "The focus on academic achievement argues that teachers must place student learning at the center of all activities." Students must maintain the grade point average required by their major for student teaching to retain the C.U.R.E. scholarship. Recognizing that grade point average is not necessarily an indication of learning, C.U.R.E. offers multiple opportunities for students to demonstrate their learning through the use of portfolio presentations, group projects, public presentations about what they have learned, and excellence in their field experiences and first years of teaching. More to the point, C.U.R.E. faculty and staff have high expectations of students, and students know it, a factor Zeichner (1995) found to be critical for the academic success of students in urban schools.

Most impressive about C.U.R.E. students is that many, upon admission to SUNY Cortland, are good students in high school, yet not among the top in their class. The majority of students enter the program with high school averages in the mid-80s and SAT scores around 1,000. However, while in college, the average C.U.R.E. student sports a 3.17 grade point average (GPA), while the average GPA for all full-time SUNY Cortland students is a 2.77. In addition, at least 40% of all C.U.R.E. students earn Dean's List recognition each semester by achieving a minimum 3.30 GPA. With the support of the C.U.R.E. program, these students become academic and community leaders.

C.U.R.E. students are aware that while they may achieve academic success as individuals, they could not achieve what they do without support of others. The adage "Lift as We Climb" from an African American women's club from the 1800s, is used as a mantra in the C.U.R.E. program (Ladson-Billings, 1992). As Deanne, a C.U.R.E. freshman, noted,

> My peer mentor, the Project Coordinator, the Graduate Assistant, and the Director of C.U.R.E. are individuals who I especially thank for making my transition to college life easier. It is very important to have a support network of people that you can go to for professional advice, help with career decisions, or just hang out with. I know that if it weren't for the support C.U.R.E. gives me, I would not have enjoyed my first year as much. Now that the school year is almost at its end, I feel like I have accomplished so much.

Likewise, Jarrell, a junior who is proficient in Spanish, has been asked several times by C.U.R.E. faculty to be a volunteer tutor for a C.U.R.E. student who was struggling with a beginning Spanish course. He has gone out of his way to contact students and offer his help, saying, "C.U.R.E. is like a family, and that's what you do in families, help each other out." Alton, a senior who joined C.U.R.E. at the beginning of his sophomore year, felt that the program inspired him to do his personal best, commenting that his GPA went up each semester that he was in C.U.R.E. Indeed, when Alton graduated, he earned the C.U.R.E. Award, given to the student with the highest GPA who has demonstrated best practices in urban education while student teaching.

Academic Program

C.U.R.E. scholars earn a bachelor's degree in a major that certifies them to teach in New York State's elementary or secondary schools. The urban education specialization includes culturally relevant courses in urban multicultural education, field experiences, and student teaching in urban schools. Monthly seminars with experienced urban educators enhance the academic curriculum. Required courses include *Introduction to Urban Education; Gender, Race, and Class Issues in Education;* and *Exploring Education–Urban Emphasis.*

Small seminar-style courses, such as *Introduction to Urban Education,* help to create a sense of community and, in fact, students talk about the course in family-like terms:

> I think the class was effective because of its small size and the camaraderie. Because we are all headed in the same direction in careers, it is good that we have such a close-knit class. I feel that the friends I've made in this class will be important assets in the future. Despite where we end up teaching, we will all still be able to look back to those we started with for support. (freshman male, Childhood Education major)

C.U.R.E. students see this community as more than social support. They also identify their peers as a valuable part of their learning experience:

> There is also peer support, peer guidance and the friends I've made in C.U.R.E. I think that is something that is very important in the college experience. I think that is something that has helped me succeed in Cortland. I think that is a big difference in C.U.R.E. and regular teacher education programs. (senior female, Childhood Education major)

The use of peer support is consistent with interpretations of Vygotsky's zone of proximal development (ZPD) that broaden concepts of the zone from "...portrayals of the ZPD as those tasks that a learner can complete with the assistance of an adult" (Gredler & Shields, 2004, p. 22). While C.U.R.E. makes use of more knowledgeable experts in its mentoring program, in selecting instructors for required courses, and in advising students, an important component of C.U.R.E. is the creation of a community that also fosters learning from peers. The ZPD is created not just by faculty and advisors, but also by the students as they define for themselves how to succeed in college and later as an urban teacher.

Field Experiences in Urban Schools

Field experiences are a hallmark of the C.U.R.E. Program. C.U.R.E. students have a designated field experience each academic year. This contrasts with other education students at SUNY Cortland who must often wait until their junior year. In addition, many C.U.R.E. students have been selected for the New York City Department of Education's Summer in the City Internship program, which provides preservice teachers opportunities to work with certified teachers in their classrooms as part of

New York City's summer school programming. Partnerships with high-need schools in New York City and Syracuse ensure that C.U.R.E. scholars observe and intern in urban settings before student teaching. Student teaching placement in New York City is facilitated by the SUNY Urban Teacher Education Center (SUTEC), a collaborative arrangement between the New York City Department of Education and SUNY colleges to organize student teaching opportunities in the City, and SUNY Cortland.

Unique to C.U.R.E. is the first-semester *Introduction to Education* course, which includes a field experience in a high-need urban school in Syracuse. The course instructor accompanies students to these weekly field experiences, and together they discuss their shared experiences in classrooms. This first field experience allows students to begin an apprenticeship of learning (Lave & Wenger, 1991), whereby C.U.R.E. students enter the experience as observers and take on small roles in the classroom, such as working one-on-one with a student or with a small group of students under the teacher's direction. Even as first-semester freshmen, these students are able to see the connections between what they experience in the field and what they read for class:

> Since the beginning of the semester, the classroom work tied in well with our field experiences. Whether it be multicultural teaching or problems with bilingual students, everything we were taught in class could be seen at one point or another in our field experience. In addition, when we discussed a new topic, the field experiences gave us examples of situations we had experienced that we could relate to the new topics. (freshman male, Childhood Education major)

As first-semester freshmen, this experience gives students an opportunity to become a part of a practicing teaching community. Rogoff (1994) characterized learning as changes in participation in a community. Lave and Wenger (1991) describe learning as identity formation. The complimentary perspectives both require the learner to be involved in an authentic community of practitioners.

> On September 11th I had my first experience with a fourth-grade class at Urban Elementary School. When we arrived [the class] had just come back from recess. I was so nervous to begin with, and the fact that they were rowdy and hectic didn't ease my fears. While the teacher was reprimanding them, all I kept thinking about was, "How am I going to do that when I am a teacher?" She eventually calmed the children down by telling little jokes and making the children giggle. It was like magic, I was amazed.
> When we first got into the classroom I was nervous standing in front of the seven or eight fourth graders staring up at me. As the first day went on, I started to fit right in. I was even asked to work one-on-one with a little boy

who was having trouble reading and writing in English. He had just moved from Puerto Rico about a year ago. Seeing him succeed in the simplest thing as a worksheet made me feel so amazing. (female freshman, Physical Education major)

While these first experiences are tentative and may involve C.U.R.E. students with only a few elementary students, they are the first steps in a long process that consistently involves C.U.R.E. students in urban schools over a 4-year period. By the end of one semester of reading about urban schools and participating in an urban school, the freshmen begin to form positive identities for themselves as teachers in urban schools. The impact of this firsthand experience is captured by the following freshman:

Most people think the problem with urban education is the building and the children's behavior. Although those are factors, in my opinion that is not what covers the bigger piece of the pie. The biggest problem is that we give up on those children the moment we hear their sad stories. Some teachers walk in, give the children easy work, and call it a day. The students aren't challenged. After all, they couldn't possibly be successful coming from such an environment.

Let me tell you not one of those [three urban] teachers [I observed] took the easy route with those children. They always challenged the students to do their individual best. When I say individual best, I don't mean the best that society has set out for them, but the best possible work that those children hold within them.

I've learned a lot in my urban education class and from visits [to an urban school].... I learned that school is a very subjective experience.... Each child takes his or her experience differently.... As a future urban educator, I think my job will be to challenge the children to do their personal best. Children who learn to work to high standards for their own approval, in my opinion, hardly ever give up because they don't want to let the most important people in the world down—themselves. The way I see it is that teachers and students have to work together to strive for excellence....

If I can teach my [students] anything, I would at least like to teach them that school is important.... Many children don't succeed not because they don't have what it takes, but because they *think* they don't have what it takes. This is why I want to teach urban children, because urban children are often fed that story that says they have a hard life and white people are always watching them. This could very well be true, but some children interpret it as the end of the road. They don't see it as a crack in the sidewalk; they think it's a canyon they'll never climb out of. Too often urban children don't succeed, because we don't believe they can and they learn from us. I know they can and if I can't give my students anything else, I'll try to give them hope. Just hope. (female freshman, Early Childhood major)

The field experience for this student goes beyond academic learning and techniques of teaching. Through the field experience she is able to see the potential in urban children and the role she can play as an urban teacher.

Leadership Opportunities in C.U.R.E.

Another component nurtured by the C.U.R.E. community is that of leadership development. The final assignment for the *Introduction to Urban Education* class described above is a group research project on some issue related to teaching in urban schools. After the groups present their projects to the class, they do the presentations again in a day-long conference at the college that is held each spring. To prepare for this public presentation, students learn to script out talks from their written papers meant for reading, appropriately develop and use PowerPoint presentations, incorporate activities to engage the audience, and intersperse film and music clips. After the conference, some groups have had the opportunity to present their projects to the College Foundation Board and community groups. In addition, students learn how to present themselves as public speakers through community lunchtime sandwich seminars sponsored by the college, poster sessions for NCATE and the College Council, and as part of recruiting groups that visit high schools with the C.U.R.E. coordinator to talk about the program and the college. All of these activities are designed to help students become comfortable speaking in public in front of a variety of groups and learning the skills required to create engaging presentations in hopes that they will use their skills and talents as future teacher leaders.

Students are also apprenticed into leadership roles through networking and mentoring. Each C.U.R.E. student is assigned a faculty or staff mentor upon entering the program. The intention here is that students will have the opportunity to develop a personal relationship with a professional on campus who is not their academic advisor. The mentors are encouraged to share social and professional experiences with students throughout their 4-year relationship, such as attending an event on campus, meeting for lunch, or attending a local or regional professional conference together. Thus, students have the opportunity to know their mentor on a personal and professional level. C.U.R.E.'s objective is to help students become comfortable interacting with people at a variety of professional levels and learn about the paths their mentors took to get to the place they are now. These mentors also help students make career decisions, such as the kind of graduate programs and schools to consider and help them learn about professional organizations.

All-C.U.R.E. Seminars are held on a monthly basis as another form of networking and mentoring. All students, faculty, and staff involved with C.U.R.E. come together for these evening meetings that are both social and professional in their intention. Often, guest speakers who work in some capacity with urban school districts are invited to share their experiences, providing students the opportunities to learn about teaching in different urban contexts and different kinds of positions they might consider as they move along in their careers. The process of an evolving community and moving from newcomer to old-timer status (Lave & Wenger, 1991) becomes apparent to undergraduates during these monthly meetings as C.U.R.E. graduates who are now new teachers in Syracuse or New York City have returned to share their experiences in the classrooms. Graduates who have been asked to return to speak at this forum have been eager to do so, and current students describe these particular sessions as the most engaging and informative. A male junior social studies major described the first All-C.U.R.E. Seminar that hosted teachers who were C.U.R.E. alum in this way: "Our seminar last week was like making history for C.U.R.E. It was the first time that graduates of the program who are now teaching came back and talked to us." These seminar guests are seen as leaders that students look up to and aspire to emulate.

Upper-division students have the opportunity to take on leadership roles in the program by becoming formal mentors to freshmen, thereby gaining experience as leaders while still undergraduates. As much as possible, students are matched by major and gender. In this capacity sophomores, juniors, and seniors guide freshmen through the process of learning about campus resources, social opportunities, and the expectations of their major programs. Students also take their leadership skills into the campus community. For example, C.U.R.E. students have started new clubs on campus, held leadership positions in clubs, student government, and Greek organizations, served as teaching assistants for courses, campus tour guides for the Office of Admissions, summer orientation assistants, and peer tutors.

BRINGING IT ALL TOGETHER: TAKING THE CONCEPT OF COMMUNITY TO THE CLASSROOM

This leadership carries over into their teaching positions. Many of the first-year teachers who comprise C.U.R.E.'s first graduating class are already recognized as leaders in their schools. In a videotaped interview (2002), the principal of one Bronx elementary school praised their positive school-wide impact:

> My people from the SUNY Cortland C.U.R.E. Program who teach here, you would not know they are first-year teachers because they do better than some teachers who have been here and other teachers who have gone to other universities.... They're well prepared. They're motivated. They're outgoing. They share. They stay here till 6:00, 7:00 at night. They're dedicated. They have this attitude that they're happy to be there, that it's a wonderful place to be here, and they're doing the very best for their children.
>
> They take the children with open arms. They're all youngsters, but they're like real parents to the children and the children respond to them because they're warm. I see the bonding relationship they have.

In addition, a former cooperating teacher of one C.U.R.E. student teacher stated that the student teacher used such innovative strategies that the teacher incorporated them into her own teaching.

The importance of connecting with families and community members in culturally relevant and respectful ways is a message that is modeled and taught in the C.U.R.E. program. The many ways the C.U.R.E. program integrates students into a community is described in this chapter. C.U.R.E. graduates are carrying these lessons concerning the importance of community into their own teaching. C.U.R.E. teachers are reaching out into the community: one PE teacher and coach invites her students to spend time with her on the weekends and after school. An elementary teacher tells about contacting a parent who said she had been associated with the New York City Board of Education all her life and that this teacher was the first person to ever contact her in the beginning of the school year with a positive introductory call. One way that C.U.R.E. attempts to help its graduates is by staying connected with new graduates during their first 2 years of teaching. Faculty visit new teachers in their classrooms at least once, and preferably twice, during those first 2 years, in addition to keeping in touch through emails and phone calls. The purpose of the visits is not so much to supervise, but to check in and let the teachers know that there is a network of support in addition to the ones they may create within their school. As one first-year, fourth-grade teacher in the Bronx expressed after a visit from C.U.R.E. faculty:

> Being part of the C.U.R.E. program was one of the greatest experiences of my life and having Michelle as a mentor is what got me to the point that I am in my life.... Then having her visit my classroom, knowing that it was because of her that I am where I am. It was the greatest feeling. They weren't there to look down on what we were doing, or trying to find fault, but looking to see us in our success. They made me feel like I was doing a good job. They talked with my children and interacted with them. My class loved them, and they were thrilled to be meeting the lady that taught me how to teach them. (female, Elementary Education graduate)

When C.U.R.E. faculty make the 4-hour trip to New York City to visit graduates, they also organize a dinner at a restaurant and invite all the graduates and their former New York City supervisor from their student teaching experience. Here, the faculty hope to provide a connection for the graduates with teachers they know who are working at other schools in the city. The same teacher quoted above had this reaction to the first dinner she attended:

> Then having dinner with everyone was great as well. It was great to connect with people and share some of our stories with each other. It was comforting to know that there were people we know going through the same struggles and successes as a new teacher. A lot of us were living and working in the same area and didn't know it. And for someone who is new to the city, it's good to know I have a friendly face I can go to and hang out with to unwind from a very stressful and tiring week.

These dinners offer a time for reconnecting with old friends and professional opportunities. One first-year teacher who was working in an area out of her certification expressed her frustration to several other teachers at the dinner. They told her about their school and encouraged her to apply there for the following year. She did and became one of their new colleagues in the next school year. Likewise, these new teachers help recent teachers secure their first positions. For example, the Brooklyn teacher cited in the opening vignette has helped new graduates secure an interview at her school.

C.U.R.E. graduates recognize the importance of these actions that help them become members of a community. This chapter opened with a C.U.R.E. graduate describing the importance of becoming a part of her students' community. Another C.U.R.E. graduate describes what she learned coming in as a new teacher about teaching and the importance of becoming a member of her colleagues' professional community at her school:

> Thus far, I have learned that each day is a new and exciting challenge. Each child has the potential and possibility of shining and fulfilling his or her dreams. Moreover, I have realized that even the most experienced or veteran teacher learns from his or her students. Each day is a new adventure and the rules are not always written down on paper. It is the responsibility of all teachers to not just love teaching, but to find the spark in each student to help them want to learn. Lastly, I have learned that even if you are a new teacher walking into a school, the friendships you make and the teachers you get advice from on important lessons help you develop into a more well rounded teacher and person. (female, Secondary Education graduate)

C.U.R.E. aims to prepare socially conscious teachers who understand the importance of bringing the culture of school and community together, who believe that the children and families who live in New York State's poorest urban centers have the right to a full and equitable education that prepares them to turn their dreams into reality, and who work to challenge and refute the general population's negative view of urban youth. C.U.R.E. aims to prepare teachers who believe in their students, who do not view a job in a high-need urban school as a stepping stone that must be endured while they gain experience to apply for a suburban position, and who have a full understanding of their role as teachers and change agents.

To achieve these goals, C.U.R.E. is interested in more than *teacher training*. This is not to diminish the necessity for teacher preparation programs to equip students with the necessary techniques and tricks of the trade necessary for superior teaching. There is no doubt or argument that excellent teachers possess a thorough knowledge of the methods necessary for instruction. But the goals of C.U.R.E. involve more than the transmission of knowledge or skills, they involve creating communities that value and support urban education and bringing prospective teachers into those communities. The words of the C.U.R.E. students and graduates in this chapter show that there is no single route to creating these communities or single individual (though key individuals may exist) responsible for creating the community. The students and graduates in this chapter name different people and different activities that contributed to their current successes. The lessons leaned from C.U.R.E. are that success lies with the involvement of people from many segments (faculty, staff, administration, and fellow students) of the campus community, and a viable community results from flexibly integrating newcomers with old timers.

REFERENCES

Bartoli, J. (2001). *Celebrating city teachers: How to make a difference in urban schools*. Portsmouth, NH: Heinemann.

Cole, M. (1990). Cognitive development and formal schooling: The evidence from cross-cultural research. In L. Moll (Ed.) *Vygotsky and education: Instructional implications and applications of sociohistorical psychology* (pp. 89-110). New York: Cambridge University Press.

Gredler, M., & Shields, C. (2004). Does no read Vygotsky's words? Commentary on Glassman. *Educational Researcher, 33*(2), 21-25.

Gutierrez, K., & Stone, L. (2000). Synchronic and diachronic dimensions of social practice: An emerging methodology for cultural-historical perspectives on literacy learning. In C. Lee & P. Smagorinsky (Eds.), *Vygotskian perspectives on literacy research* (pp. 51–85). New York: Cambridge University Press.

Haberman, M. (1996). Selecting and preparing culturally competent teachers for urban schools. In J. Sikula (Ed.), *Handbook of research on teacher education* (2nd ed., pp. 747–760). New York: Macmillan.

Ladson-Billings, G. (1992). Liberatory consequences of literacy: A case of culturally relevant instruction for African American students. *Journal of Negro Education, 61*, 378–391.

Ladson-Billings, G. (1994). *The dream keepers: Successful teachers of African-American children*. San Francisco: Jossey-Bass.

Ladson-Billings, G. (2001). The power of pedagogy: Does teaching matter? In W. Watkins, J. H. Lewis, & V. Chou (Eds.), *Race and education: The roles of history and society in educating African American students* (pp. 73–88). Boston: Allyn & Bacon.

Lave, J. (1996). Teaching, as learning, in practice. *Mind, Culture, and Activity, 3*, 149–165.

Lave, J., & Winger, E. (1991). *Situated learning: Legitimate peripheral participation*. Cambridge, UK: Cambridge University Press.

Leont'ev, A. K. (1981). The problem of activity in psychology. In J. V. Wertsch (Ed.), *The concept of activity in Soviet psychology* (pp. 37–71). New York: M.E. Sharpe.

Moll, L. (1990). Introduction. In L. Moll (Ed.), *Vygotsky and education: Instructional implications and applications of socio-historical psychology* (pp. 1–27). New York: Cambridge University Press.

Moll, L. (2000). Inspired by Vygotsky: Ethnographic experiments in education. In C. Lee & P. Smagorinsky (Eds.), *Vygotskian perspectives on literacy research* (pp. 51–85). New York: Cambridge University Press.

National Commission on Teaching and America's Schools. (1997). *What matter's most: Teaching for America's future*. New York: Author. Available online at http://www.zuni.k12.nm.us/las/21TE/NWREL/what.htm

Rogoff, B. (1990). *Apprenticeship in thinking: Cognitive development in social context*. New York: Oxford University Press.

Rogoff, B., Mistry, J., Goncu, A., & Mosier, C. (1993). *Guided participation in cultural activity by toddlers and caregivers*. Society for Research in Child Development. Chicago: Universiy of Chicago Press.

Rogoff, B. (1994). Developing understanding of the idea of communities of learners. *Mind, Culture, and Activity, 1*, 209–229.

Vygotsky, L. S. (1978). *Mind in society: The development of higher psychological processes* (M. Cole, V. John-Steiner, S. Scribner, & E. Souberman, Eds.). Cambridge, MA: Harvard University Press.

Wells, G. (2000). Dialogic inquiry in education: Building on the legacy of Vygotsky. In C. D. Lee & P. Smagorinsky (Eds.), *Vygotskian perspectives on literacy research* (pp. 51–85). New York: Cambridge University Press.

Wertsch, J. (1991). *Voices of the mind: A sociocultural approach to mediated action*. Cambridge, MA: Harvard University Press.

Zeichner, K. (1995). Educating teachers to close the achievement gap: Issues of pedagogy, knowledge, and teacher preparation. In Urban Education

National Network (Ed.), *Closing the achievement gap: A vision to guide changes in beliefs and practice.* Washington, DC: United States Department of Education, Office of Educational Research and Improvement.

CHAPTER 16

CURRICULUM AND PEDAGOGICAL DEVELOPMENT FOR BUILDING A COMMUNITY OF LEARNERS AMONG OLDER CHINESE ADULTS IN USING ICT

Chi-hung Ng

Understanding how old learners can take advantage of the technological revolution for learning, and providing them with access to computers, the Internet, and other technologies will be one of the greatest challenges and opportunities for older adult educators in the next few years. (Timmerman, 1998, p. 61)

We know little as to how older learners are motivated to learn and how they go about learning. This may be related to the following: first, compared to other age groups, older adults are considered as a minority among ICT users (White & Weatherall, 2000); second, it is generally held that older adults are technophobic and slow in the acquisition of new technology (Ryan, Szechtman, & Bodkin, 1992); and finally, older adults consistently experience cognitive decline, rendering the learning of computer knowledge and skills difficult.

Focus on Curriculum, 377–401
Copyright © 2005 by Information Age Publishing
All rights of reproduction in any form reserved.

Nevertheless, the number of older adults among ICT users has been growing in most developed countries. In Hong Kong, the elderly population has increased from 87,918 (2.8%) in 1961 to 747,052 (11.1%) in 2001 with an average annual growth rate of 5.5% (Hong Kong Census and Statistics Department, 2002a). Among the elderly population, the number of ICT users has increased significantly. For example, between 2000 and 2002, the percentage of older adults using personal computers has increased from around 1.2% to 13.8% for those ages 55–65, and from 0.1% to 2.8% for those over age 65 (Hong Kong Census and Statistics Department, 2000, 2002b). Despite this rapid growth of the elderly population and the increased number of ICT users among them, limited effort has been expended on preparing for these changing demographics in Hong Kong. Lifelong education remains rhetoric in the Hong Kong Government's various reformative policies when older adults are concerned.

Hong Kong Sheng Kuk Hui Welfare Council, being one of the largest social services organizations in Hong Kong, has committed to provide comprehensive care and services for older adults with an aim to enable them to continue to live in their communities with satisfaction, happiness, and dignity. Carrying the mission of "individual caring and total concern," the Council has also recognized the importance of lifelong learning for older adults in promoting productive and successful aging. In September 1998, the Council set up the "Institute of Continuing Education for Senior Citizens," serving the learning needs of citizens age 55 or above. The computer literacy program is one of the most successful learning programs offered by the Institute.

THE COMPUTER LITERACY CURRICULUM

The curriculum objectives of the computer literacy program were originated from the philosophical emphasis on productive aging. The concept of productive aging has been defined differently from economic, social, and psychological perspectives (cf. O'Reilly & Caro, 1994). The Institute maintains that to be productive does not necessarily mean that older adults are to be placed in the labor market, competing with younger adults for paid employment. Of course, the acquisition of new knowledge and skills may boost their chance in the job hunt. The Institute, however, dwells more on the social and psychological aspects of productive aging. The concept of productive aging is defined in terms of meaningful engagement. From this perspective, through learning and knowledge development, older adults will collaborate with others, develop abilities to cope with their life problems and difficulties, and also contribute to the well-being of others in both passive (remain independent and self-sufficient) and active (help others to cope) manners. As a result, the courses provided in the program of computer literacy reflect these foci, emphasizing the learning of practical skills, learning for self-actualization, and learning for community contribution.

- To cope: The development of basic and essential computer skills that enhance older adults' life skills (sample courses: basic computer skills);
- To grow: The acquisition of computer knowledge and skills that meet their own interest (sample courses: Web page design);
- To contribute: The development of skills and knowledge that help them relate to others and contribute to their well-being (sample courses: card design).

Courses offered within the computer literacy program ranged from basic computing to advanced level studies like Web page design. The diversity of courses is facilitative in accommodating individual differences in terms of goals, interests, and abilities among these older adults. Older adults therefore were able to make a choice of what to learn according to their own preference and situation. As a result, autonomy was stressed and older adults' anxieties and doubts were reduced. "There are a lot of things to learn and to explore; there must be something that you find interest in." This was how one of the interviewees encouraged other older adults to join the program.

The number of older adults enrolled in the computer literacy program corroborated their keen interest in learning ICT. Initially about 20 older adults started a computer course; student population jumped to 609 between December 1998 and March 1999 with the formal inception of the Institute of Continuing Education for Senior Citizens. The figure further increased to about 2000 in the subsequent years (2,100 in 2001; 1,993 in 2002; and 2,110 in 2003).[1] The elderly center has certainly turned into a hub of learning, modeling, and sharing of computer knowledge and skills.

This chapter reports a qualitative study on the successful learning experiences of a group of older adults in a center for the elderly run by Sheng Kuk Hui Welfare Council in Hong Kong. The focus is on discussing various facilitative curriculum and pedagogical conditions contributing to the successful learning and development of a community of learners among these older Chinese adults. The results highlight how these facilitative instructional conditions accommodated the needs of these older adults, helped them to open their zones of proximal development, and connect with others.

THEORETICAL CONTEXT

From a sociocultural perspective, learning is culturally embedded and constituted by a matrix of social relationship, interaction, and contextual processes. Learning is not just the acquisition of valued knowledge or skills but should be considered as appropriating cultural tools, which will transform the tasks, the requirements to complete them (Crook, 1991), and hence the relationship between individuals and the task as well as the relationship among the members within a learning community. In other words, the appropriation of significant cultural tools mediates one's cognition. Learning can therefore be seen in terms of the changing patterns of engagement in collective activities and social practice (Renshaw, 1998).

The concept of legitimate peripheral participation (Lave & Wenger, 1991) highlights the importance of this changing pattern of engagement in learning within a community of practice. From this perspective, learning is a trajectory, from apprenticeship to expertise, and from peripheral participation to engagement in practice. Over time, the apprentices participate in all types of activities, including apprenticing others. The notion of apprenticeship focuses not just on the provision of effective instruction or guidance from the more experienced old timers, but more on the active role of newcomers and their increased participation within a community. In addition, learning from this perspective directs us not just on knowledge acquisition, it also brings to the fore the importance of learners' evolving selves and the formation of new identities, from newcomers to old timers, novices to experts, and peripheral participants to core players.

Vygotsky's concept of the zone of proximal development (ZPD) is vital in understanding this changing process of learning and engagement within a community of learners. ZPD describes the gap between one's actual level of development or performance and his or her potential level of development or performance under the assistance of or in collaboration with more capable peers. It is through constant collaboration and interaction with old timers or advanced peers that newcomers are apprenticed to take up essential knowledge and skills, and eventually assume full membership within the community. The concept of ZPD signifies the importance of instruction and guidance. Bruner (1986) used the term *scaffolding* to explain how teachers' effective instruction or pedagogical practice can help students to stretch their learning capacity or expand their ZPD. Past research has demonstrated how teachers' initiation in dialogues, discourses, and activities has provided effective scaffolds to assist students to expand their ZPD (e.g., Brown & Campione, 1990; Brown & Renshaw, 2000; Kovalainen, Kumpulainen, & Vasama, 2001).

Past studies on learning using this sociocultural perspective have yielded a substantial literature related to the promotion of learning among students in different educational levels (e.g., Brown & Campione, 1990; Gilbert & Driscoll, 2002; Harland, 2003; Roth, 1995). We know thus far little as to how this theoretical position may fare out with older adults in a less formal learning setting. Most educational gerontologists (e.g., Mayhorn, Stronge, McLauglin, & Rogers, 2004; Zandri & Charness, 1989) have adopted an individualistic perspective in researching the cognitive functioning of older adults. One of the major streams of research related to the learning process of older adults is cognitive aging. The main concern of a cognitive aging perspective is to understand the decline in learning capacity of older adults and its resulting effects. The decline in learning capacity is explained in terms of aging processes related to cognitive slowing, diminished processing resources, lack of inhibition, and sensory deficits (Jones & Bayen, 1998). Obviously, cognitive aging will pose a barrier to the effective acquisition of computer knowledge and skills.

Nevertheless, cognitive decline and normal aging do not necessarily lead to a simultaneous decline in all cognitive functions. For example, age-related differences in the organization and the use of general world knowledge or facts are slight or nonexistent (Light, 1992; Mayhorn et al., 2004). In addition, there may be individual differences in the onset and pattern of cognitive aging; some functions may decline, while others remain stable or even improve. From an educational perspective, effective instruction should help improve the performance of older adults. Some have researched and discussed various cognitive strategies for promoting older adults in the learning of computer knowledge and skills, for example, specifying actions required to perform a task (Mead & Fisk, 1998), arranging practice for each task component (Jamieson & Rogers, 2000), introducing accommodative strategies to compensate for declining abilities (Rogers, Mayhorn, & Fisk, 2000), and seeking feedback from older adults (Mayhorn et al., 2004).

In addition, it can be argued that cognitive deficit may be due to a lack of learning support in an undemanding intellectual environment (Baron & Cerella, 1993; Kasworm & Medina, 1990). Older adults' poor performance in episodic memory tasks might be due to the lack of environmental support or external stimulation supporting cognitive processing of memory retrieval (Craik, 1986). Furthermore, some researchers have provided initial findings regarding how sociocultural influences can facilitate the learning processes of older adults. For example, Zandri and Charness (1989) found that older adults trained in pairs (social support) resulted in a reduction in anxiety compared to those being trained alone.

In other words, the barrier of cognitive aging is not insurmountable. Facilitative learning conditions should alleviate the problem. Bringing the sociocultural framework for researching older adults, therefore, provides a chance to explore how effective learning conditions can be developed to help older adults to deal with learning difficulties that arise from cognitive aging. A number of researchers have adopted the sociocultural perspective discussed above to design effective instructional conditions to promote knowledge development and learning. Reciprocal teaching (Brown & Champion, 1990) and collective argumentation (Brown & Renshaw, 2000) are well-known examples. In addition, some have identified the essential elements for the development of a community of learners. For example, Crawford, Krajcik, and Marx (1999), when researching the elements of a community of learners in a middle school science classroom, have located six essential components for the development of a community of learners, which are authentic tasks, independency in small-group work, negotiation of understanding, public sharing, collaboration, and shared responsibility. These elements are similar to the four principles for fostering a community of learners (autonomy, reflection, collaboration, and culture) Bruner (1996) and Brown (1997) discussed.

Thus far, we know little as to whether these effective instructional conditions developed from a sociocultural perspective using other student populations can be applied to older adults learning computer knowledge and skills. However, it is not the aim of the current research to predetermine a set of effective instructional principles consistent with a sociocultural perspective and to investigate them with a group of older adults in learning ICT. The research findings reported here were derived from a naturally evolved case. In other words, effective curriculum arrangements and pedagogical strategies reported here are not predesigned following a sociocultural perspective. Instead, these facilitative conditions have evolved in the process of the development of this computer literacy program over the past 2 years. The current research therefore should not be taken as theory applied to practice.

The facilitative instructional conditions reported here include participatory curriculum development, tutor supports, the design of learning tasks, peer tutoring, different forms of collaboration, connection with other communities, and sharing of work. It is argued that these facilitating curriculum and pedagogical arrangements have contributed to the development of a community of learners among these older adults. The effectiveness of these instructional conditions is discussed in terms of meeting the needs of older adults (accommodation) and extending their selves (extension).

PARTICIPANTS, DATA CORPUS, AND DATA ANALYSIS

The data presented in this chapter are taken from the data corpus collected over 2 years from qualitative research investigating the learning of ICT among a group of older Chinese adults. Given the lack of research studying the learning processes of older Chinese adults, the main purposes of this qualitative research are to describe the learning experiences of these older Chinese adults and explore the conditions that might have facilitated or constrained their learning of ICT. The main research questions include: Why and how do older adults learn ICT? What have they learned? In what way has their learning of ICT affected them? What are the facilitative conditions that have contributed to the successful learning of selected older adults?

The data consist of field notes, interview scripts, video excerpts, recordings of lessons, surveys, and samples of work (including digital photos, websites, etc.). The data collection processes began with in-depth interviews with 10 key informants, age 55–87 (four males and six females). They were among the first cohort of older adults who joined the computer literacy program. To verify these initial findings, another 30 older adults (12 males and 18 females; age 60–79) were interviewed, of which 10 were experienced learners, 10 dropouts, and 10 nonparticipants. The inclusion of these different types of interviewees would help corroborate the information gathered from the previous interviews and hypotheses developed could be confirmed. In order to triangulate the interview findings, different methods of data collection were subsequently adopted. First, casual observations were conducted; field notes taken, and relevant documents collected, which included samples of work, curriculum documents, enrollment records, and the details of courses offered. Second, formal observations were carried out with a group of advanced learners for a period of 8 weeks. During this period, the author observed the lessons of a group of advanced learners and later was invited to participate in their lessons. Finally, a survey questionnaire was developed and piloted with 25 randomly selected participants in the elderly center. The revised survey was then administered to all the elderly centers run by the Sheng Kuk Hui Welfare Council.

Data analyses were continuous. The ongoing analyses helped undo biases and misinterpretation, developed hypotheses, and refined data collection methods. The analytical processes involved mainly coding data into meaningful categories and segments, which were later grouped into major themes. In light of the research questions, the data were coded; codes were refined and constantly compared, and from which themes were developed. For example, the current paper was concerned with curriculum and pedagogical arrangements contributing to the successful learning of these older adults. In light of this research question, the data were recoded, recategorized, and new themes were developed. Data generated from different methods were then recoded accordingly using the same coding and categorizing scheme. This lengthy process of data analysis provided verifiable codes and themes, and more importantly, a better representation and understanding of the data and its evolving context could be achieved.

The results discussed below were taken mainly from the theme, "effective curriculum and pedagogical conditions." This chapter reports qualitative evidence generated mainly from the interview data, field notes, and observation findings. Aside from constant comparison of findings generated from these diverse qualitative methods, the survey findings were consulted in order to develop a valid and reliable account of different curriculum and pedagogical conditions conducive to the learning of ICT among these older adults.

PRESENTATION OF DATA

The main concern of this chapter is to describe and discuss effective instructional practices contributing to the successful learning of these older adults. To facilitate the discussion of the findings, an organizing framework was adopted (see Figure 16.1). This framework should be treated as heuristic for understanding what has contributed to the success of the computer literacy program and it was not intended to be a rigid causal model of development. The following discussion of the findings generated from the data will demonstrate how specific features of the computer literacy curriculum and associated pedagogical arrangements have successfully provided social scaffolds for the learning of ICT, opening up one's ZPD, and gradually fostering the development of a community of learners and linking individuals with different communities. Aside from the following curriculum and pedagogical arrangements, other social supports conducive to the successful learning of these older adults have been reported elsewhere (Ng, 2002).[2]

AN EMERGING COMMUNITY OF LEARNERS

To begin with, all the interviewees reported a high level of anxiety, a low sense of efficacy, and limited knowledge of computer operation, as shown in Figure 16.1. Before joining the computer literacy program, they commonly held a perception that learning about computers was difficult for older adults.

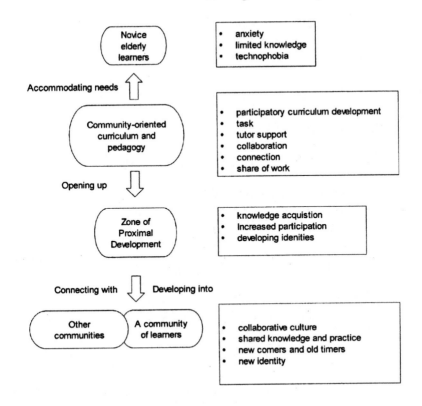

Figure 16.1.   An organizing framework.

Nevertheless, despite these problems, most older adults in the program have been able to develop a working knowledge of a computer, software, and computing operation. For the core interviewees, keen interest and strong motivation have developed, which can be shown by:

(a) their time devoted to learning and practicing computing skills;
(b) a strong intention to further their learning;
(c) a great interest in computing skills and knowledge (e.g., reading books on computing, participating in computing exhibitions);
(d) sharing their knowledge with others; and
(e) encouraging friends to do computing.

The selected excerpts below are indicators of their strong motivation:

It's hard to say; I anticipate that it takes me 1.5 hours [to come to the center]; sometimes it may take less time but sometimes it takes me 2 hours to come because of the traffic jam. After finishing the 1-hour course, I'll stay here all day long. If a computer is available, I'll play as long as possible, if not, I'll watch other people playing.

I am obsessed, yeah, I am.

My friends were retired. They are now living in Canada. I always ask them to learn to use the computer. They just ask their sons to send messages and photos to me. I urged them to do it themselves.

The following excerpt taken from the observation field notes demonstrated that the high level of interest in learning computer knowledge and skills was not confined to individuals but has been spread across older adults involved in the computer literacy program.

It was a small computer room with nine computers installed on both sides. On the walls, older adults' works and achievement were shown. There were greeting cards, bookmarks, and even Chinese paintings, produced by computer technology. It was 1:30 in the afternoon. The group seemed to have just finished their class. However, they were unwilling to leave. One of the students was talking to the tutor about some computer problems. At the end of the room, two female older adults were looking at the websites they have just developed. Two other learners were busy uploading their own files onto the Web; one of them seemed to have problems in uploading photos onto her Web page and called for help. Other students came to her rescue and a discussion on effective ways of uploading photos onto the Web was started. The tutor ended his talk and joined in.

A community of learners has evolved among these older adults. The field note above vividly showed the collaboration among these older adults in an IT-rich environment. The following interview excerpt further demonstrates that a culture of collaboration and a sense of relatedness have developed among these older adults. It also reveals the central characteristics of a community of learners specified in Figure 16.1. Note also how the interviewee has grown from a newcomer into an old timer capable of apprenticing others through the sharing of knowledge and practice in a culture of collaboration.

This big sister encouraged me and went, "It's like that at the beginning, put more effort and things will get better," so I put more efforts into it. And now it's my turn to play the role of a big sister—when I see people learning together I am very happy, because we can solve problems together; and gradually, we have become good friends, like primary kids, learning things that we should have learned a long time ago, and when we learn together, we'll remember each other. Like, if someone has not turned up for a while, we'll go, "Haven't seen you for a while", I sense the closeness between us.

In addition, these older adults have also demonstrated that they have rebuilt their confidence in connecting with other communities. The interview data repeatedly demonstrated that discussing computer knowledge has helped these older adults earn respect from their family members and friends. In addition, they used the newly acquired knowledge and skills to connect with others in novel ways, such as through emails.

COMMUNITY-ORIENTED CURRICULUM AND PEDAGOGY

The crucial question was how these anxious and unconfident novice learners have gradually developed into motivated users, capable of showcasing their computing achievement to others, and subsequently attracted other older adults to join the computer literacy program. This section will discuss various effective curriculum and pedagogical conditions contributing to the successful development of such a community of learners among these older adults. Figure 16.1 shows that these effective curriculum and pedagogical conditions include participation in curriculum development, the design of learning tasks, tutor supports, different forms of collaboration, the sharing of work, and connection with other communities.

Participation in Curriculum Development

All interviewees reported that the curriculum was collaboratively designed and developed. In the beginning of the program, the social worker responsible for setting up the computer literacy program initiated a talk with a group of older adults asking what kind of computer literacy program they would like to have. This practice of involving older adults in making various decisions related to curriculum development and course delivery has since then become a permanent feature of the curriculum development process. Older adults were asked to participate in seminars held at the end of each academic year to air their opinions and discontent and to make suggestions for better development. This occasion was also a venue for developing mutual understanding between older adults, tutors, and the management team of the computer literacy program. In addition, older adults also actively contributed to the teaching processes. They often made suggestions as to how the teaching can be improved and asked tutors for guidance, notes, and information.

Furthermore, older adults often negotiated with their tutors and the management team to develop courses they found interesting. The following critical incident demonstrates that these older adults were reflective and could effectively negotiate with the management team in making important decisions in relation to the development of the computer literacy curriculum.

A Critical Incident: "Can We Continue with Our Learning?"

"The management team of the computer literacy program has informed one of the advanced classes that their usual time slot and their current computer literacy program would come to an end after the course on assembling a computer has finished. The rationale for this decision was based on (1) There were a lot of older adults waiting to join the program; and (2) The current class of older adults has joined the program for over 2 years and finished some of the most advanced courses. The group rejected the decision immediately. After thorough discussion among themselves and with their tutor, these older adults made counter-arguments. Their intention was to continue with their learning. They have put forward some convincing arguments: (1) They should be given the chance to demonstrate their success and achievement to the newcomers; (2) they can meet at some other time; and (3) they can negotiate with their tutor to develop an integrated course helping them practice different skills and knowledge they acquired. Their suggestion was accepted after several discussions and negotiations with the management team and the district supervisor. They were then allowed to continue their class and a new course would be tailor-made to suit their needs."{\ex}

Learning Tasks

Older adults are usually experiencing cognitive problems such as short memory span, attention displacement, and cognitive slowing (cf. Jones & Bayen, 1998). The design of learning tasks has taken these needs and concerns into consideration. Learning tasks were highly structured. They were usually broken into small and manageable bits. Important steps were pinpointed and common problems forewarned. Older adults were given abundant chances to practice these tasks during the class and handouts were distributed to help them to do their own practice. The following quote taken from an interview with a tutor explains the importance of structuring the lesson tasks.

It's very important that older adults are given sufficient time to learn. They may have problems in understanding complicated computing steps. I need to break them down for them and give them notes, which took up quite a bit of my time and effort to prepare.

In addition, most interviewees corroborated that the lesson tasks were interesting and they enjoyed learning and practicing them. More importantly, students were given the chance and direction as to how these skills and knowledge could be put into practice; for example, older adults learned how to produce greeting cards for their friends and family members. In this sense, the learning tasks were situated in real-world application (Brown, Collins, & Duguid, 1989; Lave, 1988; Roth, 1995).

Tutor Support

Providing effective scaffoldings to students is crucial to the successful development of knowledge and skills (Bruner, 1986). The assistance of the tutors includes demonstrating computing skills, guiding older adults in completing complex computing procedures, troubleshooting problems, and acting as a source of reference and consultancy. Among all these supports, older adults praised especially about tutors' patience and care. Various sociocultural researchers (e.g., Addison Stone, 1993; Forman, 1989; Forman & Cazden, 1985) have already stressed the importance of the interpersonal dimension of scaffolding. The following quotes demonstrate that older adults considered tutors' emotional supports are vital for their learning.

> The tutors are very patient. I still remember one of them, Chiu, who taught basic computing, only about 17 years old. He's really good, only 17, should be restless, but he has such a patience; people ask him questions, he'd answer and teach you patiently; he did not feel irritated by our questions. But overall, all the tutors are good.

> The tutors in other centers I have been to did not have patience. They just read through the notes and did not care if you understood the stuff. Ah Long is young but he's knowledgeable and most importantly, he has patience with us and is willing to answer our questions.

The observation notes also revealed that Ah Long had a good relationship with the older adults and cared about their learning. His support for learning can be shown clearly in the following incident. The incident was recorded before an observation session of an advanced class.

> The usual class was disrupted by a team of TV producers rushing to produce a documentary about the life of older adults in Hong Kong. These TV people have taken up the classroom. All the older adults were unhappy with this

disruption. Ah Long shared their discontent but tried his best to calm them down. He promised to rearrange the class for them and gave them an extra lesson at no cost. In the midst of this discontent, I observed that Ah Long shared a high level of understanding with these older adults and his ways of calming the grudges of them—packing their shoulders and knees, airing his discontent and asking for patience, and making promises about an additional lesson—showed adequately that he cared for this group of learners and has built a personal relationship with them. The incident served to bind the group together and reinforced their intention to learn.

In an interview with Ah Long after a lesson, he showed his support for the older adults through his understanding of the diverse needs of his students.

All of them are very capable. But they have different needs and different talents. For example, Mr. Ng was good at computer graphics but he was dumb at learning the Chinese input software. Wang sitting next to him was an expert in the input software. He learned the codes and rules very quickly.

However, these tutors did not use effective instructional strategies in their lessons. During an 8-week observation of an advanced class, it was recorded that over 80% of the teaching time in each lesson was conducted through teacher-centered instruction. The tutor dominated the class and was not effective in initiating collaboration and participation. What can then be concluded is that these tutors were inexperienced. Their teaching strategies were unpolished. However, older adults seemed to have been satisfied with tutors' understanding, patience, and support.

Peer Tutoring

Advanced learners among the older adults were given the chance to help newcomers to learn computer knowledge and skills through a scheme called IT Volunteers. This arrangement can be taken as a form of peer tutoring. In practice, IT volunteers helped mainly in "basic computing courses," demonstrating to novices skills like turning on and off a computer, using and controlling the mouse, clicking the keys, and playing some interesting games. From a sociocultural perspective, capable or experienced learners offering guidance and help to new learners has been widely recognized as an effective principle of instruction. The following excerpt is a comment on how capable learners acting as an IT volunteer can assist newcomers to learn. This case also shows that the opening up of one's ZPD involves not just providing scaffolds for knowledge development, but offering emotional supports is of equal importance.

> I haven't touched a computer before. I was absolutely terrified. However, Mr. Ng [the IT volunteer] was kind and he showed me step by step. I watched him closely and he encouraged me to use the mouse and stressed that I wouldn't kill it. I was then able to do it myself very quickly and was happy that he was with me.

The IT volunteers also gained benefits in providing help to others. One of the IT volunteers stressed that he wanted to help and was willing to share with others.

> Not really help. I'd tell them that I am here to share with them my skills and knowledge. I felt good about this and was very happy to be one of the IT volunteers.

However, the implementation of this peer tutoring system was met with some difficulties. First, some experienced learners considered the idea as too egoistic and were reluctant to join. Second, some did not feel confident enough to take up this role. Certainly, formal training is needed to clear these doubts and give support for its implementation. Nevertheless, this form of collaboration and assistance helped build the linkage between old timers and newcomers. According to Lave and Wenger (1991), such a form of linkage is essential for peripheral participants to develop their skills and knowledge vital to the development of membership within a given community.

Collaboration

Collaboration has been widely recognized as a key principle for the development and advancement of a knowledge-building community (e.g., Brown & Campione, 1990; Brown & Renshaw, 2000; Kovalainen et al., 2001; Roth, 1995). Among these older adults, collaboration came in different forms during several key learning phases and events.

Learning together. During the class, collaboration takes the form of share and help. The older adults usually worked in pairs in the class; one of them follows the demonstration and performs the task on the computer while the partner takes notes and observes the tutor's demonstration closely. This form of collaboration has been reported by all the interviewees and was considered effective in tackling problems that arise from cognitive decline. As one of the interviewees commented, they learn faster with help from each other.

Collaboration was also apparent during the practice sessions. Older adults were required to book their practice sessions in order to practice what they have learned. Usually, older adults would book a session with their friends or partners together. They also indicated that they liked to practice in the elderly center with their friends than working alone at home with their own computer. One of the reasons is because they can help each other out.

> Though you have taken notes, sometimes you understand it clearly when you jot down the notes, but later you don't; and often only a little bit is missed. Like if you have classmates around, you go, "Hey, why here, I have followed the notes, why didn't it work?" You then ask your classmates to help, then they'll take a look and point out that you are nearly there. Then you got it. Right, it is very important (to have someone to help).

Neither partner in these forms of "learning together" can be seen as objectively more capable; they assumed complementary social roles. All the assistance offered is contingent on or responsive to older adults' problems at hand. This form of responsive collaboration is considered effective in assisting learners to develop from other regulation to self-regulation, and to automatize the knowledge and skills (Tharp & Gallimore, 1991).

Practicing Together

The elderly center also encouraged older adults to participate in different computer exhibitions to showcase their learning and achievement to the general public. Collaboration is needed for different jobs during an exhibition. Less skilled learners helped out the setting up of the stall and display of work. More advanced learners took turns to explain their work to the visitors. The responsibilities were shared (Brown & Campione, 1990; Rogoff, 1994). Collaboration between different learners was essential for the completion of this common task. Again through collaboration with each other, these older adults have completed a major task that they could not have completed on their own. In addition, showcasing their achievement to the public has certainly boosted older adults' self-esteem and confidence in using computer knowledge and skills.

In addition, participating in IT exhibition has given students the chance to interact with computer users and experts outside their classroom community. They also had the chance to promote their learning and achievement, as well as attracting others to learn.

> During the exhibition, we came into contact with some other people. They went, "Is it possible?", "Really possible?", "I am illiterate, is it okay?" I replied, "Of course, you don't need to know a lot before you can learn." So,

if we didn't do this exhibition, other older people would not see us and would not be able to ask us questions; and they'd tend to think they're old and there's no point of learning to use a computer.

Socializing Together

Aside from collaboration for learning, informal networks have also developed. Older adults would meet together before or after their lesson for tea or a short gathering. During these gatherings, one of the most common topics for chat was the use of IT. I was invited to join a dinner gathering of one of these groups. Most of the time, older adults chatted about their courses, new computer models, and their interest in some new courses.

Connection

Service learning is another community-oriented pedagogical arrangement adopted in the computer literacy program. During the past 2 years, advanced learners have given talks to school kids and other older adults. They shared their learning experiences and showed their achievement. In addition, older adults also collaborated with each other in different forms of social work and services using their IT skills. For example, comforts cards have been produced and sent to the victims of an earthquake in Taiwan. During major festivals, older adults also produced cards, photos, and bookmarks for their family members, relatives, and friends.

Goodnow (1990) stressed the need to examine a particular skill in relation to its implicit or explicit value in a given culture and also to one's social identity within the culture. What is significant here is that older adults' capability of effective application of computing knowledge and skills is probably attached with symbolic values, which will influence how other people perceive them and how they construct their own identities. Service learning not only has helped older adults to apply their learning but also has given them chances to connect with others in a new way.

Sharing of Work

One of the key principles for the development of a knowledge-building community is that the articles or objects produced by learners should be made public and shared by its individual members (Gilbert & Driscoll, 2002; Lebow, Wager, Marks, & Gilbert, 1996). Older adults' achievement and works were publicly shared. First, there were a lot of posters, pictures, and cards displayed in the computer room, as well as at the main entrance of the elderly center. In addition, some successful learners were filmed and the tape was made available to other learners. Older adults' website addresses were shared. The share of IT objects and resources can be taken as evidence of the development of a community of learners among these older adults.

OPENING UP OF ZPD

The computer literacy program has been designed with the notion of achieving one's potentials in mind. The recognition of cognitive deficit of older adults has enabled the tutors and management team to structure the learning processes to meet the needs of these older adults. "What is the zone of proximal development today will be the actual developmental level tomorrow" (Vygotsky, 1978, p. 87). To many, including the author, the level of achievement of this group of older adults was phenomenal. "Wow! How can you do this?" was the usual reaction when the works of these older adults were showed to the public. The discussion above has highlighted some effective instructional conditions contributing to the success of these older adults, and the development of a learning community.

Another important factor contributing to the development of a learning community among these older adults is related to the notion of ZPD. Experienced learners repeatedly explained the benefits gained through the learning of computer skills during the interview. Aside from the benefits such as a good time-killer and maintaining cognitive functioning, the learning of computing knowledge and skills has contributed to the gradual increase of engagement and development of new identities. As shown in Figure 16.1, knowledge acquisition, increased participation, and the development of new identities are essential characteristics or steps involved in the opening up of ZPD of these older adults.

First, increased engagement can be demonstrated in the levels of involvement in learning. In the following excerpt, the interviewee explained how he has increased his involvement in learning. Note that associated with the increased level of engagement, the interviewee has set for himself new goals (writing his own Web pages) and new activities (designing Web pages). In addition, he also reflected on his learning approaches when he increased his level of engagement. He explained that they had not much to learn from the tutor, suggesting that with increased engagement, they might need to seek new ways of learning.

I have become more confident gradually; that's right, the more I learned the more confident I became. I am now also, as asked by my friends, learning to write my own Web pages; I am now doing a little bit. Writing a Web page, I thought, "They can do it, I can do it too"; I have tried these tricks and some of these (showing me his Web pages); these pages I designed myself; some of them are not too bad. Right I need to learn these and write some new pages. And now we have not much to learn from the tutor. We are also doing some computer painting; I started it from the beginning, using Little Writer, and we are going to learn about mixing colors; these are for painting, and I'm not doing too bad. I thought to myself, I can do more when I have time, and can have my own pictures and works soon.

Increased engagement can also be demonstrated in the connection with other communities. The following excerpts show that the acquisition of computer knowledge and skills has enabled the interviewees to build a close relationship with their friends and families, and also enabled them to communicate with others in a novel way.

> After learning IT, I have had a closer relationship with the society, and communication with my family and friends is much more frequent.

> Just like Mui has just said, after learning computer, I have had a much closer relationship with other people. Because some of my friends have moved to Canada and retired there.

> I think we are quite smart, know how to attach a piece of music with an email, like adding a song with some cartoons. Like during the birthday of one of the classmates, I wanted to send her a bunch of flowers, but we are getting old and it's a bit uneasy for me to take a bunch of real flowers to her, so I sent her an email with some flowers that can bloom with different colors, from red into yellow and with glitter; and I'd asked her if she liked the roses; and she was happy to receive them.

The opening up of ZPD involves also the development of new identities. The following excerpt was taken from the interview of an 85-year-old woman. She has been a housewife for most of her life. The new learning experiences such as participating in a computer exhibition has helped her develop a new identity that is more outward-looking than being a housewife.

> What is so good [about learning computer]? You know I have been a housewife, and now I can step out of my home and participate in this [computer exhibition], shouldn't I be very happy. I was like "a lump of rice before" (Cantonese slang, meaning stupid), knew nothing, have never stepped out of my home. Now I can join different communities, and it's fun. Of course, I'm happy.

WHY ARE THESE INSTRUCTIONAL PRACTICES EFFECTIVE?

The previous section discusses some specific curriculum features and effective pedagogical arrangements that have contributed to the successful learning of ICT, and later the development of a community of learners, among older adults in a social center in Hong Kong. These facilitative instructional conditions include participatory curriculum development, tutor supports, the design of learning tasks, peer tutoring, different forms of collaboration, connection with other communities, and the sharing of work. These findings were in line with the principles for fostering the development of a community of learners Bruner (1996) and Brown (1997) discussed and reaffirmed the effective instructional practice for promoting classroom collaboration that Crawford and his colleagues (1999) reported.

Previous studies (e.g., Brown & Campione, 1990; Brown & Renshaw, 2000) on effective instructional practices using a sociocultural framework have taken a theory-into-practice approach. They explored how the injection of specific instructional procedures derived from a sociocultural perspective into the classroom community can effectively promote collaboration and interaction. In contrast, the current study reported a set of facilitative instructional practices naturally evolved among the participants of a computer literacy program, but which can be illustrative of good sociocultural approaches. The crucial question is to understand what has made these naturally evolved practices work.

The effectiveness of these facilitative instructional practices can be understood from two dimensions, meeting the learning needs of these older adults (accommodation) and extending the self (extension). As shown in Figure 16.1, these facilitative instructional features help create a learning environment in which older adults' needs for learning have been met and their ZPD opened up. The motive for the provision of this computer literacy program was originated from the recognition that older adults have an equal right to learn computer knowledge and skills despite their presumed cognitive problems. Inviting the older adults to participate in curriculum development, to reflect on their learning, and to collaborate through peer tutoring are some of the effective ways to understand and respond to the special needs of these older adults.

Furthermore, accommodation includes not just meeting the needs but also offering choices and accepting diversity and difference within the learning community. Older adults could make a choice as to what to learn, how to go about learning it, and what level they wanted to achieve. They also differed in terms of their goals for learning, pace of learning, and means of learning. For example, it was considered natural for some to quit in the middle of a course or miss some lessons as a result of some personal factors. Having health problems is a common one. Both tutors and older adults held an understanding and accepting attitude toward choice, difference, and diversity.

Lave and Wenger (1991) distinguished between a *learning* curriculum and a *teaching* curriculum. A learning curriculum is a characteristic of a community. Its focus is not on teaching or instruction but on the perspective of the learners. Accommodation can be considered as a key principle to the development of a learning curriculum from the learners' perspective.

Extending the self is another way to explain the effectiveness of these facilitative instructional practices. Extending the self includes the acquisition of valued knowledge and skills, the development of new identities, and the connection with other communities for the current group of older adults. It was through the acquisition of the valued knowledge and skills that older adults had the chance to rebuild their own identities as a contributing member of the society and renew and strengthen their connection with different communities including friends, family members, and other communities. Putting their newly acquired skills into practice has made their learning authentic and meaningful. More importantly, their achievement has earned them respect and helped develop their self-esteem. Their voices have therefore been heard within the Hong Kong society, and the image of older adults as technophobic and technologically clumsy was challenged.

The understanding of the effectiveness of these facilitative instructional conditions cannot be complete without a discussion of the active role of older adults. Wenger (1998, p. 77) explained that "a source of community coherence is the negotiation of a joint enterprise." What is clear in this study is that older adults have successfully negotiated "a joint enterprise" not just among themselves, but also with their tutors and the management team of the social center. The active participation of older adults has contributed to the development of the curriculum. In addition, experienced learners through active collaboration and interaction have showcased to newcomers that it is possible for them to become literate in computer knowledge and skills. The critical incident discussed in the Results section demonstrated vividly that these older adults have actively negotiated for their own benefits and contributed to the development of their learning program.

CONCLUSION

In conclusion, the mastery of computer knowledge and skills not only has helped these older adults to maintain their cognitive functioning but has also led them to relate to their usual tasks, people, and the outside world in a new way. By appropriating this novel cultural tool, these older adults achieved a higher level of independence, renewed their connection with others, and crafted for themselves new identities and new ways of relating to others and contributing to their well-being.

The findings reported here give substance to the sociocultural claim that learning is a trajectory of engagement and participation constituted in the context of changing relationships within a community. Development and learning are still feasible and transformative in the golden years. When concluding his book *Community of Practice: Learning, Meaning and Identity*, Wenger (1998, p. 263) claims that "education, in its deepest sense and at whatever age it takes place, concerns the opening of identities—exploring new ways of being that lie beyond the current state." The community-oriented curriculum and pedagogical arrangements have contributed to this empowering process, helping these older adults to open up their ZPDs and extend their connection with different communities using socially valued knowledge and skills.

ACKNOWLEDGMENT

The author would like to thank the editors for their constructive comments on the earlier version of this chapter.

NOTES

1. These figures showed the older adults actually enrolled in the courses, excluding those who have been placed on the waiting list.
2. In a conference presentation (Ng, 2002), a model of evolving motivation was developed to explain why the core interviews have developed keen interest in learning computer knowledge and skills. Social supports derived from different social contexts, including social values and norms, of family members were discussed.

REFERENCES

Addison Stone, C. (1993). What is missing in the metaphor of scaffolding? In E. A. Forman, N. Minick, & C. Addison Stone (Eds.), *Contexts for learning: Sociocultural dynamics in children's development* (pp. 169–183). New York: Oxford University Press.

Baron, A., & Cerella, J. (1993). Laboratory tests of the disuse account of cognitive decline. In J. Cerella, J. Rybash, W. Hoyer, & M. L. Commons (Eds.), *Adult information processing: Limits on loss* (pp. 125-149). San Diego, CA: Academic Press.

Brown, A. L. (1997). Transforming schools into communities of thinking and learning about serious matters. *American Psychologist, 52*, 399–413.

Brown, A. L., & Campione, J. C. (1990). Communities of learning and thinking, or a context by any other name. *Human Development, 21*, 108–125.

Brown, J. S., Collins, A., & Duguid, P. (1989). Situated cognition and the culture of learning. *Educational Researcher, 18*(1), 32–34.

Brown, R. A. J., & Renshaw, P. D. (2000). Collective argumentation: A sociocultural approach to reframing classroom teaching and learning. In H. Cowie & G. van der Aalsvoort (Eds.), *Social interaction in learning and instruction* (pp. 52–66). Amsterdam: Pergamon Press.

Bruner, J. (1986). *Actual minds, possible worlds.* London: Harvard University Press.

Bruner, J. S. (1996). *The culture of education.* Cambridge, MA: Harvard University Press.

Craik, F. I. M. (1986). A functional account of age differences in memory. In F. Klix & H. Hagendorf (Eds.), *Human memory and cognitive capabilities, mechanisms, and performances* (pp. 409–422). Amsterdam: Elservier.

Crawford, B. A., Krajcik, J. S., & Marx, R. W. (1999). Elements of a community of learners in a middle school science classroom. *Science Education, 83*(6), 701–723.

Crook, C. (1991). Computers in the zone of proximal development: Implication for evaluation. *Computers and Education, 17*, 81–91.

Forman, E. A. (1989). The role of peer interaction in the construction of mathematical knowledge. *International Journal of Educational Research, 13*, 55–69.

Forman, E. A., & Cazden, C. B. (1985). Exploring Vygotskian perspectives in education: The cognitive value of peer interaction. In J. V. Wertsch (Ed.), *Culture, communication, and cognition: Vygotskian perspectives* (pp. 323–347). Cambridge, UK: Cambridge University Press.

Gilbert, N. J., & Driscoll, M. P. (2002). Collaborative knowledge building: A case study. *Educational Technology Research and Development, 50*(1), 59–79.

Goodnow, J. (1990). The socialization of cognition: What's involved? In J. W. Stigler, R. A. Shweder, & G. H. Herdt (Eds.), *Cultural psychology: Essays on comparative human development* (pp. 259–286). New York: Cambridge University Press.

Harland, T. (2003). Vygotsky's zone of proximal development and problem-based learning: Linking a theoretical concept with practice through action research. *Teaching in Higher Education, 8*(2), 263–272.

Hong Kong Census and Statistics Department. (2000). *Thematic household survey report no. 2.* Hong Kong: The Government Printer.

Hong Kong Census and Statistics Department. (2002a). *2001 Population Census: Thematic Report—older persons.* Hong Kong: The Government Printer.

Hong Kong Census and Statistics Department. (2002b). *Thematic household survey report no. 10.* Hong Kong: The Government Printer.

Jamieson, B. A., & Rogers, W. A. (2000). Age-related effects of blocked and random practice schedules on learning a new technology. *Journal of Gerontology: Psychological Science, 55B*, 343–353.

Jones, B. D., & Bayen, U. J. (1998). Teaching older adults to use computers: Recommendations based on cognitive aging research. *Educational Gerontology, 24*, 675–689.

Kasworm, C. E., & Medina, R. A. (1990). Adult competence in everyday tasks: A cross-sectional secondary analysis. *Educational Gerontology, 16*(1), 27–48.

Kovalainen, M., Kumpulainen, K., & Vasama, S. (2001). Orchestrating classroom interaction in a community of inquiry: Modes of teacher participation. *Journal of Classroom Interaction, 36*(2), 17–28.

Lave, J. (1988). *Cognition in practice*. Cambridge, UK: Cambridge University Press.

Lave, J., & Wenger, E. (1991). *Situated learning: Legitimate peripheral participation*. Cambridge, UK: Cambridge University Press.

Lebow, D., Wager, W., Marks, P., & Gilbert, N. (1996). *Construe: Software for collaborative learning over the World Wide Web*. Paper presented at the AECT/FSU Conference on Distance Learning, Tallahassee, FL.

Light, L. L. (1996). Memory and aging. In E. L. Bjork & R. A. Bjork (Eds.), *Handbook of perception, cognition and memory* (pp. 443–490). San Diego, CA: Academic Press.

Mayhorn, C. B., Stronge, A. J., McLaughlin, A. C., & Rogers, W. A. (2004). Older adults, computer training, and the systems approach: A formula for success. *Educational Gerontology, 30*(3), 237–253.

Mead, S. E., & Fisk, A. D. (1998). Measuring skill acquisition and retention with an ATM simulator: The need for age-specific training. *Human Factors, 40*, 516–523.

Ng, C. H. (2002, December). *A sociocultural analysis of evolving motivation in the study of computing knowledge and skills*. Paper presented at the Annual Conference of Australian Association for Research in Education, Brisbane.

O'Reilly, P., & Caro, F. G. (1994). Productive aging: An overview and literature. *Journal of Aging and Social Policy, 6*(3), 39–71.

Renshaw, P. D. (1998). Sociocultural pedagogy for new times: Reframing key concepts. *Australian Educational Researcher, 25*(3), 83–100.

Rogoff, B. (1994). Developing understanding of the idea of communities of learners. *Mind, Culture, & Activity: an International Journal, 14*(4), 209–229.

Roth, W.-M. (1995). Inventors, copycats, and everyone else: The emergence of shared resources and practices as defining aspects of classroom communities. *Science Education, 79*(5), 475–502.

Ryan, E. B., Szechtman, B., & Bodkin, J. (1992). Attitudes towards younger and older adults learning to use computers. *Journal of Gerontology, 47*, 96–101.

Tharp, R., & Gallimore, R. (1991). A theory of teaching as assisted performance. In P. Light, S. Sheldon, & M. Woodhead (Eds.), *Learning to think* (pp. 42–61). London: Routledge.

Timmermann, S. (1998). The role of information technology in older adult learning. *New Directions for Adult and Continuing Education, 7*(7), 61–71.

Vygotsky, L. S. (1978). *Mind in society: The development of higher psychological processes*. Cambridge, UK: Cambridge University Press.

Wenger, E. (1998). *Communities of practice: Learning, meaning, and identity*. Cambridge, UK: Cambridge University Press.

White, J., & Weatherall, A. (2000). A grounded theory analysis of older adults and information technology. *Educational Gerontology, 26*, 371–386.

Zandri, E., & Charness, A. (1989). Training older and younger adults to use software. *Educational Gerontology, 15*, 615–631.

INDEX

ABOUT THE AUTHORS

Lyn Brodie graduated from the University of Southern Queensland (USQ) in 1985 with a degree in Electrical and Electronic Engineering, and she later gained her Masters of Engineering in 2003. After working for several years in CSIRO (National Measurement Laboratory, Sydney), biomedical research at Westmead Hospital, and designing equipment for the blind and visually impaired at various companies, Brodie returned to take up a lecturing position at USQ. She has won several teaching awards including the 2002 Australasian Association of Engineering Educators (AAEE) Engineering Educator Award and the 2003 USQ Award for Excellence in Design and Delivery of Teaching Materials (Team Leader). This award recognized her work on the design and delivery of the Problem Based Learning course delivered to all first-year engineering and surveying students studying in either internal or distance education modes. Brodie's current career research interests include Engineering Education and Problem Based Learning.

Katherine Richardson Bruna is Assistant Professor of Multicultural and International Curriculum Studies in the Department of Curriculum and Instruction, College of Education, Iowa State University. She received her doctorate in education from the University of California at Davis in 2002, where she pursued a sociocultural studies specialization with designated emphases in feminist and critical theory. Dr. Richardson Bruna's general area of interest is the preparation of teachers for culturally and linguistically diverse settings. She has presented her doctoral research, a 3-year ethnographic study of life in one multicultural teacher education classroom, with a focus on the phenomena of white teacher resistance, at national conferences such as the American Anthropological Association and the American Educational Research Association. Dr. Bruna also is involved in research related to the education of language minority children. Her current grant-supported research examines the nature of explicit academic language instruction for English learners in science. She has written a chapter related to this topic for the forthcoming edited book, *What Every Teacher Should Know About Language*.

Lorelle Burton is a psychology lecturer for the Department of Psychology at the University of Southern Queensland (USQ). She completed her PhD in 1998, is a fully registered psychologist, and a full member of the Australian Psychological Society. She was recognized with the USQ Award for Excellence in Teaching in 2001. Dr. Burton's primary teaching areas include foundation psychology and individual differences. Her research interests include the study of individual differences in cognitive abilities, learning styles, and personalities. She has published a book entitled *An Interactive Approach to Writing Essays and Research Reports in Psychology*, which includes interactive practice exercises on CD-ROM, and she is currently coauthoring an introductory textbook that examines psychology from an Australasian perspective. Additionally, Dr. Burton has presented and published multiple papers at national and international conferences in her specialized areas of teaching and research.

Bill Buxton is Assistant Professor in the Literacy Department at SUNY Cortland. He received his PhD in Curriculum and Instruction from the University of Utah in 2003. Dr. Buxton teaches courses exploring the social foundations of literacy and the complex relationship between language and print literacy for students working toward master's degrees leading to certification as a literacy specialist in the state of New York. His research interests focus on the ways conceptions of literacy both enhance and inhibit access to institutions, information, and people in modern society.

Margaret Carr is Associate Professor of early childhood studies at the University of Waikato in New Zealand. Formerly a kindergarten teacher, she was a Co-Director of the Early Childhood Curriculum Development project, which developed a national early childhood curriculum for New Zealand. That curriculum was published in 1996. Since that time Dr. Carr has been involved in a number of research projects on curriculum implementation and assessment in relation to the national curriculum. In particular, she developed, with teachers, an assessment format called "Learning Stories," the subject of a 2001 book, *Assessment in Early Childhood Settings: Learning Stories*. Dr. Carr gained her PhD from the University of Waikato in 1998, and has published widely on early childhood curriculum and assessment, learning dispositions, and technology in early childhood. Current research includes a study of the learning dispositions and "dispositional milieux" of 27 children over 2 years as they move from early childhood centers into school. With colleagues she is currently completing a collection of books on formative assessment in early childhood for the Ministry of Education. These books include a discussion of assessment issues and annotated examples from early childhood settings.

Marilyn Dorman is an instructional designer in the Distance and e-Learning Centre, University of Southern Queensland, and has taught at pretertiary as well as postgraduate levels. She has over 20 years experience in instructional design and development within USQ and for other Australian universities as well as for health education providers. Dorman has also worked as a journalist/editor, including several years as publishing editor of *Distance Education, An International Journal*. Her research interests focus on constructive alignment in higher education course development, including aspects of cultural diversity, learning styles and preferences, technology-supported learning, and investigation of graduate attributes in higher education. She has published and presented internationally on these issues.

David Dowling, Associate Professor, is the Associate Dean (Academic) in the Faculty of Engineering and Surveying at the University of Southern Queensland. While he has a background in land surveying, the major focus of both his work and research are related to enhancing the teaching and learning environment for students, which includes curriculum design, the induction and development of academic staff, orientation programs for students, and research into the factors that influence student success, particularly those that impact on student success in their first year of study at USQ.

Martin Dowson received his PhD from the University of Western Sydney in 2000. As well as being a trained teacher with classroom experience, he has lectured in educational and developmental psychology at the University of Western Sydney. Prior to his current appointment, Dr. Dowson was principal of a Christian college and a teacher of religious education. He is also a qualified Minister of Religion. He is currently a Postdoctoral Research Fellow at the SELF Research Centre of the University of Western Sydney. Dr. Dowson's research interests include student motivation and cognition, quantitative research methodologies, and the psychology of religion. He has published in key educational psychology research journals including the *Journal of Educational Psychology, Contemporary Educa-*

tional Psychology, and *Educational and Psychological Measurement,* and in religion research journals such as the *Journal of Research in Christian Education* and *Review of Religious Research.* He is also the author of an upcoming chapter in Volume 14 of *Advances in Motivation and Achievement,* which examines the motivational impact of religious beliefs.

Margaret Honey, Vice President of the Education Development Center and Director of EDC's Center for Children and Technology (www.edc.org/CCT), has worked in the field of educational technology since 1981. Her primary research interests include the role of technology in school reform and student achievement, the use of telecommunications technology to support online learning communities, and issues of equity associated with the development and use of technology. Dr. Honey holds a PhD in developmental psychology from Columbia University. She regularly contributes to educational publications, and presents at major technology and education conferences. She has served on the board of the Consortium for School Networking, and currently serves on advisory boards of math, science, and technology projects nationwide. In 1999 Dr. Honey was appointed to the Department of Education's Expert Panel on Educational Technology, charged with the responsibility for creating a framework to be used in assessing the effectiveness of all educational technology programs.

Mike Horsley is Senior Lecturer in the Faculty of Education and Social Work at the University of Sydney, where he manages partnerships between the Faculty and educational institutions. He has significant and extensive expertise in the learning of Pacific Islander students and the cultural learning of teachers who teach them. Horsley has delivered over 20 professional learning and teacher professional development courses on assisting teachers to improve the way they meet the learning needs of Pacific Island students. He currently manages a highly successful Samoan learning center with and for the Samoan community and has worked with Pasifika communities in New South Wales, Australia, for many years.

Michelle Kelly is Coordinator of Cortland's Urban Recruitment of Educators' (CURE) Program and Associate Professor in the Foundations and Social Advocacy Department at State University of New York College at Cortland. She received her PhD in Cultural Foundations of Education from the University of Utah in 2001. Dr. Kelly teaches courses in urban education and mentors new teachers in urban schools. Her research interests include preservice teachers' attitudes about teaching in urban schools, race and identity, and cultural historical approaches to learning. Dr. Kelly is currently researching SUNY Cortland's preservice teachers' constructions of urban schools and communities and their interests and reasons for an interest, or lack of interest, in teaching in an urban district with hopes that the findings might be used to encourage the development of teacher education programs that are committed to social justice and in-depth opportunities to study and experience life in urban schools.

Susan Lutz is a doctoral student in the Department of Human Development at the University of Maryland, College Park. Her primary research interests include language and literacy development, particularly factors that influence children's motivation for reading. Lutz is currently a graduate assistant on the Concept-Oriented Reading Instruction project. Susan completed her undergraduate study at Drew University in New Jersey in 2001, earning a BA in neuroscience. She then worked as a research assistant at Princeton University, first in the Center for Arts and Cultural Policy Studies and then in the Cutaneous Communication Laboratory. Her interest in studying reading developed largely from her experiences tutoring struggling elementary and middle school students and working in her hometown library during high school and college.

William McGinley is Associate Professor in English Education at the University of Colorado, Boulder. Bill's research areas of interest include literature and the humanities in public education, literacy and culture, book clubs and popular reading, community-based literacy practices, teacher education and community mentorships, skateparks, and the pedagogy of young boys. Recent publications include *Literature and the Life of our Classrooms: Transforming our Students/Transforming Ourselves* (with George Kamberelis), *Literary Retailing and the Re-making of Popular Reading* (with Katanna Conley), *"We've Been Through It": The Pedagogy of Adult Community Members in an Urban After School Program*, and *Pedagogy for a Few: The Modern Book Industry as Literature Teacher.*

Dennis McInerney is Professor of Educational Psychology at the University of Western Sydney, Australia, and Associate Director of the Self-Concept and Learning Facilitation Research Centre (SELF), a key research center of the University. He received his PhD in Educational and Cross-Cultural Psychology from the University of Sydney in 1989. Dr. McInerney has a strong interest in motivation research and has published extensively in refereed international journals. He has written numerous book chapters and conference papers, particularly in the area of motivation and achievement. His textbook *Educational Psychology: Constructing Learning* (3rd ed, 2002, Prentice Hall Australia) is the top-selling educational psychology text in Australia and is widely used as a standard text in many Australian universities. Dr. McInerney received the Outstanding Author

Award by Prentice Hall Australia (Pearson) in 2002. His other texts are *Helping Kids Achieve Their Best: Understanding and Using Motivation in the Classroom* (Allen & Unwin, 2001), *Publishing Your Psychology Research: A Guide to Writing for Journals in Psychology and Related Fields* (Sage, 2001), *Research on Sociocultural Influences on Motivation and Learning* (Vols. 1–4, Information Age), and *International Advances in Self Research* (with Herb Marsh & Rhonda Craven, Information Age).

Ellen Mandinach is Associate Director for Research at the Educational Development Center's Center for Children and Technology. She received her PhD in Educational Psychology from Stanford University in 1984. She has done extensive work in the field of educational technology and has a strong background in research methodology and measurement. Before joining CCT, Dr. Mandinach served as Senior Research scientist at Educational Testing Service. Her research has focused on the implementation and impact of computer environments on teaching and learning and the measurement of individual differences in cognitive and affective processes. Dr. Mandinach wrote a book on the cognitive and curricular impact of the systems thinking approach on teaching and learning activities, titled *Classroom Dynamics: Implementing a Technology-Based Learning Environment*, and was also part of a team that wrote *Remaking the Concept of Aptitude: Extending the Legacy of Richard E. Snow.* She has written many articles and chapters on educational technology. Her most recent focus is on an NSF-funded project to create an evaluation framework for technology-based data-driven instructional decision making.

Chi-hung Ng is Assistant Professor at the School of Education and Languages, Open University of Hong Kong. He received his PhD from the University of Queensland, Australia, in 2000. Dr. Ng's research focuses mainly on students' motivation and learning processes. He is now working on a large grant research project investigating the professional development and learning of in-service teachers in Hong Kong from an integrated perspective based on both cognitive and sociocultural theories.

Steven Ramirez Fong is currently a biology teacher at Berkeley High School in Berkeley, California. He received his undergraduate degree in Integrative Biology from the University of California–Berkeley (UCB) in 2002 and his master's in Education and Single Subject Teaching Credential from UCB in 2004. Fong obtained his graduate degree through the Master's and Credential in Science and Mathematics Education (MAC-SME) Program. Dedicated to the education of urban youth, this program's focus on issues of diversity in education was in large part the driving force behind his interest in student sociocultural background.

Marcelle A. Siegel's research in science education focuses on learning, assessment, equity, and developing resources to support instruction. For the past 2 years, she has led a research group for preservice teachers at the University of California–Berkeley. Marcelle is currently Principal Investigator of "Investigating and Improving Science Learning and Assessment for Middle School Linguistic Minority Students," funded by the University of California Linguistic Minority Research Institute. As a fellow at the National Institute for Science Education at the University of Wisconsin–Madison from 1999–2001, Siegel investigated preservice teachers' use of evidence from the learning sciences in making instructional decisions. She received an MA in Integrative Biology and a PhD in Science and Mathematics Education from the University of California–Berkeley.

Paris Strom received his PhD from Arizona State University in 1997 and is Assistant Professor in the Department of Educational Foundations, Leadership, and Technology at Auburn University in Alabama. He has taught in public high schools serving both affluent and low-income families. Dr. Strom's research, for the Motorola Foundation, explores how new technologies can be applied in creative ways to improve teacher collaboration in detection and reduction of misbehavior among students they have in common, acknowledge commendable conduct of students, and increase parent involvement in their corrective guidance roles. His cross-cultural studies focus on how adolescents and parents perceive maternal success in Japan and the United States. Dr. Strom is coauthor of the Interpersonal Intelligence Inventory (III) (Scholastic Testing Service, Chicago, 2002), a peer and self-evaluation measure to evaluate teamwork skills in secondary schools. He is also coauthor of *Educating Adolescents and Learning From Them* (2005, Allyn & Bacon) and has published over 50 articles in educational and psychological journals.

Robert Strom received his PhD from the University of Michigan in 1962. He is Professor of Psychology in Education at Arizona State University and Director of the Office of Parent Development International. Teaching experience with adolescents was followed by service as a Research Director with the National Education Association in Washington, D.C., and faculty appointments with Purdue University and Ohio State University. Dr. Strom's purposes are to help educators of every age group and parents at each state of their long-term role as teachers. These research and development goals implicate measurement instruments he designed to identify achievement, detect learning needs, and assess effects of intervention, and by efforts to build curriculum to support growth of target populations. Dr. Strom has been recognized as a Danforth Scholar, North Atlantic Treaty Scholar, and by Fulbright awards to the University of Stockholm in Sweden, the University of Philippines in Manila, and Canberra University in Australia. His publications include 20 books, 300 articles, and four instruments about lifespan development.

Rosemary Suliman is Senior Lecturer in Education and Arabic at the University of Western Sydney. She received her PhD from the University of Western Sydney in 2001. Dr. Suliman has a record of wide-ranging, innovative, and ongoing research in the field of Arabic education; language teaching methodology; curriculum development in languages; and language proficiency of students from a home situation where a language other than English is spoken and the relationship of this to students' school achievement. Her most recent research is on the motivational and linguistic context of the school achievement of Lebanese-background students. The findings of this research (the first of its kind) has had significant impact on education and community members and has resulted in an important applied action research project, "The School–Parent Alliance," a collaborative project funded by the University of Western Sydney, The NSW Premiers' Department, and with the full support of the NSW Department of Education and Training. It aims at developing an active partnership between parents, schools, and the community in order to address the educational needs of Lebanese-background students.

Wilma Vialle received her PhD from the University of South Florida in 1991 and currently lectures in Educational Psychology and Gifted Education at the University of Wollongong in Australia. Her major research interests lie in the identification and education of gifted students, particularly those who are culturally diverse, and the qualities of effective teachers of the gifted. Dr. Vialle has published her work on gifted education in refereed journals, books, and conference proceedings, and is currently the editor of the *Australasian Journal of Gifted Education*. Most recently, she coedited a volume on Australian research in giftedness, *The Gifted Enigma* (Hawker Brownlow, 2002). She has produced a textbook with colleagues, *Handbook on Child Development* (Social Science Press, 2000), which is used in several Australian universities. Dr. Vialle is also well known, nationally and internationally, for her work on multiple intelligences theory and is currently working on a study investigating spiritual intelligence.

Richard Walker teaches educational psychology at the undergraduate and postgraduate levels in the Faculty of Education and Social Work at the University of Sydney. He obtained his PhD from the University of Sydney in 1995. Recent publications in the sociocultural area include chapters in *Practice, Knowledge and the Health Professions* (J. Higgs & A.

Titchen, Eds.; Butterworth-Heineman, 2001), *Sociocultural Influences on Motivation and Learning, Volume 2* (D. M. McInerney & S. Van Etten, Eds.; Information Age, 2002), *Sociocultural Influences and Teacher Education Programs* (D. M. McInerney & S. Van Etten, Eds.; Information Age, 2003). The application of Vygotskian sociocultural understandings to student motivation, a current interest, is the focus of forthcoming articles in *European Psychologist* and *Australia Educational Researcher*. Dr. Walker is currently researching schooling for marginalized and homeless youth from a sociocultural perspective.

Jennifer Whitcomb is Assistant Dean for Teacher Education and Academic Services at the University of Colorado, Boulder. Her research interests focus on the intersection between and among the practice and structure of teacher education and teacher learning. She has coedited a casebook and facilitator's guide, *Groupwork in Diverse Classrooms* (with Judith Shulman and Rachel Lotan; Teachers College Press, 1998), and has published recently in *Teaching Education* and *Journal of Curriculum Studies*. Whitcomb is an incoming coeditor of the *Journal of Teacher Education*. She has taught courses that introduce the teaching profession to teacher candidates as well as master's and doctoral seminars in the following areas: the practice of teaching, research on teaching, teaching and learning environments, and literacy policy.

Allan Wigfield is Professor of Human Development and Distinguished Scholar-Teacher at the University of Maryland. He received his PhD in educational psychology from the University of Illinois in 1982. His research focuses on how children's motivation develops across the school years in different areas, including reading. In the reading area, Dr. Wigfield has done research on the development of children's motivation for reading, and how different instructional practices influence children's reading motivation. His research has been supported by grants from NSF, NICHD, and IERI. He has authored more than 85 peer-reviewed journal articles and book chapters on children's motivation and other topics, and also has edited three books. Dr. Wigfield was Associate Editor of the *Journal of Educational Psychology* from 2000 to 2002 and currently is Associate Editor of *Child Development*. He is also a Fellow of Division 15 (Educational Psychology) of the American Psychological Association, and has won several awards for his research and teaching.

Alexander Yeung is Lecturer and Senior Program Developer of the Division of Continuing Professional Education of the Hong Kong Institute of Education. He completed his PhD in education at the University of New South Wales. He is an active researcher and is widely published in academic journals of international repute. Dr. Yeung has also presented over 30 papers at international conferences in the last 5 years. For over 30 years, he has taught in various educational settings from preschool to postgraduate levels. Dr. Yeung has taught a wide range of school subjects and has a diversity of skills and expertise in various curriculum areas. He has served as designer, administrator, and consultant in various educational programs and research projects. In research, he has a wide range of interests and has served as reviewer for numerous journals. Dr. Yeung's major expertise includes self-concept, achievement motivation, measurement and evaluation, and cognition.

Jessica C. Zacher received her PhD in 2004 from the University of California–Berkeley, Graduate School of Education, in the Department of Language, Literacy, and Culture. She is a lecturer there and teaches undergraduate courses on literacy and language arts instruction, and has a strong interest in issues of identity and literacy in diverse settings. Dr. Zacher taught kindergarten in San Francisco and conducted research for this chapter at the same school. Other research has included work on adult literacy and on community technology projects. Her research and teaching interests include literacy development, identity construction, youth cultures, popular culture, gender studies, and children's literacies in urban settings. Dr. Zacher's latest publication is a chapter in *Bourdieu and Literacy Education* (A. Luke & J. Albright, Eds., in press).

Sarah Zerwin is a former high school English teacher and a doctoral student in the School of Education at the University of Colorado, Boulder. Currently, she is working with teacher candidates during their student teaching placement.

Printed in the United States
30022LVS00001B/153

9 781593 112080